D1596641

A CLASSIFIED BIBLIOGRAPHY
OF THE SEPTUAGINT

ARBEITEN ZUR LITERATUR UND GESCHICHTE DES HELLENISTISCHEN JUDENTUMS

HERAUSGEGEBEN VON

K. H. RENGSTORF

IN VERBINDUNG MIT

J. DANIÉLOU, G. DELLING, S. JELLICOE, H. R. MOEHRING,
B. NOACK, H. M. ORLINSKY, H. RIESENFELD,
A. SCHALIT, H. SCHRECKENBERG, W. C. VAN UNNIK,
A. WIKGREN, A. S. VAN DER WOUDE

VI

BROCK/FRITSCH/JELLICOE

A CLASSIFIED BIBLIOGRAPHY OF THE SEPTUAGINT

LEIDEN
E. J. BRILL
1973

A CLASSIFIED BIBLIOGRAPHY
OF THE SEPTUAGINT

COMPILED BY

SEBASTIAN P. BROCK

Faculty of Oriental Studies, University of Cambridge

CHARLES T. FRITSCH

Princeton Theological Seminary, New Jersey

SIDNEY JELLICOE

Bishop's University, Lennoxville, Quebec

LEIDEN
E. J. BRILL
1973

ISBN 90 04 03596 6

TABLE OF CONTENTS

Introduction IX
Abbreviations XIII

1. Introductions. 1
2. Concordances 3
3. a. Editions 4
   b. Translations of LXX 7
4. Survey articles 8
5. Personalia 9
6. Significance of LXX 10
7. General 11
8. Inspiration of LXX 13
9. Canon 14
10. a. LXX as a translation. 16
    b. Biblical translation in general (Select) 17
11. Characteristics and background 17
12. Particular concepts 18
13. Anthropomorphism/-pathism 20
14. Hellenistic exegesis 20
15. Language 21
    a. General 21
    b. (i) Grammars 23
       (ii) Grammatical Studies 25
    c. (i) Lexica 29
       (ii) Lexical Studies 30
16. Translation technique 34
17. Divine Names 37
18. a. Proper names 39
    b. Onomastica 40
19. Transliterations. 41
20. Wutz's theory 43
21. Pseudo-Aristeas. 44
    a. Texts and Translations 44
    b. Studies 45
22. Proto-LXX 47
23. Later history of LXX 48

24. LXX and MT   48
    a. General   48
    b. Chronology   50
25. LXX and Qumran   50
26. a. LXX and Peshitta   51
    b. LXX and Targum   52
27. LXX and NT   53
    a. General   53
    b. Individual Books   54
    c. Testimonia (Select)   56
28. Philo   57
29. Josephus   58
30. Apostolic Fathers, Justin   59
31. Patristica   60
32. Origen   64
33. Jerome   65
34. Editions (Studies on)   66
35. Manuscripts   68
    a. General   68
    b. Papyri   69
    c. Manuscripts (Other than Papyri)   74
    d. Inscriptions, amulets, etc.   80
    e. Catenae   81
    f. Lections; Use of LXX in Liturgy   82
36. Textual Studies   84
    a. General   84
    b. Corruptions   85
    c. Recensions (General)   86
    d. Hebraising Recensions (Other than Hexaplaric) . .   86
    e. Hexaplaric Recension   87
    f. Lucianic Recension   87
    g. Hesychian Recension   88
37. Hexapla   88
    a. General   88
    b. Hexapla and Tetrapla   90
    c. Second Column   91
38. Other Greek translations   92
    a. General   92
    b. Aquila   93
    c. Theodotion   94

     d. Symmachus 94
     e. Quinta 95
     f. Samaritikon 96
     g. Syros 96
     h. Other Translations 96
     i. Medieval Greek 97
     j. Graecus Venetus 97
39. Individual books 98
     a. (i) Pentateuch (General) 98
       (ii) Genesis 99
       (iii) Exodus 100
       (iv) Leviticus 101
       (v) Numbers 101
       (vi) Deuteronomy 102
     b. Joshua, Judges, Ruth 103
       (i) Joshua 103
       (ii) Judges 104
       (iii) Ruth 105
     c. (i) I-II Samuel (I-II Kingdoms) 105
       (ii) I-II Kings (III-IV Kingdoms) 107
     d. (i) Chronicles (Paraleipomena) 109
       (ii) I-II Esdras 110
     e. (i) Esther 112
       (ii) Judith 113
       (iii) Tobit 114
     f. I-IV Maccabees 115
     g. (i) Psalms 119
       (ii) Odes and Ps. 151 121
     h. (i) Proverbs 122
       (ii) Ecclesiastes 122
       (iii) Song of Songs (Cantica) 123
       (iv) Job 123
     i. (i) Wisdom of Solomon 125
       (ii) Ben Sira (Ecclesiasticus) 129
       (iii) Psalms of Solomon 132
     j. Prophetical Books (General) 134
     k. XII Prophets 134
     l. Isaiah 137
     m. (i) Jeremiah 139
       (ii) Lamentations 140

(iii) Baruch, Ep. Jeremiae 140
n. Ezekiel 141
o. Daniel 142
40. Versions 144
a. Arabic 144
b. Armenian 147
c. Coptic 150
d. Ethiopic 160
e. Georgian 163
f. Gothic 167
g. Old Latin 168
h. Slavonic 186
i. Peshitta 189
j. Syro-Hexaplar 191
k. Syriac: Jacob of Edessa 193
l. Palestinian Syriac (Christian Palestinian Aramaic) . 193
41. Illustration of LXX 195

Index of authors 202

INTRODUCTION

Literature on the LXX is scattered over a very wide field, and the present classified bibliography would not claim to be complete, although it is hoped that everything, or nearly everything, of importance has been included.

For purposes of convenience the 'Septuagint' is taken to consist of those books which feature in A. Rahlfs, *Septuaginta* (Stuttgart, 1935), and it is Rahlfs' order of the constituent books that is adhered to in sections 39 and 40.

Coverage is down to 1969 (inclusive),[1] but at the other end of the scale it has seemed preferable not to impose any rigid starting point, hence the practice has been to be increasingly selective for the literature prior to 1900, and it is only in exceptional cases that items earlier than *c.* 1860 are included.

The aim throughout has been to provide as practical a guide as possible to the literature,[2] and for this reason a fairly elaborate subject classification has been adopted. Obviously it has not always been easy to decide in which section to place any given item, and in some cases the same item is entered in full in two (or more) sections (notably in sections 16 and 39); in other cases cross references have been given.

The cross references are collected at the head of each section, and these refer, either to other sections in their entirety, or to individual items in those sections; the latter can readily be identified by running the eye down the left hand margins and isolating the entries marked with the appropiate section number.

Needless to say there are many marginal areas where it is extremely difficult to know what to include and what to exclude. Normally the criterion has been whether or not an item is *primarily* concerned with the LXX: thus the innumerable discussions of textual points

[1] The only exception is the presence of a few reviews which have appeared in 1970 journals.

[2] Bibliographical perfection has not been sought. Thus, for example, no attempt has been made to list all reprints, and titles in non-European languages are only given in translation.

in MT which make incidental use of the LXX have been excluded.[1]
In certain other sections, notably 15, some works of purely general
concern have been included where it is thought they would be
helpful.

Explanatory notes are occasionally given, in square brackets.
Important reviews are sometimes included, but no systematic
attempt has been made to seek these out.

In the individual sections the following points should be noted:

3: With one exception editions printed in Greece have not been
included.

31: Patristic commentaries are not included. Items primarily
concerned with textual problems will be found listed under 39.

35: Publications which contain only isolated LXX texts (e.g.
Oxyrhynchus Papyri) are not included. Studies of manuscripts
primarily concerned with textual problems will be found listed
under 39.

36: Cross references only (to 39) are given for studies relating to
individual books.

39: Commentaries are cited only exceptionally (this also applies
to books surviving only in Greek): lists of these are easily
accessible, e.g. in Eissfeldt. The subsections on books surviving
only in Greek are for the most part confined to items concerned with text and exegesis, those on literary and historical
questions being omitted.

40: It should be noted that not all OT texts in the languages
covered derive from the LXX (e.g. many Arabic texts derive
from the Peshitta). Secondary versions are not normally
included. Similar to the practice in 35, only publications of
texts which *primarily* contain versions of the LXX are
included. Linguistic studies of the versions are not included,
and the same applies to secondary literature on lectionaries,
etc.

41: No attempt has been made to include illustration of the
versions of the LXX, although a few items are given.

---

[1] See, e.g., the many articles by G. R. Driver, D. W. Thomas, to name only
British scholars (bibliographies in *Hebrew and Semitic Studies presented to
G. R. Driver*, ed. D. W. Thomas and W. D. McHardy (Oxford, 1963), and
Words and Meanings, ed. P. R. Ackroyd and B. Lindars (Cambridge, 1968),
respectively).

In compiling the bibliography the Editors have been indebted not only to the wide range of authors represented (with the special bibliographies included, in many cases, in their articles or volumes), but also to the extensive entries in works of reference such as the *Elenchus Bibliographicus (Biblica)* and Eissfeldt's *Einleitung* with its English translation by P. R. Ackroyd (1965). Valued assistance, which is gratefully acknowledged, has been given by Drs. J. N. Birdsall (University of Birmingham), J. A. L. Lee (now of the University of Sydney), and Emanuel Tov (Hebrew University, Jerusalem).

The Editors would also like to express their gratitude to Professor K. H. Rengstorf for his manifold help.

S.P.B.
C.T.F.
S.J.

ABBREVIATIONS

(1) JOURNALS AND SERIES

AASF	Annales Academiae Scientiarum Fennicae (Helsinki)
AB	Analecta Biblica (Rome)
AbhAKWissBerlin	Abhandlungen der Deutschen (Preussischen) Akademie der Wissenschaften zu Berlin
AbhGWG	Abhandlungen der Gesellschaft der Wissenschaften zu Göttingen.
AbhKM	Abhandlungen für die Kunde des Morgenlandes (Leipzig).
Abh(K)GWGött	Abhandlungen der (Königlichen) Gesellschaft der Wissenschaften zu Göttingen.
Aeg	Aegyptus (Milan)
AfO	Archiv für Orientforschung (Berlin; Graz)
AJA	American Journal of Archaeology (Concord, N.H.)
AJP	American Journal of Philology (Baltimore)
AJSL	American Journal of Semitic Languages & Literatures (Chicago)
AJT	American Journal of Theology (Chicago)
ALL	Archiv für lateinische Lexicographie und Grammatik (Munich; Leipzig)
AmEcclRev	American Ecclesiastical Review (Washington, D.C.)
AmerEdRev	American Educational Review (Chicago)
A(ngl)T(h)R(ev)	Anglican Theological Review (Evanston)
AO	Der Alte Orient. Gemeinverständliche Darstellungen (Leipzig)
ARW	Archiv für Religionswissenschaft (Leipzig; Freiburg i.B.)
ASAE	Annales du Service des Antiquités de l'Égypte (Cairo)
ATA	Alttestamentliche Abhandlungen (Münster)
AttiRAcadScdiTorino	Atti dell'Accademia Reale della Scienze di Torino (Turin)
AttiRANL	Atti della Reale Accademia Nazionale dei Lincei (Rome)
BA	The Biblical Archaeologist (New Haven)
BALC	Bulletin d'ancienne littérature chrétienne latine (Maredsous)
BASOR	Bulletin of the American Schools of Oriental Research (New Haven)
BEThL	Bibliotheca Ephemeridum Theologicarum Lovaniensium (Paris, Gembloux)
BFCT	Beiträge zur Förderung christlicher Theologie (Gütersloh)
Bibl-histHWB	Bo Reicke & L. Rost: Biblisch-historisches Handwörterbuch. 3 vols. (Göttingen, 1962-6)
BibOr	Bibliotheca Orientalis (Leiden)
BIE	Bulletin de l'Institut d'Égypte (Cairo)

BIFAO	Bulletin de l'Institut Français d'Archéologie Orientale (Cairo)
BJHIL	G. Delling: Bibliographie zur jüdisch-hellenistischen und intertestamentarischen Literatur, 1900-65 (= TU 106, 1969)
BJRL	Bulletin of the John Rylands Library (Manchester)
BS	Bibliotheca Sacra (Dallas)
BSAC	Bulletin de la Société d'Archéologie Copte (Cairo)
BW	Biblical World (Chicago)
BWA(N)T	Beiträge zur Wissenschaft vom Alten (und Neuen) Testament (Leipzig, Stuttgart)
ByzZ	Byzantinische Zeitschrift (Leipzig, Munich)
BZ	Biblische Zeitschrift (Freiburg i.B.; Paderborn)
BZAW	Beihefte zur Zeitschrift für die Neutestamentliche Wissenschaft (Giessen, Berlin)
BZNW	Beihefte zur Zeitschrift für die Alttestamentliche Wissenschaft (Giessen, Berlin)
CBL	Collectanea Biblica Latina (Rome)
CBQ	Catholic Biblical Quarterly (Washington, D.C.)
CdE	Chronique d'Égypte (Brussels)
ChQR	Church Quarterly Review (London)
CRAI	Comptes rendus des séances de l'academie des inscriptions et belles-lettres (Paris)
CSCO	Corpus Scriptorum Christianorum Orientalium (Louvain)
DACL	Dictionnaire d'Archéologie Chrétienne et de Liturgie (Paris)
DB	Vigouroux: Dictionnaire de la Bible (Paris)
DBS	Supplement to Vigouroux: Dictionnaire de la Bible (Paris)
DCB	Dictionary of Christian Biography (London)
DLZ	Deutsche Literaturzeitung (Berlin)
EB	Encyclopaedia Biblica (London)
EncBibl	Encyclopaedia Biblica (Jerusalem)
EJ	Encyclopaedia Judaica (Berlin)
EKL	Evangelisches Kirchenlexikon (Göttingen)
E(nc)C(att)	Enciclopedia Cattolica (Vatican City)
EnciclItal	Enciclopedia Italiana di Scienze, Lettere ed Arti (Rome)
EncyclBrit	Encyclopaedia Britannica (Edinburgh; Cambridge; London & New York, Chicago)
ERE	Encyclopaedia of Religion and Ethics (Edinburgh)
EstBibl	Estudios Bíblicos (Madrid)
ET	Expository Times (Edinburgh)
ETL	Ephemerides Theologicae Lovanienses (Louvain)
ÉTRel	Études Théologiques et Religieuses (Montpellier)
Expos	The Expositor (London)
FRLANT	Forschungen zur Religion und Literatur des Alten und Neuen Testaments (Göttingen)
FuF	Forschungen und Fortschritte (Berlin)
GCS	Die Griechischen Christlichen Schriftsteller der ersten Jahrhunderte (Leipzig, Berlin)
GGA	Göttingische Gelehrte Anzeigen

GötHÅ	Göteborgs Högskolas Årsskrift (Gothenburg)
HA	Handes Amsorya: Zeitschrift für Armenische Philologie (Vienna).
HDB	James Hastings (ed.): A Dictionary of the Bible. 5 vols. (Edinburgh & New York, 1898-1904)
HSDB²	(Hastings's Shorter) Dictionary of the Bible, rvsd. F. C. Grant and H. H. Rowley (Edinburgh & New York, 1963)
HTR	Harvard Theological Review (Cambridge, Mass.)
HUCA	Hebrew Union College Annual (Cincinnati)
IB	G. A. Buttrick (ed.): The Interpreter's Bible. 12 vols. (New York & Nashville, 1952-7)
IDB	G. A. Buttrick (ed.): The Interpreter's Dictionary of the Bible. 4 vols. (New York & Nashville, 1962)
IEJ	Israel Exploration Journal (Jerusalem)
ISBE	James Orr (ed.): International Standard Bible Encyclopaedia (Chicago, 1915), rvsd. M. G. Kyle, 1929 (Grand Rapids, Mich. from 1939)
JAs	Journal Asiatique (Paris)
JAC	Jahrbuch für Antike und Christentum (Münster)
JAOS	Journal of the American Oriental Society (Baltimore)
JbKlF	Jahrbuch für Kleinasiatische Forschung (Heidelberg)
JBL	Journal of Biblical Literature (Philadelphia)
JE	The Jewish Encyclopedia (New York, London)
JEA	Journal of Egyptian Archaeology (London)
JEOL	Jaarbericht... Ex Oriente Lux (Leiden)
JJS	Journal of Jewish Studies (London)
JLW	Jahrbuch für Liturgiewissenschaft (Münster)
JNES	Journal of Near Eastern Studies (Chicago)
JÖstByzGes	Jahrbuch der Österreichischen Byzantinischen Gesellschaft (Vienna)
JPOS	Journal of the Palestine Oriental Society (Jerusalem)
JQR	Jewish Quarterly Review (London; n.s. Philadelphia)
JRAS	Journal of the Royal Asiatic Society (London)
JSS	Journal of Semitic Studies (Manchester)
JTS	Journal of Theological Studies (Oxford)
LQF	Liturgiegeschichtliche Quellen und Forschungen (Münster)
LTK	Lexikon für Theologie und Kirche (Freiburg i.B.)
LUÅ	Lunds Universitets Årsskrift
MBE	Monumenta Biblica et Ecclesiastica (Rome)
MGM	Miscellanea Giovanni Mercati (Vat. City) = SeT 121-6 (Rome)
MGWJ	Monatsschrift für Geschichte und Wissenschaft des Judentums (Breslau)
MiscAgost	Miscellanea Agostiniana (2 vols., Rome, 1930-1)
MissionArchfrMem	Mémoires de la Mission archéologique française au Caire (Cairo)
MSU	Mitteilungen des Septuaginta-Unternehmens (Berlin; Göttingen)
MUSJ	Mélanges de l'Université St. Joseph (Beirut)
NAWGött	Nachrichten (von) der Akademie der Wissenschaften in Göttingen

NCE	New Catholic Encyclopedia (New York, Toronto, London, Sydney)
NGWG(ött)	Nachrichten von der (Kgl.) Gesellschaft der Wissenschaften zu Göttingen
NKZ	Neue kirchliche Zeitschrift (Leipzig, Erlangen)
NSHE	The New Schaff-Herzog Encyclopedia of Religious Knowledge (New York, London)
NT	Novum Testamentum (Leiden)
NTS	New Testament Studies (Cambridge)
NTSuppl	Supplements to Novum Testamentum (Leiden)
NTT	Nederlands Theologisch Tijdschrift (Wageningen)
OBL	Orientalia et Biblica Lovaniensia (Louvain)
OC	Oriens Christianus (Leipzig; Wiesbaden)
OCP	Orientalia Christiana Periodica (Rome)
OLZ	Orientalistische Literaturzeitung (Leipzig; Berlin)
OTMS	The Old Testament and Modern Study, ed. H. H. Rowley (Oxford, 1951)
OTS	Oudtestamentische Studiën (Leiden)
PAAJR	Proceedings of the American Academy for Jewish Research (Philadelphia)
PBA	Proceedings of the British Academy (London)
PC²	Peake's Commentary on the Bible, rvsd. M. Black & H. H. Rowley (London, Edinburgh, New York, 1962)
PRE	Realencyklopädie für protestantische Theologie und Kirche (Leipzig)
ProcAOS	Proceedings of the American Oriental Society (Baltimore)
PSBA	Proceedings of the Society of Biblical Archaeology (London)
PW	Pauly-Wissowa; Real-Encyclopädie der Classischen Altertumswissenschaft (Stuttgart)
RAC	Reallexikon für Antike und Christentum (Stuttgart)
RB	Revue Biblique (Paris)
RBén	Revue Bénédictine (Maredsous)
RBML	J. G. Eichhorn: Repertorium für Biblische und Morgenländische Litteratur. 18 parts, 1777-86 (Leipzig)
REByz	Revue des Études Byzantines (Paris)
RechSR	Recherches de Science Religieuse (Paris)
REG	Revue des Études Grecques (Paris)
REJ	Revue des Études Juives (Paris)
RestQuart	Restoration Quarterly (Abilene, Texas)
RevEtAugustiennes	Revue des Études Augustiniennes (Paris)
RevSR	Revue des Sciences Religieuses (Strasbourg; Paris)
RGG	Die Religion in Geschichte und Gegenwart (Tübingen)
RhMus	Rheinisches Museum für Philologie (Frankfurt a.M.)
RHR	Revue de l'Histoire des Religions (Paris)
RHPR	Revue d'Histoire et de Philosophie Religieuses (Strasbourg, Paris)
RicBibl	Ricerche Bibliche e Religiose (Genova)
RicRel	Ricerche Religiose (Rome)

RicStRel	Ricerche di Storia Religiosa (Rome)
ROC	Revue de l'Orient Chrétien (Paris)
RRIL	Rendiconti del Reale Istituto Lombardo di Scienze e Lettere (Milan)
RSO	Rivista degli Studi Orientali (Rome)
RSPhTh	Revue des Sciences Philosophiques et Théologiques (Paris)
RTAM	Recherches de Théologie Ancienne et Médiévale (Louvain)
SbAkWissWien	Sitzungsberichte der Österreichischen Akademie der Wissenschaften in Wien
SchwKiZ	Schweizerische Kirchenzeitung (Lucerne)
SeT	Studi e Testi (Rome)
SkHVSU	Skrifter utgivna av humanistiska vetenskapssamfundet i Uppsala
StTheol	Studia Theologica (Lund, Aarhus, Oslo)
StudiItalFilolClass	Studi Italiani di Filologia Classica (Florence)
STZ	Schweizerische Theologische Zeitschrift (Zürich)
SvExÅrsb	Svensk Exegetisk Årsbok (Uppsala; Lund)
SvTKv	Svensk Teologisk Kvartalskrift (Lund)
TA	Teologinen Aikakauskirja (Helsinki)
T(h)B(l)	Theologische Blätter (Leipzig)
ThLBl	Theologisches Literaturblatt (Leipzig)
ThreskEthEnk	Θρησκευτική καὶ Ἠθικὴ Ἐγκυκλοπαιδεία. 12 vols., 1962-8 (Athens)
ThRev	Theologische Revue (Münster)
TLZ	Theologische Literaturzeitung (Leipzig, Berlin)
TR	Theologische Rundschau (Tübingen)
TransSBA	Transactions of the Society of Biblical Archaeology (London)
TS	Theologische Studien (Utrecht)
T&S	Texts and Studies (Cambridge)
TSK	Theologische Studien und Kritiken (Hamburg; Gotha; Leipzig; Berlin)
TU	Texte und Untersuchungen (Leipzig, Berlin)
TuA	Texte und Arbeiten (Beuron)
TZ	Theologische Zeitschrift (Basel)
UJE	Universal Jewish Encyclopedia. 10 vols. (New York, 1939-43)
UUÅ	Uppsala Universitets Årsskrift
VC	Vigiliae Christianae (Amsterdam)
VD	Verbum Domini (Rome)
VT	Vetus Testamentum (Leiden)
VTS	Supplements to Vetus Testamentum (Leiden)
WdO	Die Welt des Orients (Wuppertal; Stuttgart; Göttingen)
WZKM	Wiener Zeitschrift für die Kunde des Morgenlandes
ZäS	Zeitschrift für Ägyptische Sprache und Altertumskunde (Leipzig; Berlin)
ZAW	Zeitschrift für die Alttestamentliche Wissenschaft (Giessen; Berlin)
ZDGM	Zeitschrift der Deutschen Morgenländischen Gesellschaft (Leipzig; Wiesbaden)

ZDPV	Zeitschrift des Deutschen Palästina-Vereins (Leipzig; Stuttgart; Wiesbaden)
ZfA	Zeitschrift für Assyriologie (Leipzig; Berlin)
ZfS	Zeitschrift für Semitistik und verwandte Gebiete (Leipzig)
ZKG	Zeitschrift für Kirchengeschichte (Gotha; Stuttgart)
ZKT	Zeitschrift für Katholische Theologie (Innsbruck, Vienna)
ZNW	Zeitschrift für die Neutestamentliche Wissenschaft (Giessen; Berlin)
ZRGG	Zeitschrift für Religions- und Geistesgeschichte (Marburg, Erlangen, Cologne)
ZvS	Zeitschrift für vergleichende Sprachforschung ... (Göttingen)
ZWT	Zeitschrift für wissenschaftliche Theologie (Jena, Halle, Leipzig)

(2) GENERAL

A', α'	Aquila
AT	Altes Testament
Bl.	Blätter
B.M.	British Museum
Diss.	Dissertation
Ét.	Études
E.T.	English translation
Fs.	Festschrift
n.F.	Neue Folge
n.s.	New Series
O' o'	Οἱ Ἑβδομήκοηντα (LXX)
Or.	Oriental
Π.Δ.	Ἡ Παλαιὰ Διαθήκη
Phil.-hist.Kl.	Philologisch-historische Klasse
Rev.	Revue; review
Rp.	Reprint
rp.	reprinted
Σ', σ'	Symmachus
Sb.	Sitzungsberichte
Syh.	Syrohexaplar
Θ', θ'	Theodotion
Trans.	Transactions; translation
Z(eit)	Zeitschrift

I. INTRODUCTIONS

(See also relevant sections of the
standard Introductions to the Old Testament).

BEBB, L. J. M.: art. 'Versions' in *HDB* 4, 848-55.

BOER, P. A. H. DE: art. 'Septuagint' in *Encycl Brit* 20 (1968), 229-30.

BRATSIOTIS, P.: Σύντομος εἰσαγώγη εἰς τὴν μετάφρασιν τῶν Ο'.(Athens, 1929).

——: art. 'Ο': Μετάφρασις τῆς Παλαιᾶς Διαθήκης' in *ThreskEthEnk* 5, (1966), 667-73.

BRUCE, F. F.: *The Books and the Parchments: some chapters on the transmission of the Bible* (Ch. XII, The OT in Greek). (London, 1963).

24 BURKITT, F. C.: art. 'Text and versions' in *EB* 5011-31.

COHEN, S.: art. 'Bible translations' in *UJE* 2, 334-8.

24 DILLMANN, A. (rvsd. F. BUHL): art. 'Bibeltext des A.T.' in *PRE* 2 (1897), 713-28.

FISCHER, J.; VOGELS, H. J.; BAUMSTARK, A.: art. 'Bibelübersetzungen' in *LTK* 2, 296-323.

FUCHS, H.: art. 'Septuagint' in *UJE* 9, 479-81.

GERLEMAN, G.: art. 'Altgriechische Bibelübersetzungen' in *RGG*[3] I, 1193-5.

GIL, L.: art. 'Septuaginta' in *EncBibl* 6 (1965), 612-20.

GOTTHEIL, R.: art. 'Bible translations' in *JE* 3, 185-97.

24 GRAY, G. B. (rvsd. H. S. GEHMAN): art. 'Text and versions of the OT' in *HSDB*[2] 972-9.

GRIEVE, A. J.: art. 'Septuagint' in *Encycl Brit* 11th ed., 24, 653-5; 14th ed., 20, 335-7.

HANHART, R.: art. 'Septuaginta' in *Bibl-histHWB* 3 (1966), 1772-5.

HARTMANN, L. F.: art. 'Septuagint' in *NCE* 13, 97.

HAUTSCH, E.: art. 'Septuaginta' in *PW* II.2 (1921), 1586-1621.

HOWARD, G.: Introduction to Septuagint Study, *RestQuart* (Houston, Texas) 7 (1963), 132-42; 8 (1965), 10-25.

HODY, H.: *De Bibliorum Textibus Originalibus, Versionibus Graecis et Latina Vulgata.* (Oxford, 1705).

24 JEFFERY, A.: 'Text and ancient versions of the OT', *IB* I, 46-62.

JELLICOE, S.: *The Septuagint and Modern Study.* (Oxford, 1968).
Rev. Brock in *JTS* ns 20 (1969), 574-81;
Tov in *RB* 77 (1970), 84-91.

KENYON, F. G. (rvsd. H. S. GEHMAN): art. 'Greek versions of the OT' in *HSDB²* 347-54.

KORSUNSKIJ, J.: *Die Übersetzung LXX* (Moscow, 1898).
   Rev. Nekrasov in *Christianskoje Čtenije* 1900, 425f.

MARGOLIS, M. L.: *The Story of Bible translations* (Philadelphia, 1917).

METZGER, B. M.: art. 'Versions, ancient' in *IDB* 4, 749-60.

MICHAELIS, W.: art. 'Bibelübersetzungen' in *EJ* 4, 556-70.

NESTLE, E. (et al.): art. 'Bibelübersetzungen' in *PRE³* 3, 1-178: 23, 207-26. (Adapted ET in *NSHE* 2 (1908), 94-134).

——: art. 'Septuagint' in *HDB* 4, 437-54.

OIKONOMOS, C.: Περὶ τῶν ο′ Ἑρμηνευτῶν τῆς Παλαιᾶς Θείας Γραφῆς (Athens, 1844-9; 4 vols).

ORLINSKY, H. M.: *The Septuagint: the oldest translation of the Bible* (Cincinnati, 1949).

OTTLEY, R. R.: *A Handbook to the Septuagint* (London, 1920).

PFEIFFER, R. H.: Introduction to the Old Testament (N.Y. 1948; London, 1952). Esp. Chap. V.

PODLAKA: *(The Greek translations of Holy Scripture)* [In Czech] (Prague, 1896-7).

PRICE, I. M. (rvsd. W. A. IRWIN & A. P. WIKGREN): *The Ancestry of our English Bible* (New York³, 1956).

REDPATH, H. A.: art. 'Versions, Greek (other than LXX)' in *HDB* 4, 864-6.

RINALDI, G.: art. 'Bibbia, Vecchio Testamento' in *EnciclItal* Appx III, 1 (1961), 231a-234b.

ROBERTS, B. J.: *The Old Testament Text and Versions* (Cardiff, 1951).

——: art. 'Ancient versions of the OT' in *PC²*, 81-5.

ROBINSON, H. W. (ed.): *The Bible in its ancient and English versions* (Oxford, 1940; rp 1954).

SANDAY, W.: art. 'Bible' in *ERE* 2, 562-79.

SCHÜRER, E.: *Geschichte des jüdischen Volkes im Zeitalter Jesu Christi* (Leipzig⁴, 1909) III, 424-67. (Rp. 1964).
   = ET of ed. 3 (Edinburgh, 1886), III, 156-95.

SKEHAN, P. W.: art. 'LXX, Α′ Σ′ Θ′ Hexapla' in *NCE* 2, 425-31.

SMITH, W. R.: *The OT in the Jewish Church* (London/Edinburgh², 1892), 73-148.

SWETE, H. B.: *An Introduction to the OT in Greek* (Cambridge,

1900); rvsd. ed. R. R. Ottley, 1914 (rp New York, 1968).
Rev. Lietzmann in *GGA* 1902, 329-38.

THACKERAY, H. ST.J.: art. 'Septuagint' in *ISBE* 4, 2722-32.

VACCARI, A.: art. 'Bibbia' in *EnciclItal* 6 (1930), 879-918; Appx II
(1948), 396f; Appx III (1961), 231-4.

24 ——: *De textu*: *Institutiones biblicae scholis accommodatae* (Rome⁶,
1951), 233-54, 276-362.

24 VANDERVORST, J.: *Introduction aux textes hébreu et grec de l'ancien
testament* (Malines, 1935).

VOGT, E.: art. 'Settanta, versione dei' in *EC* 11 (1953), 436-42.

24 WELLHAUSEN, J.: art. 'Septuagint' in *EncyclBrit* 9th ed., 21 (1886),
667-70.

WEVERS, J. W.: art. 'Septuagint' in *IDB* 4, 273-8.

WÜRTHWEIN, E. & NESTLE, E.: art. 'Bibelübersetzungen' in *EKL* 1,
471-9.

WÜRTHWEIN, E.: *The Text of the OT*. (Oxford, 1957); 2nd German
ed. (Stuttgart, 1963).

ZIEGLER, J.; SCHÄFER, K. T.; HAMP, V.; VÖÖBUS, A. et al.: art.
'Bibelübersetzungen' in *LTK²* 2, 375-401.

2. CONCORDANCES

(See also 40)

(a) *Of LXX*

HATCH, E. and REDPATH, H. A.: *A Concordance to the Septuagint and
the other Greek Versions of the OT (including the Apocryphal
Books)* (Oxford, 1897; rp. Graz, 1954).

KIRCHER, C.: *Concordantiae Veteris Testamenti Graecae, Ebreis vocibus respondentes* (Frankfurt a.M., 1607).

MORRISH, G.: *A Handy Concordance of the Septuagint* (London,
1887).

TROMM, A.: *Concordantiae Graecae versionis vulgo dictae Septuaginta
Interpretum* (Amsterdam/Utrecht, 1718; 2 vols).

(b) *Of MT* (select)

FÜRST, J.: *Librorum Sacrorum Veteris Testamenti Concordantiae
Hebraicae atque Chaldaicae* (Leipzig, 1840).

KUHN, K. G.: *Konkordanz zu den Qumrantexten* (Göttingen, 1960).

Lisowsky, G.: *Konkordanz zum hebräischen Alten Testament* (Stuttgart, 1958).

Mandelkern, S.: *Veteris Testamenti Concordantiae Hebraicae et Chaldaicae* (Leipzig, 1896 and rps).

Weinheimer, H.: *Hebräisches Wörterbuch in sachlicher Ordnung* (Tübingen, 1918).

(c) *Studies*

Drescher, J.: The earliest Biblical Concordances, *BSAC* 15 (1958), 63-7.

Göttsberger, J.: Berichtigung zur LXX Konkordanz von Hatch-Redpath, *BZ* 3 (1905), 39.

——: Zu εἰρήνη bei Hatch-Redpath, *BZ* 4 (1906), 246.

Heller, Ch.: *(The LXX references in Mandelkern's Concordance)* [In Hebrew] (New York, 1943).

Redpath, H. A.: Concordances to the OT in Greek, *Expos* 5 (1896), 69-77.

Steininger, P. P.: Μαζία bei Hatch-Redpath, *BZ* 8 (1910), 132.

Walde, B.: Berichtigungen zur LXX Konkordanz von Hatch-Redpath, *BZ* 15 (1920), 234.

3a. EDITIONS

(See also 39, 40)

(For older editions see Nestle in *HDB* 4, 437-54; British and Foreign Bible Society, *Historical Catalogue of Printed Bibles* (London, 1903), Part III, 573-678).

British and Foreign Bible Society: Ἡ Παλαιὰ Διαθήκη κατὰ τοὺς Ο' (London, 1914: 2 vols).

39b Brooke, A. E. and McLean, N.: *The Book of Judges in Greek according to the Text of Codex Alexandrinus* (Cambridge, 1897).

——, —— and (vol. II, 1 onwards) Thackeray, H. St. J.: *The Old Testament in Greek according to the text of Codex Vaticanus, supplemented from other uncial manuscripts with a critical apparatus containing the variants of the chief ancient authorities for the text of the LXX* (Cambridge, 1906-40).

39a Vol. I, part 1: *Genesis* (1906).

Rev. Nestle, *Berliner philologische Wochenschrift*, Sept. 1907, 1221-7; cp *LXX Studien* V (1907).

39a	2:	*Exodus, Leviticus* (1909).
		Rev. (of 1-2) Hautsch in *GGA* 1909, 563-80.
39a	3:	*Numbers, Deuteronomy* (1911).
39b	4:	*Joshua, Judges, Ruth* (1917).
39c	Vol. II, part 1:	*I-II Samuel* (1927).
39c	2:	*I-II Kings* (1930).
39d	3:	*I-II Chronicles* (1932).
39d	4:	*Esdras, Ezra, Nehemiah* (1935).
		Rev. Katz in *TLZ* 62 (1937), 341-5.
39e	Vol. III, part 1:	*Esther, Judith, Tobit* (1940).
		Rev. Torrey in *JBL* 61 (1942), 130-6.

15b CONYBEARE, F. C. and STOCK, ST. G.: *Selections from the Septuagint*
(ii)   *according to the text of Swete* (Boston/London, 1905).

DARLOW, T. H. & MOULE, H. F.: Historical Catalogue of the Printed
Editions of Holy Scripture in the Library of the British &
Foreign Bible Society, London, 1903-1911.

Dropsie College Edition:
Jewish Apocryphal Literature (New York/London).
(Introduction, text, translation, commentary).

39f   *The First Book of Maccabees* (ed. Zeitlin, S.: tr. Tedesche, S.;
       1950).

39f   *The Second Book of Maccabees* (ed. Zeitlin, S.; tr. Tedesche, S.;
       1954).

39f   *The Third and Fourth Books of Maccabees* (ed. Hadas, M.; 1953).

21   *Aristeas to Philocrates* (ed. Hadas, M.; 1951).

39i   *The Book of Wisdom* (ed. Reider, J.; 1957).

39e   *The Book of Tobit* (ed. Zimmermann, F.; 1958).

39i GEBHARDT, O. VON: Ψαλμοὶ Σολομῶντος (Leipzig, 1895).

3b GIANNAKOPOULOS, I: Ἡ Παλαιὰ Διαθήκη κατὰ τοὺς Ο΄. (Athens,
1955-68). [With introductions and modern Greek version].

Göttingen Septuagint:
Vetus Testamentum Graecum Auctoritate Societatis Litterarum
Gottingensis editum. (Göttingen, 1931-).

39e   VIII, 3: *Esther* (ed. Hanhart, R.; 1966).

39f   IX, 1: *Maccabaeorum lib. 1* (ed. Kappler, W.; 1936, ²1967).

39f   2: *Maccabaeorum lib. 2* (ed. Kappler, W., and Hanhart,
R.; 1959). Rev. Starcky in *RB* 66 (1959) 424-30.

39f   3: *Maccabaeorum lib. 3* (ed. Hanhart, R.; 1960). Rev.
Kilpatrick in *GGA* 1963 10-22 (of 2 and 3).

39g   X   :   *Psalmi cum Odis* (ed. Rahlfs, A.; 1931, ²1967). Rev.
                Vaccari in *Biblica* 1932, 335-41.

39i   XII, 1:   *Sapientia Salomonis* (ed. Ziegler, J.; 1962).

39i   2:   *Sapientia Iesu Filii Sirach* (ed. Ziegler, J.; 1965).

39k   XIII :   *Duodecim Prophetae* (ed. Ziegler, J.; 1943, ²1967).

39l   XIV :   *Isaias* (ed. Ziegler, J.; 1939, ²1967).

39m   XV   :   *Ieremias, Baruch, Threni, Epistula Ieremiae* (ed.
                Ziegler, J.; 1957).

39n   XVI, 1:   *Ezechiel* (ed. Ziegler, J.; 1952, ²1967)
                Rev. Barthélemy in *RB* 59 (1952), 607-10.

39o   2:   *Susanna, Daniel, Bel et Draco* (ed. Ziegler, J.;
1954).

39i   HART, J. H. A.: *Ecclesiasticus. The Greek text of codex 248, edited
with a textual commentary and prolegomena* (Cambridge, 1909).

     HOLMES, R. and PARSONS, J.: *Vetus Testamentum Graecum cum
variis lectionibus* (Oxford 1798-1827; 5 vols).

     JAGER, J. N.: Ἡ Παλαιὰ Διαθήκη κατὰ τοὺς Ο'. *Vetus Testamentum
Graecum ... iuxta exemplar originale Vaticanum* (Paris, 1882).

39a   LAGARDE, P. A. DE: *Genesis Graece* (Leipzig, 1868).

     ——: *Librorum Veteris Testamenti canonicorum pars prior Graece*
(Göttingen, 1883).

39g   ——: *Novae Psalterii Graeci editionis specimen.* (Göttingen, 1887 =
AbhKGWGött 33).

39b   ——: *Septuaginta-Studien* (Göttingen, 1891), 1-75 [Edition of
Judges i-xvi].

39g   ——: *Psalterii Graeci quinquagena prima* (Göttingen, 1892).

39a   LANZ-LIEBENFELS, J.: *Die griechischen Bibelversionen, LXX und
Hexapla.* Vol. 1, *Genesis, herausgegeben mit Anmerkungen und
deutscher Übersetzung versehen* (Leipzig, 1908).

39b   MARGOLIS, M. L.: *The Book of Joshua in Greek.* Parts I-IV [never
completed; to xix 38] (Paris, 1931-8).

39k   MEINHOLD, J. and LIETZMANN, H.: *Der Prophet Amos hebräisch und
griechisch.* = Kleine Texte 15, 16 (Bonn, 1905; Cambridge,
1906).

39g   NESTLE, E.: *Psalterium tetraglottum.* (Tübingen, 1879).

     ——: (ed. J. Dahse and Erwin Nestle): *Das Buch Jeremia griechisch
und hebräisch* (Stuttgart, 1924, ²1934).

39l   OTTLEY, R. R.: *The Book of Isaiah according to the Septuagint
(Codex Alexandrinus)* (Cambridge, 1904, ²1909; 1906. 2 vols).

39b RAHLFS, A.: *Das Buch Ruth griechisch als Probe einer kritischen Handausgabe der Septuaginta* (Stuttgart, 1922).
——: *Septuaginta Societatis Scientiarum Gottingensis Auctoritate:* I, *Genesis* (Stuttgart, 1926).
——: *Septuaginta, id est Vetus Testamentum Graece iuxta LXX Interpretes* (Stuttgart, 1935 and rps; 2 vols).
Rev. Katz in *TLZ* 61 (1936), 265-87.

39i RYLE, H. E. and JAMES, M. R.: *Psalms of the Pharisees, commonly called the Psalms of Solomon* (Cambridge, 1891).
SWETE, H. B.: *The OT in Greek according to the Septuagint* (Cambridge, 1887-94).
I: Genesis-IV Kings (1887; [4]1909).
II: Chron.-Tobit (1890, [2]1907).
III: Hosea-IV Macc.; Pss. Sol.; Enoch. (1894, [4]1912).

39g ——: *The Psalms in Greek according to the Septuagint* (Cambridge [2], 1896).
TISCHENDORF, C. VON: Ἡ Παλαιὰ Διαθήκη κατὰ τοὺς Ο'. *Vetus Testamentum Graece secundum LXX Interpretes* (Leipzig[6], 1880).

39c, VANNUTELLI, P.: *Libri synoptici Veteris Testamenti seu librorum*
d *Regum et Chronicorum loci paralleli* (Rome, 1931-4; 2 vols).

39i VATTIONI, F.: *Ecclesiastico. Testo ebraico con apparato critico e versione greca, latina e siriaca* (Naples, 1968).
WIKGREN, A.P., with E. C. COLWELL and R. MARCUS: *Hellenistic Greek Texts*. (Chicago, 1947) [Including selections from LXX].

3b. TRANSLATIONS OF LXX
(See also 5)

BRENTON, L. C. L.: *The LXX version of the OT according to the Vatican Text, translated into English with the principal various readings of the Alexandrine copy* (London, 1844; 2 vols).
BRUNELLO, A.: *La Bibbia secondo la versione de Settanta* (Rome, 1960; 2 vols).
Rev. Vaccari in *Biblica* 42 (1961), 465-7.
GIANNAKOPOULOS, I.: — see 3a.
GIGUET, P.: *Le livre de Job, précédé des livres de Ruth, Tobit, Judith et d'Esther. Traduit du grec des Septante* (Paris, 1859).
——: *La Sainte Bible. Traduction de l'AT d'après les Septante* (Paris, 1865-72; 4 vols).

HOWARD, H. E. J.: *The Book of Genesis according to the version of the LXX* (Cambridge, 1855) [ET with notes].

——: *The Books of Exodus and Leviticus according to the version of the LXX* (Cambridge, 1857) [*id*].

——: *The Books of Numbers and Deuteronomy according to the version of the LXX* (Cambridge, 1857) [*id*].

JAGER, J. N.: *V.T. Graecum ... cum Latina translatione* (Paris, 1839).

LAZARUS, A.: *The Holy Psalter: The Psalms of David from the LXX* (Madras, 1966).

MUSES, C. A.: *The LXX Bible: The oldest version of the OT in the translation of Charles Thomson* (Indian Hills, Colorado, 1954).

PASCAL, P., et al.: *Le livre de Job, épopée biblique en xlii chapitres paraphrasée en vers par P. Pascal d'après les textes conjoints des LXX et de la Vulgate* (Turin, 1967).

PELLS, S. F.: *The Old Covenant, commonly called the Old Testament translated from the LXX by Charles Thomson* (London, 1904; 2 vols).

Rev. Hart in *JQR* 16 (1904), 596-600.

THOMSON, C.: *The Holy Bible, containing the Old and the New Covenant, commonly called the Old and the New Testament* (Philadelphia, 1808; 4 vols).

VIGOUROUX, F. G.: *La Sainte Bible polyglotte, contenant le texte hébreu original, le texte grec des LXX, le texte latin de la Vulgate et la traduction française de M. l'Abbé Glaire*. O.T. Paris 1901.

4. SURVEY ARTICLES

BERTRAM, G.: Zur LXX-Forschung. *TR* nF 3 (1931), 283-96; 5 (1933), 173-85; 10 (1938), 69-80, 133-59.

——: Septuaginta und Urchristentum. *ThB* 4 (1925), 208-13.

——: Das Problem der Umschrift und die religionsgeschichtliche Erforschung der Septuaginta. *BZAW* 66 (1936), 97-109.

BRATSIOTIS, P. I.: Ἡ Παλαιὰ Διαθήκη ἐν τῇ Ἑλληνικῇ Ἐκκλησίᾳ ἀπὸ τῆς ἁλώσεως μεχρὶ σήμερον (Athens, 1940). [17 pp.]

DEBRUNNER, A.: — see 15a.

GROSSE-BRAUCKMANN, E.: 'LXX-Forschung' in *EKL* 3, 937-8.

JELLICOE, S.: The LXX today. *ET* 77 (1965/66), 68-74.

——: LXX Studies in the Current Century. *JBL* 88 (1969), 191-9.

JENNI, E.: Zwei Jahrzehnte Forschung an den Büchern Josua bis

Könige. *TR* nF 27 (1961) 20-32 [on 'Texte und alte Übersetzungen'].

KATZ, P.: Septuagintal Studies in the Mid-Century. Their Links with
the Past and their Present Tendencies. In *The Background to the
NT and its Eschatology*, ed. W. D. Davies, D. Daube [Fs. C. H.
Dodd] (Cambridge, 1956), 176-208.

——: art. 'LXX-Forschung' in *RGG*³ 5, 1404-7.

MARTINI, C. M.: Studi sulla Bibbia greca. *Biblica* 47 (1966), 115-21.

NESTLE, E.: New literature on the LXX. *AJT* 13 (1909), 446-50; 14
(1910), 286-93.

39h   ORLINSKY, H. M.: Current progress and problems in LXX research.
(iv)   In *The Study of the Bible To-Day and Tomorrow*, ed. H. R.
Willoughby (Chicago, 1947), 144-61.

PLESSNER, M.: Neue Arbeiten zur LXX-Forschung. *MGWJ* 70
(1926), 237-50.

REDPATH, H. A.: The present position of the study of the LXX.
AJT 7 (1903), 1-19.

REIDER, J.: LXX literature. *JQR* ns 28 (1937/8), 337-40.

SEELIGMANN, I. L.: Problemen en perspectieven in het moderne
LXX-onderzoek. *JEOL* II, 7 (1940), 359-90e, 763-6.

SPERBER, A.: Septuaginta-Probleme. *BWANT* 3: 13 (Stuttgart,
1929).

VACCARI, A.: Rassegna di recenti pubblicazioni su Testi e Versioni
della Bibbia. *Biblica* 20 (1939), 416-35.

WEVERS, J.W.: LXX-Forschungen. *TR* nF 22 (1954), 85-137, 171-90.

——: LXX-Forschungen seit 1954. *TR* nF 33 (1968), 18-76.

5. PERSONALIA
(See also 15a, 28, 40j)

BAUER, W.: Alfred Rahlfs. *NGWGött* 1935, 60-5. [rp in A. Rahlfs,
*LXX Studien*² (Göttingen, 1965)].

BERTRAM, G.: Theologische Kritik und Textkritik bei P. A. de
Lagarde. *Kirche im Angriff* 13 (1937), 370-81.

BURKITT, F. C.: H. St. J. Thackeray and his work. *JTS* 32 (1931),
225-7.

BURN, J. H.: Frederick Field M.A., LL.D. *ET* 8 (1896/7), 160-3, 274-
8, 325-8.

——: Dr. Field's OT revision notes. *ET* 30 (1918), 85-6, 181-2, 427,
476-7; 32 (1910), 139-40; 35 (1923), 45-6, 332-3.

3b   CLARK, P. O.: Letters of Charles Thomson on the translation of the
        Bible. *JPresbyterian Historical Society* 33 (1955), 239-56.
      EVERY, G.: Dr. Grabe and his manuscripts. *JTS* ns 8 (1957), 280-92.
      GORDIS, R.: The life of Professor Max Leopold Margolis: an appre-
        ciation. In *M. L. Margolis, scholar and teacher* (Philadelphia,
        1952), 1-16.
      GOTTHEIL, R.: *The bibliography of the works of P. A. de Lagarde*
        (Washington, 1892) [= rp with addenda of *ProcAOS* 1892
        ccxi-ccxxix].
      HARTMANN, W.: Paul de Lagardes religiöse Entwicklung. *TB*20
        (1941), 334-41.
40g   MANGENOT, E.: *Les travaux des Bénédictins de St. Maur, de St.
        Vanne et de St. Hydulfe sur les anciennes versions latines de la
        Bible* (Amiens, 1888).
      NESTLE, E.: A forgotten letter on the English Bible and the LXX
        [on T. Brett]. *ET* 16 (1904), 380-1.
37a   ——: Drusius als erster Sammler von Hexaplafragmenten. *ZAW*
        26 (1906), 164-7.
      ORLINSKY, H. M.: Margolis' work on the Septuagint. In *M. L.
        Margolis, scholar and teacher* (Philadelphia, 1952), 35-44.
      RAHLFS, A.: Gedächtnisrede zu Paul de Lagarde's 100 Geburtstage.
        NGWGött 1927/8, 74-89.
      ——: *Paul de Lagardes wissenschaftlisches Lebenswerk im Rahmen
        einer Geschichte seines Lebens dargestellt. MSU* 4, 1 (Berlin,
        1928).
      ROS, J.: De studie van het Bijbel-grieksch van H. Grotius tot Adolf
        Deissmann (Nijmegen, 1940.)
      SPITALER, A.: Otto Pretzl. *ZDMG* 96 (1942), 161-70.
      TECHEN, L.: Lagarde, P. A. de (Bötticher). *Allgemeine deutsche
        Biographie*, 51 (Leipzig, 1906), 531-6.
      TREITEL, L.: Z. Frankel's Verdienste um die LXX-Forschung.
        MGWJ 45 (1901), 253-62.
      ZIEGLER, J.: P. Katz (Walters). *TLZ* 87 (1962), 793-6.

6. SIGNIFICANCE OF LXX

      BARTHÉLEMY, D.: La place de la LXX dans l'Église. *Recherches
        Bibliques* 8 (1967), 13-28.

Boehmer, J.: Mission und LXX. *Studierstube* 1903, 340-54.

Bratsiotis, P.: Ἡ διὰ τὴν ἐπιστήμην καὶ μάλιστα τὴν Ἑλληνικὴν σπουδαιότης τῆς μεταφράσεως τῶν Ο'. *Ekklesia* 1928, 145-7.

Hadidian, D. Y.: The LXX and its place in theological education. *ET* 76 (1964), 102-3.

Hanhart, R.: Die Bedeutung der LXX-Forschung für die Theologie. In *Drei Studien zum Judentum* (Munich, 1967).

15c, Harrison, E. F.: The importance of the LXX for Biblical studies.
27   *BS* 112 (1956), 344-55; 113 (1956), 37-45.

Jahn, G.: *Beiträge zur Beurtheilung der LXX* (Kirchhain, 1902).

24   Kirkpatrick, A. F.: The LXX version: its bearing on the text and interpretation of the OT. *Expos* V, 3 (1896), 263-87.

24   Nestle, E.: Die LXX in ihrer Bedeutung für die literarische Kritik. Eine Mahnung zur Vorsicht. *OLZ* 11 (1908), 240-2.

7. GENERAL

Barnes, W. E.: 'The Recovery of the Septuagint'. *JTS* 36 (1935), 123-31.

Bertram, G.: Griechisches AT und Entmythologisierung. *Deutsches PfarrerBl* 66 (1966), 413ff.

Bratsiotis, P. I.: Ἑβδομηκονταλογικὰ μελετήματα (Athens, 1926/7).

Bruce, F. F.: The OT in Greek. *Bible Translator* 4 (1953), 129-35, 156-62.

Danker, F. W.: The LXX — Its history. *Concordia Theological Monthly* 30 (1959), 271-84.

Derjugin, T.: *Bibel und Griechen.* (Leningrad, 1925).

Edwards, C. E.: The LXX in Criticism. *Evangelical Quarterly* 7 (1935), 172-8.

Farrar, F. W.: The LXX translation. *Expos* 1 (1881), 15-29, 104-19.

Forster, A. H.: The study of the LXX. *AnglThRev* 14 (1932), 152-208.

Frankel, Z.: *Historisch-kritische Studien zu der LXX*, Erster Band, Erste Abtheilung: *Vorstudien zu der LXX* (Leipzig, 1841).

Fruhstorfer, K.: Die griechische Bibelübersetzung der LXX. *Theologisch-practische Quartalschrift* (Linz) 88 (1935), 465-72.

Geiger, A.: *Urschrift und Übersetzungen der Bibel in ihrer Abhängig-*

keit von der inneren Entwicklung des Judentums (Frankfurt a.M.,
1928).

GRINFIELD, E. W.: *An Apology for the LXX in which its claims to
Biblical and Canonical Authority are briefly stated and vindicated*
(London, 1850).

HAAG, H.: Probleme der griechischen Bibel. *SchwKiZ* 123 (1955),
520-2, 534-5.

HEMPEL, J.: Eine Vorfrage zum LXX-Problem. *Fs. E. Barnikol.*
(Berlin, 1964), 21-6.

HIGHFIELD, H.: Gleanings from the LXX. *ET* 38 (1926), 44-5.

HOOYKAAS, I.: *Iets over de griekse vertaling van het OT* (Rotterdam,
1888).

21b, KAHLE, P. E.: *The Cairo Geniza* (London, 1947; Oxford², 1959).
22,   Rev. Brønno in *ZDMG* nF 25 (1950), 521-65; Manson in
24,   *Dominican Studies* 2 (1949), 183-92; Vermes in *NTS* 6 (1959-
36c   60), 323-5; Orlinsky in *AJA* 52 (1948), 473-4; and *JAOS* 69
       (1949), 164-7.

——: Die LXX. Prinzipielle Erwägungen. *Fs. O. Eissfeldt zum 60
Geburtstag*, ed. J. Fück (Halle, 1947), 161-80.

——: Problems of the LXX. *Studia Patristica* I = *TU* 63 (1957),
328-38.

KÖHLER, L.: Kleine Beiträge zur Septuaginta-Forschung. *STZ* 24
(1907), 41-44; 25 (1908), 36-8; 26 (1909), 135-7.

LAGARDE, P. A. DE: *LXX-Studien I-III.* (Göttingen, 1891).

——: *Mitteilungen I-IV.* (Göttingen, 1884-91).

MALHA, L.: (The Septuagint version). [In Arabic]. *Mashriq* 1930,
401-9.

MERCATI, G.: *Note di letteratura biblica e cristiana antica. SeT* 5(1901).

——: *Nuove note di letteratura biblica e cristiana antica. SeT* 95
(1941).

MORIARTY, F. L.: LXX. *TS* 14 (1953), 402-5.

NESTLE, E.: *LXXstudien I-II* (Ulm, 1886-96); III-VI (Stuttgart,
1899-1911).

——: *Marginalien und Materialien* (Tübingen, 1893).

PALLIA, J. J.: Quelques faits et écrits bibliques alexandrins. *Cahiers
d'Alexandrie* 2 (1964), 5-18.

PRIJS, L.: *Proofs of the authenticity of the LXX* (Chicago, 1947).

RAHLFS, A.: *LXX-Studien I-III* (Göttingen, 1904-11; repr. 1965).

——: *Kleine Mitteilungen aus dem LXX-Unternehmen. MSU* I, 7
(1915).

SCHLEUSNER, J. F.: *Opuscula critica ad versiones Graecas Veteris Testamenti pertinentia* (Leipzig, 1812).

SCHREINER, J.: Hermeneutische Leitlinien in der LXX. *Die hermeneutische Frage in der Theologie* (Freiburg, 1968), 356-94.

SCHÜRER, E.: Geschichte des jüdischen Volkes im Zeitalter Jesu Christi (Leipzig⁴, 1901-9).

SELLIN, E.: Die Spuren griechischer Philosophie im AT. *ThLBl* 26 (1905) 307-8.

SMITH, H. P.: Old Testament Notes. *JBL* 24 (1905), 27-30.

SOISALON-SOININEN, I.: Die LXX-Forschung in ihrem Verhältnis zum Alten Testament. *TA* 56 (1951), 208-14.

31   SOUTER, A.: The Pseudo-Augustinian *Quaestiones Veteris et Novi Testamenti. JTS* 6 (1905), 61-6.

36c   SPERBER, A.: *LXX-Probleme* (Stuttgart, 1929). Rev. Rahlfs in *TLZ* 55 (1930), 104-6.

STENGEL, PAUL: *Die griechischen Kultusaltertümer* (München³, 1920).

SWETE, H. B.: *Essays on Some Biblical Questions of the Day* (London, 1909).

22,   THACKERAY, H. ST. J.: *The LXX and Jewish Worship* (London,
23,   1921). Rev. Dhorme in *RB* 33 (1924), 268-71. Nairne in *JTS*
39c, 23 (1923), 88-91.
k-m

———: *Some aspects of the Greek OT* (London, 1927).

TRITTON, A. S.: Some notes on the LXX. *TransGlasgow OrSoc* 18 (1961), 49-52.

VELLAS, B.: Hauptprobleme der LXX-Forschung. *Byz.-neugr. Jahrbücher* 14 (1938), 310-21.

VISSER, E.: *Götter und Kulte im ptolemäischen Alexandrien* (Amsterdam, 1938).

ZIEGLER, J.: *Die LXX : Erbe und Auftrag* (Würzburg, 1962).

8. INSPIRATION OF LXX
(See also 10a)

AUVRAY, P.: Comment se pose le problème de l'inspiration des LXX? *RB* 59 (1952), 321-36.

BARDY, G.: L'inspiration des Pères de l'Église. In *Mélanges J. Lebreton*, II (Paris, 1952), 7-26 [= *RechSR* 40].

BENOIT, P.: La LXX est-elle inspirée? In *Vom Wort des Lebens: Fs. M. Meinertz.* (Münster, 1951), 41-9.

——: L'inspiration des LXX d'après les Pères. In *Mélanges H. de Lubac.* (Paris, 1963) I, 169-87.

DREYFUS, F.: L'inspiration de la LXX. Quelques difficultés à surmonter. *RSPhTh* 49 (1965), 210-20.

DUBARLE, A. M.: Note conjointe sur l'inspiration de la LXX. La valeur de certains arguments proposés en sa faveur. *RSPhTh* 49 (1965), 221-9.

GRELOT, P.: Sur l'inspiration et la canonicité de la LXX. *Sciences Ecclésiastiques* 16 (1964), 387-418.

28,   KARPP, H.: 'Prophet' oder 'Dolmetscher'? Die Geltung der LXX in
31   der alten Kirche. *Fs. Günter Dehn.* (Neukirchen, 1957), 103-17.

SANDAY, W.: *Inspiration* (London³, 1896).

9. CANON
(See also 31, 39)

AUDET, J.-P.: A Hebrew-Aramaic list of books of the OT in Greek transcription. *JTS* ns 1 (1950), 135-54.

BARTHÉLEMY, D.: L'A.T. a mûri à Alexandrie. *TZ* 21 (1965), 358-70.

40d   BAUMSTARK, A.: Der äthiopische Bibelkanon. *OC* 5 (1905), 162-73.

CAMPENHAUSEN, H. VON: Das AT als Bibel der Kirche vom Ausgang des Urchristentums bis zur Entstehung des NT. In *Aus der Frühzeit des Christentums.* (Tübingen, 1963), 152-96.

——: *Die Entstehung der christlichen Bibel.* Beiträge z. Hist. Theologie (Tübingen, 1968).

DAUBNEY, W. H.: *The use of the Apocrypha in the Christian Church.* (London, 1900).

31   DENNEFELD, L.: *Der alttestamentliche Kanon der antiochenischen Schule* (Biblische Studien XIV: 4, 1909).

39i   EBERHARTER, A.: *Der Kanon des AT zur Zeit des Ben Sira.* ATA III, 3. (Münster, 1911).

29   FELL, W.: Der Bibelkanon des Flavius Josephus. *BZ* 7 (1909), 1-15, 113-22, 235-44.

GUIDI, I.: Il canone biblico della chiesa copta. *RB* 10 (1901), 161-74.

35c   HALKIN, F.: Livres de l'Ancien et du Nouveau Testament insérés dans les manuscrits hagiographiques grecs. In *Mélanges H. de Lubac.* I (Paris, 1963), 373-5.

39d HOWORTH, H. H.: The modern Roman canon and the Book of Esdras A. *JTS* 7 (1906), 343-54.

JEPSEN, A.: Zur Kanongeschichte des AT. *ZAW* 71 (1959), 114-36. [On Audet].

32 KASTEREN, J. P. VAN: L'AT d'Origène. *RB* 10 (1901), 414-23.

KATZ, P.: The OT Canon in Palestine and Alexandria. *ZNW* 47 (1956), 191-227, 288.

KOOLE, J. L.: *De Overname van het Oude Testament door de Christelijke Kerk* (Hilversum, 1938).

31 LEFORT, L.-TH.: Théodore de Tabennesi et la lettre pascale de S. Athanase sur le canon de la Bible. *Le Muséon* 29 (1910), 205-16.

31 MERCATI, G.: Sul canone biblico di S. Epifanio. *SeT* 5 (1901), 17-27, 243-5.

32 MERK, A.: Origenes und der Kanon des AT. *Biblica* 6 (1925), 200-5.

23 NESTLE, E.: Zur Geschichte der Bibel. *ZWT* 50 (1908), 91-106.

28 PICK, B.: Philo's Canon of the OT and his mode of quoting the Alexandrian version. *JBL* 4 (1884), 126-43.

39f RAHLFS, A.: Über das Fehlen der Makkabäerbücher in der äthiopischen Bibelübersetzung. *ZAW* 28 (1908), 63-4.

ROBERTS, B. J.: The OT Canon: a suggestion. *BJRL* 46 (1963/4), 164-78.

32 RUWET, J.: Duo textus Origenis de canone antiqui testamenti. *Biblica* 2 (1921), 57-60.

31 ——: Clément d'Alexandrie: canon des écritures et apocryphes. *Biblica* 29 (1948), 77-99, 240-68, 391-408.

31 ——: Le canon alexandrin des écritures. S. Athanase. *Biblica* 33 (1952), 1-29.

RYLE, H. E.: *The Canon of the OT* (London, 1892).

SANDAY, W.: The Cheltenham List of the Canonical Books of the OT and NT and of the Writings of Cyprian. *Studia Biblica et Ecclesiastica* 3 (1891), 217-325.

23 SCHNIERLA, W.: The Orthodox OT Canon and the so-called Apocrypha. *St. Vladimir's Seminary Quarterly* ns I, 4 (1957), 40-6.

31 STENZEL, M.: Der Bibelkanon des Rufin von Aquileja. *Biblica* 23 (1942), 43-61.

SUNDBERG, A. C.: The OT and the early Church (a study in Canon). *HTR* 51 (1958), 205-26.

——: *The OT of the early Church* (Cambridge, Mass., 1964).

——: The 'Old Testament': A Christian Canon. *CBQ* 30 (1968), 143-55.

TORREY, C. C. and EISSFELDT, O.: Ein griechisch transkribiertes und interpretiertes hebräisch-aramäisches Verzeichnis der Bücher des AT aus dem 1. Jahrh. n. Chr. *TLZ* 77 (1952), 250-4 [On Audet].

TURNER, C. H.: Latin Lists of the Canonical Books. *JTS* 1 (1900), 554-60; 2 (1901), 236-53, 577; 4 (1903), 426-34; 13 (1912), 77-82, 511-4.

ZEITLIN, S.: An historical study on the canonisation of the Hebrew Scriptures. *PAAJR* 2 (1931/2), 121-58.

ZINK, J. K.: *The use of the OT in the Apocrypha* (Diss. Duke Univ., 1963).

10a. LXX AS A TRANSLATION

BAAB, O. J.: A Theory of Two Translators for the Greek Genesis *JBL* 52 (1933), 239-243.

22   BICKERMANN, E. J.: *The LXX as a translation. PAAJR* 28 (1959), 1-39.

BLAU, L.: The Relation of the Bible Translations of the Jews in Romance Languages to the Ancient Versions and the Jewish Inscriptions in the Catacombs. *JQR* N.S. 19 (1928-9), 157-82.

40g   BLONDHEIM, D. S.: *Les parlers judéo-romans et la Vetus Latina; étude sur les rapports entre les traductions bibliques en langue romane des Juifs au moyen âge et les anciennes versions* (Paris, 1925).

8,   BROCK, S. P.: The phenomenon of Biblical translation in Antiquity.
21b,   *Alta* (Birmingham) II, 8 (1969), 96-102.
22

22   COSTE, J.: La première expérience de traduction biblique: la Septante. *La Maison Dieu* 53 (1958), 56-88.

39i   LEIPOLDT, J.: Von Übersetzungen und Übersetzern. In *Fs. W. Schubart*, ed. S. Morenz. (Leipzig, 1950), 54-60 [On Ben Sira].

—— and MORENZ, S.: *Heilige Schriften. Betrachtungen zur Religionsgeschichte der antiken Mittelmeerwelt* (Leipzig, 1953).

22   RABIN, C.: The Translation Process and the Character of the LXX. *Textus* 6 (1968), 1-26.

10b. BIBLICAL TRANSLATION IN GENERAL (Select)
(See also 33)

GRANT, F. C.: *Translating the Bible* (Greenwich, Conn. 1961).

JACOBSEN, E.: *Translation, a traditional craft* (Copenhagen, 1958).

MOREAU, J. L.: *Language and religious language: a study in the dynamics of translation* (Philadelphia, 1961).

NIDA, E. A.: Translation or Paraphrase. *Bible Translator* 1 (1950), 97-106.

——: *Towards a science of translating* (Leiden, 1964).

ORLINSKY, H. M.: The new Jewish version of the Torah: toward a new philosophy of Bible translation. *JBL* 82 (1963), 249-64.

33 SCHWARZ, W.: *Principles and problems of Biblical translation* (Cambridge, 1955).

——: The history of the principles of Bible translation in the western world. *Babel* 9 (1963), 5-22.

STOERIG, H. J.: *Das Problem des Übersetzens* (Stuttgart, 1963).

11. CHARACTERISTICS AND BACKGROUND
(See also 12, 39)

BARROIS, A.: Une Nouvelle Théorie de l'Origine des LXX. *RB* 39 (1930), 332-61.

BERTRAM, G.: Die Bedeutung der LXX in der Geschichte des Diasporajudentums [Summary only]. *ZDMG* 81 (1927), liv-lv.

——: Die religiöse Umdeutung altorientalischer Lebensweisheit in der griechischen Übersetzung des AT. *ZAW* 54 (1936), 153-67.

——: Der religionsgeschichtliche Hintergrund des Begriffs 'Erhöhung' in der LXX. *ZAW* 68 (1956), 57-71.

——: Vom Wesen der LXX-Frömmigkeit. *WdO* II, 3 (1956), 274-84.

——: LXX-Frömmigkeit. *RGG*³ 5 (1961), 1707-9.

——: Zur Bedeutung der Religion der LXX in der hellenistischen Welt. *TLZ* 92 (1967), 245-50.

BOUSSET, W.: *Jüdisch-christlicher Schulbetrieb in Alexandria und Rom. FRLANT*. N.F.6 (Göttingen, 1915).

DEISSMANN, G. A.: Die Hellenisierung des semitischen Monotheismus. *Neue Jahrbücher für das klassische Altertum* (1903), 161-77.

FRANKEL, Z.: *Über den Einfluss der palästinischen Exegese auf die alexandrinische Hermeneutik.* (Leipzig, 1851).

FREUDENTHAL, J.: Are there Traces of Greek Philosophy in the LXX? *JQR* 2 (1890), 205-22.

39a FÜRST, J.: Spuren der palästinisch-jüdischen Schriftdeutung und
(ii) Sagen in der Übersetzung der LXX. In *Semitic Studies in memory of A. Kohut* (Berlin, 1897), 152-66. [In Gen.]

39a GINZBERG, L.: Die Haggada bei den Kirchenvätern und in der apo-
(ii) kryphischen Litteratur. *MGWJ* 42 (1898), 537-50; 43 (1899), 17-22, 117-125, 149-159, 217-231, 293-303, 409-416, 461-470, 485-504, 529-547. [In Gen.]

HEINISCH, P.: *Griechische Philosophie und AT* (Münster, 1913-4). 2 vols.

KAUPEL, H.: Sirenen in der LXX. *BZ* 23 (1935-6), 158-65.

MARCUS, R.: Jewish and Greek elements in the LXX. In *Louis Ginzberg Jubilee Volume*. (New York, 1945), II, 227-45.

MORENZ, S.: Ägyptische Spuren in der LXX. In *Mullus: Fs. T. Klauser = JAC Ergänzungsband* 1 (1964), 250-8.

PRIJS, L.: *Jüdische Tradition in der LXX* (Leiden 1948).

REDPATH, H. A.: The Geography of the LXX. *AJT* 7 (1903), 289-307.

——: Mythological terms in the LXX. *AJT* 9 (1905), 34-35.

39d SCHMID, U.: *Die Priamel der Werte im Griechischen von Homer bis*
(ii) *Paulus* (Wiesbaden, 1964).

STEIN, E.: Ein jüdisch-hellenistischer Midrasch über den Auszug aus Ägypten. *MGWJ* 78 (1934), 558-75.

WAINWRIGHT, G. A.: The Septuagint's Καππαδοκία for Caphtor. *JJS* 7 (1956), 91-2.

WEINSTEIN, N. J.: *Die alexandrinische Agada* (Göttingen, 1901).

15c WILLIGER, E.: Hagios. *Untersuchungen zur Terminologie des Heiligen*
(ii) *in den hellenisch-hellenistischen Religionen* (Giessen, 1922).

12. PARTICULAR CONCEPTS

(See also 15, 16, 39)

ARGYLE, A. W.: God's 'repentance' and the LXX. *ET* 75 (1963), 367.

BERTRAM, G.: Der anthropozentrische Charakter der LXX-Fröm-migkeit. *FuF* 8 (1932), 29.

——: Septuaginta-Frömmigkeit. *RGG*³ 5 (1961), 1707-9.

——: Der Begriff der Erziehung in der griechischen Bibel. In *Imago Dei: Fs. G. Krüger*. (Giessen, 1932), 33-51.

——: Praeparatio Evangelica in der Septuaginta. *VT* 7 (1957), 225-49.

——: Der Begriff der Religion in der LXX. *ZDMG* 87 (1934), 1-5.

——: Die religiöse Umdeutung altorientalischer Lebensweisheit in der griechischen Übersetzung des Alten Testaments. *ZAW* 54 (1936), 153-67.

——: Hochmut und verwandte Begriffe im griechischen und hebräischen AT. *WdO* 3 (1964), 32-43.

——: Vom Wesen der Septuaginta-Frömmigkeit. *WdO* 23 (1956), 274-84.

——: Weisheit und Lehre in der LXX. *ZDMG Suppl.* I (1969), 302-10.

BOEHMER, JULIUS: Dieses Volk. *JBL* 65 (1926), 134-48.

——: Golgotha ein alttestamentlicher Name. *ZAW* 34 (1914), 300-11.

BROCKINGTON, L. H.: The Greek Translator of Isaiah and his Interest in δόξα. *VT* 1 (1951), 23-32.

DESCAMPS, A.: La justice de Dieu dans la Bible grecque. *Studia Hellenistica* 5 (1948), 69-92.

15c (ii) DUBRAU, R. T.: Forgiveness in the LXX. *Concordia Theological Monthly* 16 (1945), 249-56.

15c (ii), 16 EBERHARTER, A.: Die im AT üblichen Ausdrücke für die Sündenvergebung und ihre Entsprechung in der LXX und Vulgata. *BZ* 14 (1917), 293-300.

FRITSCH, C. T.: Sin in the Septuagint. *JBL* 60 (1941), 6-7.

27 GLASSON, T. F.: Mark 13 and the Greek Old Testament. *ET* 69 (1957-8), 213-5.

GRYGLEWICZ, F.: La valeur morale du travail manuel dans la terminologie grecque de la Bible. *Biblica* 37 (1956), 314-37.

JENTSCH, W.: *Urchristliches Erziehungsdenken. Die Paideia Kyriu im Rahmen der hellenistisch-jüdischen Umwelt.* BFCT 45, 3 (1951).

LAGRANGE, M. J.: L'ange de Iahvé. *RB* 12 (1903), 212-25.

16 LYS, D.: The Israelite Soul according to the LXX. *VT* 16 (1966), 181-228.

MURPHY, J. L.: Ekklesia and the LXX. *AmEcclRev* 139 (1958), 381-90.

15c (ii), 16, 27 39g REHRL, S.: *Das Problem der Demut in der profangriechischen Literatur im Vergleich zu LXX und NT.* Aevum Christianum 4 (Münster, 1961).

39g SCHNEIDER, J.: Πνεῦμα ἡγεμονικόν. Ein Beitrag zur Pneuma-Lehre der LXX. *ZNW* 34 (1935), 62-9.

27,   SCHULZ, T. N.: La Grazia della Bibbia: nell'AT, nei LXX, in
28   Filone e nel 1° secolo. *RicBibl* 4 (1969), 289-311.

27   SPICQ, C.: La vertue de simplicité dans l'A et le NT. *RSPhTh* 22
      (1933), 5-26.

15c STÄHLIN, G.: *Skandalon. Untersuchungen zur Geschichte eines bibli-*
(ii),   *schen Begriffs.* BFCT II, 24 (1930).
27

     ZIEGLER, J.: *Dulcedo Dei. Ein Beitrag zur Theologie der griechischen
     und lateinischen Bibel. ATA* 13, 2 (1937).

13. ANTHROPOMORPHISM/-PATHISM
(See also 39h)

BERTRAM, G.: Religion in der Bibel. Zur Vermenschlichung der
    biblischen Offenbarung. *Kirche im Angriff* 12 (1936), 89-103.

FRITSCH, C. T.: *The Anti-anthropomorphisms of the Greek Pentateuch*
    (Princeton, 1943).
    Rev. Manson in *JTS* 46 (1945), 78-80.
    Rev. Orlinsky in *Crozer Quarterly* 21 (1944), 156-60.

33   LOEWE, R.: Jerome's treatment of an anthropopathism. *VT* 2
    (1952), 261-72.

ORLINSKY, H. M.: The Treatment of Anthropomorphisms and
    Anthropopathisms in the LXX of Isaiah. *HUCA* 27 (1956), 193-
    200.

——: Studies in the LXX of the Book of Job. III, On the Matter of
    Anthropomorphisms, Anthropopathisms, and Euphemisms.
    HUCA 30 (1959), 153-67; 32 (1961), 239-68.

SOFFER, A.: 'The house of God/Lord' in the LXX of the Pentateuch.
    JBL 75 (1956), 144-5.

——: The Treatment of Anthropomorphisms and Anthropopathisms
    in the LXX of Psalms. *HUCA* 28 (1957), 85-107.

TRENCSÉNYI-WALDAPFEL, I.: Défense de la version des LXX contre
    l'accusation d'anthropopathie. In *Études orientales à la mémoire
    de Paul Hirschler* (Budapest, 1950), 122-36.

14. HELLENISTIC EXEGESIS
(Excluding PHILO, for whom see section 28. See also 17, 24b, 39e (i), l.)

BERTRAM, G.: Die Bedeutung der LXX in der Geschichte des
    Diasporajudentums. *Klio* 21 (1927), 444-6.

DAUBE, D.: Alexandrian methods of interpretation and the Rabbis. *Fs. H. Lewald* (Basel, 1953), 27-44.

HEINEMANN, I.: Hellenistica. *MGWJ* 73 (1929), 425-43.

——: *Altjüdische Allegoristik* (Breslau, 1935).

——: (Allegory in Hellenistic Jewish Writers apart from Philo). [In Hebrew] In *Sefer J. Levi*, ed. M. Schwabe and J. Gutman. (Jerusalem, 1949), 46-58.

31   JOOSEN, J. C. and WASZINK, J. H.: art. 'Allegorese' in *RAC* 1 (1950), 283-93.

LEIPOLDT, J.: Zur Geschichte der Auslegung. *TLZ* 75 (1950), 229-34.

NESTLE, E.: Zum Zeugnis des Aristobul über die LXX. *ZAW* 26 (1906), 287-8.

31   PÉPIN, J.: *Mythe et Allégorie* (Paris, 1958).

SCHROYER, M. J.: Alexandrian Jewish Literalists. *JBL* 55 (1936), 261-84.

STEIN, E.: Alttestamentliche Bibelkritik in der späthellenistischen Literatur. *Collectanea Theologica* (Lvov) 16 (1935), 38-83.

WALTER, N.: *Der Thoraausleger Aristobulos. TU* 86 (1964).

——: Anfänge alexandrinisch-jüdischer Bibelauslegung bei Aristoboulos. *Helikon* 3 (1963), 353-72.

15. LANGUAGE

a. GENERAL

ABEL, F.-M.: Coup d'œil sur la koiné. *RB* ns 23 (1926), 5-26.

BANK, J. S.: The Greek of the LXX. *ET* 9 (1898), 500-3.

BARR, J.: *The semantics of Biblical language* (Oxford, 1961).

27   BÜCHSEL, F.: Die griechische Sprache der Juden in der Zeit der LXX und des NT. *ZAW* 60 (1944), 132-49.

COLWELL, E. C.: Greek language. *IDB* 2, 479-87.

DEBRUNNER, A.: Bericht über die Literatur zum nachklassischen Griechisch aus den Jahren 1907-1929. *Bursians Jahresbericht* 236 (1932), 115-226 (esp. 181-96); 240 (1933), 1-25.

——: Nachklassisches Griechisch 1930-5. *Bursians Jahresbericht* 261 (1938), 140-208 (esp. 172-7).

DEISSMANN, A.: Die Sprache der griechischen Bibel. *TR* 1 (1898), 463-72; 5 (1902), 58-69; 9 (1906), 210-29; 15 (1912), 339-64.

——: art. 'Hellenistisches Griechisch'. *PRE* 7 (1899), 627-39.

17   ——: *Bible Studies* (Edinburgh, 1901) = [ET of *Bibelstudien*, 1895, and Neue Bibelstudien, 1897].

——: *The Philology of the Greek Bible* (London, 1908) [= rp., with additions, from *Expos* VII, 4 (1907/8)].

——: *Light from the Ancient East*. (London, 1927) [ET of 4th edition, 1923].

DIETERICH, K.: *Untersuchungen zur Geschichte der griechischen Sprache von der hellenistischen Zeit bis zum 10. Jahrh. n. Chr.* (Leipzig, 1898).

16   DODD, C. H.: *The Bible and the Greeks* (London, 1934; rp. 1954).

DRIVER, G. R.: Supposed Arabisms in the O.T. *JBL* 55 (1936), 101-20.

GEHMAN, H. S.: The Hebraic Character of LXX Greek. *VT* 1 (1951), 81-90.

GHEDINI, G.: Bolletino di greco biblico. *La Scuola Cattolicà* 58 (1930), 81-90; 59 (1931), 315-24.

HARRIS, J. R.: The So-called Biblical Greek. *ET* 25 (1913-14), 54-5.

HARTUNG, K.: *LXX Studien: ein Beitrag zur Graecitas dieser Bibelübersetzung.* (Bamberg, 1886).

30, 36, 39h (iv), i(ii)   HATCH, E.: *Essays in Biblical Greek* (Oxford, 1899). Rev. Abbott in *Hermathena* 7 (1890), 147-57.

HELBING, R.: Die sprachliche Erforschung der LXX. *Verh. 49. Versammlung deutscher Philologen und Schulmänner in Basel* (Leipzig, 1908), 48-50.

IRMSCHER, J.: Der Streit um das Bibelgriechisch. *Acta Antiqua Academiae Hungaricae* 7 (1959), 127-34.

27   LAMBERTZ, M.: Sprachliches aus LXX und NT. *WissZUnivLeipzig* 3 (1952), 79-87.

LEMOINE, E.: *Théorie de l'emphase grecque classique et biblique* (Paris, 1954).

MOHRMANN, C.: Linguistic Problems in the Early Christian Church. *VC* 11 (1957), 11-36.

MONTEVECCHI, O.: Dal paganesimo al cristianesimo. Aspetti dell'evoluzione della lingua greca nei papiri dell'Egitta. *Aegyptus* 37 (1957), 41-59.

39g   ——: Quadam de Graecitate Psalmorum cum papyris comparata. *Proceedings IXth International Congress of Papyrology* (Oslo, 1961), 293-310.

——: Continuità ed evoluzione della lingua greca nella Settanta e nei papyri. *Actes Xe Congrès International des Papyrologues* (Warsaw, 1964), 39-49.

Moulton, J. H.: NT Greek in the Light of Modern Discovery. In *Cambridge Biblical Essays*, ed. H. B. Swete (Cambridge, 1909), 461-505.

Pernot, H.: Observations sur la langue de la LXX. *REG* 42 (1929), 411-25.

——: Grec d'Égypte et grec des Écritures. *REG* 44 (1931), 167-204.

Psichari, J.: Essai sur le grec de la LXX. *REJ* 55 (1908), 161-208 = *Quelques travaux de linguistique* ... (Paris, 1930), 831-91.

Radermacher, L.: Koine. *SbAkWissWien* 224, 5 (1947).

5   Ros, J.: *De Studie van het bijbelgrieksch van Hugo Grotius tot Adolf Deissmann* (Nijmegen, 1940).

27   Rydbeck, L.: *Fachprosa, vermeintliche Volkssprache und NT* (Uppsala, 1967).

Tabachovitz, D.: *Études sur le grec de la basse époque.* SkHVSU 36: 3 (Uppsala, 1943).

Thumb, A.: *Die griechische Sprache im Zeitalter des Hellenismus* (Strasbourg, 1901).

——: Die sprachgeschichtliche Stellung des Biblischen Griechisch. *TR* 5 (1902), 85-99.

Turner, N.: The Testament of Abraham: Problems in Biblical Greek. *NTS* 1 (1954/5), 219-23.

——: The unique character of Biblical Greek. *VT* 5 (1955), 208-13.

——: *Grammatical insights into the NT* (Edinburgh, 1965).

Vergote, J.: Het probleem van de Koine volgens de laatste historisch-philologische bevindingen. *Philologische Studien* 4 (1932/3), 28-46, 81-101, 190-215; 5 (1933/4), 81-105; 6 (1934/5), 81-107.

——: art. 'Grec, biblique'. *DBS* 3, 1320-69.

Wackernagel, J.: *Kleine Schriften I-II* (Göttingen, 1953). Rev. Katz in *TLZ* 1956, 603-7.

Witkowski, S.: Bericht über die Literatur zur Koine aus den Jahren 1903-6. *Bursians Jahresbericht* 159 (1912), 1-279. (For 1898-1902 see *ibid.* 120 (1904), 153-256).

b. (i) Grammars

Abel, F.-M.: *Grammaire du grec biblique suivie d'un choix de papyrus* (Paris, 1927). Rev. Lefort in *Muséon* 41 (1928), 65-74.

BLASS, F. and DEBRUNNER, A.: *A Greek Grammar of the NT and other early Christian Literature* (Chicago/Cambridge, 1961). [ET of 9/10th ed.] Trans. and rvsd. R. W. FUNK.

Rev. (of [9]1954): Katz in *TLZ* 1957, 110-15.

BONACCORSI, G.: *Primi saggi di filologia neotestamentaria*, I-II (Turin, 1933, 1950).

CRÖNERT, W.: *Memoria Graeca Herculanensis* (Leipzig, 1903).

ERRADONEA, I.: *Epitome Grammaticae Graeco-Biblicae* (Rome, 1933; [2]1935).

HELBING, R.: *Grammatik der LXX. Laut- und Wortlehre* (Göttingen, 1907).

Rev. Wackernagel in *TLZ* 23 (1908), 635-42.

——: *Die Kasussyntax der Verba bei den LXX. Ein Beitrag zur Hebraismenfrage und zur Syntax der Koine* (Göttingen, 1928).

Rev. Debrunner, in *Indogermanische Forschungen* 48 (1930), 99-101.

Johannessohn in *DLZ* 50 (1929), 1058-61.

Schmid in *Philologische Wochenschrift* 49 (1929), 465-71.

HLUBOVSKYJ, N. N.: *Gramatika na grŭckija biblejski ezikŭ vetchi i novi zaveti* (Sofia, 1927).

JANNARIS, A. N.: *An Historical Greek Grammar* (London, 1897).

KÜHNER, R.: *Ausführliche Grammatik der griechischen Sprache*. I, *Elementar- und Formenlehre* (Hannover[3], 1890-92); II, *Satzlehre* (Hannover/Leipzig[3], 1898/1904).

MAYSER, E.: *Grammatik der griechischen Papyri aus der Ptolemäerzeit*. I   (Berlin, 1923; neue Ausgabe); II, 1-3 (Berlin, 1926-34); I, 2 (Berlin[2], 1938); I, 3 (Berlin[2], 1936).

MEISTERHANS, K.: *Grammatik der attischen Inschriften* (Berlin[3], 1900).

MOULTON, J. H.: *A Grammar of NT Greek* (Edinburgh, 1906-63). I, *Prolegomena* (1906). II, *Accidence and Word Formation* (ed. W. F. Howard, 1919-29). III, *Syntax* (ed. N. Turner, 1963).

NACHMANSON, E.: *Laute und Formen der magnetischen Inschriften* (Uppsala, 1904).

PALMER, L. R.: *A Grammar of the Post-Ptolemaic Papyri*, I, 1 [all published] (London, 1946).

PSALTES, S. B.: *Grammatik der byzantinischen Chroniken* (Göttingen, 1913).

RADERMACHER, L.: *Neutestamentliche Grammatik* (Tübingen², 1925).

ROBERTSON, A. T.: *A Grammar of the Greek NT in the Light of Historical Research* (London, 1914, ⁴1923).

SCHWYZER, E.: *Grammatik der pergamenischen Inschriften* (Berlin, 1898).

——: *Griechische Grammatik* (Munich, 1953).

Rev. Katz in *TLZ* 1954, 239-41.

THACKERAY, H. ST. J.: *A Grammar of the OT in Greek according to the LXX.* I, *Introduction, Orthography and Accidence* [all published]. (Cambridge, 1909).

Rev. Moulton in *JTS* 11 (1910), 293-300.

b. (ii) GRAMMATICAL STUDIES

(See also 3, 12, 16, 27, 39)

AERTS, W. J.: *Periphrastica. An investigation into the use of* εἶναι *and* ἔχειν *as auxiliaries or pseudo-auxiliaries in Greek from Homer up to the present day* (Amsterdam, 1965).

ALLEN, H. F.: *The infinitive in Polybius compared with the infinitive in biblical Greek.* University of Chicago Historical and Linguistic Studies II, 1 (1907).

ANLAUF, G.: *Standard Late Greek oder Attizismus. Eine Studie zum Optativgebrauch im nachklassischen Griechisch* (Cologne, 1960).

ARGYLE, A. W.: The genitive absolute in biblical Greek. *ET* 69 (1957/8), 285.

BAUER, J.: Πῶς in der griechischen Bibel. *NT* 2 (1957), 81-91.

BECKWITH, I. T.: The Articular Infinitive with εἰς. *JBL* 15 (1896), 155-67.

BEYER, K.: *Semitische Syntax im Neuen Testament. I, Satzlehre* (Göttingen, 1962; ²1968).

BJÖRCK, G.: *Ἦν διδάσκων. Die periphrastischen Konstruktionen im Griechischen.* (Uppsala, 1940).

BLOMQVIST, J.: *Greek particles in Hellenistic Prose* (Lund, 1969).

BURESCH, K.: Γέγοναν und anderes Vulgärgriechisch. *RhMus* 46 (1891), 193-232.

39f   CHAMBERS, C. D.: On a use of the aorist participle in some Hellenistic writers. *JTS* 23 (1922), 183-7. [II and IV Macc.].

CHANTRAINE, P.: *Histoire du parfait grec* (Paris, 1927).

COLEMAN, N. D.: εἰ or εἶ in Hellenistic Greek — with a note on Mark viii.12. *JTS* 28 (1927), 159-67 (cp 274-6).

DEBRUNNER, A.: Hellenistisches ΕΙΔΑΝ, ΕΠΕΣΑΝ und dgl. *Fs. P. Kretschmer*. (Vienna, 1926), 15-22.

DEISSMANN, A.: Die Anfänge der LXX-Grammatik. *Internat. Wochenschrift* 1908, 1217-26.

16 DILLMANN, A.: Über Baal mit dem weiblichen Artikel. *Monatsberichte der Kön. preussischen Akademie der Wissenschaften* (Berlin, 1881), 601-20.

DUNBAR, G. R.: Submerged Aorists. *ET* 45 (1933-4), 46.

GHEDINI, G.: Note di sintassi greca. *Aegyptus* 15 (1935), 230-8.

——: La lingua dei vangeli apocrifi greci. In *Studi dedicati alla memoria di P. Ubaldi*. (Milan, 1937), 443-80.

GILMORE, G. W.: ῞Εως in Hellenistic Greek. *JBL* 10 (1890), 153-60.

GONDA, J.: On the so-called proleptic accusative in Greek. *Mnemosyne* 11 (1958), 117-22.

——: A remark on the periphrastic construction in Greek. *Mnemosyne* 12 (1959), 97-112.

GRASSI, G.: Imperativo presente e aoristo nelle preghiere agli Dei. *StudiItalFilolClass* 35 (1963), 186-98.

HARMAN, H. M.: The optative mood in Hellenistic Greek. *JBL* 6 (1886), 3-12.

16 HAUSCHILD, G. R.: *Die Verbindung finiter und infiniter Verbalformen desselben Stammes in einigen Bibelsprachen* (Frankfurt a.M., 1893).

HESSELING, D. C.: Zur Syntax von ἄρχομαι und Verw. *ByzZ* 20 (1911), 147-64.

HIGGINS, M. J.: The renaissance of the first century and the origin of standard late Greek. *Traditio* 3 (1945), 49-100.
    Rev. Chantraine in *Revue Philologique* III, 23 (1950), 94-5.
    Vergote in *RevBelgePhilHist* 28 (1950), 1460-2.

HOWARD, W. F.: On the futuristic use of the aorist participle in Hellenistic Greek. *JTS* 24 (1923), 403-6.

HUBER, K.: *Untersuchungen über den Sprachcharakter des griechischen Leviticus* (Giessen, 1916).
    Rev. Debrunner in *GGA* 1919, 118-29.

JOHANNESSOHN, M.: *Der Gebrauch der Kasus in der LXX* (Diss. Berlin, 1910).

——: Das biblische καὶ ἐγένετο und seine Geschichte. *ZvS* 53 (1925), 161-212.

——: *Der Gebrauch der Präpositionen in der LXX. MSU* III, 3 (1926) = *NGWGött* 1925, Beiheft, 165-388.

———: Der Wahrnehmungssatz bei den Verben des Sehens in der hebräischen und griechischen Bibel. *ZvS* 64 (1937), 145-260.

———: Das biblische καὶ ἰδού. *ZvS* 66 (1939), 145-95; 67 (1940), 30-84, 182.

———: Das biblische Einführungsformel καὶ ἔσται *ZAW* 59 (1942/3), 129-84.

KAUPEL, H.: Beobachtungen zur Übersetzung des Infinitivus absolutus in der Septuaginta. *ZAW* 61 (1949), 191-2.

KUHRING, W.: *De praepositionum Graecarum in chartis Aegyptiacis usu quaestiones selectae* (Diss. Bonn, 1906).

LEFORT, L. TH.: see under Abel (15b i).

35a   LIPSIUS, K. H. A.: *Grammatische Untersuchungen über die biblische Gräcität: Über die Lesezeichen* (Leipzig, 1863).

LJUNGVIK, H.: *Studien zur Sprache der apokryphen Apostelgeschichten* (Uppsala, 1926).

———: Einige Bemerkungen zur spätgriechischen Syntax. *Aegyptus* 19 (1933), 159-68.

———: *Beiträge zur Syntax der spätgriechischen Volkssprache* (Uppsala, 1932).

MARTIN, R. A.: *The syntax of the Greek of Jeremiah, I* (Diss. Princeton, 1957).

16   ———: Some syntactical criteria of translation Greek. *VT* 10 (1960), 295-310.

———: Syntactical Evidence of Aramaic sources in Acts i-xv. *NTS* 11 (1965/5), 38-59. [Many tables for LXX books].

MEISTER, R.: Prolegomena zu einer Grammatik der LXX. *Wiener Studien* 29 (1907), 228-59.

———: Beiträge zu Lautlehre der LXX. *Wiss. Beilage des Tätigkeitsberichts der klass. Philologen an der Univ. Wien* (Vienna, 1909), 15-45.

———: Das Genus der Substantiva im Sprachgebrauch der LXX. *Wiener Studien* 34 (1912), 77-81.

MOSSBACHER, H.: *Präpositionen und Präpositionsadverbien unter besonderer Berücksichtigung der Infinitiv-Konstruktion bei Clemens von Alexandrien* (Diss. Erlangen, 1931).

MOZLEY, F. W.: Notes on the biblical use of the present and aorist imperative. *JTS* 4 (1903), 279-82.

MURAOKA, T.: The Use of ὡς in the Greek Bible. *NT* 7 (1964), 51-72.

NACHMANSON, E.: Partitives Subjekt im Griechischen. *GötHÅ* 48, 2 (1942), 1-85 (51-64 on LXX).

OLSSON, B.: Nominativ bei Zeitbestimmung in den Papyri. *Aegyptus* 6 (1925), 294.

PALM, J.: *Über Sprache und Stil des Diodorus von Sizilien.* (Lund, 1955).

RICARDO, B. I.: *De praepositionis παρά usu atque significatione in Pentateuchi versione Alexandrina* (Diss. Amsterdam, 1917).

ROBERTSON, A. T.: The aorist participle for purpose in the koine. *JTS* 25 (1924), 286-9.

ROSSBERG, C.: *De praepositionum Graecorum in chartis Aegyptiis Ptolemaeorum aetatis usu* (Diss. Jena, 1909).

ROUFFIAC, J.: *Recherches sur les caractères du grec dans le NT d'après les inscriptions de Priène* (Paris, 1911).

SALONIUS, A. H.: *Zur Sprache der griechischen Papyrusbriefe* (Helsingfors, 1927).

SOISALON-SOININEN, I.: (Special character of the Greek of the LXX) [In Finnish]. *Commentationes Salomies* (Helsinki, 1953), 46-52.

——: (Principles of LXX 'Syntaxforschung') [In Finnish]. *Teologinen Aikakauskirja* 68 (1963), 216-31.

——: *Die Infinitive in der LXX. AASF*, B 132, 1 (Helsinki, 1965) Rev. Gooding in *JTS* ns 18 (1967), 451-5.

SVENNUNG, J.: Anredeformen. *Acta SocLitHumanRegiaeUppsal* 42, (Lund, 1958).

STERENBERG, J.: *The Use of Conditional Sentences in the Alexandrian Version of the Pentateuch* (Diss. Munich, 1908).

STRÖMBERG, R.: *Greek prefix studies: on the use of adjective particles. GötHÅ* 52, 3 (1946).

THRALL, M. E.: *Greek Particles in the NT.* (Leiden, 1962).

TORM, F.: Der Pluralis οὐρανοί. *ZNW* 33 (1934), 48-50.

VITEAU, J.: *Étude sur le grec du NT comparé avec celui des LXX.*
    I, Le verbe — syntaxe des propositions.
    II, Sujet, complément et atribut (Paris, 1893, 1896).

VOTAW, C. W.: *The use of the infinitive in Biblical Greek* (Diss. Chicago, 1896).

WALDIS, J.: *Die Präpositionsadverbien mit der Bedeutung 'vor' in der LXX.* Beilage zum Jahresberichte der Kantonsschule. (Lucerne, 1921/2).

WIFSTRAND, A.: *Die Stellung der enklitischen Personalpronomina bei den LXX.* K. Humanistiska vetenskapssamfundets i Lund årsberättelse (Lund, 1950).

c. (i) Lexica

(See also 6, 29)

ARNDT, W. F. and GINGRICH, F. W.: *A Greek-English Lexicon of the NT* (Chicago/Cambridge, 1957) [ET of Bauer[4]].

BAUER, W.: *Griechisch-deutsches Wörterbuch zu den Schriften des NT und der übrigen urchristlichen Literatur* (Berlin[5], 1963).
Rev. Katz in *Kratylos* 5 (1960), 157-63.

BIEL, J. C.: *Novus Thesaurus Philologus, sive Lexicon in LXX et alios interpretes et scriptores apocryphos VT* (ed. E. H. Mutzenbecher). The Hague, 1779-80; 3 vols.

CASTELL, E.: *Lexicon Heptaglotton* (London, 1669; 2 vols).
[Companion to London Polyglot].

CHANTRAINE, P.: *Dictionnaire étymologique de la langue grecque: histoire des mots* (Paris, 1968-).

GRADENWITZ, O. (ed.): *Heidelberger Konträrindex der griechischen Papyrusurkunden* (Berlin, 1931).

HERWERDEN, H. VAN: *Lexicon Graecum suppletorium et dialecticum* (Leiden, 1910; 2 vols).

KITTEL, G. (ed.) contd. G. FRIEDRICH: *Theologisches Wörterbuch zum NT.* (Stuttgart, 1933-) [ET Grand Rapids, 1964-].

KRETSCHMER, P. and LOCKER, E.: *Rückläufiges Wörterbuch der griechischen Sprache.* (Göttingen, 1944) [*Ergänzungen*, by G. Kisser: Göttingen[2], 1963].

LAMPE, G. W. H.: *A patristic Greek Lexicon* (Oxford, 1968).

LIDDELL, H. G. and SCOTT, R.: *A Greek-English Lexicon* (Revised edition ed. H. S. Jones: Oxford, 1940). Supplement (ed. E. A. Barber et al.; Oxford, 1968).
Rev. (of *Supplement*) Baars in *VT* 20 (1970), 371-9.

MAUERSBERGER, A.: *Polybios-Lexikon* (Berlin, 1956-).

MOULTON, J. H., and MILLIGAN, G.: *The Vocabulary of the Greek NT illustrated from the Papyri and other non-literary Sources* (London, 1930).

PREISIGKE, F.: *Wörterbuch der griechischen Papyrusurkunden mit Einschluss der griech. Inschriften, Aufschriften, Ostraka, Mumienschilder usw. aus Ägypten.*
I-II, (Berlin, 1925-7).
III, *Besondere Wörterliste* (ed. E. Kiessling, 1931).
IV, 1-3 *Zweite Reihe* (A to E to date). (Berlin, 1944, 1958, 1966).

Supplement I, 1-2 (1940-66) (ed. E. Kiessling; Amsterdam, 1969).

29 RENGSTORF, K. H.: *A complete Concordance to Flavius Josephus* (Leiden, 1973-).

——: *Supplement* I: *Namenwörterbuch zu Flavius Josephus*, ed. A. Schalit (Leiden, 1968).

RIESENFELD, H. and B.: *Repertorium Lexicographicum Graecum. Coniectanea Neotestamentica* 14 (Uppsala, 1953) [List of indexes and dictionaries to classical and Christian writers].

SCHLEUSNER, J. F.: *Novus Thesaurus Philologico-Criticus, sive Lexicon in LXX* (Leipzig, 1820/1; Glasgow, 1822; London, 1829).

SOPHOCLES, E. A.: *Greek Lexicon of the Roman and Byzantine Periods* (New York, 1900).

STEPHANUS, H.: *Thesaurus Graecae Linguae* (ed. C. B. Hase, etc.) (Paris, 1831-65; 8 vols).

29 THACKERAY, H. ST. J.: *A Lexicon to Josephus* (Paris, 1933-55). I, (1930); II-IV (ed. R. Marcus) (1934-55).

WAHL, C. A.: *Clavis librorum Veteris Testamenti apocryphorum philologica* (Leipzig, 1853).

c. (ii) LEXICAL STUDIES

(See also 11, 12, 16, 17, 27, 31, 39)

ALLEN, W. C.: On the meaning of προσήλυτος in the LXX. *Expos.* 4 (1891), 264-75.

AMSTUTZ, J.: Ἁπλότης. *Eine begriffsgeschichtliche Studie zum jüdischchristlichen Griechisch* (Bonn, 1968).

12 AMUSIN, I. D.: (Terms for slaves in Hellenistic Egypt according to the LXX). [Russian]. *Vestnik Drevnej Istorii* 40 (1952), 46-67.

ANZ, H.: *Subsidia ad cognoscendum Graecorum sermonem vulgarem e Pentateuchi versione Alexandrina repetita* (Diss. Halle, 1894).

AUERBACH, M.: *De nonnullis vocibus peregrinis in Veteris Testamenti Alexandrina versione obviis. Programm Sambor* (1911).

——: *De vocibus peregrinis in Vetere et Novo Testamento Graeco obviis. Eus Supplementa* 7 (1930).

BARR, J.: *Biblical words for time* (London, 1962).

390 BARRY, P.: On Luke xv 25: συμφωνία, bagpipe. *JBL* 23 (1904), 180-90; 27 (1908), 99-127.

12   BARTELINK, G. J. M.: Zur Spiritualisierung eines Opferterminus. *Glotta* 39 (1960), 43-8.

24   BERTRAM, G.: Der Sprachschatz der LXX und der des hebräischen AT. *ZAW* nF 16 (1939), 85-101.

BLANK, H. S.: The LXX Renderings of OT Terms for Law. *HUCA* 7 (1930), 259-83.

12   BRATSIOTIS, N. P.: נפש-ψυχή. Ein Beitrag zur Erforschung der Sprache und der Theologie der LXX. *VTS* 15 (1966), 58-89.

39f   DE BRUYNE, D.: ἐγκλείειν, κατακλείειν, παρακλείειν (II Mach. v 8, iv 34, xiii 21). *RB* 30 (1921), 408-9.

CAIRD, G. B.: Towards a lexicon of the LXX, I-II. *JTS* ns 19 (1968), 453-75; 20 (1969), 21-40. [Corrections to LSJ.]

CERESA-GASTALDO, A.: 'Ἀγάπη nei documenti anteriori al NT. *Aegyptus* 31 (1951), 269-306.

——: 'Ἀγάπη nei documenti extranei all' influsso biblico, *Rivista di Filologia* ns 31 (1953), 347-56.

COSTE, J.: *Trois essais sur la LXX à partir du mot* ταπεινός (Lyon, 1953).

12,   DANIEL, S.: *Recherches sur le vocabulaire du culte dans la LXX.*
16   *Études et Commentaires* 61 (Paris, 1965).

DAUBE, D.: Κερδαίνω as a missionary term. *HTR* 40 (1947), 109-20.

DEISSMANN, A.: Die Rachegebete von Rheneia. *Philologus* 61 (1902), 252-65.

——: ἱλαστήριος and ἱλαστήριον. Eine lexicalische Studie. *ZNW* 4 (1903), 193-212.

——: ΠΡΟΘΥΜΑ. *RhMus* 60 (1905), 457-8.

DODD, C. H.: ἱλάσκεσθαι, its cognates, derivatives and synonyms in the LXX. *JTS* 32 (1931), 352-60.

390   DUMÉZIL, G.: Les puits de Nechtan. *Celtica* (Dublin) 6 (1963), 50-61 [Dan iii 46].

FASCHER, E.: Προφήτης. *Eine sprach- und religionsgeschichtliche Untersuchung* (Giessen, 1927).

——: Theologische Beobachtungen zu δεῖ im AT. *ZNW* 45 (1954), 244-52 [cp. *idem BZNW* 21 (1954), 228-54].

FENTON, J. C.: Rare Words in the Bible. *ET* 64 (1952/3), 124-5.

39c   FINET, A.: Termes militaires accadiens dans l'AT conservés dans les LXX. *Iraq* 25 (1963), 191-2.

FONSECA, L. G. da: Διαθήκη — foedus an testamentum? *Biblica* 8 (1927), 31-50, 161-81, 290-319, 418-41; 9 (1928), 26-40, 143-60.

Forster, A. H.: The meaning of δόξα in the Greek Bible. *ATR* 12 (1929/30), 311-6.

Friedrichsen, A.: Ἰσόψυχος. *Symbolae Osloenses* 18 (1938), 42-9.

——: *Hagios-Qādōš: Ein Beitrag zu den Voruntersuchungen zur christlichen Begriffsgeschichte* (Kristiania, 1916).

16   Gehman, H. S.: ἅγιος in the LXX. *VT* 4 (1954), 337-48.

——: Adventures in LXX Lexicography. *Textus* 5 (1966), 125-32.

——: Rambles in LXX Lexicography. *Indian Journal of Theology* 14 (1965), 90-101.

Georgacas, D. J.: A contribution to Greek word history, derivation and etymology. *Glotta* 36 (1958), 100-22, 161-93.

Grobel, K.: Σῶμα as 'self, person' in the LXX. *BZNW* 21 (1954), 52-9.

Grosart, J. B.: ὁ Χριστός and Χριστός (LXX). *ET* 1 (1889), 275-6.

Highfield, H.: Gleanings from the Septuaginta. *ET* 38 (1926-7), 44-5.

24,   Hill, D.: *Greek Words and Hebrew Meanings* (Cambridge, 1967).
27   Rev. Barr in *Biblica* 49 (1968), 377-87.

Holladay, W. L.: *The root šûbh in the OT* (Leiden, 1958) [20-33 on LXX].

Jacques, X.: Le Vocabulaire de la LXX. Vers une méthode de recherche et d'exposition. *Biblica* 48 (1967), 296-301.

27,   Joüon, P.: Les mots employés pour designer 'le temple' dans l'AT,
29   le NT et Josèphe. *RechSR* 25 (1935), 329-43.

Katz, P.: Ἐν πυρὶ φλογός. *ZNW* 46 (1955), 133-8.

——: ΚΑΤΑΠΑΥΣΑΙ as a corruption of ΚΑΤΑΛΥΣΑΙ in the LXX. *JBL* 65 (1946), 319-24.

27   Kennedy, H. A. A.: *The sources of NT Greek, or the influence of the LXX on the vocabulary of the NT* (Edinburgh, 1895).

12,   Korn, J. H.: Πειρασμός. *Die Versuchung des Gläubigen in der*
27   *griechischen Bibel. BWANT* IV, 20 (1937).

Lee, J. A. L.: A note on LXX material in the Supplement to Liddell and Scott. *Glotta* 47 (1969), 234-42.

27a Leeuwen, W. S. van: *Eirene in het NT: Een semasiologische, exegetische bijdrage op grond van de LXX en de joodsche literatuur* (Wageningen, 1940).

Lieberman, S.: Two lexical notes. *JBL* 65 (1946), 67-72.

27   Lindhagen, C.: Ἐργάζεσθαι *Die Wurzel* ΣΑΠ *in N und AT. Zwei Beiträge zur Lexicographie der griechischen Bibel. UUÅ* 1950, 5.

Lowe, A. D.: The origin of οὐαί. *Hermathena* 105 (1967), 34-9.

27 LYONNET, S.: De notione expiationis. *VD* 38 (1960), 65-75, 241-61.
27 MANSON, T. W.: Ἱλαστήριον. *JTS* 46 (1945), 1-10.
    MICHAELIS, W.: Der Beitrag der LXX zur Bedeutungsgeschichte von πρωτότοκος. *Fs. A. Debrunner* (Bern, 1954), 313-20.
    MOHRMANN, C.: Note sur δόξα. *Fs. A. Debrunner* (Bern, 1954), 321-8.
390 MOORE, G. F.: Συμφωνία not a bagpipe. *JBL* 24 (1905), 166-75.
    MORGENTHALER, R.: *Statistik des NT Wortschatzes* (Zurich, 1958).
    MURPHY, J. L.: Ἐκκλησία and the LXX. *AmerEcclRev* 139 (1958), 381-90).
    NÖLDEKE, T.: Assyrios, Syrios, Syros. *Hermes* 5 (1871), 443-68.
27a PAESLACK, M.: Zur Bedeutungsgeschichte der Wörter φιλεῖν 'lieben'; φιλία 'Liebe, Freundschaft'; φίλος 'Freund' in der LXX und im NT. *Theologia Viatorum* 5 (1953/54), 15-142.
    PAX, E.: Ex Parmenide ad LXX. De notione vocabuli δόξα. *VD* 38 (1960), 92-102.
    PICCOLI, G.: Etimologie e significati di voci bibliche indicanti Satana. *Rivista di Filologia* ns 30 (1952), 69-73.
    PRESTIGE, G. L.: Ἅιδης. *JTS* 24 (1923), 476-85.
    RAURELL, F.: *Studia ad vocabulum δόξα in LXX pertinentia* (Diss. Antonianum, Rome, 1963).
    REPO, E.: *Der Begriff 'Rhēma' im Biblisch-Griechischen. I, Rhēma in der LXX. AASF* B. 75, 2 (Helsinki, 1951).
27 RIESENFELD, H.: Étude bibliographique sur la notion d'ΑΓΑΠΗ. *Coniectanea Neotest.* 5 (1941), 1-27.
    ROMEO, A.: Il termine λειτουργία nella grecità biblica. *Miscellanea liturgica in honorem L. Mohlberg* (Rome, 1950) II, 467-519.
27a SCHMIDT, K. L.: Die Kirche des Urchristentums. Eine lexikographische und biblisch-theologische Studie. *Festgabe A. Deissmann* (Tübingen, 1927), 258-319 (esp. 258-80).
    SCHWARTZ, E.: Einiges über Assyrien, Syrien, Koile Syrien. *Philologus* 86 (1931), 373-99; 87 (1932), 261-3 [cp. Bickermann, *RB* 54 (1947)].
    SCHWYZER, E.: Altes und Neues zu (hebr.-) gr. σάββατα (gr.-) lat. sabbata usw. *ZVS* 62 (1934), 1-16.
    SPICQ, C.: ἐπιποθεῖν — desirer ou chérir? *RB* 64 (1957), 184-95.
27 STEINMÜLLER, J. E.: ἐρᾶν, φιλεῖν, ἀγαπᾶν in extra-biblical and biblical sources. *Fs. A. Miller* (Rome, 1951), 404-23.
    SWANSON, D. C.: Diminutives in the Greek NT. *JBL* 77 (1958), 134-51.

Swetnam, J.: Diatheke in the LXX account of Sinai: a suggestion. *Biblica* 47 (1966), 438-44.

Tarelli, C. C.: ἀγάπη. *JTS* ns 1 (1950), 64-7.

16   Watson, N. M.: Some observations on the use of δικαιόω in the LXX. *JBL* 79 (1960), 255-66.

Wickenhauser, A.: ἐνώπιος, ἐνώπιον, κατενώπιον. *BZ* 8 (1910), 263-70.

16   Wolfson, H. A.: On the LXX Use of τὸ ἅγιον for the Temple. *JQR* ns 38 (1947), 109-10.

27a   Yoder, Y. O.: NT Synonyms in the LXX (Diss. Northern Baptist University, 1954).

16. TRANSLATION TECHNIQUE

(See also 12, 15, 39)

Andrews, D. K.: The translation of Aramaic *dî* in the Greek Bible. *JBL* 66 (1947), 15-51.

Baab, O. J.: A theory of two translators for the Greek Genesis. *JBL* 52 (1933), 239-43.

Barr, J.: Vocalization and the analysis of Hebrew among the ancient translators. *VTS* 16 (1967), 1-11.

15c (ii)   ——: Seeing the wood for the trees. An enigmatic ancient translation [אֶשֶׁל, ἄρουρα]. *JSS* 13 (1968), 11-20.

Baumgärtel, F.: Die LXX zu Jesaja das Werk zweier Übersetzer. *BWAT* nF 5 (1923), 20-31.

——: Zur Entstehung der Pentateuch-LXX. *BWAT* nF 5 (1923), 53-80.

Blank, S. H.: The LXX renderings of OT terms for law. *HUCA* 7 (1930), 259-83.

Blau, J.: Zum Hebräisch der Übersetzer des AT. *VT* 6 (1956), 98-100. [On Dt. viii: 4, Neh. ix: 21, Ez. i: 14, xxi: 25.]

Daniel, S.: — see 15c ii.

Debrunner, A.: Zur Übersetzungstechnik der LXX. *BZAW* 41 (1925), 69-78 [article with Κύριος].

Egli, C.: Zur Kritik der LXX. *ZWT* 5 (1862), 76-96, 287-321. [On translators of Pentateuch and Joshua.]

Gray, G. B.: The Greek version of Isaiah: is it the work of a single translator? *JTS* 12 (1911), 286-93.

Gwynn, R. M.: Notes on the authorship of some books of the Greek Old Testament. *Hermathena* 20 (1930), 52-61.

HELLER, J.: Grenzen sprachlicher Entsprechung der LXX. Ein Beitrag zur Übersetzungstechnik der LXX auf dem Gebiet der Flexionskategorien. *MittInstOrientforschung* 15 (1969), 234-48.

HERRMANN, J. and BAUMGÄRTEL, F.: *Beiträge zur Entstehungsgeschichte der LXX. BWAT* nF 5 (1923). [Listed separately.]

———: and BAUMGÄRTEL, F.: Die LXX zum Zwölfprophetenbuch das Werk zweier Übersetzer. *BWAT* nF 5 (1923), 32-8.

———: Die LXX zu Ezechiel das Werk dreier Übersetzer. *BWAT* nF 5 (1923), 1-19.

HINDLEY, J. C.: The translation of words for Covenant. *Indian Journal of Theology* 10 (1961), 13-24.

JOHNSON, S. E.: *The LXX translators of Amos.* (Private edition; Chicago, 1938.)

KATZ, P.: מקרא in der griechischen und lateinischen Bibel. *ZAW* 65 (1953), 253-5.

———: Zur Übersetzungstechnik der LXX. *WdO* 2 (1956), 267-73.

KAUPEL, H.: Beobachtungen zur Übersetzung des Infinitivus absolutus in der LXX. *ZAW* 61 (1945/8), 191-2.

KELLEY, B. H.: *The LXX translators of I Sam. and II Sam. i-xi 1* (Diss. Princeton, 1948).

KELSO, J. A.: The LXX rendering of שִׁגָּיוֹן. *JBL* 27 (1908), 157-9.

KÖHLER, L.: Das Substantiv גל in der LXX. *ZAW* 31 (1911), 154-5.

15c
(ii) LEDOGAR, R. J.: Verbs of praise in the LXX translation of the Hebrew Canon. *Biblica* 48 (1967), 29-56.

LEVI, I.: La racine 'yp-y'p et sa traduction dans la LXX. *REJ* 64 (1912), 142-5.

———: Le mot 'intelligence' traduit par 'foi' dans les anciennes versions de la Bible. *REJ* 64 (1912), 146-7.

15c
(ii) MARGOLIS, M. L.: Entwurf zu einer revidierten Ausgabe der hebr.-aram. Aequivalente in der Oxforder Concordance to the Septuagint. *ZAW* 25 (1905), 311-9. [Sample μένειν].

15c
(ii) ———: χαίειν (einschliesslich der Komposita und Derivata) und seine hebräisch-aramäischen Aequivalente im Gräzismus des AT. *ZAW* 26 (1906), 85-9.

15c
(ii) ———: λαμβάνειν and its Hebrew-Aramaic equivalents in OT Greek. *AJSL* 22 (1905/6), 110-9.

———: The Greek preverb and its Hebrew-Aramaic equivalents. *AJSL* 26 (1909/10), 33-61.

15b
(ii) ———: The particle ἤ in OT Greek. *AJSL* 25 (1908), 257-75.

——: Complete induction for the identification of the vocabulary of the Greek versions of the OT with its Semitic equivalents: its necessity and the means of obtaining it. *JAOS* 30 (1910), 301-12.

——: The mode of expressing the Hebrew 'Ā'I D in the Greek Hexateuch. *AJSL* 29 (1913), 237-60.

MEEK, T.J. : The translation of Ger in the Hexateuch. *JBL* 49 (1930), 172-80.

15c MONTGOMERY, J. A.:. Hebrew חסד and Greek χάρις. *HTR* 32 (1939),
(ii)   97-102.

15c NESTLE, E.: חבר = ἔθνος. *ZAW* 15 (1895), 288-90.
(ii)

RABIN, C.: The ancient versions and the indefinite subject. *Textus* 2 (1962), 60-76.

REDPATH, H. A.: A contribution towards settling the dates of the translators of various books of the LXX. *JTS* 7 (1906), 606-15.

RIDDLE, D. W.: The logic of the theory of translation Greek. *JBL* 51 (1932), 13-30.

RIFE, J. M.: The mechanics of translation Greek. *JBL* 52 (1933), 244-52.

SCHÄFERS, J.: Ist das Buch Ezekiel in der LXX von einem oder mehreren Dolmetschern übersetzt? *Theologie und Glaube* 1 (1909), 289-91.

12, SEGALLA, G.: La volonta di Dio nei LXX in rapporto al TM;
24   θέλημα, rāṣōn, hēfeṣ. *RBiblica Italiana* 13 (1965), 121-43.

SIMOTAS, P. N.: τὸ ἑβραϊκὸν דבר ἐν τῇ μεταφράσει τῶν O' (Saloniki, 1964). [pp. 21.]

THACKERAY, H. ST. J.: The translators of Jeremiah. *JTS* 4 (1903), 245-66.

——: The translators of Ezekiel. *JTS* 4 (1903), 398-411.

——: The translators of the prophetical books. *JTS* 4 (1903), 578-85.

——: The Greek translators of the four books of Kings. *JTS* 8 (1907), 262-78.

——: The bisection of books in primitive LXX manuscripts. *JTS* 9 (1908), 88-98.

——: The infinitive absolute in the LXX. *JTS* 9 (1908), 597-601.

TURNER, N.: The Greek translators of Ezekiel. *JTS* ns 7 (1956), 12-24.

VELLAS, B.: *L'importance des traductions doubles dans le texte des LXX* (Athens, 1936).

35b WEVERS, J. W.: Evidence of the text of the John H. Scheide papyri

39n   for the translation of the status constructus in Ezekiel. *JBL* 70 (1951), 211-6.

WILSON, J. B.: Hebrew Syntax in the LXX. *Transactions of the Glasgow University Oriental Society* 4 (1926), 71-2.

17. DIVINE NAMES

(See also 15a, 21b, 29, 35b, 39i(ii))

ALFRINK, B.: La prononciation 'Jehova' du Tétragramme. *OTS* 5 (1948), 43-62.

——: and Katz, P: Die Aussprache שמא für יהוה. *TZ* 5 (1949), 72-4.

39n BAUDISSIN, W. W. VON: *Kyrios als Gottesname im Iudentum* (Giessen, 1926-29; 4 vols).

Rev. Eissfeldt in *OLZ* 1926, 783-8.

BAUMGÄRTEL, F.: Zu den אדני יהוה Stellen bei Ezechiel. *BWAT* nF 5 (1923), 81-95.

39a (i) ——: Zu den Gottesnamen im Pentateuch. *BWAT* nF 5 (1923), 96-7.

38a BERTRAM, G.: Zur Prägung der biblischen Gottesvorstellung in den griechischen Übersetzungen des AT: die Wiedergabe von schaddad und schaddaj im Griechischen. *WdO* 2 (1959), 502-13; cp. *Akten des XXIV. Internat. Orient. Kongresses* (Munich, 1959), 211-3.

38a ——: ἱκανός in den griechischen Übersetzungen des AT als Wiedergabe von Schaddaj. *ZAW* 70 (1958), 20-31.

24 ——: Der Sprachschatz der Septuaginta und der des hebräischen Alten Testaments. *ZAW* 57 (1939), 85-101.

BLAU, L.: Origine et histoire de la lecture du Schema. *REJ* 31 (1895), 179-201.

31 BRINKTRINE, J.: Der Gottesname 'Αϊά bei Theodoret von Cyrus. *Biblica* 30 (1949), 520-3.

BUDDE, K.: Der Abschluss von Baudissin's 'KYPIOS'. *JBL* 49 (1930), 204-6.

CERFAUX, L.: Le nom divin 'Kyrios' dans la Bible grecque. *RSPhTh* 20 (1931), 27-51 = *Recueil Cerfaux* (Gembloux, 1954) I, 113-36.

——: 'Adonai' et 'Kyrios'. *RSPhTh* 20 (1931), 417-52 = *Recueil Cerfaux*, I, 137-72.

39n CORNILL, C. H.: Der Gottesname bei Ezechiel. In *Das Buch des Propheten Ezechiel* (Leipzig, 1886), 172-5.

DELCOR, M. L.: Des diverses manières d'écrire le tétragramme sacré dans les anciens documents hébraïques. *RHR* 147 (1955), 145-73.

EISSFELDT, O.: Jahwe-Name und Zauberwesen. *ZMissionskunde und Religionswissenschaft* 42 (1927), 161-86.

——: Neue Zeugnisse für die Aussprache des Tetragrammatons als Jahwe. *ZAW* nF 12 (1935), 59-76.

EERDMANS, B. D. The name Jahu. *OTS* 5 (1948), 1-29.

39n HARFORD, J. B.: The Divine Name in Ezekiel. In *Studies in the Book of Ezekiel* (Cambridge, 1935), 102-62.

HERRMANN, J.: Die Gottesnamen im Ezechieltexte: eine Studie zur Ezechielkritik und zur Septuagintawertung. *BWAT* 13 (1913), 70-87.

HOMMEL, H.: Pantokrator. *Theologia Viatorum* 5 (1953/4), 322-78.

KATZ, P.: Zur Aussprache von יהוה. *TZ* 4 (1948), 467-9.

——: יהוה Jejā, Jājā? *VT* 4 (1954), 428-9.

35b KENYON, F. G.: Nomina Sacra in the Chester Beatty Papyri. *Aegyptus* 13 (1933), 5-10.

KITTEL, R.: Der Gott Bet'el. *JBL* 44 (1925), 123-53.

LAUTERBACH, J. Z.: Substitutes for the Tetragrammaton. *PAAJR* 2 (1930/1), 39-67.

14 MARCUS, R.: Divine names and attributes in Hellenistic Jewish Literature. *PAAJR* 3 (1931/2), 43-120.

38a MERCATI, G.: Sulla scrittura del tetragramma nelle antiche versioni greche del VT. *Biblica* 22 (1941), 339-54.

39o MONTGOMERY, J. A.: A survival of the Tetragrammaton in Daniel. *JBL* 40 (1921), 86.

15c MONTEVECCHI, O.: Pantokrator. In *Studi ... Calderini-Paribeni*
(ii) (Milan, 1956), II, 401-32.

NESTLE, E.: Jacob von Edessa über den Schem hammephorasch und andere Gottesnamen. Ein Beitrag zur Geschichte des Tetragrammaton. *ZDMG* 32 (1878), 465-508, 735-7.

29 ——: Josephus über das Tetragrammaton. *ZAW* 25 (1905), 206.

31 ——: Irenaeus über die hebräischen Gottesnamen. *ZAW* 27 (1907), 301-2.

35b PAAP, A. H. R.: *Nomina Sacra in the Greek Papyri of the first five centuries AD. The sources and some deductions.* = Papyrologica Lugd. Batav. 8 (Leiden, 1959).

Rev. Gerstinger in *Gnomon* 32 (1960), 371-4.

Roberts in *JTS* 11 (1960), 410-2.

——: Die griechischen Nomina Sacra. *Proc. IX. International Congress of Papyrology*, (Oslo, 1961), 311-9.

39a REDPATH, H. A.: A new theory as to use of the divine names in the
(i)   Pentateuch. *AJT* 8 (1904), 286-301.

SCHOEMAKER, Wm. R.: The use of רוּחַ in the OT and of πνεῦμα in the
NT. *JBL* 23 (1904), 13-67.

39a SKINNER, J.: The divine names in Genesis. *Expos* VIII, 5 (1913),
(ii)   289-313, 400-420, 494-514 [on LXX]; VIII, 6 (1913), 23-45,
97-116.

SMITH, J. A.: The meaning of Kyrios. *JTS* 31 (1930), 155-60.

STADE, B.: Ιευε ἀδωνάει. *ZAW* I (1881), 346.

THIERRY, G. J.: The pronunciation of the tetragrammaton. *OTS* 5
(1948), 30-42.

TRAUBE, L.: *Nomina Sacra. Versuch einer Geschichte der christlichen Kürzung* (Munich, 1907).

35b WADDELL, W. G.: The tetragrammaton in the LXX. *JTS* 45 (1944),
39a   158-61. [On P. Fuad Inv. 266.]
(vi)

38b WALKER, N.: The writing of the divine name in Aquila and in the
Ben Asher text. *VT* 3 (1953), 103-4.

38a ZORELL, F.: Der Gottesname 'Šaddai' in den alten Übersetzungen.
Biblica 8 (1927), 215-9.

18a. PROPER NAMES

(See also 39f, k; 40f)

ALBRIGHT, W. F.: The names 'Israel' and 'Judah' with an excursus
on the etymology of 'Todah' and 'Torah'. *JBL* 46 (1927), 151-
185.

25 BEEGLE, D. M.: Proper names in the new Isaiah Scroll. *BASOR* 123
(1951), 157-67.

BRØNNO, E.: Einige Namentypen der Septuaginta. *ActaOr* 19 (1943),
33-64.

——: Some Nominal Types in the Septuagint. *Classica et Mediaevalia* 3 (1940), 180-213.

39a ČERNÝ, J.: Greek etymology of the name of Moses. *Annales du
(iii)   Service* 41 (1942), 349-54.

DELLING, G.: Biblische Namen im ägyptischen Judentum. *TLZ* 92
(1967), 249-51.

GRIFFITHS, J. G.: The Egyptian derivation of the name Moses. *JNES* 12 (1953), 225-31.

KÖHLER, L.: LXX-Eigennamen und ihre Entartung. In *Festgabe A. Kaegi* (Frauenfeld, 1919), 182-8.

19   KÖNNECKE, C.: *Die Behandlung der hebräischen Namen in der LXX.* Programm des k. Gymnasiums zu Stargard in Pommern, 1885.

LINDBLOM, J.: Ophir-Sophir: zum Problem der Namenbildung in der LXX. *Eranos* 19 (1919/20), 108-17.

19,   LISOWSKY, G.: *Die Transskription der hebraeischen Eigennamen des*
39a   *Pentateuch in der LXX* (Diss., Basel, 1940).
(i)

19,   MUNELES, O.: *Die Transskription der hebraeischen Eigennamen in der*
24   *LXX in ihrem Verhältnis zum MT* (Diss. Prague, 1925).

39a   NESTLE, E.: Moses-Moyses. *ZAW* 27 (1907), 111-2.
(iii)

WAINWRIGHT, G. A.: The LXX Καππαδοκία for Caphtor. *JJS* 7 (1956), 91-2.

ZORELL, F.: Spiritus asper und lenis hebräischer Wörter und Eigennamen im Griechischen. *ZKT* 24 (1900), 734-8.

18b. ONOMASTICA

(See also 28, 29, 32, 33, 39e(ii))

BENEDIKTSSON, J.: Ein frühbyzantinisches Bibellexicon. *Classica et Mediaevalia* 1 (1938), 243-80.

BERGMANN, J.: Einige Bemerkungen zu Eusebius' Onomasticon. *MGWJ* 43 (1899), 505-13.

DRACHMANN, A. B.: *Die Überlieferung des Cyrillglossars* (Copenhagen, 1936).

40a   GUIDI, I.: Un fragment arabe d'onomastique biblique. *RB* ns 1 (1904), 75-8.

HARRIS, J. R.: A primitive onomasticon. *Expos* VIII, 20 (1920), 401-14.

KLOSTERMANN, E.: Onomasticum Marchalianum. *ZAW* 23 (1903), 135-40.

——: *Das Onomastikon der biblischen Ortsnamen.* = *GCS* Eusebius Werke III, 1 (Leipzig, 1904).

——: art. 'Glossen, Glosseme, Glossarien, biblische und kirchliche, in *PRE³* 6, 709-15.

LAGARDE, P. A. DE: *Onomastica Sacra* I-II (Göttingen, 1870; ²1887) [rp. of *Liber interpretationis hebraicorum nominum* in *Corpus Christianorum* lxxii, 1959].

MERCATI, G.: Appunti sul palinsesto Vat.gr. 1456. *RhMus* 65 (1910), 331-8 = *SeT* 78 (1937), 186-93.

——: Attorno all'onomastico della siroesaplare. *Vivre et Penser* 1 (1941), 1-11.

40d MERX, A.: Un fragment d'onomastique biblique en éthiopien. *JA* VIII, 17 (1891), 274-86.

NESTLE, E.: Zur Geschichte der hebräischen Lexicographie. *ZAW* 24 (1904), 309-12.

——: Ein unbenützter Zeuge für die Textkritik der griechischen Bibel. *ZAW* 24 (1904), 321-3 (cp 26 (1906), 171).

——: Zur traditionellen Etymologie des Namens Rebekka. *ZAW* 25 (1905), 221-2.

——: Zu den Onomastica sacra. *ZAW* 26 (1906), 159-62.

——: Zu den Onomastica. *ZAW* 32 (1912), 17-21.

RAHMER, M.: Welcher biblische Ortsname ist 'Cedson' im Onomastikon des Hieronymus? *MGWJ* 42 (1898), 193-9.

28 ROKEAH, D.: A new onomasticon fragment from Oxyrhynchus and Philo's etymologies. *JTS* ns 19 (1968), 70-82.

TISSERANT, E.: Un fragment d'onomastique biblique. *RB* 10 (1913), 76-87.

TREU, K.: Ein merkwürdiges Stück byzantinischer Gelehrsamkeit. *ByzZ* 58 (1965), 306-12.

31 WILBRAND, W.: Die Deutung der biblischen Eigennamen beim hl. Ambrosius. *BZ* 10 (1912), 337-50.

WUTZ, F. X.: 'Zu den Onomastica' (ZAW XXIII, 17ff). *BZ* 10 (1912), 142.

——: *Onomastica Sacra. Untersuchungen zum Liber interpretationis nominum hebraicorum des hl. Hieronymus. I, Quellen und System der Onomastica. II, Texte und Register. TU* 41 (1915).

31 ZIEGLER, J.: Die Peregrinatio Aetheriae und das Onomasticon des Eusebius. *Biblica* 12 (1931), 71-84.

19. TRANSLITERATIONS
(See also 18, 20, 21b, 37, 39f, i(ii))

21 ALTHEIM, F. and STIEHL, R.: Μεταγραφή. In *Philologia Sacra* (= Aparchai 2; Tübingen, 1958), 9-48.

AUDET, J. P.: A Hebrew Aramaic List of Books of the OT in Greek Transcription. *JTS* N.S. 1 (1950), 135-54.

BLAU, L.: La Transcription de l'Ancien Testament en caractères grecs. *REJ* 88 (1929), 18-22.

BRØNNO, E.: Some nominal types in the LXX. *Classica et Mediaevalia* 3 (1940), 180-213.

——: Einige Namentypen der LXX. Zur historischen Grammatik des Hebräischen. *Acta Orientalia* 19 (1943), 33-64.

——: The Isaiah Scroll DSIa and the Greek transliterations of Hebrew. *ZDMG* 106 (1956), 252-8.

——: The Hebrew Laryngals in non-masoretic traditions. *Fourth World Congress of Jewish Studies* (Jerusalem, 1967), 113-5.

BRUSTON, C. H.: Le sens de ἱλαστήριον et ce qui en résulte. *Nouvelle Revue de Théol.* 13 (1904), 382-8.

FLASHAR, M.: Das Ghain in der LXX. *ZAW* 28 (1908), 194-220, 303-13. [Genesis only.]

GINSBURGER, M.: La Transcription de l'Ancien Testament en caractères grecs. *REJ* 87 (1929), 40-2, 88 (1929), 184-6.

HEJCL, J.: Αμμεσφεκωδειμ. *BZ* 3 (1905), 149-50.

MARGOLIS, M. L.: Transliterations in the Greek OT. *JQR* ns 16 (1925), 117-25.

MEISTER, R.: Zur Transkription der hebräischen Gutturale durch die LXX. *Wiener Studien* 28 (1907), 160-1.

NESTLE, E.: Spiritus asper und spiritus lenis in der Umschreibung hebräischer Wörter. *Philologus* 68 (1909), 456-63.

RŮŽIČKA, R.: Über die Existenz des ڢ im Hebräischen. *ZfA* 21 (1908), 293-340.

——: Zur Frage der Existenz des ǵ im Ursemitischen. *WZKM* 26 (1912), 96-106.

——: Die Wiedergabe des nordsemitischen ע durch ḫ im Assyrischen als eine Parallele der Transkription von ע durch γ bei den LXX. *BZ* 13 (1913), 342-9.

——: La question de l'existence du ǵ dans les langues semitiques en géneral et dans la langue ugaritienne en particulier. *Archiv Orientálni* 22 (1954), 176-237 [189-94 on LXX].

SPERBER, A.: Hebrew based on Greek and Latin transcriptions. *HUCA* 12/3 (1937/8), 103-274.

STAPLES, W. E.: The Hebrew of the LXX. *AJSL* 44 (1927/8), 6-30.

WUTZ, F. X.: *Die Transkriptionen von der LXX bis zu Hieronymus.* *BWAT* II, 9 (=34) (1933) .

20. WUTZ'S THEORY

BARROIS, A.: Une nouvelle théorie de l'origine des LXX. *RB* 39 (1930), 332-61.

BERTRAM, G.: Das Problem der Umschrift und die religionsge-schichtliche Erforschung der LXX. *BZAW* 66 (1936), 97-109.

——: Zur LXX-Forschung. III, Das Problem der Umschrift-texte. *TR* 10 (1938), 69-80, 133-59.

FISCHER, J.: Zur LXX-Vorlage im Pentateuch. II, Ein kritisches Referat über Wutz, Die Transkriptionen ... *BZAW* 42 (1926), 22-42.

FORSTER, A. H.: The Study of the LXX. *ATR* 14 (1932), 152-5.

GÖTTSBERGER, J.: Eine Transkription aus G in MT. *BZ* 17 (1925), 50.

HAUPERT, R.S.: The transcription theory of the LXX. *JBL* 53 (1934), 251-5.

HELLER, C.: *Untersuchungen zur LXX: Die Tychsen-Wutzsche Transkriptionstheorie* (Berlin, 1932).

HUMBERT, P.: Les travaux de Wutz sur la Septante. *Revue théologi-que* n s 13 (1925), 258-37.

KÖNIG, E.: Die neuesten Kämpfe um den Wert der LXX. *Jeschurun* 12 (1925), 349-64; 444-60.

——: Sind 'Transkriptionstexte' als Vorlagen der LXX eine neue Vermutung von Wutz? *Jeschurun* 13 (1926), 327-8.

MARGOLIS, M. L.: Transliterations in the Greek OT. *JQR* ns 16 (1925/6), 117-25.

PHILIPPIDIS, L. I.: Ἡ περὶ μεταγραφῶν θεωρία τοῦ F. X. Wutz. *Nea Sion* 19 (1927), 594-610, 683-92, 751-8; 20 (1928), 27-43, 83-106, 145-69.

SCHMIDTKE, F.: Die neue LXX-Theorie. *Theologie und Glaube* 17 (1925), 628-39.

TYCHSEN, O. G.: *Tentamen de variis codicum hebraicorum VT MSS generibus.* (Rostock, 1772), 54-65.

WUTZ, F. X.: Die ursprüngliche LXX. Grundsätzliches zur LXX-Forschung. *ThBl* 2 (1923), 111-6.

——: Die Bedeutung der Transkriptionen in der LXX. *BZ* 16 (1922/4), 193-213.

——: *Die Transkriptionen von der LXX bis zu Hieronymus. BWAT* II, 9. Lieferung 1 (1925) = pp. 1-176; Lieferung 2 (1933) = pp. 177-571.

Rev. Bertram in *OLZ* 1927, 266-70; 1935, 33-9.
Horst in *TLZ* 1937, 409-15.
Kittel in *DLZ* 1925, 657-64.

39g ——: *Die Psalmen textkritisch untersucht* (Munich, 1925).
Rev. Eissfeldt in *OLZ* 1926, 992-8.

39g ——: Alte hebräische Stämme im Psalmentexte der LXX. *BZ* 17
(1925), 1-28.

——: Ist der hebräische Urtext wieder erreichbar? *ZAW* nF 2
(1925), 115-9.

26a ——: Alte Stämme und Formen, die von LXX (Pe) noch bezeugt
werden. *BZ* 18 (1929), 1-31.

——: Abweichende Vokalisationsüberlieferung im hebräischen Text.
BZ 21 (1933), 9-21.

——: Beiträge zur Technik alter Textkritik. *BZ* 22 (1934), 16-29.

——: Exegese und Textkritik. *BZ* 23 (1935), 1-19, 129-46.

——: *Systematische Wege von der LXX zum hebräischen Urtext*
(Stuttgart, 1937).
Rev. Kahle in *ZDMG* 92 (1938), 276-86; Orlinsky in *JBL* 57
(1938), 215-8.

39h ——: *Das Buch Job* (Stuttgart, 1939).
(iv)

21. PSEUDO-ARISTEAS (cp *BJHIL* 61-3)
(See also 3a, 10, 19, 39f)

a. Texts and Translations

Andrews, H. T.: The Letter of Aristeas. In *Apocrypha and Pseudepigrapha*, ed. R. H. Charles (Oxford, 1913; rp 1963) II, 83-122.

Hadas, M.: *Aristeas to Philocrates* (New York/London, 1951).
Rev. Orlinsky in *Crozer Quarterly* 29 (1952), 201-5.

Hody, H.: Contra historiam LXX interpretum Aristeae nomine
inscriptum dissertatio. In *De Bibliorum Textibus* . . (Oxford,
1705), 1-89.

Kahana, A.: הספרים החיצונים (Tel. Aviv², 1956), II, 1-71.

Meecham, H. G.: *The oldest version of the Bible: Aristeas on its
traditional origin* (London, 1932).

——: *The Letter of Aristeas. A linguistic study* (Manchester, 1935).

Pelletier, A.: *Lettre d'Aristée à Philocrate.* = Sources Chrétiennes
89 (Paris, 1962).

Riessler, P.: Brief des Aristeas. In *Altjüdisches Schrifttum ausser-
halb der Bibel* (Berlin/Augsburg, 1928; rp. 1966).

THACKERAY, H. ST. J.: The Letter of Aristeas. [Greek text] in Swete, *Introduction* . .², 533-606.

——: *The Letter of Aristeas.* = Translations of Early Documents, Series II: Hellenistic Jewish Texts (London 1917). [Revised version of 'Translation of the Letter of Aristeas', *JQR* 15 (1902/3), 337-91.]

TRAMONTANO, R.: *La lettera di Aristea a Filocrate* (Naples, 1931). Rev. Barrois in *RB* 41 (1932), 104-12.

Vosté in *Angelicum* 9 (1932), 77-84.

WENDLAND, P.: *Aristeae ad Philocratem epistula* (Leipzig, 1900).

——: Der Aristeasbrief. In *Apokryphen und Pseudepigraphen des AT*, ed. E. Kautzsch (Tübingen, 1900), II, 1-31.

b. STUDIES

ABRAHAMS, I.: Recent criticism of the Letter of Aristeas. *JQR* 14 (1901/2), 321-42.

BAYER, E.: *Demetrios Phalareus, der Athener* (Stuttgart/Berlin, 1942).

BERTHOLET, A.: Der Aristeasbrief. In *Geschichte der althebräischen Literatur*, ed. K. Budde (Leipzig², 1909), 387-92.

BICKERMANN, E. J.: Zur Datierung des Pseudo-Aristeas. *ZNW* 29 (1930), 280-96.

DRÄSEKE, J.: Zu Ptolemaios Philadelphos' Brief bei Epiphanios. *ZWT* 32 (1889), 358-60.

FÉVRIER, J. G.: *La date, la composition et les sources de la lettre d'Aristée à Philocrate* (Paris, 1925).

22   GOODING, D. W.: Aristeas and Septuagint origins. *VT* 13 (1963), 357-79.

GUTMANN, J.: (Origin and purpose of the Letter of Aristeas). [In Hebrew] *Ha-Goren* 10 (1928), 42-59.

HERMANN, L.: La Lettre d'Aristée à Philocrate et l'empereur Titus. *Latomus* 25 (1966), 58-77.

27   JELLICOE, S.: St. Luke and the Seventy(-two). *NTS* 6 (1960), 319-21.

27   ——: St. Luke and the Letter of Aristeas. *JBL* 80 (1961), 149-55.

27,   ——: Aristeas, Philo and the Septuagint *Vorlage. JTS* ns 12 (1961),
28   261-71.

——: The occasion and purpose of the Letter of Aristeas: a reexamination. [On Klijn] *NTS* 12 (1965/6), 144-50.

KLIJN, A. F. J.: The Letter of Aristeas and the Greek translation of the Pentateuch in Egypt. *NTS* 11 (1965), 154-8.

LEWIS, J. J.: The table talk section in the Letter of Aristeas. *NTS* 13 (1966/7), 53-6.

17   MICHEL, O.: Wie spricht der Aristeasbrief über Gott? *TSK* 102 (1930), 302-6.

MOMIGLIANO, A.: Per la data e la caratteristica della Lettera di Aristea. *Aegyptus* 12 (1932), 161-72.

MOTZO, B.: Aristea. *Atti della R. Accademia di Scienze di Torino*, 50 (1915), 202-26, 547-70.

MURRAY, O.: Aristeas and Ptolemaic kingship. *JTS* ns 18 (1967), 337-71.

19   PHILIPPIDIS, L. I.: Ἀριστέα Ἐπιστολὴ πρὸς Φιλοκράτην καὶ τὸ ἐν Αἰγύπτῳ ἔθος τῶν μεταγραφῶν. *Theologia* 19 (1941/8), 508-11.

PARSONS, E. A.: *The Alexandrian Library, Glory of the Hellenic World* (Amsterdam/London/New York, 1952).

29   PELLETIER, A.: *Flavius Josèphe, adaptateur de la lettre d'Aristée: une réaction atticisante contre la Koinè* (Études et Commentaires 45) Paris, 1962.

SKEHAN, P. W.: Aristeas, Letter of, in *NCE* 1 (1967), 797-8.

29   STÄHLIN, G.: Josephus und der Aristeasbrief. *TSK* 102 (1930), 323-31.

STEIN, E.: (The author of the Epistle of Aristeas as an apologist for Judaism). [In Hebrew] *Zion* 1 (1936), 129-47.

22   STRICKER, B. H.: *De brief van Aristeas. De hellenistische codificaties der praehelleense godsdiensten.* VerhKonAkWet, Afd. Letterkunde nr. 62, 4 (Amsterdam, 1956).
Rev. Préaux in *CdE* 33 (1958), 153-6. (cp also 22).

TARN, W. W.: The Milindapanha and Pseudo-Aristeas. In *The Greeks in Bactria and India* (Cambridge, 1938) 414-36.

——: *Hellenistic Civilization*, ch. V-VI (London[3], 1952).

TCHERIKOVER, V.: The ideology of the Letter of Aristeas. *HTR* 51 (1958), 59-85. [Also in Hebrew, in *Fs. Dinaburg*, (Jerusalem, 1949), 83ff.]

VACCARI, A.: La lettera di Aristea sui LXX interpreti nella litteratura italiana. *Civiltà Cattolica* 82 (1930), 308-26.

VINCENT, H.: Jérusalem d'après la Lettre d'Aristée. *RB* ns 5 (1908), 520-32; 6 (1909), 555-75.

WENDLAND, P.: art. Aristeas, Letter of, in *JE* 2, 92-4.

28   ——: Zur ältesten Geschichte der Bibel in der Kirche. *ZNW* 1 (1900), 267-90.

WESTERMANN, W. L.: Enslaved Persons. *AJP* 59 (1938), 1-30.
WILLRICH, H.: Die Abfassungszeit des Aristeas-Briefes. In *Urkun-denfälschung in der hellenistisch-jüdischen Literatur*. *FRLANT* nF 21 (1924), 86-91.
ZUNTZ, G.: Zum Aristeas-Text. *Philologus* 102 (1958), 240-6.
22 ——: Aristeas Studies. I, The seven banquets; II, Aristeas on the translation of the Torah. *JSS* 4 (1959), 21-36, 109-26.
——: art. Aristeas in *IDB* 1, 219-21.

22. PROTO-LXX

(See also 7, 10a, 21b, 36d)

APTOWITZER, V.: Die rabbinischen Berichte über die Entstehung der LXX. *Ha-Qedem* 2 (1909), 11-27, 102-22; 3 (1910), 4-17.
FARMER, G.: A problem in the history of the LXX. *ET* 3 (1891), 172-3.
GASTER, M.: *The Samaritans*, ch. III. (London, 1925).
GRAETZ, H.: The genesis of the so-called LXX. *JQR* 3 (1891), 150-6.
——: The LXX: a reply to Prof. Swete. *ET* 2 (1890), 277-8.
HANHART, R.: Fragen um die Entstehung der LXX. *VT* 12 (1962), 139-62. [On 21 Stricker.]
JOHNSTON, J. B.: The date of the LXX. *ET* 13 (1901), 382-3.
——: The dating of the LXX. *ET* 30 (1918/19), 535-6.
KAHLE, P. E.: *The Cairo Geniza*, ch. III. 2 (Oxford², 1959).
36a KATZ, P.: Das Problem des Urtextes der Septuaginta. *TZ* 5 (1949), 1-24.
     Rev. Michaelis in *Judaica* (Zurich) 5 (1949), 228-37.
36a ——: The recovery of the original LXX — a study in the history of transmission and textual criticism. *Actes du Ier congrès de la fédération internationale des associations d'études classiques* (Paris, 1951), 165-82.
ORLINSKY, H. M.: On the Present State of Proto-Septuagint Studies. *JAOS* 61 (1941), 81-91.
     Rev. Gehman in *JBL* 60 (1941), 428-30.
ROWLEY, H. H.: The Proto-Septuagint Question. *JQR* ns 33 (1943), 497-9.
SPERBER, A.: *LXX-Probleme. BWAT* III, 13 (1929).
     Rev. Rahlfs in *TLZ* 55 (1930), 104-6.
SWETE, H. B.: Graetz's theory of the LXX. *ET* 2 (1890), 209.

WEVERS, J. W.: Proto-Septuagint studies. In *The Seed of Wisdom*; *Fs. T. J. Meek* (Toronto, 1954), 58-77.

23. LATER HISTORY OF LXX
(see also 7, 9, 35d)

ANON: *La Bibbia nell'Alto Medievo* (Spoleto, 1963).

BERTRAM, G.: Der religionsgeschichtliche Hintergrund des Begriffs der Erhöhung in der Septuaginta. *ZAW* N.F. 27 (1956), 57-71.

DEVREESSE, R.: In *Introduction à l'étude des manuscrits grecs* (Paris, 1954), 101-44.

DOBSCHÜTZ, E. VON: art. Bible in the Church. *ERE* 2, 579-615.

36c DÖRRIE, H.: Zur Geschichte der LXX im Jahrhundert Konstantins. *ZNW* 39 (1940), 57-110.

VAJDA, G.: La version des LXX dans la littérature musulmane. *REJ* 89 (1929/30), 65-70.

VELLAS, V.: Die heilige Schrift in der griechischen Orthodoxen Kirche. In *Die Orthodoxe Kirche in griechischer Sicht*. (1958), 121-40.

WENDLAND, P.: Zur ältesten Geschichte der Bibel in der Kirche. *ZNW* 1 (1900), 267-90.

——: *Aristeae ad Philocratem Epistula* (Leipzig, 1900), 87-166. [Patristic testimonia.]

24. LXX AND MT
(See also 1, 5, 7, 15, 18, 36, 37, 38, 39)

a. GENERAL

BACHER, W.: Miscellen. *ZAW* 27 (1907), 285-6.

BARR, J.: *Comparative Philology and the Text of the OT* (Oxford, 1968).

BLAU, J.: Zum Hebräisch der Übersetzer des AT. *VT* 6 (1956), 97-9.

GEHMAN, H. S.: The Hebraic Character of Septuagint Greek. *VT* 1 (1951), 81-90.

39(c) GOODING, D. W.: Temple Specifications: a dispute in logical arrange-
ii   ment between MT and LXX. *VT* 17 (1967), 143-172.

GOSHEN-GOTTSTEIN, M. H.: Theory and Practice of Textual Criticism. The Text-critical Use of the LXX. *Textus* 3 (1963), 130-58.

KAHLE, P. E.: Untersuchungen zur Geschichte des Pentateuch-textes. *TSK* 88 (1915), 399-439 = *Opera Minora* (Leiden, 1956), 3-37.

KENNEDY, J.: *An aid to the textual amendment of the OT* (ed. N. Levison) (Edinburgh, 1928).

MARGOLIS, M. L.: The Scope and Methodology of Biblical Philology. *JQR* ns I (1910/11), 5-41.

NYBERG, H. S.: — see 39k.

ORLINSKY, H. M.: The LXX: its use in textual criticism. *BA* 9 (1946), 22-34.

——: The textual critisicm of the OT. In *The Bible and the Ancient Near East* = *Fs. W. F. Albright*, ed. G. E. Wright (New York, 1961), 113-32.

PHILLIPS, W. J.: *The LXX fallacy. An indictment of modern criticism* (London, 1918).

REIDER, J.: The Present State of Textual Criticism of the OT. *HUCA* 7 (1930), 285-315.

ROBERTS, B. J.: art. Text, OT. *IDB* 4, 580-94.

——: The transmission of the text: OT. In *A Companion to the Bible*, ed. H. H. Rowley (Edinburgh², 1963), 144-62.

SCHLUTZ, S. J.: The Differences between the Masoretic and Septua-ginta Texts of Deuteronomy (Diss. Harvard, 1949).

SCHREINER, J.: *Septuaginta-Massora des Buches der Richter. Eine text-kritische Studie. AB* 7 Rome (1957), 1-4.

SEELIGMANN, I. L.: — see 36b.

SPERBER, A.: Das Alphabet der LXX-Vorlage. *OLZ* 32 (1929), 533-40.

TALMON, S.: Double Readings in the Masoretic Text. *Textus* I (1960), 144-84.

THOMAS, D. W.: The Language of the OT. In *Record and Revelation*, ed. H. Wheeler Robinson (Oxford, 1938), 374-402, 490-1.

——: The textual criticism of the OT. In *The OT and Modern Study*, ed. H. H. Rowley (Oxford, 1951), 238-63.

WIENER, H. M.: Samaritan, Septuagint, Masoretic text. *Expos.* VIII, 2 (1911), 200-19.

b. Chronology
(See also 39c(ii), d(ii))

29   Bosse, A.: *Die chronologischen Systeme im Alten Testament und bei Josephus. Mitteilungen der Vorderasiatischen Gesellschaft* 13 (1908), nr. 2.

Meysing, J.: La chronographie juive à l'époque gréco-romaine. *RevSR* 41 (1967), 289-304.

Pfeiffer, R. H.: Aeva Mundi. *RicStRel* 1 (1957), 245-53.

Preuss, E.: *Die Zeitrechnung der LXX* (Berlin, 1859).

29   Thiele, E. R.: *The mysterious numbers of the Hebrew Kings* (Chicago, 1951; ²Grand Rapids, 1965). [2nd edition omits chapters on LXX and Josephus.]

25   Wacholder, B. Z.: Biblical chronology in the Hellenistic world chronicles. *HTR* 61 (1968), 451-81.

14   ——: How long did Abram stay in Egypt? A study in Hellenistic, Qumran and Rabbinic chronography. *HUCA* 35 (1964), 43-56.

25. LXX AND QUMRAN

(For further literature see C. Burchard, *Bibliographie zu den Handschriften vom Toten Meer, BZAW* 76 (1957) and *BZAW* 89 (1965) (esp. 328-9); also W. S. Lasor, *Bibliography of the Dead Sea Scrolls* 1948-57 (Pasadena, 1958), continued in B. Jongeling, *A Classified Bibliography of the Finds in the Desert of Judah*, 1958-69 (Leiden, 1971); M. Yizhar, *Bibliography of Hebrew Publications on the Dead Sea Scrolls* 1948-64 = *Harvard Theological Studies* 23 (1967). See also 19, 24, 27, 31, 39)

Albright, W. F.: New Light on early recensions of the Hebrew Bible. *BASOR* 140 (1955), 27-33.

39c   Cross, F. M.: A new Qumran Biblical fragment related to the orig-
(i)   inal Hebrew underlying the LXX. *BASOR* 132 (1953), 15-26.

39c   ——: The oldest manuscripts from Qumran. *JBL* 74 (1955), 147-72.
(i)

——: *The Ancient Library of Qumran* (New York², 1961). Esp. ch. IV.

——: The History of the Biblical text in the Light of Discoveries in the Judean Desert. *HTR* 57 (1964), 281-99.

——: The Contribution of the Qumrân Discoveries to the Study of the Biblical Text. *IEJ* 16 (1966), 81-95.

Greenberg, M.: The stabilization of the text of the Hebrew Bible reviewed in the light of the Biblical materials from the Judaean Desert. *JAOS* 76 (1956), 157-67.

ORLINSKY, H. M.: Qumran and the present state of OT text studies: the LXX text. *JBL* 78 (1959), 26-33.

RABIN, C.: The Dead Sea Scrolls and the history of the OT text. *JTS* ns 6 (1955), 174-82.

SEGAL, M. H.: The promulgation of the authoritative text of the Hebrew Bible. *JBL* 72 (1953), 35-47.

39a
(iv,
v),
36c

SKEHAN, P. W.: The Qumran manuscripts and textual criticism. *VTS* 4 (1957), 148-60.

——: The Biblical scrolls from Qumran and the text of the OT. *BA* 28 (1965), 87-100.

——: The Scrolls and the OT Text. *McCormick Quarterly* 21 (1968), 273-83.

VOGT, E.: Textus praemasoreticus ex Qumran. *Biblica* 35 (1954), 263-6.

26a. LXX AND PESHITTA

(See also 20, 36f, 38g, 40g)

39m
(ii),
26b

ABELESZ, A.: *Die syrische Übersetzung der Klagelieder und ihr Verhältnis zu Targum und LXX* (Diss. Giessen, 1895).

BARNES, W. E.: The Influence of the LXX on the Pešiṭta. *JTS* 2 (1901), 186-97.

39g

BERG, J. F.: *The influence of the LXX upon the Peshiṭta Psalter* (New York, 1895).

39c
(ii),
26b

BERLINGER, J.: *Die Peschitto zum 1 (3) Buche der Könige und ihr Verhältnis zum MT, LXX und Targum* (Berlin, 1897).

BLOCH, J.: The influence of the Greek Bible on the Peshitta. *AJSL* 36 (1920), 161-6.

39a
(i)

——: (The relationship of the Syriac version of the Pentateuch to the LXX) [Hebrew]. *Abhandlungen zur Erinnerung an A. P. Chajes* (Vienna, 1933), 168-73.

39l,
26b

DELEKAT, L.: Die Peschitta zu Jesaja zwischen Targum und LXX. *Biblica* 38 (1957), 185-99, 321-35.

39l

DIETTRICH, G.: *Ein Apparatus criticus zur Pešitto zum Propheten Jesaja.* BZAW 8 (Giessen, 1905).

39c ENGLERT, D. M. C.: *The Peshitto of Second Samuel* [incl. LXX]
(i)   (Philadelphia, 1949).
      Rev. Orlinsky in *JQR* ns 41 (1950), 117-20.
39m FRANKL, P. F.: *Studien über die LXX und Peschitto zu Jeremia*
      (Breslau, 1873) = *MGWJ* 21 (1872), 444-56, 497-509, 545-57.
39a HÄNEL, J.: *Die ausermassorethischen Übereinstimmungen zwischen*
(ii)   *der LXX und der Peschittha in der Genesis* (Giessen, 1911).
39h KAMENTZKY, A. S.: Die Peschitto zu Koheleth textkritisch und in
(ii)   ihrem Verhältnis zu dem MT, der LXX und den andern alten
      griechischen Versionen. *ZAW* 22 (1904), 181-239.
39g, OPPENHEIM, B.: *Die syrische Übersetzung des fünften Buches der*
26b   *Psalmen und ihr Verhältnis zu dem MT und den älteren Über-*
      setzungen, namentlich den LXX und Targum (Leipzig, 1891).
39h PINKUSS, H.: Die syrische Übersetzung der Proverbien textkritsch
(i),   und in ihrem Verhältnisse zu dem MT, den LXX und dem
26b   Targum untersucht. *ZAW* 14 (1894), 65-141, 161-222.
39h SALKIND, J. M.: *Die Peschito zu Schirhaschirim textkritisch und in*
(iii)   *ihrem Verhältnis zu MT und LXX untersucht* (Leiden, 1905).
39c SCHWARTZ, E.: *Die syrische Übersetzung des I Buches Samuel und*
(i),   *ihr Verhältnis zu MT, LXX und Targum* (Berlin, 1897).
26b
39k SEBÖK, M. (SCHÖNFELDER): *Die syrische Übersetzung der zwölf*
      kleinen Propheten und ihr Verhältnis zu dem MT und zu den
      älteren Übersetzungen (Leipzig, 1887).
39k ZANDSTRA, S.: *The witness of the Vulgate, Peshitta and Septuagint to*
      the text of Zephaniah (New York, 1909).

26b. LXX AND TARGUM
(See also 26a, 38b, 39, 40g)

39l BROCKINGTON, L. H.: LXX and Targum. *ZAW* 66 (1954), 80-6.
      CHURGIN, P.: Targum and LXX. *AJSL* 50 (1933/4), 41-65.
      DELEKAT, L.: Ein Septuagintatargum. *VT* 8 (1958), 225-52.
39h KAMINKA, A.: LXX und Targum zu Proverbia. *HUCA* 8/9 (1931/2),
(i)   169-91.

27. LXX AND NT

(See also 6, 12, 15, 21b, 30, 35b, 36g, 38b, 39)

a. GENERAL

ATKINSON, B. F. C.: The textual background of the use of the OT by the New. *JTrans Victoria Institute* 79 (1947), 36-69.

BERTRAM, G.: Praeparatio evangelica und die LXX. *VT* 7 (1957), 225-49.

BÖHL, E.: *Die alttestamentlichen Citate im NT* (Vienna, 1878).

15c BROCKINGTON, L. H.: The LXX Background to the NT use of δόξα.
(ii)   In *Studies in the Gospels*; *Fs. R. H. Lightfoot* (Oxford, 1955), 1-8.

DITTMAR, W.: *Vetus Testamentum in Novo. Die alttest. Parallelen des NT im Wortlaut der Urtexte und der LXX* (Göttingen, 1899, 1903; 2 vols).

EDGAR, S. L.: Respect for Context in Quotations from the OT. *NTS* 9 (1962), 55-62.

FILSON, F. V.: The LXX and the NT. *BA* 9 (1946), 34-42.

FITZMYER, J. A.: The Use of Explicit OT Quotations in Qumran
25   Literature and in the NT. *NTS* 7 (1961), 297-333.

HÜHN, E.: *Die alttestamentlichen Citate und Reminiscenzen im NT* (Tübingen, 1900).

JOHNSON, S. E.: The LXX and the NT. *JBL* 56 (1937), 331-45.

KAHLE, P.: The Greek Bible and the Gospels. *TU* 73 (1959), 613-21.

KARNETZKI, M.: *Die alttest. Zitate in der synoptischen Tradition* (Diss. Tübingen, 1955) (cp. *TLZ* 1956, 492-3).

MARBURY, C. H.: *OT textual traditions in the NT: studies in text types* (Diss. Harvard; cf. *HTR* 61 (1968), 643f).

MERCATI, G.: Alcuni appunti ad un saggio novissimo di critica
36a   testuale dei LXX. *SeT* 95 (1941), 135-57. [On Sperber].

SHEEHAN, J. F. X.: The LXX and the NT. *Bible Today* 1 (1965), 1133-6.

SMITS, C.: *Oud-testamentische citaten in het NT* (The Hague, 1952-5; 2 vols).

SPERBER, A.: (NT and LXX). [In Hebrew.] *Tarbiz* 6 (1934), 1-29.
——: NT and LXX. *JBL* 59 (1940), 193-293.

36a STAERK, W.: Die alttest. Citate bei den Schriftstellern des NT. *ZWT* 35 (1892), 461-85; 36 (1893), 70-98; 38 (1895), 218-30.

TABACHOVITZ, D.: *Die LXX und das NT. — Stilstudien* (Lund,
15b   1956).
(ii)   Rev. Katz in *Gnomon* 30 (1958), 27-30.

Toy, C. H.: *Quotations in the NT* (New York, 1884).

Vannutelli, P.: Les Évangiles synoptiques. [On quotations.] *RB* ns 22 (1925), 32-53, 505-23; 23 (1926), 27-39.

Vénard, L.: Citations de l'AT dans le NT. *DBS* 2 (1934), 23-51.

Vogels, H. J.: Alttestamentliches im Codex Bezae. *BZ* 9 (1911), 149-58.

b. Individual Books

Allen, W. C.: The OT quotations in St. Matthew and St. Mark. *ET* 12 (1900/1), 187-9, 281-5.

39g Bacon, B. W.: Heb. i. 10-12 and the LXX Rendering of Ps. cii: 23. *ZNW* 3 (1902), 280-5.

39l Bartsch, H. W.: Eine bisher übersehene Zitierung der LXX in Mk. iv. 30. *TZ* 15 (1959), 126-8. [Isa xl. 18.]

39k Baumstark, A.: Die Zitate des Mt-Evangeliums aus dem XII Prophetenbuch. *Biblica* 37 (1956), 296-313.

39o Bludau, A.: Die Apokalypse und Theodotions Danielübersetzung. *ThQuartalschrift* 79 (1897), 1-26.

Büchel, C.: Der Hebräerbrief und das AT. *TSK* 79 (1906), 508-91.

39h Cambe, P.: L'influence du Cantique des cantiques sur le NT. *Revue* (iii)   *Thomiste* 62 (1962), 5-26.

Clarke, W. K. L.: The use of the LXX in Acts. In *The Beginnings of Christianity*, ed. F. J. Foakes Jackson and K. Lake (London, 1922), I. ii, 66-105.

39g, Dahood, M.: Two Pauline quotations from the OT. *CBQ* 17 (1955), h   19-24. [Prov. xxv: 22, Ps. cxvi: 10].

39g Dupont, J.: Filius meus es tu; l'interprétation de Ps. ii: 7 dans le NT. *RechSR* 35 (1948), 522-43.

——: L'interprétation des Psaumes dans les Actes des Apôtres. *OBL* 4 (1962), 357-88.

Freed, E. D.: *OT quotations in the Gospel of John.* NT Suppl. 11. (Leiden, 1965).

39a Goulder, M. D. & Sanderson, M. L.: St. Luke's Genesis. *JTS* ns 8 (ii)   (1957), 17-30.

Gundry, R. H.: *The use of the OT in St. Matthew's Gospel.* NT Suppl. 18 (Leiden, 1967).

Haenchen, E.: Schriftzitate und Textüberlieferung in der Apostelgeschichte. In *Gott und Mensch* (Tübingen, 1965), 157-71.

39g Hanson, A. T.: The interpretation of the second person singular in quotations from the Psalms in the NT. *Hermathena* 73 (1959), 69-72. [On Rom. xv. 3.]

HARDER, G.: Die LXX-Zitate des Hebräerbriefes. *Theologia Viatorum* 1939, 33-52.

39e HARRIS, J. R.: A quotation from Judith in the Pauline epistles.
(ii) *ET* 27 (1915), 13-5.

HOLTZ, T.: *Untersuchungen über die alttestamentlichen Zitate bei Lukas. TU* 104 (Berlin, 1968).

39a HOSKYNS, E. C.: Genesis i-iii and St. John's Gospel. *JTS* 21 (1920),
(ii) 210-8.

39g, HYLDAHL, N.: A Reminiscence of the OT at Rom. i: 23. *NTS* 2
m (1955/6), 285-8. [Ps. cvi: 20 and Jer. ii: 11].

39a JERVELL, J.: *Imago Dei. Genesis I. 26f in Spätjudentum, Gnosis und*
(ii) *den paulinischen Briefen. FRLANT* 58 (1959).

JOHNSON, S. E.: The biblical quotations in Matthew. *HTR* 36 (1943), 135-53.

JONES, D.: 'Ανάμνησις in the LXX and the interpretation of I Cor. xi: 25. *JTS* ns 6 (1955), 183-91.

KATZ, P.: Οὐ μή σε ἀνῶ οὐδ' οὐ μή σε ἐγκαταλίπω. Hebr. xiii: 5: the biblical sources of the quotation. *Biblica* 33 (1952), 523-5.

——: 'Εν πυρὶ φλογός. *ZNW* 46 (1955), 133-40.

39a ——: The quotations from Deuteronomy in Hebrews. *ZNW* 49
(vi) (1958), 213-23.

39g KISTEMAKER, S.: *The Psalm quotations in the Epistle to the Hebrews* (Amsterdam, 1961).

MICHEL, O.: *Paulus und seine Bibel. BFCT* II, 18 (1929).

39d NESTLE: E., Matthew's genealogy and the LXX of Chronicles. *ET* 11 (1899), 191.

PLOEG, J. VAN DER: L'exégèse de l'AT dans l'Épître aux Hébreux. *RB* 54 (1947), 187-228.

RESE, M.: *Alttestamentliche Motive in der Christologie des Lukas* (Gütersloh, 1969).

39g ROSE, A.: L'influence des psaumes sur les annonces et les récits de la Passion et de la Résurrection dans les Évangiles. *OBL* 4 (1962), 297-356.

39h SMIT SIBINGA, J.: Une citation du Cantique dans la Secunda Petri.
(iii) *RB* 73 (1966), 107-18.

39h SPICQ, C.: Une reminiscence de Job xxxvii: 13 dans I Cor. iv: 21?
(iv) *RB* 60 (1953), 509-12.

STENDAHL, K.: *The School of St. Matthew and its use of the OT*

(Uppsala, 1954; ²Lund/Philadelphia, 1968).

THOMAS, K. J.: *The Use of the LXX in the Epistle to the Hebrews* (Diss. Manchester, 1959).

——: The OT citations in Hebrews. *NTS* 11 (1964/5), 303-25.

TRUDINGER, L. P.: *The text of the OT in the book of Revelation* (Diss. Boston, 1963).

——: Some observations concerning the text of the OT in the Book of Revelation. *JTS* ns 17 (1966), 82-8.

UNNIK, W. C. VAN: The quotation from the OT in John xii: 34. *NTS* 3 (1959), 174-9.

VOLLMER, H.: *Die alttestamentlichen Zitate bei Paulus textkritisch und biblisch-theologisch gewürdigt* (Leipzig, 1895).

31 WALLACE-HADRILL, D. S.: An analysis of some quotations from the first Gospel in Eusebius' Demonstratio Evangelica. *JTS* ns 1 (1950), 168-75. [LXX quotations].

15b WIFSTRAND, A.: Lukas och Septuaginta. *SvTKv* 16 (1940), 243-62.
(ii)

39h WINARDY, J.: La Cantique des cantiques et le NT. *RB* 71 (1964),
(iii)   161-90.

c. TESTIMONIA (Select)

AUDET, J.-P.: L'hypothèse des Testimonia. Remarque autour d'un livre récent. *RB* 70 (1963), 381-405. [On Prigent.]

31 BENOIT, A.: Irenée *Adv. Haer.* IV. 17. 1-5 et les Testimonia. *Studia Patristica* 2 = *TU* 79 (1961), 20-7.

39m DANIÉLOU, J.: Christos Kyrios. Une citation des Lamentations de
(ii)   Jérémie dans les Testimonia. *RechSR* 39 (1951/2), 338-52.

30 ——: Un testimonium sur la vigne dans Barnabé XII, 1. *RechSR* 50 (1962), 389-99.

——: L'origine de l'Épiphanie et les Testimonia. *RechSR* 52 (1964), 538-53.

39n ——: La vision des ossements desséchés (Ez xxxvii 1-14) dans les Testimonia. *RechSR* 53 (1965), 220-33.

30 ——: *Études d'exégèse judéo-chrétienne (Les Testimonia)* (Paris, 1966).

HARRIS, J. R.: *Testimonies I-II* (Cambridge, 1916/20).

HOMMES, N. J.: *Het Testimoniaboek* (Amsterdam, 1935).

MONTGOMERY, J. A.: Anent Dr. R. Harris's 'Testimonies'. *Expos* VIII, 22 (1931), 214-9.

30 PRIGENT, P.: *Les Testimonia dans le Christianisme primitif: L'Épî-tre de Barnabé I-XVI et ses sources* (Paris, 1961).
    Rev. Kraft in *JTS* 13 (1962) 401-8.
SUNDBERG, A. C.: On Testimonies. *NT* 3 (1959), 268-81.

28. PHILO
(See also 8, 9, 12, 18, 21b, 38b)

18b AMIR, J.: (Explanation of Hebrew names in Philo). [In Hebrew.]
     Tarbiz 31 (1962), 297.
18b BELKIN, S.: (The interpretation of names in Philo). [In Hebrew.]
     Horeb 12 (1956), 3-61.
CHRISTIANSSEN, I.: *Die Technik der allegorischen Auslegungswissen-schaft bei Philon von Alexandrien* (Tübingen, 1969).
COLSON, F. H.: Philo's quotations from the OT. *JTS* 41 (1940), 237-51.
CONYBEARE, F. C.: Upon Philo's text of the LXX. *Expos* IV. 4 (1891), 456-66.
——: The Philonean text of the LXX. *JQR* 5 (1893), 246-80; 8 (1896), 88-122.
DELLING, G.: Wunder-Allegorie-Mythus bei Philon von Alexandrien. In *Gottes ist der Orient: Fs. O. Eissfeldt*. (Berlin, 1959), 42-68.
EDERSHEIM, A.: art. Philo in *DCB* 4, 357-89.
FELDMAN, L. H.: *Studies in Judaica: Scholarship on Philo and Josephus 1937-62* (New York, 1962). [Annotated bibliography; revised edn. in preparation.]
GOODENOUGH, E. R.: *The Politics of Philo Judaeus ... with a general bibliography* (New Haven, 1938). [Esp. 246-7.]
18b HANSON, A. T.: Philo's etymologies. *JTS* ns 18 (1967), 128-39.
31   HEINISCH, P.: *Die Einfluss Philos auf die älteste christliche Exegese. ATA* I, 1/2 (1909).
36a KATZ, P.: *Philo's Bible. The aberrant text of the Bible quotations in some Philonic writings and its place in the textual history of the Greek Bible* (Cambridge, 1950).
     Rev. Kilpatrick in *JTS* ns 2 (1951), 87-9.
          Bonsirven in *Biblica* 31 (1950), 414-5.
KNOX, W. L.: Philo's use of the OT. *JTS* 41 (1940), 30-34.
39a MARCUS, R.: A textual-exegetical note on Philo's Bible. *JBL* 69
(ii)   (1950), 363-5. [On Gen. xxvii 41.]

RYLE, H. E.: *Philo and Holy Scripture* (New York, 1895).
Rev. Wendland in *Berliner philologische Wochenschrift* 15 (1895), 1281-5.

SCHROEDER, A.: *De Philonis Alexandrini Vetere Testamento* (Greifswald, 1907).

SIEGFRIED, C.: Philo und der Text der LXX. *ZWT* 16 (1872), 217-38, 411-28, 522-41.

——: *Philo von Alexandria als Ausleger des AT* (Jena, 1875).

5   SMIT SIBINGA, J.: Wettstein als Anonymus. *Vox Theologica* 33 (1962/3), 22-6.

STEIN, E.: *Die allegorische Exegese des Philo aus Alexandreia. BZAW* 51 (1929).

WENDLAND, P.: Zu Philos Schrift de Posteritate Caini. Nebst Bemerkungen zur Rekonstruktion der LXX. *Philologus* 57 (1898), 248-88.

29. JOSEPHUS

(See also 9, 15, 17, 21, 24b' 39; BJHIL 51-60, and fully, H. Schreckenberg: *Bibliographie zu Flavius Iosephus* (Leiden, 1968).

COHEN, N. G.: Josephus and Scripture. *JQR* ns 54 (1963), 311-32. (On Ant. I-XI).

FELDMAN, L. H.: see 28.

HÖLSCHER, G.: art. Josephus in *PW* 9 (1916), 1934-2000.

KLEIN, S.: Hebräische Ortsnamen bei Josephus. *MGWJ* 59 (1915),
18b   156-69.

39c   MEZ, A.: *Die Bibel des Josephus untersucht für Buch V-VII der*
(i)   *Archäologie* (Basel, 1895).

MICHEL, O., BAUERNFEIND, O. and BETZ, O.: Der Tempel der goldenen Kuh: Bemerkungen zur Polemik im Spätjudentum. *ZNW* 49 (1958), 197-212.

NESTLE, E.: Die Bibel des Josephus. *ZAW* 30 (1910), 152-3.

NIESE, B.: art. Josephus in *ERE* 7, 569-79.

PELLETIER, A.: *Flavius Josèphe adaptateur de la lettre d'Aristée: une réaction atticisante contre la Koinè* (Paris, 1962).

RENGSTORF, K. H.: *A Complete Concordance to Flavius Josephus.* I: A-Δ (Leiden, 1973); II (E-K), III (Λ-Π), IV (P-Ω) in active preparation.

SCHALIT, A.: *Namenwörterbuch zu Flavius Josephus* (Leiden, 1968).

SCHALLER, B.: art. Iosephos in *Der Kleine Pauly* II (Stuttgart, 1967), 1440-44.

39a   SCHECKER, H.: Die Hellenisierung des Hexateuchs in der Archäo-
(i),b   logie des Josephus. *Verhandlungen der 55. Versammlung Deut-*
(i)   *scher Philologen*, 1925, 54.

17   SCHLATTER, A.: *Wie sprach Josephus von Gott?* BFCT XIV, 1
      (1910).

18b   ——: *Die hebräischen Namen bei Josephus.* BFCT XXVII, 3 (1915).

      SHUTT, R. J. H.: Studies in Josephus (London, 1961). [Esp. Chap. 4,
      against Thackeray's hypothesis of 'Greek assistants' to Jose-
      phus.]

18b   SIEGFRIED, C.: Die hebräischen Worterklärungen des Josephus.
      ZAW 3 (1882), 32-53.

39a   SPRÖDOWSKY, H.: *Die Hellenisierung der Geschichte von Joseph in*
(ii)   *Ägypten bei Fl. Josephus* (Greifswald, 1937).

      STÄHLIN, GUSTAV: Josephus und der Aristeasbrief. Zur Quellen-
      benutzung des Josephus. *TSK* 102 (1930), 324-31.

      THACKERAY, H. ST. J.: art. Josephus in *HDB* 5, 461-73.

36a   ——: *Josephus. The man and the historian* (New York, 1929). [Esp.
      ch. IV on LXX text.]

30. APOSTOLIC FATHERS, JUSTIN
(See also 15a, 27c)

AIURA, T.: A study of the OT quotations in 1st Clement. *Annual
      Studies* (Kwansei Gakuin Univ.) 1 (1953), 1-16.

BARNARD, L. W.: The OT and Judaism in the writings of Justin
      Martyr. *VT* 14 (1964), 395-406.

27   BOUSSET, W.: *Die Evangeliencitate Justins des Märtyrers in ihrem
      Wert für die Evangelienkritik* (Göttingen, 1891).

39m   BURKITT, F. C.: Justin Martyr and Jer. xi: 19. *JTS* 33 (1932), 371.
(i)

HARRIS, J. R.: On an obscure quotation in the First Epistle of
      Clement. *JBL* 29 (1910), 190-5.

HELFRITZ, H.: Οἱ οὐρανοὶ τῇ διοικήσει αὐτοῦ σαλευόμενοι ἐν εἰρήνῃ
      ὑποτάσσονται αὐτῷ (I Clem xx 1). *VC* 22 (1968), 1-7.

35c, KATZ, P.: Justin's OT quotations and the Greek Dodekapropheton.
39k   *Studia Patristica* 1 (1957) = *TU* 63, 543-53.

27c, KRAFT, R. A.: Barnabas' Isaiah text and the 'Testimony Book'
39l   hypothesis. *JBL* 79 (1960), 336-50.

39l   ——: Barnabas' Isaiah text and Melito's Paschal Homily. *JBL* 80
        (1961), 371-3.
        ——: *The Epistle of Barnabas: its quotations and their sources*
        (Diss. Harvard, 1961).
        OIKONOMOU, E. B.: τὸ κείμενον τῆς Π.Δ. κατὰ τὴν Α' Κλήμεντος.
        Theologia 33 (1962), 600-26.
        PRIGENT, P.: *Justin et l'Ancien Testament* (Paris, 1964).
        ROCCO, B.: Due citazioni bibliche in S. Clemente Romano. *BibOr*
        10 (1968), 207-10.
        SHOTWELL, W. A.: *The biblical exegesis of Justin Martyr* (London,
        1965).
39a   SMIT SIBINGA, J.: *The OT text of Justin Martyr*. I: *The Pentateuch*
(i)   (Leiden, 1963).
        Rev. Gooding in *JTS* 16 (1965), 187-92.
            Hanhart in *GGA* 217 (1965), 208-12.
            Kraft in *Gnomon* 36 (1964), 472-7.

31. PATRISTICA
(See also 7-9, 14, 17, 18, 27, 28, 33, 35-9)

39g   ALDEMA, J. A. DE: La naissance du Seigneur dans l'exégèse patristi-
        que du Ps. xxi: 10a. *RechSR* 51 (1963), 5-29.
39g   ARBESMANN, E.: The daemonium meridianum (Ps. xci: 6) and
        Greek and Latin exegesis. *Traditio* 14 (1958), 17-31.
39a   ARMSTRONG, G. T.: *Die Genesis in der Alten Kirche* (Tübingen,
(ii)   1962).
        BARNARD, P. M.: *The biblical text of Clement of Alexandria*. Texts and
        Studies V, 5. (Cambridge, 1899).
        BARTELINK, G. J. M.: Observations stylistiques et linguistiques
        chez Isidore de Péluse. *VC* 18 (1964), 163-80.
        BERTRAM, G.: LXX und Urchristentum. *ThBl* 4 (1925), 208-13.
        BLUDAU, A.: *Die Schriftfälschungen der Häretiker* (1925).
39a   BRATSIOTIS, P.: Gen. i: 26 in der orthodoxen Theologie. *Evang*
(ii)   *Theologie* 11 (1952), 289-97.
        BRUYNE, D. DE: St. Augustin reviseur de la Bible. *Misc. Agost.*
        (Rome, 1931), II, 521f.
        ——: Les citations bibliques dans le De Civitate Dei. *RB* 41 (1932),
        550-60.

25 CADIOU, R.: Apollinaire de Laodicée et Isaie de Qumran. *RHR* 171
39l (1967), 145-8.
39g DANIÉLOU, J.: Le psaume 21 dans la catéchèse patristique. *Maison Dieu* 49 (1957), 17-34.
39g ——: Le psaume 22 dans l'exégèse patristique. In *Richesses et déficiences des anciens psautiers latins*. (Rome, 1959), 189-211.
——: *The Theology of Judaeo-Christianity* (London, 1964).
DEAN, J. E.: *Epiphanius' Treatise on Weights and Measures* (Chicago, 1935).
39a, DEVREESSE, R.: Anciens commentateurs grecs de l'Octateuque.
b *RB* 44 (1935), 161-91; 45 (1936), 201-20, 364-84.
39a- ——: *Les anciens commentateurs grecs de l'Octateuque et des Rois.*
c *SeT* 201 (1959).
DÖRRIES, H.: Die Bibel im ältesten Mönchtum. *TLZ* 72 (1947), 215-22.
DOUAIS, C.: S. Augustin et la Bible. *RB* 2 (1893), 62-81, 351-77; 3 (1894), 110-35, 410-32.
ELLIOTT, C. J.: art. Hebrew Learning among the Fathers, in *DCB* 2, 851-72.
39a FASCHER, E.: Abraham, φυσιολόγος and φίλος θεοῦ. Eine Studie zur
(vi) ausserbibl. Abrahamstradition im Anschluss an Deut. iv: 19. In *Mullus: Fs. T. Klauser* (Münster, 1964), 111-24.
40g FISCHER, B.: Der Bibeltext in den ps-augustinischen Solutiones diversarum quaestionum ab haereticis objectarum im Codex Paris BN lat. 12217. *Biblica* 23 (1942), 139-64.
FROIDEVAUX, L. M.: Sur trois textes cités par S. Irénee. *RechSR* 46 (1956), 408-21.
GERHARDT, M. I.: The Ant-Lion: nature study and the interpretation of a biblical text [Job iv: 11] from the Physiologus to Albert the Great. *Vivarium* (Assen) 3 1965), 1-23.
39a GIVERSEN, S.: The Apocryphon of John and Genesis. *StTheol* 17
(ii) (1963), 60-76.
GRANT, R. M.: The decalogue in early Christianity. *HTR* 40 (1947), 1-17.
——: The Bible of Theophilus of Antioch. *JBL* 66 (1947), 173-96.
36f, ——: 'Patristica, 5' *VC* 3 (1949), 228-9. [Lucianic text in Genesis
39a quotations of Theophilus].
(ii)
39g GUIRAU, J. M.: Sobre la interpretácion patrística del Ps. 21 (22). *Augustinianum* 7 (1967), 95-132.

39n HAENDLER, G.: Altkirchliche Auslegungen zu Ez. iii: 17-19. *TLZ* 90 (1965), 167-74.

39a HARL, M.: La prise de conscience de la 'nudité' d'Adam. Une interprétation de Génèse 3, 7 chez les Pères grecs. *Studia Patristica* 7 = *TU* 92 (1966), 486-95.

39g, JEANNOTTE, H.: Le texte du Psautier de S. Hilaire de Poitiers. *RB*
40g ns 13 (1916), 61-89.

34 JOUASSARD, G.: Requête d'un patrologue aux biblistes touchant les LXX. *Studia Patristica* I (1957) = *TU* 63, 307-27.

39g KAHLER, E.: *Studien zum Te Deum und zur Geschichte des 24. Psalms in der Alten Kirche* (Göttingen, 1958).

KARPP, H.: 'Prophet' oder 'Dolmetscher'? Die Geltung der LXX in der Alten Kirche. *Fs. G. Dehn* (Neukirchen, 1957). 103-17.

39c KELLERMANN, B.: *Der Midrasch zum I. Buche Samuelis und seine*
(i) *Spuren bei Kirchenvätern und in der orientalischen Sage* (Diss. Giessen 1896).

KERRIGAN, A.: *St. Cyril of Alexandria: interpreter of the OT* (Rome, 1952).

39k KREMER, J.: *Die Hirtenallegorie im Buche Zacharias. ATA* XI, 2 (1930).

LAGARDE, P. A. DE: *LXX Studien II*. (Göttingen, 1892). [Ps.-Athan. *Synopsis*.]

39g LAMPE, G. W. H.: The exegesis of some biblical texts by Marcellus of Ancyra and Ps.-Chrysostom Homily on Ps. xcvi: 1. *JTS* 49 (1948), 169-75.

39a LAURENTIN, R.: Gen. iii: 15 dans la tradition jusqu'au début du 13e
(ii) siècle. *Études mariales* 12 (1954), 79-156.

39a LERCH, D.: *Isaaks Opferung christlich gedeutet. Eine auslegungs-*
(ii) *geschichtliche Untersuchung. BeitrHistTheol* 12 (Tübingen, 1950).

15c LOI, V.: Influssi dell'esegesi biblica nello sviluppo del termine
(ii) Contritio. *Vetera Christianorum* 3 (1966), 69-83.

32, MERCATI, G.: *Osservazioni a proemi del salterio di Origene Ippolito*
39g *Eusebio Cirillo Allessandrino e altri, con frammenti inediti. SeT* 142 (1948).

39a MUHL, J.: Der Weibessame (Gen. iii: 15) in spätjüdischer und früh-
(ii) christlicher Auffassung. *Biblica* 33 (1952), 371-401, 476-505.

NESTLE, E.: Ein wichtiges Citat der Didascalia. *ZNW* 1 (1900), 176-7.

——: Alttestamentliches aus Eusebius. *ZAW* 29 (1909), 57-62.

39a ORBE, A.: Spiritus Domini ferebatur super aquas. Exegesis gnostica
(ii)   de Gen. i: 2b. *Gregorianum* 44 (1963), 691-731.

39m PIATTELLI, D.: *Spr hḥtwm* e *spr hglwy* di Ger. 32, 7-14 nel l'inter-
         pretazione dei Padri della Chiesa. *Rivista Italiana per le
         Scienze Giuridiche* 2 (1967), 381-6.

39k PILARCZYK, D. E.: Jonah's gourd: Augustine and Jerome on a new
         translation of sacred Scripture. *Bible Today* 26 (1966), 1848-52.

39h POQUE, S.: L'exégèse augustinienne de Proverbes xxiii: 1-2. *RBén*
(i)   78 (1968), 117-27.

39a POSNANSKI, A.: *Schilo. Ein Beitrag zur Geschichte der Messiaslehre.*
(ii)   I: *Die Auslegung von Gen. xlix: 10 im Altertum bis zum Ende
         des Mittelalters* (Leipzig, 1904).

39a QUACQUARELLI, A.: La Genesi nella lettura dei Padri anteniceni.
         Rivista Biblica Italiana 15 (1967), 471-95.

      QUISPEL, G.: Das Thomasevangelium und das AT. *NT Suppl.* 6
         (1962), 243-8.

35c RAHLFS, A.: Nachwirkungen der Chronik des Eusebius in LXX-
         HSS. *ZAW* 28 (1908), 60-2.

      RICHARD, M.: Les 'Parallela' de S. Jean Damascène. *Actes du
         congrès internat. des études byzantines* (Belgrade, 1964), 485-9.

15c ROSE, A.: L'influence des LXX sur la tradition chrétienne. I, Le
(ii),   vocabulaire. II, Quelques passages psalmiques (iii: 6, vii: 12,
39g   xviii: 7). *Questions liturgiques et paroissiales* 46 (1965), 192-210,
         284-301.

      ROSSI, S.: La citazione dei testi sacri [LXX] nell' Adversus Praxean
         di Tertulliano. *Giornale Italiano di Filologia* 13 (1960), 249-60.

      SANT, C.: *The OT interpretation of Eusebius of Caesarea* (Malta, 1967).

39h SIMKE, H.: Cant. i 7f in altchristlicher Auslegung. *TZ* 18 (1962),
(iii)   256-67.

39h SIMONETTI, M.: Sull'interpretazione patristica di Prov. viii: 22.
(i)   *Verba seniorum* ns 5 (1965), 9-87.

39a ——: Note sull'interpretazione patristica di Deut. iv: 24. *Vetera
(vi)   Christianorum* 5 (1968), 131-6.

39a SMOROŃSKI, K.: Et Spiritus Dei ferebatur super aquas. Inquisitio
(ii)   historico-exegetica in interpretationem textus Gen. i: 2f.
         Biblica 6 (1925), 140-56, 275-93, 361-95.

39k SMYTHE, H. R.: The interpretation of Amos iv: 13 in St. Athanasius
         and Didymus, *JTS* ns 1 (1950), 158-68.

      STÄHLIN, O.: *Clemens Alexandrinus und die LXX* (Nürnberg, 1901).

      STARRATT, A. B.: *The use of the LXX in the Five Books against*

Heresies by Irenaeus of Lyons (Diss. Harvard, 1952).

39l STEGMÜLLER, G.: Prudentem eloquii mystici. Zur Geschichte der Auslegung von Is. iii: 3. In *Fs. M. Schmaus* (Münster, 1967), 599-618.

39a THUNBERG, L.: Early Christian Interpretations of the Three Angels in Genesis 18. *Studia Patristica 7 = TU* 92 (1966), 560-70.

39g VACCARI, A.: Il testo dei Salmi nel Commento di Teodoro Mopsuesteno. *Biblica* 23 (1942), 1-17.

——: Le citazioni del VT presso Mario Vittorino. *Biblica* 42 (1961), 459-64.

39g VEILLEUX, A.: L'écriture sainte dans la koinonia pachômienne. La tradition des douze psaumes. *Studia Anselmiana* 57 (1968), 262-75, 324-39.

35f VOELTZEL, R.: Le rôle de l'AT dans l'instruction des catéchumènes. *RHPR* 33 (1953), 308-21.

VOLTERRA, E.: *Collatio legum romanarum et mosaicarum.* Atti RANL VI, 4. 1 (1930).

VOSTÉ, J. M.: L'introduction de Mar Išoʿdad de Merw aux livres de l'AT. *Biblica* 26 (1945), 182-202.

39a WILSON, R. McL.: The early history of the exegesis of Gen. i: 26.
(ii) *Studia Patristica* I (1957) = *TU* 63, 420-37.

39a WINDEN, J. C. M. VAN: In the Beginning. Some observations on the
(ii) patristic interpretation of Gen. i: 1. *VC* 17 (1963), 105-21.

39i WÖLKER, W.: Die Verwertung der Weisheits-Literatur bei den christlichen Alexandrinern. *Z. f. Kirchengeschichte* 64 (1952/3), 1-33.

ZIEGLER, J.: Die Peregrinatio Aetheriae und die Hl. Schrift. *Biblica* 12 (1931), 162-98.

39k,l ——: Ochs und Esel an der Krippe. Biblisch-patristische Erwägungen zu Isaias i: 3 und Hab iii: 2 (LXX). *Münchener TheolZeitschrift* 3 (1952), 385-402.

32. ORIGEN

(See also 9, 31, 36e, 37, 38, 39ck)

BARDY, G.: Les citations bibliques d'Origène dans le De Principiis. *RB* ns 16 (1919), 106-35.

——: Les traditions juives dans l'œuvre d'Origène. *RB* 34 (1925), 217-52.

BOON, R.: Origenes' tekstkritiek van de H. Schrift. *Homiletica en Biblica* (Hague) 22 (1963), 173-8.

DANIÉLOU, J.: L'unité des deux testaments dans l'œuvre d'Origène. *RevSR* 22 (1948), 27-56.

——: Origène comme exégète de la Bible. *Studia Patristica* I (1957) = *TU* 63, 280-90.

HANSON, R. P. C.: Origen's interpretation of Scripture exemplified from his Philocalia. *Hermathena* 63 (1944), 47-58.

——: *Origen's Doctrine of Tradition* (London, 1954). [Esp. ch. I and VIII].

18b ——: The interpretation of Hebrew names in Origen. *VC* 10 (1956), 103-23.

——: *Allegory and Event* (London ,1959). [Esp. ch. VI].

KAHLE, P.: The Greek Bible Manuscripts Used by Origen. *JBL* 79 (1960), 111-8.

——: Die von Origenes verwendeten griechischen Bibelhandschriften. *Studia Patristica* IV (1961) = *TU* 79, 107-17.

KLOSTERMANN, E.: Formen der exegetischen Arbeiten des Origenes. *TLZ* 72 (1947), 203-8.

PREUSCHEN, E.: Bibelcitate bei Origenes. *ZNW* 4 (1903), 67-74.

36a TIÈCHE, ED.: *Spuren eines vororigenistischen Septuagintatextes in der Vulgär-paraphrase des Konstantinos Manasses* (Leipzig, 1910).

33. JEROME

(See also 10, 13, 37a, 38)

39g BURKITT, F. C.: Jerome's Work on the Psalter. *JTS* 30 (1929), 395-97.

36b HULLEY, K. K.: The principles of textual criticism known to St. Jerome. *Harvard Studies in Classical Philology* 55 (1945), 87-109.

38a JOHANNESSOHN, M.: Hieronymus und die jüngeren griechischen Übersetzungen des AT. *TLZ* 73 (1948), 145-52.

31 JOUASSARD, G.: Reflexions sur la position de S. Augustin relativement aux LXX dans sa discussion avec S. Jérôme. *Revue des études augustiniennes* 2 (1956), 93-9.

40g MEERSHOEK, G. Q. A.: *Le latin biblique d'après S. Jérôme.* = Latinitas Christiana Primaeva 20 (Nijmegen), 1966.

NEWTON, W. L.: Influences on St. Jerome's translation of the OT. *CBQ* 5 (1943), 17-33.

18b   REHM, M.: Die Bedeutung hebräischer Wörter bei Hieronymus. *Biblica* 35 (1954), 174-97.

10   SEMPLE, W. H.: St. Jerome as a biblical translator. *BJRL* 45 (1965), 227-43.

39k   STUMMER, F.: Spuren jüdischer und christlicher Einflüsse auf die Übersetzung der grossen Propheten durch Hieronymus. *JPOS* 8 (1928), 35-48.

39c,   ——: Einige Beobachtungen über die Arbeitsweise des Hierony-
40g   mus bei der Übersetzung des ATs aus der hebraica veritas. I, Jüdische Tradition in den Büchern Sam. und Kön.; II, Einfluss bestimmter Textgruppen der LXX; III, Einfluss der Vetus Latina auf die sprachliche Gestalt der Vulgata. *Biblica* 10 (1929), 3-30.

——: Griechisch-römische Bildung und christliche Theologie in der Vulgata des Hieronymus. *ZAW* nF 17 (1940/1), 251-69.

SUTCLIFFE, E. F.: The Κοινή 'diversa' or 'dispersa'? St. Jerome PL 24, 548B. *Biblica* 36 (1955), 213-22.

37a   VACCARI, A.: Esaple ed esaplare in S. Girolamo. *Biblica* 8 (1927), 463-8.

39g   WARD, A.: Jerome's work on the Psalter. *ET* 44 (1932), 87-92.

34. EDITIONS (Studies on)
(See also 31, 39, 40)

AMANN, F.: Die römische LXX-revision im 16. Jahrhundert. *BZ* 12 (1914), 116-24.

BARNES, W. E.: The recovery of the LXX. *JTS* 36 (1935), 123-31. [On Göttingen edition].

BAUER, W.: Die Göttinger LXX-Ausgabe. *GGA* 201 (1939), 273-8.

BERTRAM, G.: Die Göttinger LXX-Ausgabe. *OLZ* 31 (1928), 449-53.

——: Zur LXX-Forschung. I, Textausgaben der LXX. *TR* nF 3 (1931), 283-96.

BROOKE, A. E. and McLEAN, N.: The forthcoming Cambridge LXX. *JTS* 3 (1902), 601-21.

CALÈS, J.: La grande LXX de Cambridge et la LXX de Goettingue. *RechSR* 22 (1932), 54-62.

DAHSE, J.: Zur Herkunft des alttestamentlichen Textes der Aldina. *ZAW* 29 (1909), 177-85.

DEISSMANN, A.: Neuere britische LXX-Arbeiten. *Neue Jahrbücher für das klass. Altertum* 23 (1909), 99-106.

DELITZSCH, F.: *Studien zur Entstehungsgeschichte der Polyglotten-bibel des Cardinals Ximenes* (1871).

——: *Complutensische Varianten zu dem a.t.lichen Texte* (1878).

——: *Fortgesetzte Studien zur Entstehungsgeschichte der Compluten-sischen Polyglotte.* (Leipzig, 1886).

40g DENK, J.: Die Italazitate in der grossen Cambridger LXX. *BZ* 4 (1906), 19.

HANHART, R.: L'edizione dei LXX e la fondazione Gottingense che la prepara. *RivStorLettRel* 1 (1965), 351-2.

HEDLEY, P. L.: The Göttingen investigation and edition of the LXX. *HTR* 26 (1933), 57-72.

HOWORTH, H. H.: The coming Cambridge LXX: a plea for a pure text. *JTS* 6 (1905), 436-7. [Rejoinder by Swete *ibid.* 437-8.]

JOHANNESSOHN, M.: Die Göttinger LXX. *TLZ* 65 (1940), 289-96.

KAPPLER, W.: Ziele und Aufgaben des Göttinger LXX-Unter-nehmens. *GGA* 202 (1940), 115-24.

——: Die Göttinger Ausgabe der LXX. *FuF* 8 (1932), 15f.

LAGARDE, P. A. DE: Vorbemerkungen zu meiner Ausgabe der LXX. In *Symmicta II* (Göttingen, 1880), 137-48.

——: *Ankündigung einer neuen Ausgabe der griechischen Über-setzung des ATs* (Göttingen, 1882).

——: Noch einmal meine Ausgabe der LXX. *Mitteilungen* III, 21 (Göttingen, 1889), 229-56.

39a LANDSCHREIBER, K. W.: *Quellen zu Text und Noten der LXX Über-setzung in Band I (die fünf Bücher Mosis) der Polyglottenbibel von R. Stier und K. G. W. Theile* (Bielefeld, 1856).

MARGOLIS, M. L.: The Aldina as a source of the Sixtina. *JBL* 38 (1919), 51-2.

MERCATI, G.: Il testo dell'Aldina. *BZ* 8 (1910), 337-8 = *SeT* 78 (1937), 122-3.

NESTLE, E.: Zum Codex Alexandrinus in Swete's LXX. *ZAW* 15 (1895), 291-2.

——: Zur Geschichte der Sixtina. = *LXX Studien* I (1886) (cp. also II, 11-13).

——: *Die grosse Cambridge LXX* (Leiden, 1903).

——: Scotch Editions of the LXX. *ET* 15 (1903), 427-8.

——: *LXX-Studien* V (Stuttgart, 1907) [On Cambridge LXX Genesis].

——: *LXX-Studien* VI (Stuttgart, 1911).

—— and BETHUNE-BAKER, J. F.: The Cambridge Septuagints of 1665 and 1684. *JTS* 6 (1905), 611-4.

OORT, H.: De Lagarde's plan van eene uitgaaf der LXX. *TheolTijdschrift* 1882, 1-17.

PROCKSCH, O.: Die Stuttgarter LXX. *Luthertum* 1935, 237-47.

RAHLFS, A.: Die Abhängigkeit der sixtinischen LXX-Ausgabe von der aldinischen. *ZAW* 33 (1913), 30-46.

REVILLA, RICO M.: *La Poliglota de Alcala* (Madrid, 1917).

RISCH, A.: Die Neuausgabe der griech. Bibel. *AllgEvangLuthKirchenzeitung* 68 (1935), 441-6.

39g ROZEMOND, K.: Het Psalterion van Aldus Manutius. *Het Boek* 36 (1963), 94-9.

SCHNEIDER, H.: Neue Bände der Göttinger LXX. *ThRev* 65 (1960), 101-6.

36a SPERBER, A.: Probleme einer Edition der LXX. In *Fs. P. Kahle* (Leiden, 1935), 39-46.

36a ——: How to edit the LXX. In *H. A. Wolfson Jubilee Volume* (Jerusalem, 1965), 751.73, [and separate].

TASKER, R. V. G.: The Complutensian Polyglot. *ChQR* 154 (1954), 197-210.

WEVERS, J. W.: LXX-Forschungen. I, Ausgaben und Texte. *TR* nF 22 (1954), 85-138.

——: LXX-Forschungen seit 1954. I, Ausgaben. *TR* nF 33 (1968), 18-45.

39k ZIEGLER, J.: Studien zur Verwertung der LXX im Zwölfprophetenbuch I. *ZAW* nF 19 (1944), 121-9.

39k ——: Der griechischer Dodekapropheton-Text der Complutenser Polyglotte. *Biblica* 25 (1944), 297-310.

39k ——: Der Text der Aldina im Dodekapropheton. *Biblica* 26 (1945), 37-51.

39i
(ii) ——: *Die Münchener griech. Sirach-Handschrift 493. Ihre textgeschichtliche Bedeutung und erstmalige Edition durch den Augsburger Humanisten David Hoeschel, (1604)*. SbMünchen 1962, 4.

35. MANUSCRIPTS

(See also 9, 15b(ii), 17, 30, 31, 36-40)

a. GENERAL

ALBERTSON, J.: An application of mathematical probability to manuscript discoveries. *JBL* 78 (1959), 133-41.

37a BLAU, L.: Über den Einfluss des althebräischen Buchwesens auf die Originale und auf die ältesten Handschriften der LXX, des NT und der Hexapla. In *Fs. A. Berliner* (Frankfurt, 1903), 41-9.

CAVALLO, G.: *Ricerche sulla maiuscola biblica* (Florence, 1967).

DAIN, A.: *Les manuscrits* (Paris, 1964).

DEVREESSE, R.: *Introduction à l'étude des manuscrits grecs* (Paris, 1954).

GARDTHAUSEN, V.: *Griechische Paläographie* (Leipzig², 1913).

IRIGOIN, J.: Les manuscrits grecs (1931-60). *Lustrum* 7 (1962), 5-93.

KATZ, P.: The early Christians' use of codices instead of rolls. *JTS* 46 (1945), 63-5.

KENYON, F. G.: *Our Bible and the ancient manuscripts* (London⁵, 1958).

RAHLFS, A.: *Verzeichnis der griechischen Handschriften des ATs. MSU* 2 = *NGWGött* Beiheft (1914).

ROBERTS, C. H.: The Christian Book and the Greek papyri. *JTS* 50 (1949), 155-68.

——: The Codex. *PBA* 40 (1954), 169-204.

SCHUBART, W.: *Griechische Paläographie* (Munich, 1925).

SEIDER. R.: *Paläographie der griechischen Papyri. I, Urkunden; II, Literarische Papyri* (Stuttgart, 1967, 1970).

SKEAT, T. C.: The Use of dictation in ancient book production. *PBA* 42 (1956), 179-208.

THOMPSON, E. M.: *An Introduction to Greek and Latin Palaeography* (Oxford, 1912).

WITTEK, M.: *Album de paléographie grecque* (Ghent, 1967).

b. PAPYRI

39a (i) ALLGEIER, A.: *Die Chester Beatty-Papyri zum Pentateuch. Untersuchungen zur älteren Überlieferungsgeschichte der Septuaginta* (Paderborn, 1938).

39a (vi) BAARS, W.: Papyrus Fouad Inv. no. 266. *NTT* 13 (1959), 442-6.

39d (i) ——: P. Barc. Inv. no. 3 and Egerton Pap. 4. [2 Chron]. *VT* 15 (1965), 528-9.

BARDY, G.: Les papyrus des LXX. *Revue de Philologie* ns 33 (1909), 255-64.

BARNS, J. W. B. and KILPATRICK, G. D.: A New Psalms Fragment. *PBA* 43 (1957), 229-32.

BATAILLE, A.: *Les Papyrus. Traité d'études byzantines* 2 (Paris, 1955).

BEARE, F. W.: The Chester Beatty papyri. *CdE* 12 (1937), 81-91; 13 (1938), 364-72.

BELL, H. I.: *Recent discoveries of Biblical papyri* (Oxford, 1937).

BURKITT, F. C.: The Chester Beatty papyri. *JTS* 34 (1933), 363-9.

39a   COLLART, P.: Papyrus Th. Reinach, n. 59-61. *BIFAO* 39 (1940), 1-6.
(iii),
g

COLLOMP, P.: Les papyrus Chester Beatty, observations bibliologi-
ques. *RHPR* 14 (1936), 130-43.

DEISSMANN, G. A.: *Die LXX-Papyri und andere altchristliche
Texte der Heidelberger Papyrus-Sammlung* (Heidelberg, 1905).

——: The New Biblical Papyri at Heidelberg. *ET* 17 (1905), 248-54.

39l   DONOVAN, B. E.: An Isaiah fragment in the Library of Congress.
HTR 61 (1968), 625-9.

DUMESTE, M.-L.: Die Bedeutung der Chester Beatty Papyri für die
Septuagintaforschung. *FuF* 15 (1939), 20-22.

39a   DUNAND, F.: *Papyrus grecs bibliques (Papyrus F. Inv. 266). Volu-
(ii),   mina de la Genèse et du Deutéronome. Introduction.* = Recherches
(vi);   d'archéologie, de philologie et d'histoire XXVII (Cairo, 1966).
17

——: Papyrus grecs bibliques (Papyrus F. Inv. 266). Volumina de la
Genèse et du Deutéronome [Text]. *Études de Papyrologie* 9
(1966), 81-150.

EICHGRÜN, E.: Identification eines alttest. Bruchstückes. *Prolegomena* 2 (1953), 5-8, 20.

39c   FEINBERG, L.: A papyrus text of I Kingdoms. *HTR* 62 (1969), 349-
(i)   56.

39n   GALIANO, M. F.: 'Notes on the Madrid Ezekiel Papyrus' (= 967).
American Studies in Papyrology 7 (Toronto, 1970), 133-8.

39n   ——: Notes on the Madrid Ezekiel Papyrus. *BASP* 5 (1968), 72.

39a   —— and GIL, M.: Observaciones sobre los papiros 961 y 962.
(ii)   *Emerita* 21 (1953), 1-13.

39e   GEISSEN, A.: *Der LXX-Text des Buches Daniel. Kap. 5-12 zusammen
(i),o   mit Susanna, Bel et Draco, sowie Esther i 1a-ii 15 nach dem
Kölner Teil des Papyrus 967.* Papyrologische Texte und Abhandlungen 5 (Bonn, 1968).

38b, GRENFELL, B. P. & HUNT, A. S.: The Amherst Papyri; being an
39a   account of the Greek Papyri in the collection of Lord Amherst
(iii),   (*London*, 1900-1).
(vi),h
(iv),g

39m HAELST, J. VAN: Deux nouveaux fragments de Jérémie. *Recherches*
(i)   *de Papyrologie* 1 (1961), 113-20.
——: Catalogue raisonné des papyrus litteraires chrétiens d'Égypte,
grecs et latins. *Actes du Xe congrès des papyrologues* (Warsaw,
1964), 215-25.

390 HAMM, W.: *Der LXX-Text des Buches Daniel. Kap. 1-2 nach dem*
Kölner Teil des Papyrus 967. Papyrologische Texte und Abhandlungen 10 (Bonn, 1969).

39g HEINRICI, G. F. G.: *Die Leipziger Papyrusfragmente der Psalmen.*
= Beiträge zur Geschichte und Erklärung des NT 4 (Leipzig,
1903).
JEREMIAS, J.: Der gegenwärtige Stand der frühchristlichen Papyrologie. *TLZ* 75 (1950), 55-8.

39n JOHNSON, A. C., GEHMAN, H. S. and KASE, E. H.: *The J. H.*
Scheide Biblical Papyri: Ezekiel (Princeton/London, 1938).

39g KASSER, R. and TESTUZ, M.: *Papyrus Bodmer XXIV: Psaumes*
xvii-cxviii (Cologny/Geneva, 1967).
KATZ, P.: P. Fuad 203 und die LXX. *TZ* 9 (1953), 228-31 [On prayer
published by Benoit in *RB*, 1951].
KENYON, F. G.: art. 'Papyri' in *HDB* 5, 352-7.
——: *The Chester Beatty Biblical Papyri* (London, 1933-41;
Dublin, 1958).
    I, General introduction (1933).
II-III, (NT).

39a   IV, Genesis (Text 1934; plates 1935-6).
(ii)

39a   V, Numbers, Deuteronomy (Text 1935; plates 1958).
(v),
(vi)

39i   VI, Isaiah, Jeremiah, Ecclesiasticus (Text 1937; plates
(ii),l,   1958).
m

39n,   VII, Ezekiel, Daniel, Esther (Text 1937; plates 1938).
o,e(i)

    VIII, (Enoch, Melito).

39g   KILPATRICK, G. D. A fragment of Ps. xliii (LXX) 20-23. *JTS* 50
      (1949), 176-7.

39g   ——: Ps. xc: 1-4 (LXX). *ZAW* 78 (1966), 224.

39g   KRAFT, R. A., and TRIPOLITIS, A.: Some uncatalogued papyri of
      theological and other interest in the John Rylands Library.
      BJRL 51 (1968/9), 137-63.

39g   LIETZMANN, H.: Ein Psalterfragment der Jenaer Papyrussammlung.
      In *NT Studien für G. Heinrici* (Leipzig, 1914), 60-5.

      MALDFELD, G.: Funde und Veröffentlichungen von Papyrus und
      Pergamenthandschriftbruchstücken des A und NT in neuester
      Zeit. *Deutsches Pfarrerblatt* 50 (1950), 200-3.

      ——: Der Beitrag ägyptischer Papyruszeugen für den frühen
      griechischen Bibeltext. *Mitt. Papyrussammlung d. Österr.
      Nationalbibliothek* ns 5 (1956), 79-84.

39g   MERCATI, G.: Ps. xc: 1-2 riconosciuto nel Papiro PSI 739. *Biblica* 8
      (1927), 96.

      NALDINI, M.: Due papiri cristiani della collezione fiorentina. *Studi
      Italiani de Filologia Classica* 33 (1961), 212-6.

      ——: *Documenti dell'antichità cristiana. Rassegna di papiri e
      pergamene della raccolta fiorentina* (Florence, 1964) [9 LXX
      fragments].

39g   NIEDERWIMMER, K.: Bisher uneditierte Fragmente biblischen In-
      halts aus der Sammlung Erzherzog Rainer. *JÖstByzGes* 14
      (1965), 7-11.

39g   O'CALLAGHAN, J.: Salmos i 3-6, ii 6-9 (P. Palau-Rib. 1). *Studia
      Papyrologica* 4 (1965), 91-7.

      ORLINSKY, H. M.: The Chester Beatty Biblical Papyri. *JQR* ns 32
      (1941), 89-95.

      PHILLIPS, G. A.: The Chester Beatty Biblical Papyri. *ET* 45 (1933-4),
      55-60.

27c, ——: The oldest biblical papyrus and a leaf from a testimony book.
39a   *ET* 48 (1936/7), 168-70.
(vi)

39n   REIDER, J.: The Scheide Biblical Papyri. *JQR* ns 29 (1938/9), 405-9.

27c, ROBERTS, C. H.: *Two Biblical papyri in the John Rylands Library*
39a   (Manchester, 1936).
(vi)   Rev. Katz in *TLZ* 1936, 340-1.

39g, ——: *The Antinoopolis Papyri*, I (London, 1950).
h(i)   Rev. Katz in *TLZ* 1955, 737-40.
i(i)
(ii),
n

39a   ——: P. Yale I (Gen. LXX) and the early Christian book. *Fs. C. B.*
(ii)   *Welles* (New Haven, 1966), 25-8.

39h   ROCA PUIG, R.: P. Med. Inv. n. 151 (Eccl. iii: 17-8, 21-2). *Aegyptus*
(i)   32 (1952), 215-22.

39d   ——: Un papiro grec del libre dels Paralipomens. *Bol. RAcad. de*
(i)   *Buenas Letras de Barcelona* 29 (1961), 219-27.

39d   ——: Un papiro griego del libro segundo de los Paralimpomenos.
(i)   *Helmantica* (Salamanca) 14 (1963), 173-85.

39m   ——: Papiro griego de Jeremias. *Aegyptus* 45 (1965), 70-73.
(i)

        RUDBERG, G.: Septuagintafragmente unter den Papyri Osloenses.
        Forhandl. i Videnskapselskapet i Kristiania, 1923, 2.

39k   SANDERS, H. A.: A papyrus of the Minor Prophets. *HTR* 14 (1921),
        181-7.

39k   ——: *Facsimile of the Washington manuscript of the Minor Prophets
        in the Freer Collection* (Ann Arbor, 1927).

39a   —— and SCHMIDT, C.: *The Minor Prophets in the Freer Collection
(ii),k   and the Berlin fragment of Genesis* (New York, 1927).

        SANZ, P.: *Griechische literarische Papyri christlichen Inhalts.* =
        Mitteil. Papyrussammlung Nationalbibliothek Wien, ns 4
        (Baden bei Wien, 1946).

        SCHMIDT, C.: Die neuesten Bibelfunde aus Ägypten. *ZNW* 30
        (1931), 285-93.

39g   SIMOTAS, P. N.: Ὁ Πάπυρος Bodmer IX. *Theologia* 31 (1960), 315-
        24, 414-23.

        SMOTHERS, E. R.: Les papyrus Beatty de la Bible grecque. *RechSR*
        24 (1934), 12-34.

        STEGMÜLLER, O.: *Berliner Septuagintafragmente* (Berlin, 1939).

39g   TESTUZ, M.: *L'Epître de Jude, les 2 Epîtres de Pierre, les Psaumes 33 et
        34. P. Bodmer VII-IX* (Geneva, 1959).

        TRAVERSA, A.: Alcuni papiri inediti della collezione genovese.
        Serta Eusebiana: Misc. Philologica. (Genoa, 1958), 114-24.

39a   TREU, K.: Das Berliner Genesis-Fragment P. 17035. *Actes du Xe
(ii)   congrès international des papyrologues* (Warsaw, 1964), 209-13.

        ——: Christliche Papyri, 1940-67. *AfP* 19 (1969), 169-206.

        ——: Neue Berliner Septuagintafragmente (with 7 plates). *AfP* 20
        (1970), 43-65.

        ——: Christliche Papyri II, ibid, 145-52.

        VOGT, E. and CALDERINI, A.: Beatty, Chester, papiri. *Enciclopedia
        Cattolica* 2 (1949), 1113-5.

39a WELLES, C. B.: The Yale Genesis fragment. *Yale University Library*
(ii) *Gazette* 39, 1 (1964), 1-8.
   WILCKEN, U.: The Chester Beatty Biblical papyri. *Archiv für Papyrusforschung* 11 (1935), 112-4.
   WILLIS, W. H.: The new collection of papyri at the University of Mississippi. *Proceedings IXth Internat. Congress of Papyrology* (Oslo, 1961), 381-92.
39k YOUTIE, H.: A Codex of Jonah: Berlin Sept. 18 + PSI X 1164. *HTR* 38 (1945), 195-7.
   ZWAAN, J. DE: De in Egypte gevonden papyri van den bijbel. *Stimmen der Tijd* 21 (1932), 306-21.
39h ZUNTZ, G.: Der Antinoe Papyrus der Proverbia und das Prophetolo-
(i),n gion. *ZAW* 68 (1956), 124-84.

c. MANUSCRIPTS (Other than Papyri)

39l ABBOTT, T. K.: *Par Palimpsestorum Dublinensium: ·· Fragments of the Book of Isaiah in the LXX Version* (Dublin, 1880).
39g ALLGEIER, A.: Zwei gr.-lat. Bibelhandschriften aus Cues und ihre Bedeutung für die Frage der abendländischen LXX-Über-lieferung. *OC* III, 10 (1935), 139-60.
   ANON: *Bibliorum sacrorum graecorum codex vaticanus 1209 denuo phototypice expressus (Cod. e. Vaticanis selecti IV)* (Milan, 1905/7).
39f BAARS, W. Eine neue griechische Handschrift des 3. Makkabäer-buches. *VT* 13 (1963), 82-7.
39k ——: A new witness to the text of the Barberini Greek version of Habakkuk III. *VT* 15 (1965), 381-2.
39c ——: A forgotten fragment of the Greek text of the Books of
(i) Samuel. *OTS* 14 (1965), 201-5.
   BARDY, G.: Simples remarques sur les ouvrages et les manuscrits bilingues. *Vivre et Penser* 3 (1943/4), 242-67.
   BARTHÉLEMY, D.: see 36d.
   BARTINA, S.: Códices griegos del AT. *EncBibl* 2 (1963), 359-62.
   BEES, N. A.: Über zwei Codices des AT aus den Bibliotheken von Meteoron und Megaspelaion. *ZAW* 32 (1912), 225-31.
39g ——: Zum Psalter 552 der Hamilton-Sammlung. *Byz.-neugr. Jahrbücher* 12 (1935/6), 119-28.
39o BENJAMIN, C. D.: Collation of Holmes Parsons 23 (Venetus)-62-147

in Daniel from photographic copies. *JBL* 44 (1925), 303-26.

39g BIELER, L.: *Psalterium graeco-latinum. Codex Basiliensis A VII.3* (Amsterdam, 1960).

BILLEN, A. V.: The Classification of the Greek MSS of the Hexateuch. *JTS* 26 (1925), 262-77.

39g BONICATTI, M.: Per l'origine del salterio Barberiniano greco 372 e la cronologia del tetraevangelio urbinate greco 2. *Rivista di Cultura Classica e Medievale* 2 (1960), 42-61.

39n BOTTE, B.: Codex Melphictensis. *DBS* 5 (1955), 1101-2.

BRÜGSCH, H.: *Neue Bruchstücke des Codex Sinaiticus aufgefunden in der Bibliothek des Sinaiklosters* (Leipzig, 1875).

BURKITT, F. C.: Codex Alexandrinus. *JTS* 11 (1910), 603-6.

39a CERIANI, A. M.: *Pentateuch et Iosue quae ex prima scriptura supersunt*
(i),b *in codice ambrosiano graeco seculi fere V.* = Monumenta Sacra
(i) et Profana III (Milan, 1864).

39k- ——: *De codice marchaliano seu vaticano graeco 2125 prophetarum*
o *phototypice repraesentato commentatio* (Rome, 1890) [cp Cozza].

CHABOT, J. B.: Note sur la polyglotte de la Bibliothèque Ambrosienne de Milan. *OCP* 13 (1947), 451-3.

COZZA, J.: *Sacrorum bibliorum vetustissima fragmenta graeca et latina*, I (Rome, 1867).

——: *Vetus testamentum iuxta LXX interpretum versionem e codice omnium antiquissimo graeco vaticano 1209 phototypice repraesentatum* (Rome, 1889-90; 5 vols).

39k- ——: *Prophetarum codex graecus vaticanus 2125 qui dicitur marcha-*
o *lianus phototypice editus* (Rome, 1890: 2 vols).

39g DEISSMANN, A.: Handschriften aus Anatolien in Ankara und Izmit. *ZNW* 34 (1935), 262-84 [Incl. Psalter].

39a DOLD, A.: Neue Palimpsest-Bruchstücke der griechischen Bibel.
(ii) *BZ* 18 (1929), 241-70. [Gen].

——: Neue St. Galler vorhieronymianische Propheten-Fragmente der St. Galler Sammelhandschrift 1398b zugehörig. *TA* I: 31, (1940).

GAROFALO, S.: Nuove note sulla edizione in facsimile tipografico del Codex Vaticanus (B). *SeT* 231 (1964), 217-27.

39n GEHMAN, H. S.: The Relations between the Hebrew text of Ezekiel and that of the John H. Scheide Papyri. *JAOS* 58 (1938), 92-102.

39n ——: The Relations between the Text of the John H. Scheide Papyri and that of the other Greek MSS of Ezekiel. *JBL* 57 (1938). 281-87.

GERHÄUSSER, W. and RAHLFS, A.: *Münchener Septuaginta-Fragmente. MSU* I, 4 (Berlin, 1913).

GERSTINGER, H.: — see 41.

39a (vi), b(i) GOODSPEED, E. J.: The Freer manuscript of Deuteronomy and Joshua. *Biblical World* 36 (1910), 204-9.

——: The Detroit MSS of the LXX and the N.T. *BW* 31 (1908), 218-26.

39a (ii) GOTCH, F. W.: *A supplement to Tischendorf's* Reliquiae ex incendio ereptae codicis celeberrimi Cottoniani *contained in his* Monumenta Sacra Inedita nova collectio, tomus II, *together with a synopsis of the codex* (Edinburgh/London, 1881).

HARRIS, J. R.: *Biblical fragments from Mount Sinai* (London, 1890).

39g HART, J. H. A.: The new LXX fragment. *JTS* 4 (1903), 215-7.

39c (i) HUNGER, H.: Ein neues LXX-Fragment in der Öst. Nationalbibliothek. *Anzeiger ÖstAkWiss ph.-hist. Kl.* 93 (Vienna, 1956), 188-99.

JACOB, A.: La minuscule grecque penchée et l'âge du Parisinus grec 1741. *Mélanges E. Chatelain* (Paris, 1910), 52-6.

KENYON, F. G.: *Facsimiles of Biblical Manuscripts in the British Museum.* (London, 1900).

—— and MILNE, H. J. M.: *The Codex Alexandrinus in reduced photographic facsimile* (London, 1909-57; 5 vols).

39g KLOSTERMANN, E.: Ein neues griechisches Unzialpsalterium. *ZAW* 17 (1897), 339-46.

LAGARDE, P. A. DE: Die pariser Blätter des Codex Sarravianus. *Semitica 2 (= AbhKGWGött)* (1879), 1-48.

LAGRANGE, M. J.: Le manuscrit sinaïtique. *RB* 35 (1926), 83-93.

31 LAKE, K.: The Sinaitic and Vatican manuscripts and the copies sent by Eusebius to Constantine. *HTR* 11 (1918), 32-5.

—— and H.: *Codex Sinaiticus Petropolitanus et Frederico-Augustanus Lipsiensis. The Old Testament ... reproduced in facsimile from photographs* (Oxford, 1922).

LAUCH, E.: Etwas vom Codex Sinaiticus. In *Fs.A.Alt* (Leipzig, 1954), 5-11.

39b (i),41 LIETZMANN, H.: Zur Datierung der Josuarolle. *Festgabe für H. Degering* (Leipzig, 1926), 181-5.

39k LIFSHITZ, B.: The Greek Documents from the Cave of Horror. *IEJ* 12 (1962), 201-7 (cp also *Yediot* 26 (1962), 183f.).

LYON, R. W.: A Re-examination of Codex Ephraemi Rescriptus. *NTS* 5 (1958/9), 260-72.

39g MARGOLIS, M. L.: A new uncial of the Greek Psalter [Washington ms]. *AJSL* 36 (1919/20), 84-6.

MERCATI, G.: Per la storia esterna dei codici marchaliano e claromontano. *RB* 10 (1901), 580-3.

——: Un'oscura nota del codice Alessandrino. In *Mélanges E. Chatelain* (Paris, 1910), 79-82 = *SeT* 78 (1937), 154-8.

39a ——: Due Glosse all'Esodo nel Codice vaticano. *RB* ns 2 (1905),
(iii)   555-6 = *SeT* 77 (1937), 424-5.

——: Origine antiochena di due codici greci del secolo IV. *Analecta Bollandiana* 68 (1950), 210-22.

MILNE, H. J. M. and SKEAT, T. C.: *Scribes and Correctors of the Codex Sinaiticus* (London, 1938).

MOIR, I.: *Codex Climaci Rescriptus.* = Texts and Studies, ns 2. (Cambridge, 1956).

39b ——: Two LXX palimpsest fragments. *JTS* ns 8 (1957), 1-11.
(i)

NESTLE, E.: *Veteris testamenti graeci codices Vaticanus et Sinaiticus cum textu recepto collati ab Eb. Nestle. Supplementum editionum quae sixtinam sequuntur omnium in primis Tischendorfianarum* (Leipzig, 1880, ²1887).

——: *LXX-Studien II* [On B] (Ulm, 1896).

OESTERLEY, W. O. E.: *Codex Taurinensis (Y) transcribed and collated* (London, 1908) [JTS 6-8].
    Rev. Rahlfs in *TLZ* 1909, 629-30.

OMONT, H.: *Vetus testamentum graece: codicis sarraviani colbertini quae supersunt* ... (Leiden, 1897).

PHILLIPS, G. A.: The Codex Sinaiticus and the Codex Alexandrinus. *ET* 51 (1939/40), 299-301.

RAHLFS, A.: Über eine von Tischendorf aus dem Orient mitgebrachte in Oxford, Cambridge, London und Petersburg liegende Handschrift der LXX. *NGWGött* 1898, 98-112.

——: Alter und Heimat der vatikanischen Handschrift. *NGWGött* 1899, 72-9.

——: Über die Handschrift Athen, Nat. Bibl. 43. *TLZ* 38 (1913), 476-7.

39h —: Palimpsest Fragmente des Sirach und Iob aus Jerusalem. *MSU*
(iv),i   1, 388-403 = *NGWGött* 1915, 404-19.
(ii)

——: *Verzeichnis der griechischen Handschriften des Alten Testaments. MSU* II (1914).

———: Über einige alttestamentliche Handschriften des Abessinier-
klosters S. Stefano zu Rom. *MSU* III, 1 (1918).

———: Curiosa im Codex Sinaiticus. *ZAW* nF 9 (1932), 309-10.

REDPATH, H. A.: Codex Zittaviensis. *ET* 8 (1896/7), 383.

390   ROCCO, B.: Un codice biblico del sec. IX-X. *Rivista Biblica Italiana*
16 (1968), 291-304 [Dan. iv, 28b-vi, 19].

39h   RUELLE, C.-E.: Un passage des LXX dans le Parisinus 2841 en
(iv)   parti palimspeste. *Revue de Philologie* ns 33 (1909), 162 [Job].

SANDERS, H. A. New manuscripts of the Bible from Egypt. *AJA*
II, 12 (1908), 49-55.

39a   ———: *Facsimile of the Washington manuscript of Deuteronomy and*
(vi),   *Joshua in the Freer Collection* (Michigan, 1910).
b(i)

———: *The OT manuscripts in the Freer Collection.*

39a   I, *The Washington manuscript of Deuteronomy and Joshua*
(vi),   (New York, 1910).
b(i)

39g   II, *The Washington manuscript of the Psalms.* (New York,
1917).

———: A newly discovered leaf of the Freer Psalter. *HTR* 22 (1929),
391-3.

———: Some Greek Fragments in the Freer Collection. *JBL* 34
(1915), 187-93.

SCHERMANN, TH.: Griechische Handschriftenbestände in den Bibliotheken der christlichen Kulturzentren des 5.-7. Jahrhunderts
(nach Konzilakten). *OC* 4 (1904), 151-63.

SCHMIDT, C.: Die neuesten Bibelfunde aus Ägypten. *ZNW* 30 (1931),
285-93.

ŠEVČENKO, I.: New documents on C. Tischendorf and the codex
Sinaiticus. *Scriptorium* 18 (1964), 55-80.

SKEAT, T. C.: The provenance of the codex Alexandrinus. *JTS* ns
6 (1955), 23-5.

SMITH, H. P.: Biblical MSS in America. *JBL* 42 (1923), 239-50;
44 (1925), 188-89.

SOISALON-SOININEN, I.: Ein neuer Septuaginta-Fund [Finnish].
TA 60 (1955), 83-94.

SPERBER, A.: The Codex Vaticanus B. *MGM* 6 (Vatican City, 1946).

SPINKA, M.: The acquisition of the codex Alexandrinus by England.
JReligion 16 (1936), 10-29.

39g   TAYLOR, C.: A new LXX fragment. *JTS* 4 (1903), 130.

THOMPSON, E. M.: *Facsimile of the Codex Alexandrinus* (London, 1879-83; 4 vols).

39g TILL, W. and SANZ, P.: *Eine griechisch-koptische Odenhandschrift.*
(ii) *MBE* 5 (Rome, 1939).

TINDALL, C.: *Contributions to the statistical study of the Codex Sinaiticus* (ed. T. B. Smith; Edinburgh, 1961).

TISCHENDORF, C. VON: *Codex Ephraemi syri rescriptus sive fragmenta veteris testamenti* ... (Leipzig, 1845).

——: *Codex Frederico-Augustanus* (Leipzig, 1846).

——: *Anecdota sacra et profana* (Leipzig, ¹1855; ²1861).

——: *Monumenta sacra inedita, nova collectio* (Leipzig). I (1885); II (1857); III (1860): IV, VI (1869); IX (1870).

——: *Bibliorum codex sinaiticus petropolitanus* (St. Petersburg, 1862); 4 vols).

——: *Appendix codicum celeberrimorum sinaitici vaticani alexandrini* (Leipzig, 1867).

——: *Codex Sinaiticus. The ancient biblical manuscript now in the British Museum. Tischendorf's story related by himself* (London, 1933).

TISSERANT, E.: *Codex Zuqninensis rescriptus veteris testamenti. SeT* 23 (1911).
  Rev. Margolis in *JQR* ns 3 (1912/3), 128-9.
  Rahlfs in *TLZ* 36, 741-3.

39h ——: Un manuscrit palimpseste de Job. *RB* ns 9 (1912), 481-503.
(iv)

39h ——: Nouvelles notes sur le manuscrit palimpseste de Job. *RB* ns
(iv) 16 (1919), 89-105, 500-5.

TREU, K.: Majuskelbruchstücke der LXX aus Damaskus. *NAWGött* 1966, 6 = MSU 8 (1966).

39n VACCARI, A.: *Codex Melphictensis rescriptus Ezechielis fragmenta graeca. MBE* 2 (Rome, 1918).

——: I palinsesti biblici di Beuron. *Biblica* 11 (1930), 231-5.

VERCELLONE, C. and COZZA, J.: *Bibliorum sacrorum graecus codex vaticanus* (Rome, 1869-81; 6 vols.) [I (1869) Pent. Josh.; II (1870) Jud.-Esd.; III (1871) Poetical Books; IV (1872) Esth. Tob. etc.; V (1868) NT; VI Prolegomena. cp also Anon. *De editione romana codicis graeci vaticani ss. bibliorum* (Rome, 1881).]

39g VIOLET, B.: Ein zweisprachiges Psalmfragment aus Damaskus. *OLZ* 4 (1901), 384-403, 425-41, 475-88.

39k VOGT, E.: Fragmenta Prophetarum minorum deserti Juda. *Biblica* 34 (1953), 423-6.

39g WILLOUGHBY, H. R.: Stray NT-Psalter leaves identified. *JBL* 61 (1942), 57-60.

ZIEGLER, J.: see 34.

d. INSCRIPTIONS, AMULETS, etc.

BÖHL, E.: Alte christliche Inschriften nach dem Text der LXX. *TSK* (1881), 692-713.

39k BONNER, C.: The story of Jonah on a magic amulet. *HTR* 41 (1948), 31-7.

39g BUCHER, P.: Les commencements des Psaumes li à xciii; inscription d'une tombe de Kasr es Saijad. *Kemi* 4 (1931), 157-60 [cp *NTS* 14, p. 366, n. 4].

39g COLLART, P.: Un papyrus Reinach inédit. Psaume cxl sur une amulette. *Aegyptus* 13 (1933), 208-12.

39g ——: Psaumes et amulettes. *Aegyptus* 14 (1934), 463-7.

DEISSMANN, A.: Verkannte Bibelzitate in syrischen und mesopotamischen Inschriften. *Philologus* 64 (1905), 475-8 = *Licht vom Osten* (1908), 335-8.

JALABERT, L. and LECLERQ, H.: Citations bibliques dans l'épigraphie. *DACL* III, 2 (1914), 1731-79.

——: Notes d'épigraphie chrétienne: citations bibliques dans les inscriptions. *RechSR* 1 (1910), 68-71.

39h ——: A propos de quelques versets du Cantique des Cantiques.
(iii) *RechSR* 2 (1911), 59-61.

39a JERPHANION, G. DE: Une variante isolée d'un manuscrit confirmée
(ii) par l'épigraphie. *Biblica* 3 (1922), 444-5.

NESTLE, E.: Die alten christlichen Inschriften nach dem Text der LXX. *TSK* (1883), 153-4.

PETERSON, E.: Das Amulett von Acre. *Aegyptus* 33 (1953), 172-8.

PRÉAUX, C.: Une amulette chrétienne aux musées royaux d'art et d'histoire de Bruxelles. *CdE* 10 (1935), 361-70.

39e SCHWARTZ, J.: Un fragment grec du livre de Judith (sur Ostracon).
(ii) *RB* 53 (1946), 534-7.

39g STEVE, M. A. and BENOIT, P.: Une cruche avec inscription biblique. *RB* 56 (1949), 433-42 [Ps. xxxv: 8-10].

39g, THOUVENOT, R.: Une citation biblique dans l'épigraphie africaine.

40g *Atti 3 Congresso internazionale di Epigrafia* (Rome, 1958), 381-5. [Ps. xxiii: 1, Old Latin].

39a WEITZMANN, K. and ŠEVČENKO, I.: The Moses cross at Sinai.
(iii) *Dumbarton Oaks Papers* 17 (1963), 385-98 [Exod. xix: 16-8].

39g WIKGREN, A. P.: Two ostraca of the LXX Psalter. *JNES* 5 (1946), 181-4.

e. CATENAE

39h BERTINI, U.: La catena greca in Giobbe. *Biblica* 4 (1923), 129-42.
(iv)

39a, DECONINCK, J.: *Essai sur la chaîne de l'Octateuque* (Paris, 1912).
b

DEVREESSE, R.: Chaînes exégètiques grecques. *DBS* 1 (1928), 1084-1164.

39g ——: La chaîne sur les psaumes de Daniele Barbaro. *RB* ns 21 (1924), 65-81, 498-521.

39k FAULHABER, M.: *Die Prophetencatenen nach römischen Handschriften* (Freiburg, 1899).
Rev. Lietzmann in *GGA* 1900, 920-9.

39h ——: *Hohelied-, Proverbien- und Predigerkatenen.* = Theologische
(i-iii) Studien der Leo-Gesellschaft 4 (Vienna, 1902).

——: Katenen-Handschriften in spanischen Bibliotheken. *BZ* 1 (1903), 151-9, 246-55, 351-71.

——: Katenen und Katenenforschung. *ByzZ* 18 (1909), 383-95.

39h HOPPMANN, O.: *Die Catena des Vaticanus gr. 1802 zu den Proverbien.*
(i) = Catenenstudien 2; 1912.

KARO, G. and LIETZMANN, H.: *Catenarum graecarum catalogus.* *NGWGött* 1902, 1, 3, 5.

LIETZMANN, H.: *Catenen: Mitteilungen über ihre Geschichte und handschriftliche Überlieferung* (Freiburg i.B., 1897).

39a, LINDL, E.: *Die Octateuchkatene des Procop von Gaza und die Septua-*
b *gintaforschung* (Munich, 1902).

RAHLFS, A.: Die Catenenhandschrift des Meursius. *TLZ* 38 (1913), 763-4.

——: Die Quellen der Catena Nicephori. *TLZ* 39 (1914), 92. (cp. *TLZ* 1913, 476-7).

39g RICHARD, M.: Quelques manuscrits peu connus des chaînes exégéti-ques et des commentaires grecs sur le psautier. *Bulletin d'In-*

formation de l'Institut de Recherche et d'Histoire des Textes 3 (1954), 87-106.

39g ——: Les premières chaînes sur le Psautier. *Bulletin d'Information de l'Institut de Recherche et d'Histoire des Textes* 5 (1956), 87-98.

f. Lections; Use of LXX in Liturgy

BALDI, D.: Le lezioni scritturistiche nella liturgia di Gerusalemme nei secoli IV e V. *Studii Biblici Franciscani Liber Annuus* 2 (1951/2), 163-226.

40a BAUMSTARK, A.: Ein griechisch-arabisches Perikopenbuch des koptischen Ritus. *OC* II, 2 (1913), 142-4.

40a ——: Das leydener griechisch-arabische Perikopenbuch für die Kar- und Osterwoche. *OC* II, 4 (1915), 39-58.

40i,k, ——: *Nichtevangelische syrische Perikopenordnungen des ersten Jahr-*
l *tausends im Sinne vergleichender Liturgiegeschichte untersucht.*
LQF 3 (1921).

40c ——: Die quadragesimale alttestamentl. Schriftlesung des koptischen Ritus. *OC* 25/6 (1930), 37-58.

BRATSIOTIS, P. I.: Das AT in der griech. Orthodoxen Kirche. *Kyrios* 1 (1960), 59-82.

——: Ἡ Παλαιὰ Διαθήκη ἐν τῇ Ἑλληνικῇ ὀρθοδόξῳ ἐκκλησίᾳ (Athens, 1961).

40l BURKITT, F. C.: The Palestinian Syriac Lectionary. *JTS* 6 (1905), 91-8.

——: The old lectionary of Jerusalem. *JTS* 24 (1923), 415-34.

40c BURMESTER, O. H. E.: *Le lectionnaire de la semaine sainte. Patrologia Orientalis* XXIV, 2 (1933), 171-294; XXV, 2 (1939), 175-485.

——: The Bohairic Pericopae of Wisdom and Sirach. *Biblica* 15 (1934), 451-65.

40a, ——: The Coptic-Greek-Arabic Holy Week lectionary of Scetis.
c *BSAC* 16 (1962), 83-137.

40a, ——: The Bodleian folio and further fragments of the Coptic-Greek-
c Arabic Holy Week lectionary from Scetis. *BSAC* 17 (1963), 35-56.

CERVALL, L.: Un lectionnaire de l'AT. *SvExÅrsb* 24 (1959), 89-96.

COLORNI, V.: *L'uso del greco nella liturgia del giudaismo ellenistico e la novella 146 di Giustiniano. Annali di Storia del Diritto* (Milan) 8 (1964).

CONSTANTELOS, D. J.: The Holy Scripture in Greek Orthodox worship. *Greek Orthodox Theological Review* (Brookline, Mass.) 12 (1966), 7-83.

40c DRESCHER, J.: A Coptic lectionary fragment. *ASAE* 51 (1951), 247-56.

GAMBER, K.: Fragmente eines griechischen Perikopenbuches des 5. Jh. aus Aegypten. *OC* 44 (1960), 75-87.

GERHARDSSON, B.: Ein griechischen Lektionar in Uppsala. *SvEx Årsb* 24 (1959), 72-88.

39a HEIMING, O.: Genesis und Proverbienlesung der koptischen Qua-
(ii),h dragesima und Karwoche. *JLW* 10 (1930), 174-80.
(i),
40c

HOEG, C., and ZUNTZ, G.: Remarks on the Prophetologion. In *Quantulacunque: Studies presented to Kirsopp Lake* (London, 1927), 189-226.

—— and ZUNTZ, G.: *Prophetologium:* (Copenhagen, 1939-).
    I, Lectiones nativitatis et epiphaniae (1939).
    II, Lectiones hebdomadarum I et II quadragesimae (1940).
    III, Lectiones hebdomadarum III et IV quadragesimae (1952).
    IV, Lectiones hebdomadae V quadragesimae et hebdomadae in Palmis et majoris (1960).
    V, Lectiones Sabbati Sancti (1962).
    (= *Monumenta musicae byzantinae:* Lectionaria, vol. I).

HOEG, C.: Sur le Prophétologium. *Studi bizantini e neoellenici* 6 (1940), 488-9.

JOUASSARD, G.: Aperçu sur l'importance de l'AT dans la vie litur-gique des premiers siècles chrétiens. *REByz* 16 (1958), 104-15.

——: L'AT dans la prière des premières communautés chrétiennes. In *Mémorial A. Gelin* (Le Puy, 1961), 355-62.

KUNZE, G.: *Die gottesdienstliche Schriftlesung.* I, *Stand und Aufgaben der Perikopenforschung* (Göttingen, 1947).

39g MILNE, H. J. M.: Early Psalms and lections for Lent. *JEA* 10 (1924), 278-82.

NEGOITSA, A.: L'AT dans le culte de l'Église Orthodoxe. *RHPR* 47 (1967), 347-54.

NESTLE, E.: Alttestamentliches aus den griechischen Synaxarien. *ZAW* 27 (1907), 49-56.

RAHLFS, A.: *Die alttestamentlichen Lektionen der griechischen Kirche.* *NGWGött* 1915, 28-136.

SCHERMANN, T.: Das Lektionarsystem der ägyptischen Kirche. *Der Katholik* 92 (1912), 248-52.

VELLAS, V.: Ἡ ἁγία γραφὴ ἐν τῇ ὀρθοδόξῳ ἐκκλησίᾳ (Athens, 1958).

VENETIANER, L.: Ursprung und Bedeutung der Propheten-Lektionen. *ZDMG* 73 (1919), 103-70 [Wild!].

ZUNTZ, G.: Das byzantinische LXX-Lektionar ('Prophetologion'). *Classica et Medievalia* 17 (1956), 183-98.

36. TEXTUAL STUDIES

(See also 7, 15a, 22-35; and for individual books, 39).

a. GENERAL

BERTRAM, G.: Zur LXX-Forschung. II, Das Textproblem der LXX. *TR* nF 5 (1933), 172-86.

BICKERMAN, E. J.: Some Notes on the Transmission of the LXX. In *A. Marx Jubilee Volume* (New York, 1950), 149-78.

BURKITT, F. C.: The recovery of the original Septuagint. *EB* 5021-2.

35b COLLOMP, P.: La critique textuelle et la papyrologie. *CdE* 7 (1932), 237-42.

DAHSE, J.: Textkritische Studien I.II. *ZAW* 28 (1908), 1-21, 161-73.

GOSHEN-GOTTSTEIN, M. H.: Theory and Practice of Textual Criticism: The Text-critical Use of the LXX. *Textus* 3 (1963), 130-158.

KENYON, F. G.: *The text of the Greek Bible* (London, 1937) (2nd ed. A. W. Adams; German translation, Göttingen, 1961).

——: *Recent developments in the textual criticism of the Greek Bible* (London, 1933).

24 KOENIG, J.: L'activité herméneutique des scribes dans la transmission du texte de l'AT. *RHR* 161 (1962), 141-74; 162 (1963), 1-43.

MARGOLIS, M. L.: ΧΩΡΙΣ. In *Oriental Studies ... Paul Haupt* (Baltimore, 1926), 84-92.

NESTLE, E.: Zur Rekonstruktion der LXX. *Philologus* 58 (1899), 121-31.

SACCHI, P.: Il testo dei Settanta nella problematica piu recente. *Atene e Roma* ns 9, 4 (1964), 145-58.

STEGMÜLLER, O.: Überlieferungsgeschichte der Bibel. In *Geschichte* der Textüberlieferung der antiken und mittelalt. Literatur (Zürich, 1961), I, 152-64.

THOMAS, D. W.: The Textual Criticism of the OT. *OTMS* (Oxford, 1951), 248-55.

WEVERS, J. W.: LXX Forschungen seit 1954. III: Spezielle Text-studien. *TR* nF 33 (1968), 62-76.

b. CORRUPTIONS

35b COLWELL, E. C.: Scribal habits in early papyri. A study in the cor-ruption of text. In *The Bible in Modern Scholarship* ed. J. P. Hyatt (New York, 1965), 370-89.

39a FÜRST, J.: Über eine korrumpierte Stelle in der Übersetzung der
(ii)   LXX. *MGWJ* 5 (1856), 282-4 [Gen. xviii: 12].

GEHMAN, H. S.: Some types of errors of transmission in the LXX. *VT* 3 (1953), 397-400.

GRÄTZ, H.: Fälschungen in dem Texte der LXX von christlicher Hand zu dogmatischen Zwecken. *MGWJ* 2 (1853), 432-6; 3 (1854) 121-3.

HOLZMANN, M.: Auf die LXX zurückgehende Übersetzungsfehler. *MGWJ* 72 (1928), 519-39.

——: Ein auf die LXX zurückgehender Übersetzungsfehler. In *Festgabe C. G. Montefiore* (Berlin, 1928), 73-7.

JUNG, L.: Mistranslation as a source in Jewish and Christian Lore. *PAAJR* 5 (1933/4), 55-67.

KATZ, P.: ΚΑΤΑΠΑΥΣΑΙ as a corruption of ΚΑΤΑΛΥΣΑΙ. *JBL* 65 (1946), 319-24.

——: Two kindred corruptions in the LXX. *VT* 1 (1951), 261-6.

41 KAUFMANN, D.: Errors in the LXX and the Vulgate from which illustrations and sculptures derive their origin. *JQR* 11 (1898/9), 163-6.

MARGOLIS, M. L.: Studien im griechischen AT. *ZAW* 27 (1907), 212-70.

——: (Scribal errors in the LXX) [In Hebrew]. In *Fs. zu Ehren des Dr. A. Harkavy* (St. Petersburg, 1908), 112-6.

——: The textual criticism of the Greek OT. *Transactions of the American Philosophical Society* 67 (1928), 187-97.

24 SEELIGMANN, I. L.: Indications of editorial alteration and adapta-tion in the MT and the Septuagint. *VT* 11 (1961), 201-21.

c. Recensions (General)

Bickerman, E. J.: Some Notes on the Transmission of the LXX. *Alexander Marx Jubilee Vol.*, ed. S. Lieberman (New York, 1950), 149-78.

Debrunner, A.: Zu den LXX-Rezensionen. *Museum Helveticum* 14 (1957), 255.

36e- Dörrie, H.: Zur Geschichte der LXX im Jahrhundert Konstantins.
g   *ZNW* 39 (1940), 57-110.

39a Gooding, D. W.: *Recensions of the Septuagint Pentateuch* (London, 1955).

36e- Méchineau, L.: La critique biblique au IIIe siècle: II, Les recen-
g   sions d'Origène, de St. Lucien, d'Hesychius, et nos textes grecs actuels. *Études* (Paris) 55 (1892), 424-53.

Sperber, A.: Hebrew based upon Biblical Passages in Parallel Transmission. *HUCA* 14 (1939), 153-249.

——: The problem of the LXX recensions. *JBL* 54 (1935), 73-92.

d. Hebraising Recensions (other than Hexaplaric)

35c, Barthélemy, D.: Redécouverte d'un chaînon manquant de l'his-
39k   toire de la LXX. *RB* 60 (1953), 18-29.

35c, ——: *Les Devanciers d'Aquila. VTS* 10 (1963).
39k   Rev. Jellicoe in *JAOS* 84 (1965), 178-82.
      Kraft in *Gnomon* 37 (1965), 474-83.
      Vermès in *JSS* 11 (1966), 261-4.

Grindel, J. M.: Another characteristic of the καίγε recension. *CBQ* 31 (1969), 499-513.

Katz, P.: Frühe hebraisierende Rezensionen der LXX. *ZAW* 69 (1957), 77-84.

22 Skehan, P. W.: The earliest LXX and subsequent revisions. *Jerome Biblical Commentary* (Englewood Cliffs, N.J., 1968), II, 570-2.

Smith, M.: Another Criterion for the καίγε Recension. *Biblica* 48 (1967), 443-5.

e. Hexaplaric Recension
(See also 37)

Soisalon-Soininen, I.: *Der Charakter der asterisierten Zusätze in der LXX. AASF* B 114 (Helsinki, 1959).
    Rev. Gooding in *Gnomon* 33 (1961), 143-8.
        Hanhart in *Helikon* 4 (1964), 669-71.
        Kahle in *TLZ* 1959, 743-5.
        Schreiner in *Erasmus* 15 (1963), 201-4.
        Ziegler in *ThRev* 56 (1960), 9-12.

f. Lucianic Recension

Alès, A. d': Autour de Lucien d'Antioche. *MUSJ* 21 (1937/8), 183-99.

Anon: Lucian's recension of the LXX. *ChQR* 51 (1900/1), 379-98.

Bardy, G.: St. Lucien d'Antioche et son école: les collucianistes. *RechSR* 22 (1932), 437-62.

——: *Recherches sur St. Lucien d'Antioche et son école* (Paris, 1936).

39c (i)   Brock, S. P.: Lucian *redivivus*: Some reflections on Barthélemy's *Les Devanciers d'Aquila. Studia Evangelica* 5 (1968) = *TU* 103, 176-81.

40g   Cantera, J.: Puntos de contacto de la 'Vetus Latina' con la recensión de Luciano y con otras recensiones griegas. *Sefarad* 25 (1965), 69-72.

Christou, P. K.: Λυχιανός. *ThreskEthEnk* 8 (1966), 396-8.

39a (ii)   Dahse, J.: Zum Luciantext der Genesis. *ZAW* 30 (1910), 281-7.

Förster, J.: Gerechtigkeit für Lucian und den antiochenischen Text. *Monats. f. Pastoraltheologie* 45 (1956), 267-72.

Kraft, H.: art. 'Lucian' in *RGG*³ 4, 463f.

Mercati, G.: Di alcune testimonianze antiche sulle cure bibliche di San Luciano. *Biblica* 24 (1943), 1-17.

Metzger, B. M.: Lucian and the Lucianic Recension of the Greek Bible. *NTS* 8 (1962), 189-203.

——: The Lucianic recension of the Greek Bible. In *Chapters in the History of NT textual criticism* (Leiden, 1963), 1-41 [Revised version of preceding].

MOORE, G. F.: The Antiochian recension of the LXX. *AJSL* 29
(1912/13), 37-62.

ROUTH, M. J.: *Reliquiae Sacrae.* (Oxford,[2] 1846), IV, 3-17 [Testi-
monia to Lucian].

31   SPANNEUT, M.: La Bible d'Eustathe d'Antioche — contribution à
l'histoire de la 'version lucianique'. *Studia Patristica* 4 (1961) =
TU 79, 171-90.

26a   STOCKMAYER, T.: Hat Lukian zu seiner Septuagintarevision die
Peschito benützt? *ZAW* 12 (1892), 218-23.

STOKES, G. T.: art. Lucianus in *DCB* 3, 748f.

39n   TISSERANT, E.: Notes sur la recension lucianique d'Ézéchiel.
RB 8 (1911), 384-390.

g. HESYCHIAN RECENSION

BAUER, W.: Hesychius. *RGG*[3] 3, 299.

BOUSSET, W.: Die Rezension des Hesychius. In *Textkritische Studien
zum NT. TU* 11, 4 (1894), 74-110.

GEHMAN, H. S.: The Hesychian Influence in the Versions of Daniel.
JBL 48 (1929), 321-32.

JELLICOE, S.: The Hesychian recension reconsidered. *JBL* 82 (1963),
409-18.

27   KENYON, F. G.: Hesychius and the text of the NT. In *Mémorial
Lagrange* (Paris, 1940), 245-50.

VACCARI, A.: The Hesychian recension of the LXX. *Biblica* 46
46 (1965), 60-66.

37. HEXAPLA

(See also 1, 5, 32, 33, 35a, 36e, 38, 39, 40g, j)

a. GENERAL

33   ALLGEIER, A.: Schlussbemerkungen zum Gebrauch der Hexapla bei
Hieronymus. *Biblica* 8 (1927), 468-9.

33,   ——: Die Hexapla in den Psalmen-Übersetzungen des heiligen
39g   Hieronymus. *Biblica* 8 (1927), 450-63.

BAHRDT, C. G.: *Origenis Hexaplorum quae supersunt* (Leipzig/
Lübeck, 1769-70; 2 vols).

BELLET, P.: art. 'Hexaplas' in *EncBibl* 3 (1964), 1218-20.

39b BILLEN, A. V.: The Hexaplaric Element in the LXX Version of
(ii)   Judges. *JTS* 43 (1942), 12-19.

40g BRUYNE, D. DE: Les Hexaples et l'ancienne version latine. *RB* 30
     (1921), 572-4.

39g CERIANI, A. M.: Frammenti esaplari palinsesti dei Salmi nel testo
     originale scoperti dal dott.ab. G. Mercati. *RRIL* II, 29 (1896),
     406-8.

DATHE, J. A.: *Opuscula* (ed. E. F. C. Rosenmüller) (Leipzig, 1796).

32 DÖDERLEIN, J. C.: Zu den Hexaplen des Origenes. *RBML* 6 (1780),
     195-207.

DRUSIUS, J.: *Veterum interpretum graecorum in totum vetus testa-
     mentum fragmenta collecta versa et notis illustrata* (Arnhem,
     1622).

24, EISSFELDT, O.: Zur textkritischen Auswertung der Mercatischen
37c, Hexapla-Fragmente. *WdO* 1 (1947), 93-7, = *Kleine Schriften* 3
39g (1966), 9-13.

FIELD, F.: *Origenis Hexaplorum quae supersunt; sive veterum inter-
     pretum graecorum in totum vetus testamentum fragmenta*
     (Oxford, 1867, 1874; 2 vols; rp Hildesheim, 1964).

31 HEMMERDINGER, B.: Les hexaples et Saint Irenée. *VC* 16 (1962),
     19-20.

KLIJN, A. F. J.: De reactie van de kerk op Origenes' Hexapla. *NTT*
     7 (1952), 296-302.

31, KLOSTERMANN, E.: *Analecta zur Septuaginta, Hexapla und Patristik*
35c (Leipzig), 1895).

39g ——: Die Mailänder Fragmente der Hexapla. *ZAW* 16 (1896),
     334-7.

39l LÜTKEMANN, L. and RAHLFS, A.: *Hexaplarische Randnoten zu
     Isaias i-xvi. MSU* 6 = *NGWGött* 1915 Beiheft.

40g MARGOLIS, M. L.: Additions to Field from the Lyons Codex of the
     Old Latin. *JAOS* 33 (1913), 254-8.

36e ——: Hexapla and Hexaplaric. *AJSL* 32 (1915), 126-40.

MÉCHINEAU, L.: La critique biblique au IIIe siècle: I, Les Hexaples
     d'Origène. *Études* (Paris), 54 (1891), 202-28.

39g MERCATI, G.: D'un palimpsesto ambrosiano dei Salmi esaplari.
     Atti RAcadSc di Torino 31 (1895/6), 655-76, = *SeT* 76 (1937),
     318-38.

——: Un congettura sopra il libro del Giusto. *SeT* 5 (1901), 1-7.

31 ——: Sul testo e sul senso di Eusebio H.E. VI. 16. *SeT* 5 (1901), 47-60.

40k ——: Di varie antichissime sottoscrizioni a codici esaplari. *SeT* 95 (1941), 1-48.

——: Appunti esaplari. *Biblica* 25 (1944), 1-8.

35e, ——: *Psalterii Hexapli Reliquiae.* I. *Codex rescriptus Bybliothecae*
39g *Ambrosianae 0.39 Supp. phototypice expressus et transcriptus* (Rome, 1958).

Rev. Meyer in *DLZ* 82 (1961), 505-9.

35e ——: *Psalterii Hexapli Reliquiae. Pars prima: Osservazioni; com-*
39g *mento critico al testo dei frammenti esaplari* (Rome, 1965).

19, MEYER, R.: Bemerkungen zu den Mailänder Hexaplafragmenten. In
37c, *Festgabe H. Jursch.* (Berlin, 1962), 122-32.
39g

MORIN, G.: Index lectionum quae ex hexaplis ab Hieronymo pro-
feruntur. *Anecdota Maredsolana* III, 1 (1895), 105-8.

NESTLE, E.: Zur Hexapla des Origenes. *ZWT* 38 (1895), 231-8.

ORLINSKY, H. M.: The columnar order of the Hexapla. *JQR* ns 27 (1936/7), 137-49.

PITRA, J. B.: (Hexapla fragments:) *Analecta sacra* (Venice, 1883) III, 555-78.

31 SCHWARTZ, E.: Zur Geschichte der Hexapla. *NWGGött* 1903, 6, 693-700; = *Gesammelte Schriften* Bd. 5 (Berlin, 1963), chap. VI.

TAYLOR, C.: art. 'Hexapla' in *DCB* 3, 14-23.

39g ——: *Hebrew-Greek Cairo Genizah Palimpsests.* (Cambridge, 1900).
39d THOMSEN, P.: Ein Fragment einer Minuskelhandschrift mit hexa-
(i) plarischen Notizen. *ZAW* 31 (1911), 308-9. [2 Chr.].

VACCARI, A.: Esaple e esaplare in S Girolamo. *Biblica* 8 (1927), 463-8.

b. HEXAPLA and TETRAPLA

39d HOWORTH, H. H.: The Hexapla and Tetrapla of Origen and the light
(ii) they throw on the books of Esdras A and B. *PSBA* 24 (1902), 147-72.

ORLINSKY, H. M.: Origen's Tetrapla — a scholarly fiction? *Proc. 1st World Congress of Jewish Studies* 1947 (Jerusalem, 1952), I, 173-82.

39b PRETZL, O.: Der hexaplarische und tetraplarische Septuagintatext
des Origenes in den Büchern Josua und Richter. *ByzZ* 30 (1929/30), 262-8.

39b,   Procksch, O.: *Tetraplarische Studien*, I [Dan., Pss]-II [Joshua,
g,o   Judges, Ruth]. *ZAW* nF 12 (1935), 240-69; 13 (1936), 61-
         90.

c. Second Column
(See also 19)

Altheim, F.: Porphyrios und Origenes' Hexapla. In *Geschichte der Hunnen* 5 (1962), 100-9.

Blau, L.: La transcription de l'AT en caractères grecs. *REJ* 88 (1929), 18-22.

Brønno, E.: *Studien über hebräische Morphologie und Vokalismus auf Grund der Mercatischen Fragmente der zweiten Kolumne der Hexapla des Origenes. AbhKM* 28 (1943).
   Rev. Eissfeldt in *ZDMG* 100 (1951), 401-2.

——: Zu den Theorien P. Kahles von der Entstehung der tiberischen Grammatik. *ZDMG* 100 (1951), 521-65 [On Cairo Geniza].

19,   ——: The Isaiah Scroll DSIa and the Greek transliterations of
39l   Hebrew. *ZDMG* nF 31 (1956), 252-8.

——: Samaritan Hebrew and Origen's Secunda. *JSS* 13 (1968), 193-201.

Emerton, J. A.: The purpose of the second column of the Hexapla. *JTS* ns 7 (1956), 79-87.

Ginsburger, M.: La transcription de l'AT en caractères grecs. *REJ* 87 (1929), 40-2; 88 (1929), 184-6.

Halévy, J.: L'origine de la transcription du texte hébreu en caractères grecs dans l'Hexaple d'Origène. *JAs* IX, 17 (1901), 335-41 (cp [Chabot] 349-50); 18 (1902), 399-400.

Janssens, G.: Het Hebreeuws van de tweede kolom van Origenes' Hexapla. *JEOL* 15 (1957/8), 103-11.

Margolis, M. L.: The pronunciation of the shewa according to the new hexaplaric material. *AJSL* 26 (1909), 62-72.

Mercati, G.: Il problema della colonna II dell'Esaplo. *Biblica* 28 (1947), 1-30, 173-215.

Pretzl, O.: Die Aussprache des Hebräischen nach der zweiten Kolumne der Hexapla des Origenes. *BZ* 20 (1932), 4-22.

Speiser, E. A.: The pronunciation of Hebrew according to (later: based chiefly on) the transliterations in the Hexapla. *JQR* ns 16 (1925/6), 343-82; 23 (1933), 233-65; 24 (1934), 9-46.

SPERBER, A.: Hebrew Based upon Greek and Latin Transliterations. *HUCA* 12/3 (1937/8), 103-274.

———: *A Historical Grammar of Biblical Hebrew* (Leiden, 1966) [Includes revision of preceding item].

39a   ZUNTZ, G.: On the opening sentence of Melito's Paschal Homily.
(iii)   *HTR* 36 (1943), 299-315.

38. OTHER GREEK TRANSLATIONS

(See also 1, 17, 32, 33, 35, 37, 39)

a. GENERAL

38c,   ALTHEIM, F. and STIEHL, R.: Quinta oder Theodotion? Bemer-
e   kungen zu G. Mercati's Ausgabe der ambrosianischen Psalter-
       fragmente. *OC* 48 (1964), 18-22, and in *Die Araber in der alten
       Welt* (Berlin, 1965) II, 33-8.

40g   BLONDHEIM, D. S.: *Les parlers judéo-romans et la Vetus Latina.
      Étude sur les rapports entre les traductions bibliques en langue
      romane des Juifs au moyen âge et les anciennes versions* (Paris,
      1925).
      Rev. Blau in *JQR* ns 19 (1928/9), 157-82.

40i   BRUNS, P. J.: Syrische Nachrichten von den griechischen Über-
      setzeren aus Manuscripten gesammelt. *RBML* 14 (1784), 39-59.
      FIELD, F.: *Otium Norvicense; sive tentamen de reliquiis Aquilae
      Symmachi Theodotionis e lingua Syriaca in Graecam convertendo*
      (Oxford, 1864).
      JOHANNESSOHN, M.: Zur Entstehung der Ausdrucksweise der latei-
      nischen Vulgata aus den jüngeren griechischen alttestament-
      lichen Übersetzungen. *ZNW* 44 (1952/3), 90-102.
      ———: Hieronymus und die jüngeren griechischen Übersetzungen des
      ATs. *TLZ* 73 (1948), 145-52.

31,   MERCATI, G.: *Alla ricerca dei nomi degli 'altri' traduttori nelle Omilie
35e,   sui Salmi di San Giovanni Crisostomo e variazioni su alcune catene
39g   del Salterio. SeT* 158 (1952).

39l   MÖHLE, A.: Ein neuer Fund zahlreicher Stücke aus den Jesaja-
      übersetzungen des Akylas, Symmachos und Theodotion. *ZAW*
      nF 11 (1934), 176-83.
      REDPATH, H. A.: Versions, Greek (other than LXX). *HDB* 4,
      864-6.

33   WALDIS, J. K.: *Hieronymi Graeca in Psalmos fragmenta untersucht*
39g   *und auf ihre Herkunft geprüft* (Münster, 1908).

39k- ZIEGLER, J.: *Die jüngeren griechischen Übersetzungen als Vorlage der*
o   *Vulgata in den prophetischen Schriften* (Braunsberg, 1943).

39l   ——: Textkritische Notizen zu den jüngeren griechischen Über-
        setzungen des Buches Isaias. *NAWGött* 1939, 75-102.

b. AQUILA

      ABRAHAMS, M.: *Aquila's Greek version of the Hebrew Bible* (London,
        1919).

26b ANGER, R.: *De Onkelo Chaldaico quem ferunt Pentateuchi paraphraste*
        et quid ei rationis intercedat cum Akila graeco Veteris Testamenti
        interprete. I, *De Akila* (Leipzig, 1845).

38j, BLONDHEIM, D. S.: Échos de judéo-hellénisme. Influence de la LXX
39i   et d'Aquila sur les versions néo-grecques des Juives. *REJ* 78
(ii)   (1924), 1-14.

      BURKITT, F. C.: Aquila. *JE* 2, 34-6.

      ——: Aquila. *JQR* 10 (1898), 207-16.

39c ——: *Fragments of the Books of Kings according to the translation of*
(ii)   *Aquila* (Cambridge, 1897).

      Rev. Mercati in *SeT* 77 (1937), 124-9.

      CASSUTO, U.: Aquila. *EJ* 3, 27-35.

39k DATHE, J. A. and MORUS, S. F. N.: *Disputatio ... in Aquila reliquias*
        interpretationis Hoseae (Leipzig, n.d.).

      DICKSON, W. P.: Aquila. *DCB* 1, 150f.

      FRIEDMANN, M.: *Onkelos und Akylas* (Vienna, 1896).

      GINZBERG, L.: Aquila in Rabbinic literature. *JE* 2, 36-8.

      JELLICOE, S.: Aquila and his Version. *JQR* 59 (1968/9), 326-32.

28   KATZ, P.: Notes on the LXX. II. A fresh Aquila fragment recovered
        from Philo. *JTS* 47 (1946), 31-3.

      —— and ZIEGLER, J.: Ein Aquila-Index in Vorbereitung. *VT* 8
        (1958), 264-85.

      KRAUSS, S.: Akylas der Proselyt. In *Fs. M. Steinschneider* (Leipzig,
        1896), 148-63.

      LIEBREICH, L. J.: Silverstone's Aquila and Onkelos. *JQR* ns 27
        (1936/7), 287-91.

27, RAHLFS, A.: Über Theodotion-Lesarten im Neuen Testament und
30   Aquila-Lesarten bei Justin. *ZNW* 20 (1921), 182-99.

REIDER, J.: *Prolegomena to a Greek-Hebrew and Hebrew-Greek Index to Aquila.* (Philadelphia, 1916) = *JQR* ns 4 (1913), 321-56, 577-620; 7 (1916), 287-366.

39h RÜGER, H. P.: Vier Aquila-Glossen in einem hebräischen Prover-
(i) bien-Fragment aus der Kairo-Geniza. *ZNW* 50 (1959), 275-7.

26b SILVERSTONE, A. E.: *Aquila and Onkelos* (Manchester, 1931).

TURNER, N.: *An Index to Aquila.* VTS 12 (Leiden, 1966).

Rev. Barr in *JSS* 12 (1967), 286-304.

Hanhart in *ThRev* 64 (1968), 391-4.

31 VACCARI, A.: S. Augustin, S. Ambrosius et Aquila. In *Augustinus Magister* (Paris, 1955), 473-82.

c. THEODOTION

39b COOPER, C. M.: Theodotion's influence on the Alexandrian text of
(ii) Judges. *JBL* 67 (1948), 63-8.

GIL, L.: Theodotion. *EncBibl* 6 (1965), 934-5.

GWYNN, J.: Theodotion. *DCB* 4, 970-9.

HIRSCH, E. G.: Theodotion. *JE* 12, 127f.

38d, MERCATI, G.: Una lezione dubbia di Σ'Θ' in Isaia lviii: 3. *SeT* 95
39l (1941), 93-4 = *Vivre et Penser* 1 (1941), 13-15.

38d NESTLE, E.: Adam bei Σ' und Θ'. *ZAW* 30 (1910), 153.

39a O'CONNELL, K. G.: *The Theodotionic revision of the Book of Exodus*
(iii) (Diss. Harvard, 1967).

RAHLFS, A.: — see 38b.

SALMON, G.: *A historical introduction to the study of the Books of the NT* (London, ⁸1897), 538-51 [On Θ'].

39o SCHMITT, A.: *Stammt der sogenannte 'Θ'-Text bei Daniel wirklich von Theodotion?* MSU 9 (Göttingen, 1966).

d. SYMMACHUS

33, CANNON, W. W.: Jerome and Symmachus. Some points in the
39h Vulgate translation of Koheleth. *ZAW* nF 4 (1927), 191-9.
(ii)

39g CAPELLE, P.: Fragments du Psautier d'Aquila? *RBén* 28 (1911), 64-8 [Σ'].

GEIGER, A.: Symmachus, der Übersetzer der Bibel. *Jüdische Zeitschrift für Wissenschaft und Leben* (Breslau) 1 (1862), 39-64.

GIL, L.: Simmaco. *EncBibl* 6 (1965), 701-2.

GWYNN, J.: Symmachus. *DCB* 4, 748f.

HEIDENHEIM, M.: Wer war Symmachus? *Deutsche Vierteljahrsschrift für evangelisch-theologische Forschung und Kritik* 3, 463f.

LIEBREICH, L. J.: Notes on the Greek version of Symmachus. *JBL* 63 (1944), 397-403.

31   MERCATI, G.: *L'età di Simmaco l'interprete e S. Epifanio ossio se Simmaco tradusse in greco la Bibbia sotto M. Aurelio il filosofo* (Modena, 1892) = *SeT* 76 (1937), 20-92.

39g   ——: Frammenti di Aquila o di Simmaco? *RB* 8 (1911), 266-72 = *SeT* 78 (1937), 297-303.

      ——: see 38c.

39a   NESTLE, E.: Luther über Symmachus zu Gen. iv: 4. *ZAW* 26 (1906),
(ii)   162-3.

39g   ——: Symmachus not Aquila. *ET* 22 (1910), 377.

      ——: see 38c.

PERLES, F.: Symmachus. *JE* 11, 619.

SCHOEPS, H. J.: Ebionitisches bei Symmachus. *Coniectanea Neotestamentica* 6 (Uppsala, 1942) [= Symmachusstudien I].

——: Mythologisches bei Symmachus. *Biblica* 26 (1945), 100-11. [= Symmachus-Studien II].

——: Symmachus Studien III: Symmachus und der Midrasch. *Biblica* 29 (1947), 31-51 = *Aus frühchristlicher Zeit* (Tübingen, 1950), 82-119.

39l   ——: Ein neuer Engelname in der Bibel? (Zur Übersetzung des Symmachus von Jes. xxxiii 3). *ZfReligions- und Geistesgeschichte* I (1948), 86-7.

——: *Theologie und Geschichte des Judenchristentums* (Tübingen, 1949), 33-7, 350-80.

39g   WESSELY, C.: Un nouveau fragment de la version grecque du Vieux Testament par Aquila [in fact Σ']. In *Mélanges offerts à M. É. Châtelain* (Paris, 1910), 224-9.

ZAHN, G.: Herkunft und Lehrrichtung des Bibelübersetzers Symmachus. *NKZ* 34 (1923), 197-209.

e. QUINTA

BARTHÉLEMY, D.: Quinta ou version selon les Hébreux? *TZ* 16 (1960), 342-53.

39c   BURKITT, F. C.: The so-called Quinta of 4 Kingdoms. *PSBA* 24
(ii)   (1902), 216-9.
37a   MERCATI, G.: D'alcuni frammenti esaplari sulla Va e VIa edizione
         greca della Bibbia. *SeT* 5 (1901), 28-46.
32   NESTLE, E.: Zu dem Bericht des Origenes über seine 5. u. 6. Bibel-
         übersetzung. *ZAW* 26 (1906), 168.

f. SAMARITIKON

39a   GLAUE, P. and RAHLFS, A.: Fragmente einer griechischen Über-
         setzung des samaritanischen Pentateuchs. *MSU* I, 2 =
         NGWGött 1911, 2, 167-200.
       KOHN, S.: Samareitikon und LXX. *MGWJ* 38 (1894), 1-7, 49-67.
39a   LIFSHITZ, B. and SCHIBY, J.: Une synagogue samaritaine à Thessa-
(v)   lonique. *RB* 75 (1968), 368-78. [Num. vi: 22-7].
39a   RAHLFS, A.: Nachtrag: Ein weiteres Fragment der griechischen
         Übersetzung des samaritanischen Pentateuchs. *MSU* I, 2 =
         NGWGött 1911, 263-6.

g. SYROS

26a   BLOCH, J.: ῾Ο Σύρος and the Peshitta. In *Jewish Studies in Memory
         of I. Abrahams* (New York, 1927), 66-73.
       MERCATI, G.: A quale tempo risale il 'Siro'? Nota. *Biblica* 26 (1945),
         1-11.
37a   PERLES, J.: De Syro in Hexaplis commemoratione. In *Meletemata
         Peschitthoniana* (Vratislav, 1859), 49-51.
       RAHLFS, A.: Quis sit ὁ Σύρος? *MSU* I, 404-12 = *NGWGött* 1915,
         420-8.
       VÖÖBUS, A.: Neues Licht auf das Problem des ὁ Σύρος. In *Peschitta
         und Targumim des Pentateuchs* (Stockholm, 1958), 110-11.

h. OTHER TRANSLATIONS

39g   DRÄSEKE, J.: Die Abfassungszeit der Psalmen-Metaphrase des
         Apollinarios von Laodicea. *ZWT* 32 (1889), 108-20.

39g GITSCHEL, J.: War der Verfasser der dem Apollinarius zugeschrie-
benen Psalmenmetaphrase wirklich körperlich blind? In
Munera philologica L. Ćwiklinski (Posnaniae, 1936), 104-10.

39g GOLEGA, J.: Verfasser und Zeit der Psalterparaphrase des Apollina-
rios. *ByzZ* 39 (1939), 1-22.

39g ——: *Der Homerische Psalter.* = Studia patristica et byzantina 6
(Ettal, 1960).

KIPPER, B.: Josipo tradutor grego quase desconhecido. *Revista di
Cultura Biblica* 5 (1961), 298-307, 387-95, 446-56.

KRAUSS, S.: Two hitherto unknown Bible Versions in Greek. *BJRL*
27 (1943), 97-105.

39g LUDWICH, A.: *Apollinari metaphrasis Psalmorum* (Leipzig, 1912).

39g MILLER, P. S.: The Greek Psalter of Apollinarius. *Proceedings of
the American Philological Society* 65 (1934), xli.

39g SLATER, T.: *A metaphrasis: a metrical version of the Psalms* (London,
1870) [ET of Apollinarius].

i. MEDIEVAL GREEK

39a BELLÉLI, L.: Une version grecque du Pentateuque du seizième
siècle. *REG* 3 (1890), 288-308.

——: Deux versions peu connues du Pentateuque. *REJ* 22 (1891),
250-63.

39d, DANON, M.: Meirath 'enaim. Version en néogrec et en caractères
m,o hébraïques de Jérémie x: 11; de Daniel, ii: 5 — vii: 28; et
d'Esdras iv: 7 — vi: 26 du Caraite Élie Aféda Béghi (1627).
JAs XI, 4 (1914), 5-65.

39a HESSELING, D. C.: *Les cinq livres de la Loi (Le Pentateuque)*
(Leiden/Leipzig, 1897) [Neo-Greek in Hebrew characters,
published Constantinople 1547].

Rev. Belléli in *REJ* 35 (1897), 132-55; cp Hesseling *ibid.* 314-8.

39k ——: Le Livre de Jonas. *ByzZ* 10 (1901), 208-17.

39a MARSHALL, F. H.: *Old Testament Legends* (Cambridge, 1925)
[G. Chumnos' poem on Gen. and Exod.].

j. GRAECUS VENETUS

FEDALTO, G.: Per una biografia di Simone Atumano. *Aevum* 40
(1966), 445-67.

39a,   GEBHARDT, O. VON: *Graecus Venetus*. Pentateuchi Proverbiorum
b,h,   Ruth Cantici Ecclesiasticae Threnorum Danielis versio graeca
m   ex unico bibliothecae S. Marci Venetae codice (Leipzig, 1875).
            Rev. P. F. Frankl, *MGWJ* 24 (1875), 513-9.

MERCATI, G.: Se la versione dall' ebraico del codice Veneto greco
      VII sia di Simone Atumano arcivescovo di Tebi. *SeT* 30
      (1916).

——: Chi sia l'autore della nuova versione dall' ebraico del codice
      veneto greco VII. *RB* ns 13 (1916), 510-26.

39. INDIVIDUAL BOOKS
(See also 3, 4, 9-12, 15-18, 20, 24-31, 33-38, 40)

a. (i) *Pentateuch (General)*

ALBRIGHT, W. F.: Historical and Mythical Elements in the Story of
      Joseph. *JBL* 37 (1918), 111-113.

35b,   ALLGEIER, A.: *Die Chester Beatty Papyri zum Pentateuch. Unter-*
36a   *suchungen zur älteren Überlieferungsgeschichte der LXX*
            (Paderborn, 1938).

AMERSFOORDT, J.: *Dissertatio de variis lectionibus Holmesianis
      locorum quorundam Pentateuchi Mosaici* (Leiden, 1815).

BAUMGÄRTEL, F.: Zur Entstehung der Pentateuchseptuaginta.
      BWAT nF 5 (1923), 53-80.

31   BAUMSTARK, A.: Griech. und hebräische Bibelzitate in der Penta-
            teucherklärung Isho'dads von Merv. *OC* II, 1 (1911), 1-19.

——: Das Problem des christlich-palästinensischen Pentateuch-
      textes. *OC III*, 10 (1935), 201-24.

BENDER, A.: Das Lied Exodus 15. *ZAW* 23 (1903), 1-48.

BICKERMANN, E. J.: Two legal interpretations of the LXX. *Revue
      internationale des droits de l'antiquité*. III, 3 (1956), 81-104.

36a   BILLEN, A. V.: The classification of the Greek manuscripts of the
            Hexateuch. *JTS* 26 (1925), 262-77.

35b   CASPARI, W.: Papyrusstreifen des vorchristlichen Pentateuch.
            TSK 107 (1936), 347-53.

——: Die verdrängte und die offizielle griechische Übersetzung des
      Pentateuch. *ZDMG* 90 (1936), 10.

EGLI, C.: Zur Kritik der LXX. *ZWT* 1862, 76-96, 287-321 [Trans-
      lators of Pent. and Joshua LXX].

24 FISCHER, J.: *Das Alphabet der LXX-Vorlage im Pentateuch. ATA* X, 2 (1924).

24 ——: *Zur LXX-Vorlage im Pentateuch. BZAW* 42 (1926).

FRITSCH, C. T.: *The Anti-anthropomorphisms of the Greek Pentateuch* (Philadelphia, 1943).

36c GOODING, D. W.: *The recensions of the LXX Pentateuch* (London, 1955).

GRAETZ, H.: Eine eigenthümliche alte griechische Pentateuch-Übersetzung mit längeren Zusätzen. *MGWJ* 35 (1886), 60-73.

36f HAUTSCH, E.: *Der Lukiantext des Octateuch. MSU* 1 = *NGWGött* (1909), 518-43.

KAHLE, P.: Die LXX zum Pentateuch. *TSK* 88 (1915), 410-26.

MEEK, T. J.: The translation of *Gêr* in the Hexateuch. *JBL* 49 (1930), 172-80.

NESTLE, E.: The Division of the 10 Commandments in the Greek and Hebrew Bibles. *ET* 8 (1896), 426-7.

15c PELLETIER, A.: Le vocabulaire de commandement dans le Penta-
(ii) teuch des LXX et dans le NT. *RechSR* 41 (1953), 519-24.

——: L'attentat au droit du pauvre dans le Pentateuch des LXX. *RechSR* 42 (1954), 523-7.

SOFFER, A.: "The House of God/Lord" in the LXX of the Pentateuch. *JBL* 75 (1956), 144-5.

THIERSCH, H. G. S.: *Libri tres de Pentateuchi versione Alexandrina* (Erlangen, 1841).

36f, THORNHILL, R.: Six or seven nations: a pointer to the Lucianic
40g text in the Heptateuch, with special reference to the Old Latin version. *JTS* ns 10 (1959), 233-46.

(ii) Genesis

BAAB, O. J.: A theory of two translators for the Greek Genesis. *JBL* 52 (1933), 239-43.

BERGMEIER, R.: Zur LXX-Übersetzung von Gen. iii: 16. *ZAW* 79 (1967), 77-9.

36a DAHSE, J.: Textkritische Studien I-II. *ZAW* 28 (1908), 1-21, 161-73.

——: Zu Gen. vii: 11. *ZAW* 30 (1910), 68.

36f ——: Zum Lukiantext der Genesis. *ZAW* 30 (1910), 281-7.

FÜRST, J.: Spuren der palästinisch-jüdischen Schriftdeutung und Sagen in der Übersetzung der LXX [Gen.]. In *Semitic Studies...* *A. Kohut* (Berlin, 1897), 152-66.

16   GEHMAN, H. S.: Hebraisms of the old Greek Version of Genesis. *VT* 3 (1953), 141-8.

GLENN, M. G.: The word לו in Gen. xxviii: 19 in the LXX and in Midrash. *JQR* 59 (1968), 73-5.

GORDON, C. H.: Abraham the βασιλεύς [Gen. xxiii: 6]. *JbKlF* 2, 1 (1965), 227-30.

26b KATZ, P.: Coincidences between LXX and Targum in Gen. xv:4. *JTS* 47 (1946), 166-9.

KÖHLER, L.: Kleine Beiträge zur Septuagintaforschung. *STZ* 1908, 182-5 [On Gen. xxv: 27 and Isa. xxiii].

KRAFT, R. A.: A note on the oracle of Rebecca (Gen. xxv: 23). *JTS* ns 13 (1962), 318-20.

KRAUSS, S.: 'Euilat' in the LXX. *JQR* 11 (1898/9), 675-9.

MARGOLIS, M. L.: Short notes on the Greek OT. *AJSL* 25 (1908/9), 174. [Gen. iii: 16; xlix: 21].

MARTIN, R. A.: The earliest Messianic interpretation of Gen. iii: 15. *JBL* 84 (1965), 425-7.

MUTSCHMANN, H.: Das Genesiscitat in der Schrift *Peri Hypsous*. *Hermes* 52 (1917), 161-200.

NESTLE, E.: The LXX rendering of Gen. iv: 1. *AJT* 9 (1905), 519.

——: Gen. xiv: 11. *ZAW* 27 (1907), 113-4.

——: Gen. xxv: 22. *ET* 22 (1910), 230.

NORDEN, E.: *Das Genesiszitat in der Schrift vom Erhabenen. AbhAk WissBerlin*, 1954, 1 = *Kleine Schriften* (Berlin, 1966), 286-313.

OLMSTEAD, A. T.: The Greek Genesis. *AJSL* 34 (1917/8), 145-69.

ORLINSKY, H. M.: Critical notes on Gen. xxxix: 14, 17, Jud. xi: 37.
24   *JBL* 61 (1942), 87-97.

WIENER, H. M.: The Greek Genesis, the Graf-Wellhausen theory and
24   the conservative position. *BS* 75 (1918), 41-60.

ZIEGLER, K.: Das Genesiszitat in der Schrift *Peri Hypsous. Hermes* 50 (1915), 572-603.

(iii) *Exodus*

ARNOLD, WM. R.: The Divine Name in Exodus 3: 14. *JBL* 24 (1905), 107-65.

FINN, A. H.: The tabernacle chapters. *JTS* 16 (1915), 449-82.

FRANKEL, Z.: Zur Erklärung einer auffallenden Übersetzung der LXX. *MGWJ* 15 (1866), 299-301 [Ex. xii: 22].

GOODING, D. W.: *The Account of the Tabernacle. Translation and Textual Problems of the Greek Exodus.* = Texts and Studies ns 6 (Cambridge, 1959).
> Rev. Katz in *TLZ* 85 (1960), 350-5.
>> Thornhill in *JTS* 11 (1960), 124-7.
>> Ziegler in *ThRev* 56 (1960), 57-60.

GÖTTSBERGER, J.: Zu Ex. xxxv: 7ff. nach der LXX. *BZ* 10 (1912), 12.

O'CONNELL, K. G.: *The Theodotionic revision of the Book of Exodus* (Diss. Harvard, 1967), cp *HTR* 61 (1968), 64f.

PELLETIER, A.: Le 'voile du temple' de Jérusalem en termes de métier. *REG* 77 (1964), 70-5 [Ex. xxvi: 36].

39a
(iv)
——: Une particularité du rituel des 'pains d'oblation' conservée par la LXX. *VT* 17 (1967), 364-7 [Ex. xxv: 30 and Lev. xxiv: 8].

RABINOWITZ, J. J.: Ex. xxii: 4 and the LXX version thereof. *VT* 9 (1959), 40-6.

29
SCHWARTZ, J.: Le 'cycle de Pétoubastis' et les commentaires égyptiens de l'Exode. *BIFAO* 49 (1949), 67-83.

11
——: Notes sur l'archéologie des LXX. *Revue d'Égyptologie* 8 (1951), 195-8.

SELWYN, W.: *Notae criticae in versionem Septuagintaviralem. Exodus i-xxiv* (Cambridge, 1856).

SERVIN, A.: La tradition judéo-chrétienne de l'Exode. *BIE* 31 (1948/9), 315-55.

WHITTAKER, J.: Moses atticizing. *Phoenix* 21 (1967), 196-201. [Numenius < Ex. iii: 14, LXX].

(iv) *Leviticus*

HUBER, K.: *Untersuchungen über den Sprachcharakter des griechischen Leviticus* (Giessen, 1916).

PELLETIER, A.: — see Exodus.

WELCH, A. C.: The LXX of Leviticus. *ET* 30 (1919), 277-8.

WIENER, H. M.: Studies in the Septuagintal texts of Leviticus. *BS* 70 (1913), 498-527, 669-86; 71 (1914), 80-94.

(v) *Numbers*

SCHOEPS, H. J.: כלב הקנזי: Die griechischen Übersetzer zu Num. xxxii: 12. *Biblica* 26 (1945), 307-9.

SELWYN, W.: *Notae criticae in versionem Septuagintaviralem. Liber Numerorum* (Cambridge, 1857).

(vi) *Deuteronomy*

35b ALLGEIER, A.: Dt. xxv 1-3 im Manchester Papyrus (PRG 458). *Biblica* 19 (1938), 1-18.

DEGANI, E.: Due note filologiche, I: Dt. xiv 1 LXX. *Bolletino del Comitato per la Preparazione dell'Ediz. naz. dei Classici greci e latini* (Rome) 14 (1966), 93-4.

36a, GOODING, D. W.: *The Greek Deuteronomy* (Diss. Cambridge, 1954).
d,e

35b HEMPEL, J.: Zum griechischen Deuteronomiumstexte des II. Jahrh. a.C. *ZAW* nF 14 (1937), 115-27.

24 ——: Zur LXX-Vorlage im Deuteronomium. Eine Entgegnung auf [Ziegler] ZAW 1960, 237ff. *ZAW* nF 32 (1961), 87-96.

36a HOFBAUER, J.: Zu den Textfamilien der LXX im Deuteronomium. *ZKT* 62 (1938), 385-9.

24 MERCATI, G.: Un singolare versione di Dt. xxvi: 17, 18 e l'originale di essa. *Biblica* 24 (1943), 201-4.

35b OPITZ, H. G. and SCHAEDER, H. H.: Zum LXX-Papyrus Rylands Greek 458. *ZNW* 35 (1936), 115-7.

27c, PHILLIPS, G. A.: The oldest Biblical papyrus and a leaf from a
35b testimony book. *ET* 48 (1936/7), 168-70.

24 SCHULTZ, S. J.: *The differences between the Masoretic and LXX texts of Deuteronomy* (Diss. Harvard, 1949).

35b VACCARI, A.: Fragmentum biblicum saeculi II ante Christum. *Biblica* 17 (1936), 501.

——: Papiro Fuad Inv. 266. Analisi critica dei Frammenti publicati in 'New World Translation of the Christian Scriptures'. *Studia Patristica* 1 (1957) = *TU* 63, 339-42.

39k VELLAS, B.: Τὰ χωρία Δευτ. 32: 43 καὶ Ζαχ. 14: 17 (Athens, 1935).

ZIEGLER, J.: Zur LXX-Vorlage im Deuteronomium. *ZAW* nF 31
24 (1960), 237-62.

b. Joshua, Judges, Ruth

(i) *Joshua*

39b BOLING, R. G.: Some Conflate Readings in Joshua-Judges. *VT* 16
(ii) (1966), 293-8.

EGLI, C.: see Pentateuch.

GASTER, M.: Das Buch Josua in hebr. samaritanischer Rezension.
ZDMG 62 (1908), 209-79, 494-549.

——: The Samaritan book of Joshua and the LXX. *PSBA* 31
(1909), 115-27, 149-53.

HOLLENBERG, J.: *Der Charakter der alexandrinischen Übersetzung des
Buches Josua* ... (Moers, 1876).

24 HOLMES, S.: *Joshua : The Hebrew and Greek Texts* (Cambridge, 1914).

KATZ, P.: see 36b.

36a MARGOLIS, M. L.: The Grouping of Codices in the Greek Joshua.
JQR ns 1 (1910), 259-63.

35c ——: The Washington manuscript of Joshua. *JAOS* 31 (1911),
365-7.

36f ——: The K Text of Joshua. *AJSL* 28 (1911/2), 1-55.

24 ——: Man by Man (Josh. vii: 17). *JQR* ns 3 (1912), 319-36.

24 ——: τῶν ἐνδόξων — Josh. iv: 4. In *Studies in Jewish Literature in
honour of Prof. K. Kohler* (Berlin, 1913), 204-9.

24 ——: τετροπωμένους — Josh. xi: 6. *JBL* 33 (1914), 286-9.

24 ——: Ai or 'the city'? Josh. viii: 12, 16. *JQR* ns 7 (1916), 491-7.

——: (A new border town recovered from the LXX of Joshua). See
JPOS 5 (1925), 61-3.

3a, ——: Specimen of a new edition of the Greek Joshua. In *Jewish
36a Studies in memory of I. Abrahams* (New York, 1927), 307-23.

3a ——: Corrections to the Apparatus of Joshua in the Cambridge
LXX. *JBL* 49 (1930), 234-64.

——: Andreas Masius and his commentary on the book of Joshua
[Accepted for *HTR* but manuscript apparently lost].

36b ORLINSKY, H. M.: The LXX variant κατέπαυσαν in Josh. ii: 1. *JBL*
63 (1944), 405-6.

24 ——: The Hebrew Vorlage of the LXX in the Book of Joshua.
VTS 17 (1969), 187-95.

36e, PRETZL, O.: Der hexaplarische und tetraplarische LXX-Text des
37b Origenes in den Büchern Josua und Richter. *ByzZ* 30 (1929/30),
262-8.

36a   ——: Die griechischen Handschriftengruppen im Buche Josue untersucht nach ihrer Eigenart und ihrem Verhältnis zueinander. *Biblica* 9 (1928), 377-427.

(ii) *Judges*

36e   BILLEN, A. V.: The hexaplaric element in the LXX version of Judges. *JTS* 43 (1942), 12-9.

BOLING, R. G.: — see Joshua.

COOPER, C. M.: *Studies in the Greek texts of Judges: synonyms of A and B* (Diss. Dropsie College, 1941).

——: Theodotion's influence on the A text of Judges. *JBL* 67 (1948), 63-8.

FRITZSCHE, O. F.: *Liber Iudicum secundum LXX interpretes* (Zurich, 1867).

LUDLUM, J. H.: *The dual Greek text of Judges in codices A and B* (Diss. Yale, 1957).

MOORE, G. F.: The Greek Versions of Judges. *JBL* 1890 ii.

NESTLE, E.: Der Richter Elon. *ZAW* 28 (1908), 149-50.

——: Die Waffe des Samgar (Judic. iii: 31). *ZAW* 28 (1908), 230-1.

——: Samgar. *ZAW* 32 (1912), 152-3.

ORLINSKY, H. M.: — see Genesis.

36a   PRETZL, O.: LXX-Probleme im Buch der Richter. *Biblica* 7 (1926), 233-69, 353-83.

——: — see Joshua.

24   SCHREINER, J.: *Septuaginta-Massora des Buches der Richter. Eine textkritische Studie.* Analecta Biblica 7 (1957).
Rev. Katz in *TLZ* 1961, 829-32.

36a   ——: Textformen und Urtext des Deboraliedes in der LXX. *Biblica* 42 (1961), 173-200.

36a   ——: Zum B-Text des griechischen Canticum Deborae. *Biblica* 42 (1961), 333-58.

SCHULTE, A.: *De restitutione atque indole genuinae versionis graecae in libro Iudicum* (Leipzig, 1889).

36a   SOISALON-SOININEN, I.: *Die Textformen der LXX-Übersetzung des Richterbuches.* *AASF* B 72.1 (1951).
Rev. Katz in *TLZ* 1952, 154-8.
Lambert in *VT* 2 (1952), 184-9.

(iii) *Ruth*

RAHLFS, A.: *Das Buch Ruth griechisch als Probe einer kritischen Handausgabe der LXX* (Stuttgart, 1922).

36a ——: *Studie über den griechischen Text des Buches Ruth. MSU* III, 2 = *NGWGött* 1922, 47-164.

Rev. Tisserant in *RB* 33 (1924), 123-7.

SHEPPARD, H. W.: Ruth iii: 13b an explanation of B's inserted words. *JTS* 19 (1918), 277.

SPERBER, A.: Wiederherstellung einer griechischen Textgestalt des Buches Ruth. *MGWJ* 81 (1937), 55-65.

36e THORNHILL, R.: The Greek text of the Book of Ruth: a Grouping of Manuscripts according to Origen's Hexapla. *VT* 3 (1953), 236-49.

c. (i) *I-II Samuel (I-II Kingdoms)*

APTOWITZER, V.: Rabbinische Parallelen und Aufschlüsse zu LXX und Vg: I, Die Bücher Samuelis. *ZAW* 29 (1909), 241-52.

——: Les additions de la LXX dans I Sam. v: 6,9. *REJ* 54 (1907), 56-7.

35 BAARS, W.: A Forgotten Fragment of the Greek Text of the Books of Samuel. *OTS* 14 (1965), 201-5.

24 BARNES, W. E.: LXX and MT (I Sam. xxvi: 20b; Ezek. i: 13). *ET* 6 (1894), 223-5.

BATTEN, L. W.: Helkath Hazzurim, 2 Sam. 2: 12-16. *ZAW* 26 (1906), 90-4.

24 BELING, W. A.: *The Hebrew variants in the First Book of Samuel compared with the Old Greek Recensions* (Diss. Princeton, 1947).

BENNETT, W. H.: I Sam. ii: 5 (LXX). *ET* 13 (1901), 234.

24 BOER, P. A. H. DE: *Research into the Text of I Samuel* (i-xvi) (Amsterdam, 1938).

——: I Samuel xvii. Notes on the text and the ancient versions. *OTS* 1 (1941/2), 79-103.

——: Research into the text of I Samuel xviii-xxxi. *OTS* 6 (1949), 1-100.

24 BÖKLEN, E.: Elisas 'Berufung' (I Reg. 19: 19-21). *ZAW* 32 (1912), 41-8.

24 BOSTRÖM, O. H.: *Alternative readings in the Hebrew of the Books of Samuel* (Rock Island, 1918).

36e,   Brock, S. P.: *The recensions of the LXX version of I Samuel* (Diss.
f,37b   Oxford, 1966).

Büchler, A.: La LXX sur I Sam. v: 6,9. *REJ* 54 (1907), 269-71.

Canet, L.: La version grecque de I Sam. xiv: 15. *REJ* 63 (1921),
297-8.

Dieu, L.: Retouches lucianiques sur quelques textes de la Vieille
36f   Latine (I et II Samuel). *RB* ns 16 (1919), 372-403.

——: Les manuscrits grecs des livres de Samuel. *Le Muséon* 34
36a   (1921), 17-60.

Driver, S. R.: *Notes on the Hebrew Text ... of Samuel* (Oxford,[2],
1913; rp 1960), xxxiii-lxxxiii.

Fischer, B.: Lukian-Lesarten in der Vetus Latina der vier Königs-
36f   bücher. *Studia Anselmiana* 27/8 (1951), 169-77.

Gehman, H. S.: A Note on I Sam. xxi: 13 (14). *JBL* 67 (1948),
241-3.

——: Exegetical methods employed by the Greek translator of I
11,   Samuel. *JAOS* 70 (1950), 292-6.
16   Johnson, B.: *Die hexaplarische Rezension des I. Samuelbuches der*
36e   *LXX. Studia Theologica Lundensia* 22 (1963).
         Rev. Brock in *JTS* ns 15 (1964), 112-7.
             Kirchmeyer in *REG* 78 (1965), 454-7.

Kelly, B. H.: *The LXX translators of I Samuel and II Samuel i-xi.
I* (Diss. Princeton, 1948).

Méritain, J.: *La version grecque des Livres de Samuel* (Paris,
1898).

Nestle, E.: I Sam. xviii: 9 in der LXX. *ZAW* 12 (1892), 29-30.

24   Orlinsky, H. M.: 'Ha-roqdīm for hā-rēqīm in II Sam. vi: 20. *JBL*
65 (1946), 25-35.

40g   Philonenko, M.: Une paraphrase du cantique d'Anna. *RHPR* 42
(1962), 157-68.

24   Rehm, M.: *Textkritische Untersuchungen zu den Parallelstellen der
Samuel-Königsbücher und der Chronik. ATA* XII, 3 (1937).

Rinaldi, G.: Golia e David. (I Sam. xvii: 1-xviii: 8). *Bibbia e
Oriente* 8 (1966), 11-29.

Rowley, H. H.: A note on the LXX text of I Sam. xv: 22a. *VT* 1
(1951), 67-8.

Schmid, J.: *Septuagintageschichtliche Studien zum I. Samuelbuch*
(Diss. Breslau, 1941 [now Marburg ms 41/1164)].

Simotas, P. N.: (II Sam. xxiv: 15 LXX). *Theologia* 36 (1965),
580-6.

32 STENZEL, M.: Das erste Samuelbuch in den lateinischen erhaltenen Origenes-Homilien zum Alten Testamente. *ZAW* nF 20 (1945/8), 30-43.

STOEBE, H. J.: Anmerkungen zu I Sam. viii: 16 und xvi: 20. *VT* 4 (1954), 177-84.

24 ——: Die Goliathperikope I Sam. xvii: 1-xviii: 5 und die Textform der LXX. *VT* 6 (1956), 397-413.

THACKERAY, H. ST. J.: The Greek translators of the four Books of Kings. *JTS* 8 (1907), 262-78.

——: The Song of Hannah and other lessons and Psalms for the Jewish New Year Day. *JTS* 16 (1915), 177-204.

24 THORNHILL, R.: A note on אל נכון, I Sam. xxvi: 4. *VT* 14 (1964), 462-6.

TRENČZENYI-WALDAPFEL, I.: Die Hexe von Endor und die griechisch-römische Welt. *Acta Orientalia Hungarica* 12 (1961), 201-22.

WEINGREEN, J.: A Rabbinic-type Gloss in the LXX Version of I Sam. i: 18. *VT* 14 (1964), 225-8.

11 WEVERS, J. W.: A Study in the exegetical principles of the translator of II Sam. xi: 2-I Kings. ii: 11. *CBQ* 15 (1953), 30-45.

24 WOODS, F. H.: The Light thrown by the LXX Version on the Books of Samuel. *Studia Biblica* (Oxford) 1 (1885), 21-38.

(ii) *I-II Kings (III-IV Kingdoms)*

ABERBACH, M. and SMOLAR, L.: Jeroboam's Rise to Power [in LXX]. *JBL* 88 (1969), 69-72.

——, ——: Jeroboam and Solomon: Rabbinic interpretations. *JQR* 59 (1968/9), 118-32.

36a ALLEN, L. C.: Further thoughts on an old recension of Reigns in Paralipomena. *HTR* 61 (1968), 483-91.

24 BARNES, W. E.: Jachin and Boaz. *JTS* 5 (1904), 447-51.

36f BURKITT, F. C.: I Kings viii 53b, the Lucianic text. *JTS* 10 (1909), 439-46.

DEBUS, J.: *Die Sünde Jerobeams. FRLANT* 93 (1967).

FINET, A.: Termes militaires accadiens conservés dans la LXX. *Iraq* 25 (1963), 191-2.

FISCHER, B: — see I-II Samuel.

GOODING, D. W.: Ahab according to the LXX. *ZAW* 76 (1964), 269-80.

24b   ——: Pedantic Timetabling in the 3rd Book of Reigns. *VT* 15 (1965), 153-66.

——: The LXX's Version of Solomon's Misconduct. *VT* 15 (1965), 325-35.

——: An Impossible Shrine. *VT* 15 (1965), 405-20.

——: The Shimei duplicate and its satellite miscellanies in 3 Reigns II. *JSS* 13 (1968), 76-92.

24b   ——: The LXX's Rival Versions of Jeroboam's Rise to Power. *VT* 17 (1967), 173-89.

——: Problems of Text and Midrash in the Third Book of Reigns. *Textus* 7 (1969), 1-29.

24b   ——: Text-sequence and translation-revision in 3 Reigns ix: 10-x: 33. *VT* 19 (1969), 448-63.

24   GÖTTSBERGER, J.: יִצָא, ἐποίει. 4 Kms xviii: 7. *BZ* 17 (1925), 224.

HÄNEL, J.: Die Zusätze der LXX in I Reg. ii: 36 a-o, 46 a-l. *ZAW* 47 (1929), 76-9.

36f,   HAUPERT, R. S.: *The relation of codex Vaticanus and the Lucianic*
40d,   *text in the Books of Kings from the viewpoint of the Old Latin and*
g   *the Ethiopic versions* (Diss. Philadelphia, 1930).

36a   KLEIN, R. W.: New evidence for an old recension of Reigns. *HTR* 60 (1967), 93-105.

MONTGOMERY, J. A.: The Supplement at the End of 3 Kms ii. *ZAW* nF 9 (1932), 124-9.

——: (ed. H. S. Gehman): *The Books of Kings*. ICC. (London, 1951), 8-24.

NESTLE, E.: I Kings xvii: 21, II Kings iv: 34 (LXX). *ET* 14 (1902), 185-6.

——: ἐνδιηλλαγμένος in I(III) Reg. xxii 47. *ZDMG* 60 (1906), 243-4.

24   OLMSTEAD, A. T.: Source study and the biblical text. *AJSL* 30 (1913/4), 1-35.

——: The earliest Book of Kings. *AJSL* 31 (1914/5), 169-214.

39l   ORLINSKY, H. M.: The Kings-Isaiah Recension of the Hezekiah Story. *JQR* 30 (1939/40), 33-49.

36a   RAHLFS, A.: *LXX-Studien I: Studien zu den Königsbüchern* (Göttingen, 1904).

36f   ——: *LXX-Studien III: Lucians Rezension der Königsbücher* (Göttingen, 1911).

Rev. Margolis in *JQR* ns 3 (1912/3), 129-30.

REHM, M.: see I-II Samuel.

24b SHENKEL, J. D.: *Chronology and recensional development in the Greek text of Kings* (Cambridge, Mass., 1968).
Rev. Gooding in *JTS* ns 21 (1970), 118-31.
——: A comparative Study of the synoptic parallels in Paraleipomena and I-II Reigns. *HTR* 62 (1969), 63-65.

24b SEEBASS, H.: Zur Königserhebung Jerobeams I. *VT* 17 (1967), 325-33.
——: Traditionsgeschichte des LXX-Zusatzes xii: 24 a-z. In: Die Verwerfung Jerobeams I und Salomos durch die Prophetie des Ahia von Silo. *WdO* 4, 2 (1968), 179-82.

35c SPERBER, A.: The Codex Vaticanus B (LXX). *SeT* 121 (1946), 1-18.

35c SILBERSTEIN, S.: Über den Ursprung der im Codex Alexandrinus und Vaticanus des dritten Königsbuches der alexandrinischen Übersetzung überlieferten Textgestalt. *ZAW* 13 (1893), 1-75; 14 (1894), 1-30.

THACKERAY, H. ST. J.: see I-II Samuel.
——: New light on the book of Jashar. *JTS* 11 (1910), 518-32.

24 WEVERS, J. W.: Double Readings in the Books of Kings, *JBL* 65 (1946), 307-10.
——: A study in the Hebrew Variants in the book of Kings. *ZAW* 61 (1945/8), 43-76.
——: Exegetical principles underlying the LXX text of I Kings ii: 12-xxi: 43. *OTS* 8 (1950), 300-22.
——: Principles of interpretation guiding the fourth translator of the book of the Kingdoms. *CBQ* 14 (1952), 40-56.

35c ——: A study in the Textual History of Codex Vaticanus in the Books of Kings, *ZAW* 64 (1952), 178-89.

d. (i) *Chronicles (Paraleipomena)*

ALLEN, L. C.: see I-II Kings.
BACHER, W.: Der Name der Bücher der Chronik in der LXX. *ZAW* 15 (1895), 305-8.

6a DAHSE, J.: Textkritische Studien I, 1: Die Lage der Quellen von II Chr. xxxii: 30, xxxiii: 14 nach der LXX. *ZAW* 28 (1908), 1-5.

GERLEMAN, G.: *Studies in the LXX*. II, *Chronicles. LUÅ* 43, 3(1946).
Rev. Orlinsky in *JBL* 67 (1948), 381-90.

Gwynn, R. M.: Notes on the authorship of some books of the Greek OT. *Hermathena* 20 (1930), 52-61.

Howorth, H. H.: Chronicles. *PSBA* 27 (1905), 267-78.

——: see Daniel.

Klein, R. W.: Studies in the Greek texts of the Chronicler. *HTR* 59 (1966), 449 [Summary of thesis].

——: Supplements in the Paralipomena: a rejoinder [To Allen]. *HTR* 61 (1968), 492-5.

24 Lemke, W. E.: The synoptic problem in the Chronicler's history. *HTR* 58 (1965), 349-63.

Rehm, M.: see I-II Samuel.

Rogers, V.: *The old Greek version of Chronicles* (Diss. Princeton, 1954).

Shenkel, D.: see I-II Kings.

39d Torrey, C. C.: The Greek versions of Chronicles, Ezra and Nehe-
(ii)   miah. *PSBA* 25 (1903), 139-40.

——: The apparatus for the textual criticism of Chronicles, Ezra, Nehemiah. In *OT and Semitic Studies in memory of W. R. Harper* (Chicago, 1908), 55-111.

(ii) *I-II Esdras*
(cp BJHIL 86-7)

Allgeier, A.: Beobachtungen am LXX-Text der Bücher Esdras und Nehemia. *Biblica* 22 (1941), 227-51.

35c Allrik, H. L.: I Esdras according to Codex B and Codex A as Ap-
    pearing in Zerubbabel's List in I Esdr. v: 8-23. *ZAW* 66 (1954), 272-92.

36e,g Bardy, G.: Notes sur les recensions hésychienne et hexaplaire du livre de Néhémie (II Esdras). *RB* ns 15 (1918), 192-9.

24 Bayer, E.: *Das III. Buch Esdras und sein Verhältnis zu den Büchern Esra-Nehemia. Biblische Studien* 16, 1 (1911).

9 Denter, T.: *Die Stellung der Bücher Esdras im Kanon des AT. Eine kanongeschichtliche Untersuchung* (Diss. Fribourg, 1962).

Girdlestone, R. B.: Notes on the comparative value of the two recensions of Ezra. *PSBA* 24 (1902), 14-16.

Gwynn, J.: see Chronicles.

Howorth, H. H.: The apocryphal book Esdras A and the LXX. *PSBA* 23 (1901), 147-59.

24b ——: The chronology and order of events in Esdras A, compared with, and preferred to, those in the canonical Ezra. *PSBA* 23 (1901), 305-25.

——: The Hexapla and Tetrapla of Origen and the light they throw on the books of Esdras A and B. *PSBA* 24 (1902), 147-72.

——: The LXX text of the book of Nehemiah. *PSBA* 24 (1902), 332-40; 25 (1903), 15-22, 90-8.

——: Reply to Girdlestone. *PSBA* 24 (1902), 16-20.

——: The genealogies and lists in Nehemiah. *PSBA* 26 (1904), 25-31, 63-9, 94-100.

JACOB, A.: *Septuagintastudien zu Esra* (Diss. Breslau, 1912).

JAHN, G.: *Die Bücher Esra (A und B) und Nehemja* (Leiden, 1909).

KLEIN, R. W.: Old readings in I Esdras. The lists of returnees from Babylon (Ezra 2/Neh 7). *HTR* 62 (1969), 99-107.

LOMMATZSCH, E.: 'Die stärksten Dinge'. *JahrbuchAkWissMainz* 1961, 236-8.

METZGER, B. M.: The 'lost' section of II Esdras. *JBL* 76 (1957), 153-6.

24 MOULTON, W. J.: Über die Überlieferung und den textkritischen Werth des dritten Esrabuchs. *ZAW* 19 (1899), 209-58; 20 (1900), 1-35.

36f PIROT, L.: Note sur la recension de Lucien d'Antioche dans Esdras-Néhémie. *Biblica* 2 (1921), 356-60.

RUDOLPH, W.: Der Wettstreit der Leibwächter des Darius, 3. Esr. iii: 1-v: 6. *ZAW* nF 20 (1945/8), 176-90.

15c RUNDGREN, F.: Zur Bedeutung von ΟΙΚΟΓΕΝΗΣ in 3. Esr. iii: 1.
(ii) *Eranos* 55 (1957), 145-52.

RYAN, J. K.: 'Magna est veritas et praevalebit' (3 Ezra iv: 41). *AmerEcclesRev* 135 (1956), 116-24.

27b SAHLIN, H.: I Esdras 4 et I Cor. 13. Note préliminaire. *Coniectanea Neotestamentica* 5 (1941), 28-9.

3a TEDESCHE, S. S.: *A critical edition of I Esdras* (Diss. Yale, 1928).

TORREY, C. C.: *Composition and historical value of Ezra-Nehemiah.* *BZAW* 2 (1896).

——: The nature and origin of First Esdras. *AJSL* 23 (1906/7), 116-41.

——: The story of the three youths. *AJSL* 23 (1906/7), 177-201.

——: *Ezra Studies* (Chicago, 1910, rp. New York, 1970).

——: A revised view of First Esdras. In *Louis Ginzberg Jubilee Volume* (New York, 1945), I, 395-410.

——: see Chronicles.

WALDE, B.: *Die Esdrasbücher der LXX. Biblische Studien* 17, 4 (1913).

ZIMMERMANN, F.: The Story of the Three Guardsmen. *JQR* 54 (1964), 179-200.

e. (i) *Esther*
(cp *BJHIL* 92)

BICKERMAN, E. J.: The Colophon of the Greek Book of Esther. *JBL* 63 (1944), 339-62.

36a ——: Notes on the Greek Book of Esther, *PAAJR* 20 (1951), 101-33.

12   BROWNLEE, W. H.: Le livre grec d'Esther et la royauté divine. *RB* 73 (1966), 161-85.

36a COOK, H. J.: The A Text of the Greek Version of the Book of Esther. *ZAW* 81 (1969), 369-76.

12   EHRLICH, E. L.: Der Traum des Mardochai. *ZfReligions- und Geistes-geschichte* 7 (1955), 69-74.

JACOB, B.: Das Buch Esther bei den LXX. *ZAW* 10 (1890), 241-98.

JAHN, G.: *Das Buch Esther nach LXX hergestellt, übersetzt und kritisch erklärt* (Leiden, 1901).
     Rev. Wellhausen in *GGA* 1902, 127-47.

15c KLIMA, O.: Paqid — διδάσκαλος. *Archiv Orientální* 23 (1955), 481.
(ii),
16

LANGEN, J.: Die beiden griechischen Texte des Buches Esther. *Tübinger Theologische Quartalschrift* 42 (1860), 244-72.

——: *Die deuterocanonischen Stücke im Buche Esther* (Freiburg, 1862).

LEWY, J.: The Feast on the 14th Day of Adar. *HUCA* 14 (1938/9), 127-51.

MARCUS, R.: Dositheus, Priest and Levite. *JBL* 64 (1945), 269-71.

MOORE, C. A.: *The Greek text of Esther* (Diss. Johns Hopkins, 1965).

24   ——: A Greek Witness to a Different Hebrew Text of Esther. *ZAW* 79 (1967), 351-8.

35c MOTZO, B. R.: Il testo greco di Ester in un manoscritto di Grottoferrata, 6. In *Scritti ... dedicati Abate A. Amelli* (Montecassino, 1920), 17-23.

39f ——: Il rifacimento greco di Ester e il III Macc. In *Saggi de Storia e Letteratura Giudeo-Ellenistica* (Florence, 1924), 272ff.

36a ——: La storia del testo di Ester. *RicRel* 3 (1927), 205-8.
29 ——: Il testo di Ester in Giuseppe. *Studi e Materiali di Storia delle Religione* 4 (1928), 84-105.
36a ——: I testi greci de Ester. *Studi e Materiali di Storia delle Religione* 6 (1930), 223-31.

PATON, L. B.: A Text Critical Apparatus to the Book of Esther. In *OT and Semitic Studies in memory of W. R. Harper* (Chicago, 1908), 3-52.

QUACQUARELLI, A.: Esther xiv: 13: Tribue sermonem compositum in ore meo. *AnnFacMagUnivBari* 2 (1961), 3-19.

RINGGREN, H.: Esther and Purim. *SvExÅrsb* 20 (1955), 5-24.

24 SCHEFTELOWITZ, J.: Zur Kritik des griechischen und massoretischen Buches Esther. *MGWJ* 47 (1903), 24-37, 110-9, 201-13, 289-316.

39f SCHNEIDER, B.: Esther Revised according to the Maccabees. *Studii Biblici Franciscani Liber Annuus* 13 (1962/3), 190-218.

29 SEYBERLICH, R. M.: Esther in der LXX und bei Flavius Josephus. In *Neue Beiträge zur Geschichte der alten Welt*; I, *Alter Orient und Griechenland*, ed. E. C. Welskopf (Berlin, 1964), 363-6.

14 STEIN, E.: Essai d'adaptation de la fête de Pourim dans l'Alexandrie hellénistique. *REJ* 75 (1935), 109-18.

STIEHL, R.: Das Buch Esther. *WZKM* 53 (1957), 4-22.

TORREY, C. C.: The Older Book of Esther. *HTR* 37 (1944), 1-40.

(ii) *Judith*
(See further *BJHIL* 84-5)

BRUNNER, G.: *Der Nabuchodonosor des Buches Judith* (Berlin², 1959).

CAZELLES, H.: Le personage d'Achior dans le livre de Judith. *RechSR* 39 (1951), 324-7.

DELCOR, M.: Le livre de Judith et l'époque grecque. *Klio* 49 (1967), 151-79.

36a DUBARLE, A. M.: Les textes divers du livre de Judith. *VT* 8 (1958), 344-73.

31 ——: Le mention de Judith dans la littérature ancienne juive et chrétienne. *RB* 66 (1959), 514-49.

——: *Judith: Formes et sens des divers traditions. Analecta Biblica* 24 (Rome, 1966). 2 vols.

GRINTZ, Y. M.: *Sefer Yehudith* (Jerusalem, 1957).

HAAG, E.: *Studien zum Buche Judith. Trierer Theologische Studien* 16, (1963).

JANSEN, H. L.: La composition du chant de Judith. *Acta Orientalia* 15 (1936), 63-71.

MEYER, C.: Zur Entstehungsgeschichte des Buches Judith. *Biblica* 3 (1922), 193-203.

MILLER, A.: *Das Buch Judith* (Bonn, 1940), 17f. [on text].

SKEHAN, P. W.: Why leave out Judith? *CBQ* 24 (1962), 147-54.

——: The Hand of Judith. *CBQ* 25 (1963), 94-110.

18b STEUERNAGEL, C.: Bethulia. *ZDPV* 66 (1943), 232-45.

STUMMER, F.: *Geographie des Buches Judith* (Stuttgart, 1947).

VACCARI, A.: Note critiche ed esegetiche. Judith xvi: 11. *Biblica* 28 (1947), 401-4.

ZIMMERMANN, F.: Aids for the Recovery of the Hebrew Original of Judith. *JBL* 57 (1938), 67-74.

(iii) *Tobit*

(cp *BJHIL* 85-6)

BÉVENOT, H.: The Primitive Book of Tobit. *BS* 83 (1926), 55-84.

31 GAMBERONI, J.: *Die Auslegung des Buches Tobias in der griechisch-lateinischen Kirche der Antike und der Christenheit des Westens bis 1600* (Munich, 1969).

GLASSON, T. F.: The Main Source of Tobit. *ZAW* 71 (1959), 275-7.

35c HALKIN, F.: *Inédits byzantins d'Ochride, Candïe et Moscou. Subsidia Hagiographica* 38 (Brussels, 1963) [no 11: paraphrase of Tobit].

36a HARRIS, J. R.: The double text of Tobit. *AJT* 3 (1899), 451-4.

HAUPT, P.: Asmodeus. *JBL* 40 (1921), 174-8.

12 HUET, G.: Le conte du 'mort reconnaissant' et le livre de Tobie. *RHR* 71 (1915), 1-29.

12 JANSEN, H. L.: Die Hochzeitsriten im Tobitbuche. *Temenos* (Helsinki) 1 (1965), 142-9.

16, JOÜON, P.: Quelques hébraïsmes de Codex Sinaiticus de Tobie.
35c *Biblica* 14 (1933), 168-74.

LEBRAM, J.: Μυστήριον βασιλέως [Tob. xii: 7]. In *Fs. O. Michel* (Leiden, 1963), 320-4.

12 ——: Die Weltreiche in der jüdischen Apokalyptik. Bemerkungen zu Tobit xiv: 4-7. *ZAW* 76 (1964), 328-31.

35c LÖHR, M.: Alexandrinus und Sinaiticus zum Buche Tobit. *ZAW* 20 (1900), 243-63.

MILIK, J. T.: La patrie de Tobie. *RB* 73 (1966), 522-30.

MÜLLER, J.: Beiträge zur Erklärung und Kritik des Buches Tobit. *BZAW* 13 (1908), 1-53.

NESTLE, E.: Zum Buche Tobit. In *LXX-Studien III* (Stuttgart, 1899), 22-35; *IV* (1903), 9-10.

NÖLDEKE, T.: Die Texte des Buches Tobit. *Monatsberichte der Berliner Akademie*, (1879), 54-69.

PAUTREL, R. and LEFEBVRE, M.: Trois textes sur Rafaël. *RechSR* 39 (1951), 115-24.

PLATH, M.: Zum Buch Tobit. *TSK* 74 (1901), 377-414.

PRADO, J.: La índole literaria del libro de Tobit. *Sefarad* 7 (1947), 373-94.

——: Historia, enseñanzas y poesia en el libro de Tobit. *Sefarad* 9 (1949), 27-51.

3a   PRIERO, G.: *Il libro di Tobia. Testi e introduzioni* (Como, 1924).

——: *I testi greci de Tobia. Saggio di studio filologico-critico* (Como, 1924).

RIST, M.: The God of Abraham, Isaac and Jacob. *JBL* 57 (1938), 289-303.

16,   SAYDON, P.: Some Mistranslations in the Codex Sinaiticus of the
35c   Book of Tobit. *Biblica* 33 (1952), 363-5.

SCHMITT, C.: Der weise Achikar der morgenländischen Sage und der Achikar des Buches Tobias nach der Übersetzung der LXX. *Pastor Bonus* 26 (1913/14), 83-90.

35c   SCHULTE, A.: Im welchem Verhältnis steht der Codex A zum Codex Vaticanus im Buche Tobias? *BZ* 6 (1908), 262-5.

SERENI, E.: Il libro di Tobit. *RicRel* 4 (1928), 43-55, 97-117, 420-39; 5 (1929), 35-49.

36a   SIMPSON, D. C.: The Chief Recensions of the Book of Tobit. *JTS* 14 (1913), 516-30.

TORREY, C. C.: Nineveh in the Book of Tobit. *JBL* 41 (1922), 237-45.

f. *I-IV Maccabees*
(See further *BJHIL* 60, 88-91)

ABEL, F.-M.: Les lettres préliminaires du 2e Livre des Maccabées. *RB* 53 (1946), 513-33.

——: Éclaircissement de quelques passages des Maccabées. *RB* 55 (1948), 184-94.

ABRAHAMS, I.: The Third Book of Maccabees. *JQR* 9 (1897), 39-59.

18a BEVAN, A. A.: The Origin of the Name Maccabee. *JTS* 30 (1929), 191-3.

BICKERMANN, E. J.: Ein jüdischer Festbrief vom Jahre 124 v. Chr. (II Macc. i: 1-9). *ZNW* 32 (1933), 233-54.

——: The date of Fourth Maccabees. In *Louis Ginzberg Jubilee Volume* (New York, 1945), 105-12.

——: Les Maccabées de Malalas. *Byzantion* 21 (1951), 63-83.

36a BRUPPACHER, H.: Textkritisches zu I Macc. *ZAW* 49 (1931), 149-50.

36a BRUYNE, D. DE: Le texte grec des deux premiers livres des Machabées. *RB* 31 (1922), 31-54.

——: ἐκ τῶν ὀμμάτων (II Mach. ix: 9) *RB* 30 (1921), 407-8.

——: Notes de philologie biblique. 2 Mach. *RB* 31 (1922), 405-9.

——: Le texte grec du deuxième livre des Machabées. *RB* 39 (1930), 503-19.

BURNEY, C. F.: An Acrostic Poem in Praise of Judas Maccabaeus. *JTS* 21 (1920), 319-25 [I Macc. iii: 1-9].

CAVAIGNAC, E.: Remarques sur le deuxième livre des Macchabées. *RHR* 130 (1945), 42-58.

COHEN, J.: *Judaica et Aegyptiaca. De Maccabaeorum libro III quaestiones historicae* (Diss. Groningen, 1941).

12 GELIN, A.: Les origines bibliques de l'idée de martyre. *Lumière et Vie* 36 (1958), 123-9.

GIL, L.: Sobre el estile del libro segundo de los Maccabeos. *Emerita* 26 (1958), 11-32.

GINSBURG, M. S.: Sparta and Judaea. *Classical Philology* 29 (1934), 117-22.

GRIMM, W.: Über I Macc. vii und xv: 16-21. *ZWT* 17 (1873), 231-8.

35c GRYGLEWICZ, F.: Le codex alexandrinus du premier livre des Macchabées. *Teologiczno-Kanoniczne* 8 (1961), 23-37.

12 GÜNTHER, E.: Zeuge und Märtyrer. *ZNW* 47 (1956), 145-61.

HADAS, M.: III Maccabees and the Tradition of Patriotic Romance. *CdE* 24 (1949), 97-104.

21 ——: Aristeas and III Maccabees. *HTR* 42 (1949), 175-84.

36a HANHART, R.: Zum Text des 2. und 3. Makkabäerbuches. Probleme der Überlieferung, der Auslegung und der Ausgabe. *MSU* 8 (1961) = *NGWGött* 1961, 427-86. Rev. Kilpatrick in *GGA* 1963, 10-22.

HARRIS, J. R.: Metrical Fragments in III Maccabees. *BJRL* 5 (1919), 195-207.

———: Some Notes on IV Maccabees. *ET* 32 (1920/1), 183-5.

HERKENNE, H.: *Die Briefe zum Beginn des II Makkabäerbuches* (i: 1-ii: 18). *Biblische Studien* VIII, 4 (1904).

12   HUNKIN, J. W.: Judas Maccabaeus and Prayers for the Dead. *Expos* VIII, 9 (1915), 361-5.

———: I Macc. iii: 48, an emendation. *JTS* 29 (1928), 43-6.

19   JADRIJEVIĆ, A.: Tria aenigmata hebraica librorum Maccabaeorum. *Antonianum* 33 (1958), 263-74.

16   JOÜON, P.: Quelques hébraïsmes de syntaxe dans le premier livre des Macchabées. *Biblica* 3 (1922), 231-2.

KAMINKA, A.: Quelques notes sur le Ier livre des Macchabées. *REJ* 92 (1932), 179-83.

KAPPLER, W.: *De memoria alterius libri Maccabaeorum* (Diss. Göttingen, 1929).

36a KATZ, P.: The Text of 2 Maccabees reconsidered. *ZNW* 51 (1960), 10-30.

40g ———: Eleazar's martyrdom in 2 Maccabees: the Latin evidence for a point of the story. *Studia Patristica* 4 (1961) = *TU* 79, 118-24.

KRAETZCHMAR, R.: The Original Name of the Book of I Maccabees. *ET* 12 (1900), 93-5.

12   LAUER, S.: *Eusebes logismos* in IV Maccabees. *JJS* 6 (1955), 170-1.

LEVI, I.: Le martyre des sept Macchabées dans la Pesikta Rabbati. *REJ* 54 (1907), 138-41.

———: Les deux livres des Macchabées et le livre hébraïque des Hasmonéens. *Semitica* 5 (1955), 15-36.

LOEWE, R.: A Jewish Counterpart to the Acts of the Alexandrians. *JJS* 12 (1961), 105-22.

MARCUS, R.: The name Μακκαβαῖος. In *Joshua Starr memorial volume* (New York, 1953), 59-65.

29   MELAMED, E. Z.: (Josephus and I Maccabees) [In Hebrew]. *Eretz Israel* 1 (1951), 122.

MOREAU, J.: Le troisième livre des Macchabées. *CdE* 31 (1941), 111-22.

MUGLER, C.: Remarques sur le second livre des Macchabées. La statistique des mots et la question de l'auteur. *RHPR* 11 (1931), 419-23.

36a NESTLE, E.: Einiges zum Text des zweiten Makkabäerbuches. In *LXX Studien* IV (1903), 19-22.

NIESE, B.: Kritik der beiden Makkabäerbücher nebst Beiträgen zur

Geschichte der makkabäischen Erhebung. *Hermes* 35 (1900), 268-307, 453-527.

PAX, E.: 'Ich gebe hin meinem Leib und mein Glück'. Eine Lesart zu 2 Makk. vii: 37. *Studii Biblici Franciscani Liber Annuus* 16 (1965/6), 357-68.

15c (ii)   PENNA, A.: Διαθήκη, συνθήκη nei libri dei Maccabei. *Biblica* 46 (1965), 149-80.

12   PERLER, O.: Das vierte Makkabäerbuch, Ignatius von Antiochien und die ältesten Märtyrerberichte. *Rivista di Archeologia Cristiana* 25 (1949), 47-72.

PRÉAUX, C.: Reflexions sur l'entité hellénistique [II Mac. iv: 13]. *CdE* 40 (1964), 129-39.

RAHLFS, A.: Die Kriegselefanten im I Makkabäerbuche. *ZAW* 52 (1934), 78-9.

RAVENNA, A.: I Maccabei nella litteratura talmudica. *Rivista Biblica* 10 (1962), 384-91.

12   RENAUD, B.: La loi et les lois dans les livres des Macchabées. *RB* 68 (1961), 39-67.

15c (ii)   RICHNOW, W.: *Untersuchungen zu Sprache und Stil des zweiten Makkabäerbuches* (Diss. Göttingen, 1968).

36a   RISBERG, B.: Textkritische und exegetische Anmerkungen zu den Makkabäerbüchern. *Beiträge zur Religionswissenschaft* (Stockholm) 2 (1918), 6-31.

SCHADE, L.: Zu II Makk. i: 19. *BZ* 8 (1910), 228-35.

19   SCHULTE, A.: Der hebräische Titel des ersten Makkabäerbuches. *BZ* 7 (1909), 254.

36a   SCHWABE, M. and MELAMED, E. Z.: Zum Text der Seronepisode in I Macc. und bei Josephus. *MGWJ* 72 (1928), 202-4.

SCHWEITZER, A.: *Untersuchungen über die Reste eines hebräischen Textes vom ersten Makkabäerbuch* (Berlin, 1901).
Rev. Schmidt in *TLZ* 1901, 544-5 (cp. 605).

19   SIGWALT, C.: Σαρβηθ σαβανιελ und Σαραμελ (I Makk.). *BZ* 10 (1912), 362.

12   SURKAU, H. Q.: Martyrien in jüdischer und frühchristlicher Zeit. *FRLANT* 54 (1938), 9-29.

19   TORREY, C. C.: Three troublesome proper names in Ist Maccabees. *JBL* 53 (1934), 31-3.
——: The Letters Prefixed to Second Maccabees. *JAOS* 60 (1940), 119-50.

21 TRACY, S.: III Maccabees and Ps. Aristeas. *Yale Classical Studies* 1 (1928), 241-52.

VACCARI, A.: Note critiche ed esegetiche. 2 Macc. xv: 17. *Biblica* 28 (1947), 404-6.

15b WEIERHOLT, M.: Zum Ausdruck οἱ περί τινα in den Makkabäer-
(ii) büchern. *Symbolae Osloenses* 11 (1932), 69-71.

36a WILHELM, A.: Zu einigen Stellen der Bücher der Makkabäer. *An-zeiger AkWissWien, ph.-hist. Kl.* 1937, 15-20.

g. (i) *Psalms*

24 ACKROYD, P. R.: *nṣḥ* — εἰς τέλος. *ET* 80 (1968/9), 126.

36a ALLGEIER, A.: Der Einfluss Spaniens in der Textgeschichte der Psalmen. *Gesamm. Aufsätze zur Kulturgeschichte Spaniens* 6 (1937), 60-61.

——: Exegetische Beiträge zur Geschichte des Griechischen vor dem Humanismus. *Biblica* 24 (1943), 261-88 [On Graeco-Latin Psalters].

——: Die erste Psalmenübersetzung des Heiligen Hieronymus und das Psalterium Romanum. *Biblica* 12 (1931), 447-82.

24 BAETHGEN, F.: Der textkritische Wert der alten Übersetzungen zu den Psalmen. *JahrbProtTheol* 1882.

BAUMSTARK, A.: Der älteste erhaltene griechisch-arabische Text von Ps. cx (cix). *OC* Dritte Serie 9 (1934), 55-6.

——: Zur Textgeschichte von Ps. 89 (99) 21. *OC* Dritte Serie 9 (1934), 1-12.

BERG, F.: *The influence of the LXX upon the Peshitta Psalter* (New York, 1895).

BRATSIOTIS, P. I.: Αἱ ᾠδαὶ τῶν ἀναβαθμῶν τοῦ ψαλτηρίου (Athens, 1928).

BRINKTRINE, J.: Dominus regnavit a ligno. *BZ* 10 (1966), 105-7.

BRUYNE, D. DE: La reconstitution du Psautier hexaplaire latin *Rev. Bén.* 41 (1929), 297-324.

DELEKAT, L.: Probleme der Psalmenüberschriften. *ZAW* nF 35 (1964), 269-80.

DUBARLE, A. M.: δράξασθε παιδείας — Ps. ii: 12. *RB* 62 (1955), 511-2.

11 ERWIN, H. M.: *Theological aspects of the LXX of the book of Psalms* (Diss. Princeton, 1962).

FLASHAR, M.: Exegetische Studien zum LXX-Psalter. *ZAW* 32 (1912), 81-116, 161-89, 241-68.

35c GOODING, D. W.: The Text of the Psalms in the two Durham Bibles. *Scriptorium* 12 (1958), 94-6.

GRIBOMONT, J. and THIBAUT, A.: Méthode et esprit des traductions du 'Psautier grec'. *CollBiblLat* 13 (1959), 51-105.

31 GROSSE-BRAUCKMANN, E.: *Der Psaltertext bei Theodoret. MSU* I, 3 (1911).

27 HASENZAHL, W.: *Die Gottverlassenkeit des Christus nach dem Kreuzeswort bei Matthäus und Markus und das christologische Verständnis des griechischen Psalters.* BFCT 39, 1 (1937).

24 HUCKLE, J. J.: Ps. xvi: 10b, a Consideration (LXX and MT). *Dunwoodie Review* (New York) 4 (1964), 43-54.

35d KAYSER, C.: Gebrauch von Psalmen zur Zauberei. *ZDMG* 42 (1888),
40i   456-62.

KILPATRICK, G. D.: Ps. 90, 1-4 (LXX), *ZAW* 78 (1966), 224.

LAGARDE, P. A. DE: *LXX Studien I* (Göttingen, 1891), 73-92.

MARGOLIS, M. L.: Ps. lxix: 11. *ZAW* 31 (1911), 314.

24 MERCATI, G.: Sul testo ebraico del Salmo 140 (141) 1. *SeT* 5 (1901), 8-16.

24 MOZLEY, F. W.: *The Psalter of the Church: the LXX Psalms com-*
38a   *pared with the Hebrew, with various notes* (Cambridge, 1905).

23 NEGOITSA, A.: The Psalter in the Orthodox Church. *SvExÅrsb* 32 (1967), 55-68.

NOHE, A.: *Der Mailänder Psalter; seine Grundlage und Entwicklung* (Freiburg, 1936).

12 POSNER, A.: Stoischer Einfluss im LXX-Psalter. *ZAW* nF 2 (1925), 276.

36a RAHLFS, A.: *LXX-Studien II: Der Text des LXX-Psalters* (Göttingen, 1907).

31 ROSE, A.: L'influence des LXX sur la tradition chrétienne. III, Aperçu sur le Ps. 67. *Questions liturgiques et Paroissiales* 47 (1966), 11-35.

24 SCHEDL, C.: Aus dem Bache am Wege. Textkritische Bemerkungen zu Ps. cx (cix) 7. *ZAW* 73 (1961), 290-7.

SOFFER, A.: The Treatment of Anthropomorphisms and Antianthropomorphisms in the LXX of Psalms. *HUCA* 28 (1957), 85-107.

STAERK, W.: Zur Kritik der Psalmenüberschriften. *ZAW* 12 (1892), 91-151.

THACKERAY, H. ST. J.: Ps. 76 and other psalms for the feast of Tabernacles. *JTS* 15 (1914), 425-32.

31 VACCARI, A.: Il testo dei Salmi nel Commento di Teodoro Mopsuesteno. *Biblica* 23 (1942), 1-17.

35d WIKGREN, A. P.: Two ostraka of the LXX Psalter. *JNES* 5 (1946), 181-84.

(ii) *Odes & Ps. 151*

39e HOWORTH, H. H.: The Prayer of Manasses and the Book of Esther.
(i) *PSBA* 31 (1909), 89-99, 156-68.

MEARNS, J.: *The Canticles of the Christian Church* (Cambridge, 1914).

MEYER, R.: Die LXX-Fassung von Ps. cli: 1-5 als Ergebnis einer dogmatischen Korrektur. *BZAW* 105 (1967), 164-72.

40i NAU, F.: Un extrait de la Didascalie: la prière de Manasse. *ROC* 13 (1908), 134-41.

NESTLE, E.: Zum Gebet Manasses. In *LXX Studien III* (Stuttgart, 1899), 6-22, 28-35; *IV* (Stuttgart, 1903), 5-9, 23.

——: Zu den Cantica am Schluss des Psalters. *ZAW* 26 (1906), 286-7.

ROUSSEAU, O.: La plus ancienne liste de cantiques liturgiques tirés de l'écriture. *RechSR* 35 (1948), 120-3.

23 SCHNEIDER, H.: Die biblischen Oden im christlichen Altertum. *Biblica* 30 (1949), 28-65.

——: Die biblischen Oden seit dem 6. Jh. *Biblica* 30 (1949), 239-72.

——: Die biblischen Oden in Jerusalem und Konstantinopel. *Biblica* 30 (1949), 433-52.

——: Die biblischen Oden im Mittelalter. *Biblica* 30 (1949), 479-500.

——: Der Vulgata-Text der Oratio Manasse. *BZ* nF 4 (1960), 277-82.

SOLYOM, J.: Zur Überlieferung des Gebetes Manasse. *ZKG* 75 (1964), 339-46.

SPOER, H. H.: Psalm 151. *ZAW* 28 (1908), 65-8.

STRUGNELL, J.: Notes on the text and transmission of the apocryphal Psalms 151, 154 (= Syr II) and 155 (= Syr III). *HTR* 59 (1966), 257-81.

25 VOGÜE, A. DE: Un emprunt de la Règle du maître à la Prière de Manasse. *Revue d'ascétique et de mystique* 43 (1967), 200-3.

VOLZ, H.: Zur Überlieferung des Gebetes Manasses. *ZKG* 70 (1959), 293-307.

WILKINS, G.: The Prayer of Manasseh. *Hermathena* 16 (1911), 167-78.

h. (i) *Proverbs*

24   BAUMGARTNER, A. J.: *Étude critique sur l'état du texte des Proverbes d'après les principales traductions anciennes* (Leipzig, 1890).

12   GERLEMAN, G.: Religion och moral: Septuagintas Proverbiaversättning. *SvTKv* 26 (1950), 222-32.

11   ——: The LXX Proverbs as a Hellenistic document. *OTS* 8 (1950), 14-27.

——: *Studies in the LXX. III, Proverbs. LUÅ* 52, 3 (1956).

GÖTTSBERGER, J.: Miszelle zu Prv. i: 7 nach der LXX. *BZ* 2 (1904), 14.

——: Zu Prv. iii: 18b nach LXX. *BZ* 3 (1905), 139.

JÄGER, J. G.: *Observationes in Proverbiorum Salomonis versionem Alexandrinam* (1788).

KAMINKA, A.: LXX und Targum zu Proverbia. *HUCA* 8/9 (1931/2), 169-91.

LAGARDE, P. A. DE: *Anmerkungen zur griechischen Übersetzung der Proverbien* (Leipzig, 1863); & Mitteilungen I, 2 (1884), 19-26.

THACKERAY, H. ST. J.: The Poetry of the Greek Book of Proverbs. *JTS* 13 (1912), 46-66.

35b, ZUNTZ, G.: Der Antinoe Papyrus der Proverbia und das Propheto-
f   logion. *ZAW* 68 (1956), 124-84.

(ii) *Ecclesiastes*

24   BERTRAM, G.: Hebräischer und griechischer Qohelet. *ZAW* 64 (1952), 26-49.

DILLMANN, A.: *Über die griech. Übersetzung des Qoheleth. SbKPreuss AkWiss*, Berlin, 1892.

15c   GWYNN, R. M.: Notes on the vocabulary of Ecclesiastes in Greek.
(ii)   *Hermathena* 19 (1920), 115-22.

KLOSTERMANN, E.: *De libri Coheleth versione Alexandrina* (Diss. Kiel, 1892).

SALZBERGER, M.: Septuagintalübersetzung zum Buche Kohelet. *MGWJ* 22 (1873), 168-74.

(iii) *Song of Songs (Cantica)*

15c BLAKENEY, E. H.: A note on the word σιώπησις — Cant. iv: 1, 3;
(ii) vi: 6. *ET* 55 (1943/4), 138.
36g EURINGER, S.: Une leçon probablement hésychienne [Cant. vii: 1].
  RB 7 (1898), 183-92.
  KLOSTERMANN, E.: Eine alte Rollenverteilung zum Hohenliede.
  ZAW 19 (1899), 158-62.
31 SIMKE, H.: Cant. i: 7f in altchristlicher Auslegung. *TZ* 18 (1962),
  256-67.

(iv) *Job*

24 BARTON, G. A.: The Composition of Job 24-30. *JBL* 30 (1911), 66-77.
  ——: Some Critical Notes on Job. *JBL* 42 (1932), 29-32.
  ——: Some Text-critical Notes on the Elihu speeches. Job 32-37.
  JBL 43 (1924), 228.
24 BEER, G.: Textkritische Studien zum Buche Job. *ZAW* 17 (1897),
  97-122; 18 (1898), 257-86.
  BICKELL, G.: Der ursprüngliche Septuagintatext des Buches Job.
  ZKT 10 (1886), 557-64.
  DIEU, L.: Le texte de Job du Cod. Alexandrinus et ses principaux
  témoins. *Le Muséon* 31 (1912), 223-74.
  DRUCE, G. C.: An account of the μυρμηκολέων or ant-lion. *Antiqua-
  ries Journal* 3 (1923), 347-64.
  FRANKL, P. F.: Die Zusätze in der LXX zu Hiob. *MGWJ* 21 (1872),
  306-15.
29 GAILEY, J. H.: *Jerome's Latin version of Job from the Greek, cap.
  1-26. Its text character and provenience* (Diss. Princeton, 1945).
11 GARD, D. H.: *The exegetical method of the Greek translator of the
  Book of Job. JBL* monograph 8 (1952).
  Rev. Zuntz in *L'Antiquité classique* 22 (1953), 538-41.
12 ——: The Concept of Job's Character according to the Greek
  Translator of the Hebrew text. *JBL* 72 (1953), 182-6.
12 ——: The Concept of the Future Life according to the Greek Translator of the Book of Job. *JBL* 73 (1954), 137-43.
11 GEHMAN, H. S.: The Theological Approach of the Greek Translator
  of Job i-xv. *JBL* 68 (1949), 231-40.
  GERHARDT, M. I.: The ant-lion. *Vivarium* (Assen) 3 (1965), 1-23.
  GERLEMAN, G.: *Studies in the LXX. I, The Book of Job. LUÅ* 43, 2
  (1946).

Rev. Orlinsky in *JBL* 67 (1948), 381-90.

GRAETZ, H.: Das Zeitalter der griechischen Übersetzung des Buches Hiob. *MGWJ* 26 (1877), 83-91.

GRAY, G. B.: The additions in the ancient Greek version of Job. *Expos.* VIII, 19 (1920), 422-38.

GUEY, J.: Une glose pseudonumismatique incluse dans Job xlii: 11 (LXX). *BullSocFranç de Numismatique* 19 (1964), 320-31.

HOWORTH, H. H.: Job, etc. *PSBA* 33 (1910), 26-33, 53-61.

24   JEFFREY, J.: The MT and the LXX compared, with Special Reference to the Book of Job. *ET* 36 (1924/5), 70-3.

15c   KATZ, P.: Notes on the LXX: IV, ἔα δέ, 'let alone' in Job. *JTS* 47
(ii)   (1946), 168-9.

——: Notes on the LXX: V, Job xv: 2; VI, Some further passages in Job. *JTS* 48 (1947), 194-6.

24   KÖHLER, L.: Die LXX-Vorlage von Hi. xv: 28. *ZAW* 31 (1911), 155-6.

29   LAGARDE, P. A. DE: Des Hieronymus Übertragung der griechischen Übersetzung des Job. *Mitteilungen* II, 11 (Göttingen, 1887), 189-237.

24   ORLINSKY, H. M.: Job v: 8; a problem in Greek-Hebrew Methodology. *JQR* ns 25 (1934/5), 271-8.

36b   ——: Some Corruptions in the Greek Text of Job. *JQR* ns 26 (1935/6), 133-45.

24   ——: The Hebrew and Greek Texts of Job xiv: 12. *JQR* ns 28 (1937/8), 57-68.

15c   ——: ἀποβαίνω and ἐπιβαίνω in the LXX of Job. *JBL* 56 (1937),
(ii)   361-7.

4   ——: Studies in the LXX of the Book of Job; I, An analytical survey of previous studies. *HUCA* 28 (1957), 53-74.

11,   II, The character of the LXX translation, *HUCA* 29 (1958),
13,   229-71. III, On the matter of anthropomorphisms. *HUCA* 30
36a   (1959), 153-67; 32 (1961), 239-68. IV, The present state of the
24,   Greek text of Job. *HUCA* 33 (1962), 119-51. V, The Hebrew *Vorlage* of the LXX of Job: The text and the script. *HUCA* 35 (1964), 57-78; 36 (1965), 37-47 (to be completed).

24   ZIEGLER, J.: Der textkritische Wert der LXX des Buches Iob. *Miscellanea Biblica* (Rome, 1934), II, 277-96.

ZIMMERMANN, L.: The LXX appendix to Job. *The Scotist* 1960, 48-59.

i. (i) *Wisdom of Solomon*
(cp *BJHIL* 78-82)

12 BEAUCHAMP, P.: Le salut corporel des justes et la conclusion du livre de la Sagesse. *Biblica* 45 (1964), 491-526.

27 BRAUN, F-M.: Saint Jean, la Sagesse et l'histoire. *Fs. O. Cullmann = NT Supplement* 6 (1962), 123-33.

12 BÜCKERS, H.: *Die Unsterblichkeitslehre des Weisheitsbuches, ihr Ursprung und ihre Bedeutung. ATA* XIII, 4 (1938).

BURROWS, E.: Wisdom X 10. *Biblica* 20 (1939), 405-7.

35f CABANISS, A.: Wisdom xviii 14f.: an early Christmas text. *VC* 10 (1956), 97-102.

CAMPS, G. M.: Midraš sobre la história de les plagues (Ex. 7-12). In *Miscellanea B. Ubach* (Montserrat, 1953), 97-113.

12 CEUPPENS, F.: De conceptu 'sapientiae divinae' in libris didacticis Antiqui Testamenti. *Angelicum* 12 (1935), 333-45.

12 COHN, J.: Die Weltschöpfung in der Sapienz. In *Fs. J. Guttman* (Leipzig, 1915), 22-7.

12 COLOMBO, D.: Quid de vita sentiat Liber Sapientiae. *Studii Biblici Franciscani Liber Annuus* 2 (1951/2), 87-118.

——: *Doctrina de providentia divina in Libro Sapientiae* (Diss. Rome, 1953).

12, DELCOR, M.: L'immortalité de l'âme dans le livre de la Sagesse et
25 dans les documents de Qumran. *Nouvelle Revue Théologique* 77 (1955), 614-30.

12 DUBARLE, A. M.: Une source du livre de la Sagesse? *RHPhTh* 37 (1953), 425-43.

12 ——: Le péché originel dans les livres sapientiaux. *Revue Thomiste* 56 (1956), 597-619.

12 ——: La tentation diabolique dans le livre de la Sagesse (ii: 24). In: *Mélanges E. Tisserant I = SeT* 231 (1964), 187-95.

DULIÈRE, W. L.: Antinoüs et le livre de la Sagesse. *ZRGG* 11 (1959), 201-27.

31 DUMMER, J.: Epiphanius, *Ancoratus* 102, 7 und die Sap. Sal. *Klio* 43/5 (1965), 344-50.

11 DUPONT-SOMMER, A.: Les 'impies' du Livre de la Sagesse sont-ils les Épicuriens? *RHR* 111 (1935), 90-109.

12 ——: Adam 'Père du Monde' dans la Sagesse de Salomon (x: 1-2). *RHR* 119 (1939), 182-203.

12 EISING, H.: Die theologische Geschichtsbetrachtung im Weisheits-

buche. In *Fs. M. Meinertz* (Münster, 1951), 28-40.

——: Der Weisheitslehrer und die Götterbilder. *Biblica* 40 (1959), 393-408.

FELDMANN, F.: Die literarische Art von Weisheit Kap. 10-19. *Theologie und Glaube* 1 (1909), 178-184.

——: Zur Einheit des Buches der Weisheit. *BZ* 7 (1909), 140-50.

11   FICHTNER, J.: Die Stellung der Sapientia Salomonis in der Literatur- und Geistesgeschichte ihrer Zeit. *ZNW* 36 (1937), 113-32.

24   ——: Der AT-Text der Sapientia Salomonis. *ZAW* 57 (1939), 155-92.

11   FINAN, T.: Hellenistic humanism in the Book of Wisdom. *Irish Theological Quarterly* 27 (1960), 30-48.

FOCKE, F.: *Die Entstehung der Weisheit Salomonis. FRLANT* nF 5 (1913).

FREUDENTHAL, J.: What is the original language of the Wisdom of Solomon? *JQR* 3 (1891), 722-53.

15c   GÄRTNER, E.: *Komposition und Wortwahl des Buches der Weisheit*
(ii)   (Diss. Würzburg, 1912).

GEMOLL, W.: Zur Sapienta Salomonis. *Philologische Wochenschrift* 53 (1933), 108-10.

GILL, D.: The Greek sources of Wisdom xii: 3-7. *VT* 15 (1965), 383-6.

27   GRAFE, E.: Das Verhältnis der paulinischen Schriften zur Sapientia Salomonis. In *Fs. C. von Weizsäcker* (Freiburg, i.B. 1892), 251-86.

9   GRANT, R. M.: The Book of Wisdom at Alexandria. Reflections on the history of the canon and theology. *Studia Patristica* 7 (= *TU* 92, Berlin, 1966), 462-72.

26b   GRELOT, P.: Sagesse X 21 et le Targum de l'Exode. *Biblica* 42 (1961), 49-60.

12   ——: L'eschatologie de la Sagesse et les apocalypses juives. *Memorial A. Gelin* (Le Puy, 1961), 165-78.

HARRIS, J. R.: Athena Sophia and the Logos. *BJRL* 7 (1922-3), 56-72.

HEINEMANN, I.: Die griechischen Quellen des Buches der Weisheit. In his *Poseidonios' Metaphysische Schriften* 1 (1921), 136-53.

——: Synkrisis oder äussere Analogie in der Weisheit Salomonis. *TZ* 4 (1948), 241-51.

11   HEINISCH, P.: *Die griechische Philosophie im Buche Weisheit. ATA* I, 4 (1908).

12   ——: Das jüngste Gericht im Buche der Weisheit. *Theologie und Glaube* 2 (1910), 89-106.

——: Sap. viii: 19, 20. *BZ* 9 (1911), 130-41.

KUHN, G.: Beiträge zur Erklärung des Buches der Weisheit. *ZNW* 28 (1929), 334-41.

——: Exegetische und textkritische Anmerkungen zum Buche der Weisheit. *TSK* 103 (1931), 445-52.

12 LAGRANGE, M. J.: Le livre de la Sagesse: sa doctrine des fins dernières. *RB* ns 4 (1907), 85-104.

LANGE, S.: The Wisdom of Solomon and Plato. *JBL* 55 (1936), 293-302.

LARCHER, C.: *Études sur le Livre de Sagesse* (Paris, 1969).

15c LYONNET, S.: Le sens de πειράζειν en Sap. ii: 24 et la doctrine du
(ii) péché originel. *Biblica* 39 (1958), 27-36.

MACDONALD, D. B.: *The Hebrew Philosophical Genius* (Princeton, 1936), 96-127.

MARGOLIOUTH, D. S.: Was the Book of Wisdom written in Hebrew? *JRAS* ns 22 (1890), 263-97.

MARIÈS, L.: Remarques sur la forme poétique du livre de la Sagesse (i: 1-ix: 17). *RB* ns 5 (1908), 251-7.

——: Rhythmes quantitatifs dans le livre de la Sagesse. *CRAI* 1935, 104-17.

MARX, A.: An Aramaic fragment of the Wisdom of Solomon. *JBL* 40 (1921), 57-69.

11 MENZEL, P.: *Der griechische Einfluss auf Prediger und Weisheit Salomonis* (Halle, 1889).

MOHRMANN, C.: À propos de Sap. xv: 18. *VC* 6 (1952), 28-30.

MOTZO, B. R.: L'età e l'autore della Sapienza. *RicRel* 2 (1926), 39-44.

MURPHY, R. E.: To know your might is the root of immortality (Wisd. xv: 3). *CBQ* 25 (1963), 88-93.

31 NEWMAN, H. L.: The influence of the Book of Wisdom on early Christian writings. *Crozer Quarterly* 8 (1931), 361-72.

PETERS, N.: Ein hebräischer alphabetischer Psalm in der Weisheit Salomonis Kap. ix. *BZ* 14 (1917), 1-14.

PFLAUM, H. G.: Les sodales Antoniniani. *CRAI* 1962, 118-21.

25 PHILONENKO, M.: Le maître de justice de la Sagesse de Salomon. *TZ* 14 (1958), 81-8.

PLACES, E. DES: Un emprunt de la Sagesse aux Lois de Platon. *Biblica* 40 (1959), 1016-7.

11 ——: Le livre de la Sagesse et les influences grecques. *Biblica* 50 (1969), 536-42.

PLANAS, F.: Como la sombra ... (Sab. v: 8-14). *Cultura Biblica* 5 (1948), 248-52.

12   PORTER, F. C.: The pre-existence of the soul in the Book of Wisdom and in Rabbinic writings. In *Fs. W. R. Harper* I (1908), 205-70 = *AJT* 12 (1908), 53-115.

16   PURINTON, C.: Translation Greek in the Wisdom of Solomon. *JBL* 47 (1928), 276-304.

REESE, J. M.: Plan and structure in the Book of Wisdom. *CBQ* 27 (1965), 371-99.

RICKEN, F.: Gab es eine hellenistische Vorlage für Weisheit 13-15? *Biblica* 49 (1968), 54-86.

36a   RISBERG, B.: Textkritische und exegetische Anmerkungen zur Weisheit Salomos. *ZAW* 33 (1913), 206-21.

ROMANIUK, C.: Liber Sapientiae qua lingua ubi scriptus est. *VD* 46 (1948), 175-80.

25,   SCAZZOCCHIO, L.: Ecclesiastico, Tobia, Sapienza di Solomone alla
39e   luce dei testi di Qumran. *RSO* 37 (1962), 199-209.
(iii)
i(ii)

12   SCHÜRER, E.: Zur Chronologie des griechischen Sirachbuches. *TLZ* 29 (1904), 558-9.

SCHÜTZ, R.: *Les idées eschatologiques du livre de la Sagesse* (Paris, 1935).

SIEBENECK, R. T.: The midrash of Wisdom x-xix. *CBQ* 22 (1960), 176-82.

SKEHAN, P. W.: *The literary relationship between the Book of Wisdom and the protocanonical Wisdom books of the OT* (Washington, 1938).

39l   ——: Isaias and the teaching of the Book of Wisdom. *CBQ* 2 (1940), 289-99.

——: The text and structure of the Book of Wisdom. *Traditio* 3 (1945), 1-12.

39g   ——: Borrowings from the Psalms in the Book of Wisdom. *CBQ* 10 (1948), 384-97.

SMITH, J.: De interpretatione Sap. xiii: 9. *VD* 27 (1949), 287-90.

SPEISER, E. A.: The Hebrew Origin of the First Part of the Book of Wisdom. *JQR* 14 (1923/4), 455-82.

STEIN, E.: Ein jüdisch-hellenistischer Midrasch über den Auszug aus Ägypten. *MGWJ* 42 (1934), 558-75.

39l   SUGGS, M. J.: Wisdom of Solomon ii: 10-v: 23: a homily based on the fourth servant song. *JBL* 76 (1957), 26-33.

12 SWEET, J. P. M.: The theory of miracles in the Wisdom of Solomon. In *Miracles*, ed. C. F. D. Moule (Cambridge, 1965), 115-26.

VANHOYE, A.: Mesure ou démesure en Sag. xii: 22? *RechSR* 50 (1962), 530-7.

TREVES, M.: Il libro della Sapienzia. *Parola del Passato* 17 (1962), 192-201.

11 VELLAS, B.: Ἡ ἐπίδρασις τῆς Ἑλληνικῆς φιλοσοφίας ἐπὶ τοῦ βιβλίου τῆς Σοφίας Σολομῶντος (Athens, 1961).

WEBER, W.: Die Composition der Weisheit Salomos. *ZWT* 47 (1904), 145-69.

12 ——: Vier Aufsätze über die Unsterblichkeit, die Seelenlehre, Heimat und Zeitalter, den Auferstehungsglauben der Weisheit Salomos. *ZWT* 48 (1905), 409-44; 51 (1909), 314-32; 53 (1911), 322-45; 54 (1912), 205-39.

12 WEISENGOFF, J. P.: The impious of Wisdom ii. *CBQ* 11 (1949), 40-65.

WRIGHT, A. G.: The structure of Wisdom 11-19. *CBQ* 27 (1965), 28-34.

——: The structure of the book of Wisdom. *Biblica* 48 (1967), 165-84.

ZENNER, J. K.: Der erste Teil des Buches der Weisheit. *ZKT* 22 (1898), 417-31.

——: (ed. H. Wiessmann): Der zweiter Teil des Buches der Weisheit. *ZKT* 35 (1911), 21-9, 449-65, 665-73.

40g ZIEGLER, J.: Zur griechischen Vorlage der Vetus Latina in der Sapientia Salomonis. In *Fs. H. Junker* (Trier, 1961), 275-91.

ZIENER, G.: *Die theologische Begriffssprache im Buche der Weisheit. Bonner biblische Beiträge* 11 (1956).

——: Die Verwendung der Schrift im Buche der Weisheit. *Trierer Theologische Zeitschrift* 66 (1957), 138-51.

27 ——: Weisheitsbuch und Johannesevangelium. *Biblica* 38 (1957), 396-418; 39 (1958), 37-60.

27 ——: Johannesevangelium und urchristliche Passafeier. *BZ* 2 (1958), 263-74 (esp. 266-70).

ZIMMERMANN, F.: The Book of Wisdom: its Language and Character. *JQR* 57 (1966), 1-27, 101-35.

(ii) *Ben Sira (Ecclesiaticus)*

(cp *BJHIL* 82-4)

AUVRAY, P.: Notes sur le prologue de l'Ecclésiastique. In *Mélanges A. Robert* (Paris, 1957), 281-7.

BRUYNE, D. DE: Le prologue, le titre et la finale de l'Ecclésiastique. *ZAW* 47 (1929), 257-63.

12   BÜCHLER, A.: Ben Sira's Conception of Sin and Atonement. *JQR* 13
(1922/3), 303-35, 461-502; 14 (1923/4), 53-83.

CADBURY, H. J.: The grandson of Ben Sira. *HTR* 48 (1955), 219-25.

DEISSMANN, A.: Zur Chronologie des griechischen Sirachbuches.
TLZ 29 (1904), 558.

DELCOR, M.: Le texte hébreu du cantique de Siracide 51, 13 et ss.
et les anciennes versions. *Textus* 6 (1968), 27-47.

12   DESEČAR, E.: *De conceptu stultitiae in libro graeco Jesu Sirach* (Diss.
Antonianum Jerusalem, 1963).

31   EBERHARTER, A.: Die 'Ekklesiastikuszitate' bei Klemens von
Alexandrien gesammelt und mit LXX und Vulgata verglichen.
Theologische Quartalschrift 93 (1911), 1-22.

——: The text of Ecclesiasticus in the quotations of Clement of
Alexandria and St. Cyprian. *Biblica* 7 (1926), 79-83.

——: Die Ecclesiastikus-Zitate in den Pseudocyprianischen Schriften. *Biblica* 7 (1926), 324-5.

FANG CHE-YONG: *De discrepantiis inter textum graecum et hebraicum
libri Ecclesiastici seu Ben Sira quarum origo sensus necnon
monumentum theologicum investigantur* (Diss. Rome, 1963).

11   ——: *Quaestiones theologicae selectae libri Sira ex comparatione textus
graeci et hebraici ortae* (Diss. Rome, 1964).

17   ——: Usus nominis divini in Sirach. *VD* 42 (1964), 153-68.

36b   HART, J. H. A.: Primitive exegesis as a factor in the corruption of
texts of scripture illustrated from the versions of Ben Sira.
JQR 15 (1902/3), 627-31.

——: Two notes on Enoch in Sir. xliv: 16: I (by C. Taylor;) II.
JTS 4 (1903), 589-90, 590-1.

——: Sirach xlviii: 17ab. *JTS* 4 (1903), 591-2.

——: The Prologue to Ecclesiasticus. *JQR* 19 (1907), 284-97.

HARTMANN, L. F.: Sirach in Hebrew and in Greek. *CBQ* 23 (1961),
443-51.

19   HOMMEL, E.: The Forms Σειραχ and Ἀκελδαμαχ as Transcriptions of
סירא and חקלדמא. *ET* 25 (1913), 285.

12   KEARNS, C.: *The expanded text of Ecclesiasticus. Its teaching on the
future life as a clue to its origin* (Diss. Rome, 1951).

15c   KILPATRICK, G. D.: Προσανοικοδομηθήσεται — Ecclus. iii: 14. *JTS*
(ii)   44 (1943), 147-8.

9   KOOLE, J. L.: Die Bibel des Ben Sira. *OTS* 14 (1965), 374-96.

KUHN, G.: Beiträge zur Erklärung des Buches Jesus Sira I. *ZAW* 47 (1929), 289-96; 48 (1930), 100-21.

LEIPOLDT, J.: Von Übersetzungen und Übersetzern. In *Fs. W. Schubart* (Leipzig, 1950), 54-63.

25, 36a   LELLA, A. DI: *The Hebrew Text of Sirach. A text critical and historical study* (The Hague, 1966).

26b   LIEBERMANN, S.: Ben Sira à la lumière de Yérouchalmi. *REJ* 97 (1934), 50-7.

MARGOLIS, M. L.: A passage in Ecclesiasticus. *ZAW* 21 (1901), 271-2.

11   MORENZ, S.: Eine weitere Spur der Weisheit Amenopes in der Bibel (Sir 33, 13). *ZäS* 84 (1959), 79-80.

NESTLE, E.: Zum Prolog des Ecclesiasticus. *ZAW* 17 (1897), 123-4.

——: Ecclus. xii: 10-11. *ET* 11 (1899), 143.

11   PAUTREL, R.: Ben Sira et le stoicisme. *RechSR* 51 (1963), 535-49.

PERLES, F.: Notes critiques sur le texte d'Ecclésiastique. *REJ* 35 (1897), 48-64.

15b (ii)   RYDEN, L.: LXX Sirach 37, 2. *Eranos* 59 (1961), 40-4.

SAUERMANN, O.: 'Auch des Job gedachte er.' Bemerkungen zu Sirach 49, 9. In *Fs. König = Wiener Beiträge zur Theologie* (1965), 119-26.

11   SCHLATTER, A.: *Das neugefundene hebr. Stück des Sirach. Der Glossator des griechischen Sirach und seine Stellung in der Geschichte der jüdischen Theologie* (Gütersloh, 1897).

SIEBENECK, R. T.: May their bones return to life! Sirach's praise of the Fathers. *CBQ* 21 (1959), 411-28.

40i   SMEND, R.: *Griechisch-syrisch-hebräischer Index zur Weisheit des Jesus Sirach* (Berlin, 1907).

27   SPICQ, C.: Le Siracide et la structure littéraire du prologue de S. Jean. In *Mémorial Lagrange* (Paris, 1950), 183-95.

12   STÖGER, A.: Der Arzt nach Jesus Sirach (38, 1-15). In *Arzt und Christus* (Salzburg, 1965), 3-11.

12   TENNANT, F. R.: The teaching of Ecclesiasticus and Wisdom on the introduction of sin and death. *JTS* 2 (1901), 207-23.

THOMAS, D. W.: The Septuagint's rendering of שנות לב טוב in Ecclus xxxiii: 13. *VT* 10 (1960), 456.

TREVES, M.: Studi su Gesù ben Sirach. *Rassegna Mensile di Israel* 22 (1956), 387-97, 464-73.

VACCARI, A.: Ecclesiastico xxxvii: 10-11 critica ed esegesi. *Estudios*

Ecclesiasticos 34 (1960), 705-13.

12 WINTER, P.: Ben Sira and the teaching of the two ways. *VT* 5 (1955), 315-8.

25 YADIN, Y.: *The Ben Sira Scroll from Masada* (Jerusalem, 1965).

15c ZIEGLER, J.: Zum Wortschatz des griechischen Sirach. *BZAW* 77
(ii) (1958), 274-87.

36f ———: Hat Lukian den griechischen Sirach rezensiert? *Biblica* 40 (1959), 210-29.

36e ———: Die hexaplarische Bearbeitung des griechischen Sirach. *BZ* nF 4 (1960), 174-85.

36e ———: Die Vokabel-Varianten der O-Rezension im griechischen Sirach. In *Hebrew and Semitic Studies presented to G. R. Driver* (Oxford, 1963), 172-90.

36a ———: Ursprüngliche Lesarten im griechischen Sirach. In *Mélanges E. Tisserant = SeT* 231 (1964), 461-87.

———: Zwei Beiträge zu Sirach. *BZ* nF 8 (1964), 277-84.

(iii) *Psalms of Solomon*

(For further literature see A. M. Denis, *Introduction aux Pseudépigraphes de l'AT* (Leiden, 1970), 60-9)

ABEL, F.-M.: Le siège de Jérusalem par Pompée. *RB* 54 (1947), 243-55. [On viii].

ABERBACH, M.: The Historical Allusions of Chapters 4, 11 and 13 of the Psalms of Solomon. *JQR* 41 (1950/1), 379-96.

ACKROYD, P. R.: *The problem of the Maccabaean Psalms, with special reference to the Psalms of Solomon* (Diss. Cambridge, 1947).

35c BAARS, W.: A new fragment of the Greek version of the Psalms of Solomon. *VT* 11 (1961), 441-4.

BEER, G.: articles in *PRE³* 16 (1905), 235-7 and *PW* I A. ii (1920), 2001-3.

36a BEGRICH, J.: Der Text der Psalmen Salomos. *ZNW* 38 (1939), 131-64.

12 BRAUN, H.: Vom Erbarmen Gottes über den Gerechten. Zur Theologie der Psalmen Salomos. *ZNW* 43 (1950-1), 1-50.

———: art. in *RGG³* 5 (1961), 1342-3.

DÖLGER, F. J.: Zum zweiten Salomonischen Psalm. Der versiegelte Halsriemen der Kriegsgefangenen. *Antike und Christentum* 1 (1929), 291-4.

FRANKENBERG, W.: *Die Datierung der Psalmen Salomos. BZAW* 1 (1896) [With retroversion into Hebrew].

Rev. Schürer in *TLZ* 22 (1897), 65-7.

FREY, J. B.: art. in *DBS* 1 (1928), 390-6.

GEBHARDT, O. VON: see 3a.

GEIGER, E. E.: *Der Psalter Salomo's herausgegeben und erklärt* (Augsburg, 1871).

GRAY, G. B.: in R. H. Charles, *Apocrypha and Pseudepigrapha of the OT*, II, 631-52.

12   GRY, L.: Le Messie des Psaumes de Salomon. *Le Muséon* ns 7 (1906), 231-48.

HILGENFELD, A.: Die Psalmen Salomo's und die Himmelfahrt des Moses, griechisch hergestellt und erklärt. *ZWT* 11 (1868), 133-68 = *Messias Judaeorum* (Leipzig, 1869), 1-33.

25   HOLM-NIELSEN, S.: Erwägungen zu dem Verhältnis zwischen den Hodajot und den Psalmen Salomos. In *Bibel und Qumran: Fs. H. Bardtke* (Berlin, 1968), 112-31.

12   JONGE, M. DE: *De toekomstverwachting in de Psalmen van Salomo* (Leiden, 1965).

KITTEL, R.: in Kautzsch, *Apokryphen und Pseudepigraphen des AT*, II, 130-48.

36a, KUHN, K. G.: *Die älteste Textgestalt der Psalmen Salomos, ins-*
40i   *besondere auf Grund der syrischen Übersetzung neu untersucht, mit einer Bearbeitung und Übersetzung der Psal. 13-17. BWAT* IV, 21 (1937).

LEVY, I.: Les 18 Bénédictions et les Psaumes de Salomon. *REJ* 32 (1896), 161-78.

MANSON, T. W.: Miscellanea Apocalyptica. *JTS* 46 (1945), 41-2. [On xviii 6].

11,   O'DELL, J.: The religious background of the Psalms of Solomon
25   (re-evaluated in the light of the Qumran texts). *Revue de Qumran* 3 (1961), 241-57.

PERLES, F.: Zur Erklärung der Psalmen Salomo's. *OLZ* 5 (1902), 269-82, 335-42, 365-72 (and separately, Berlin, 1902).

39m PESCH, W.: Die Abhängigkeit des 11. Sal.Ps. vom letzten Kapitel des
(iii)   Buches Baruch. *ZAW* 67 (1955), 251-63.

RYLE, H. and JAMES, M. R.: see 3a.

25   SCHOEPS, H. J.: Habakukkommentar und Psalmen Salomos. *ZfReligions- und Geistesgeschichte* 3 (1951), 328-31.

VITEAU, J.: *Les Psaumes de Salomon* (Paris, 1911).

Rev. Perles in *OLZ* 1913, 162-5.

WELLHAUSEN, J.: *Die Pharisäer und die Sadducäer* (Greifswald, 1874,[2] 1924), 131-64 [With annotated translation].

j. *Prophetical Books (General)*

HERRMANN, J.: Die Entstehung der Propheten-LXX. Nebst Untersuchungen zum Aristeasbrief. *BZAW* nF 5 (1923), 39-52.

JEFFREY, J.: *Studies in the LXX. The Poetical works* (Edinburgh, 1927).

PROCKSCH, O.: *Studien zur Geschichte der LXX. Die Propheten.* *BWAT* 7 (1910).

    Rev. Margolis in *JQR* ns 1 (1910-11), 571-5.

    Rahlfs in *GGA* 1910, 694-705.

THACKERAY, H. ST. J.: The translators of the prophetical books. *JTS* 4 (1903), 578-85.

31   WAHL, O.: *Die Prophetenzitate der Sacra Parallela in ihrem Verhältnis zur LXX-Überlieferung* (Münster, 1965).

k. *XII Prophets*

31   ALLGEIER, A.: Der Text einiger kleiner Propheten bei Lucifer von Caliaris. In *Fs. A. Miller* (Rome, 1951), 286-300.

26b BAUMSTARK, A.: Aramäischer Einfluss im altlateinischen Text von Habakuk 3. *OC* 28 (1931), 163-81.

BÉVENOT, H.: Le Cantique d'Habacuc. *RB* 42 (1933), 499-525.

BEWER, J. A.: Critical Notes on Amos 2: 7 and 8: 4. *AJSL* 11 (1902-3), 116-7.

——: Note on Amos 2: 7a. *JBL* 28 (1909), 200-2.

——: Text critical suggestions on Hosea 12: 1, 4: 4, 8. Isa. 14: 12b. Ps. 11: 1. *JBL* 21 (1902), 108-14.

35c BOSSHARD, E.: LXX codices V, 62, and 147 in the Book of Amos. *JBL* 58 (1939), 331-47.

16   BÜCHLER, A.: אדר = Fell in LXX zu Micha ii: 8. *ZAW* 30 (1910), 64-5.

BURKITT, F. C.: The Psalm of Habakuk. *JTS* 16 (1915), 62-6.

24   DINGERMANN, F.: *Massora-LXX der kleinen Propheten. Eine textkritische Studie* (Diss. Würzburg, 1948).

FEIGIN, S.: Some Notes on Zechariah 11: 4-17. *JBL* 44 (1925), 203-213.

24 FISCHER, J.: In welcher Schrift lag das Buch Amos den LXX vor? *Theologische Quartalschrift* 106 (1925), 308-35.

GOOD, E. M.: *Text and versions of Hab. iii. A study in textual history* (Diss. Columbia, 1958).

——: The Barberini Greek Version of Hab. iii. *VT* 9 (1959), 11-30.

HAUPT, P.: The Septuagintal addition to Haggai ii: 14. *JBL* 36 (1917), 148-50.

18a HOONACKER, A. VAN: Un nom grec (ᾄδης) dans le livre de Jonas (ii: 7). *RB* ns 2 (1905), 398-9.

24 JANSMA, T.: Inquiry into the Hebrew and ancient versions of Zechariah ix-xiv. *OTS* 7 (1950), 1-142.

JOHNSON, S. E.: The LXX translators of Amos (Chicago, 1938; private edition).

25, KAHLE, P.: Die Lederrolle mit dem griech. Text der Kleinen Pro-
35c pheten und das Problem der LXX. *TLZ* 79 (1954), 81-94 = *Opera Minora* (Leiden, 1956), 113-27.

KAMINKA, A.: Studien zur LXX an der Hand der zwölf kleinen Prophetenbücher. *MGWJ* 72 (1928), 49-60, 242-73 (and separately, Frankfurt a.M., 1928).

31 LAWLOR, H. J.: Early citations from the Book of Jonah. *Journal of Philology* 25 (1897), 215-6.

32 LÜTKEMANN, L.: *De prophetarum minorum locis ab Origene laudatis* (Diss. Greifswald, 1911).

MARGOLIS, M. L.: Another Haggadic element in the LXX (Amos i: 11). *AJSL* 12 (1895/6), 267.

——: The character of the anonymous Greek version of Habakkuk 3. *AJSL* 24 (1907), 76-85, and in *OT and Semitic Studies in memory of W. R. Harper* (Chicago, 1908) I, 133-42.

——: ἡνία, χαλινός. *ZAW* 31 (1911), 314. [Nah. ii: 4].

MELAMED, E. Z.: (LXX of Micah) [In Hebrew]. *Eshcoloth* 3 (1959), 90-105.

MERCATI, G.: Osservazioni preliminari circa la versione barberiniana del Cantico di Abacuc. In *Studi in memoria di Ipp. Rossellini* (Pisa, 1955), II, 153-80.

31 MERX, A.: *Die Prophetie des Joel und ihre Ausleger von den ältesten Zeiten bis zu den Reformatoren* (Halle, 1879).

24 NYBERG, H. S.: Das textkritische Problem des ATs am Hoseabuche demonstriert. *ZAW* nF 11 (1934), 241-54.

24 ——: *Studien zum Hoseabuche. UUÅ* 6 (1935).

40g OESTERLEY, W. O. E.: *Studies in the Greek and Latin versions of the Book of Amos* (Cambridge, 1902).

24 PATTERSON, G. H.: The LXX text of Hosea compared with the Massoretic Text. *Hebraica* 7 (1889/90), 190-221.

33 PROCKSCH, O.: *Die LXX Hieronymi im Dodekapropheton* (Greifswald, 1914).

REINKE, L.: *Zur Kritik der älteren Versionen des Propheten Nahum* (Münster, 1867).

SCHUURMANS STEKHOVEN, J. Z.: *De alexandrijnsche vertaling van het Dodekapropheton* (Diss. Leiden, 1887).

25, SEGERT, S.: (LXX mss. from the Judean desert) [Czech]. *Listy*
35c *Filologické* 77 (1954), 293f; 80 (1957), 31-5.

THACKERAY, H. ST. J.: Primitive lectionary notes in the Psalm of Habakkuk. *JTS* 12 (1911), 191-213.

TREITEL, L.: Die LXX zu Hosea. *MGWJ* 41 (1897), 433-54.

——: Wert und Bedeutung der LXX zu den 12 kleinen Propheten. *MGWJ* 73 (1929), 232-4.

VELLAS, B.: Παρατηρήσεις ἐπί τινων στίχων τοῦ βιβλίου τοῦ Αμβακουμ (Athens, 1938).

VOLLERS, K.: *Das Dodekapropheton der Alexandriner*. I, Nah.-Mal. (Berlin, 1880); II, Hos.-Amos. *ZAW* 3 (1883), 219-72; III, Mic.-Jon. *ZAW* 4 (1884), 1-20.

24 ZANDSTRA, S.: *The witness of the Vulgata, Peshitta and LXX to the text of Zephaniah* (New York, 1909).

ZIEGLER, J.: *Die Einheit der LXX zum Zwölfprophetenbuch* (Braunsberg, 1934).

31 ——: Beiträge zum griechischen Dodekapropheton. I, Textkritische Notizen zu den jüngeren griechischen Übersetzungen der XII
36b Proph.; II, Innergr. und innerlat. verderbte Lesarten im XII
31 Proph.; III. Der Bibeltext des Cyrill von Alexandrien zu den XII kleinen Propheten in den Druckausgaben. *NGWGött* 1943, 345-412.

——: Bei der Ausarbeitung des Dodekapropheton für die grosse Göttinger LXX-Ausgabe. *ZAW* 60 (1944), 121-9.

24 ——: Studien zur Verwertung der LXX im Zwölfprophetenbuch. *ZAW* 60 (1944), 107-31 [107-20 = corrections to apparatus of BH³].

36a ——: Konjektur oder überlieferte Lesart. Zu Hab. ii: 5 κατοινω-μένος] κατοιομενος. *Biblica* 33 (1952), 366-70.

——: Zur Dodekapropheton-LXX. *ETL* 38 (1962), 904-6.

1. Isaiah

24   ARMSTRONG, J. F.: *A study of the alternative readings in the Hebrew text of Isaiah and their relation to the Old Greek and the Greek recensions* (Diss. Princeton, 1958).

BAUMGÄRTEL, F.: Die LXX zu Jesaja das Werk zweier Übersetzer. *BWAT* nF 5 (1923), 20-31.

BEWER, J. A.: Two Notes on Isaiah 49: 1-6. *Fs. G. A. Kohut* (New York, 1935), 86-90.

39k   ———: Textual Suggestions on Isa. 2: 6, 66: 3, Zeph. 2: 2, 5. *JBL* 27 (1908), 163-66.

BRATSIOTIS, P. I.: Ὁ Προφήτης Ἡσαΐας. Εἰσαγωγὴ, κείμενον τῶν Ο΄, μετάφρασις, σχόλια (Athens, 1956).

12,   BROCKINGTON, L. H.: The Greek translator of Isaiah and his interest
15c   in δόξα. *VT* 1 (1951), 23-32.
(ii)

COSTE, J.: Le texte grec d'Isaie xxv: 1-5. *RB* 61 (1954), 36-66.

DELEKAT, L.: *LXX und Peschitta, Eine Untersuchung zu den alten Übersetzungen des Buches Jesaja* (Diss. Heidelberg, 1956; cp *TLZ* 1956, 484).

DRIVER, G. R.: Linguistic and Textual Problems: Isa. 1-39. *JTS* 38 (1937), 36-50.

27   DUPONT, J.: τὰ ὅσια Δαυιδ τὰ πιστά (Acts xiii: 34 = Isai. lv: 3). *RB* 68 (1961), 91-114.

EULER, K. F.: *Die Verkündigung vom leidenden Gottesknecht aus Jes. liii in der griechischen Bibel. BWANT* IV, 14 (1934).

24   FISCHER, J.: LXX und Masora zu Jes. iv: 5, ix: 4(5), xlvi: 1, 2. *ZDMG* nF 7 (1928), lx.

———: *In welcher Schrift lag das Buch Isaias den LXX vor? BZAW* 56 (1930).

12   FRITSCH, C. T.: The concept of God in the Greek translation of Isaiah. In *Biblical Studies ... H. C. Alleman* (New York, 1960),155-69.

GRAY, G. B.: The Greek version of Isaiah: is it the work of a single translator? *JTS* 12 (1911), 286-93.

26   HEGERMANN, H.: *Jesaja 53 in Hexapla, Targum und Peschitta*
37a   (Gütersloh, 1954).
Rev. Lohse in *TLZ* 1955, 338-40.

HUNGER, H.: Ἑλιθήσεται ὁ οὐρανὸς ὡς βιβλίον (Isai. xxxiv 4). *Kleronomia* 2 (1969), 78-82.

HURWITZ, M. S.: The LXX of Isaiah 36-9 in Relation to that of 1-35, 40-66. *HUCA* 28 (1957), 75-83.

KATZ, P.: Notes on the LXX. I, Isaiah viii: 1a. *JTS* 47 (1946), 30-1.

KÖHLER, L.: see Genesis.

LAGARDE, P. A. DE: *Kritische Bemerkungen zum Buche Isaias.* *AbhKGWGött* 23, 2 (1898).

37a   LÜTKEMANN, L. and RAHLFS, A.: *Hexaplarische Randnoten zu Isaias i-xvi.* *MSU* 6 (1915).

12   NEVES, J. C. M. DAS: A teologia dos Setanta no livre de Isaia. *Itinerarium* 10, 43 (1964), 1-33.

ORLINSKY, H. M.: see I-II Kings.

——: The Treatment of Anthropomorphisms and Anthropopathisms in the LXX of Isaiah. *HUCA* 27 (1956), 193-200.

OTTLEY, R. R.: On the LXX of Isaiah v: 14, 17, 18. *JTS* 4 (1903), 269-70.

——: *The Book of Isaiah according to the LXX* (Codex A) (London/ Cambridge, 1904, 1906; 2 vols).

Rev. Thackeray in *JTS* 10 (1909), 299.

SHEPPARD, H. W.: Isaiah viii: 6: τοῦ Σιλωαμ. *JTS* 16 (1915), 414-6.

31   SCHOLZ, A.: *Die alexandrinische Übersetzung des Buches Jesaias* (Würzburg, 1880).

SCHLÜTZ, K.: *Isaias xi: 2 (die sieben Gaben des hl. Geistes) in den ersten vier christlichen Jahrhunderten.* *ATA* XI, 4 (1932).

SEELIGMANN, I. L.: *The LXX version of Isaiah* (Leiden, 1948).

14   STAERK, W.: Zur Exegese von Jes. 53 im Diasporajudentum. *ZNW* 35 (1936), 308.

31   STEGMÜLLER, G.: Prudentem eloquii mystici. Zur Geschichte der Auslegung von Isaias iii: 3. In *Fs. M. Schmaus* (Münster, 1967), 599-618.

24   TALMON, S.: A case of faulty harmonization. *VT* 5 (1955), 206-8.

VACCARI, A.: Πόλις ασεδεκ — Isaia xix: 18. *Biblica* 2 (1921), 353-6.

——: Parole rovesciate e critiche errate nella bibbia ebraica. In *Studi Levi della Vida* (Rome, 1956) II, 553-66.

WIESSERT, D.: Der Basilisk und das Windei in LXX Jes. lix: 5. Ein textuales und ein folkloristisches Problem. *ZAW* 79 (1967), 315-22.

WINTER, P.: Isaiah lxiii: 9 (Greek) and the Passover Haggadah. *VT* 4 (1954), 439-41.

15c   ZIEGLER, J.: *Untersuchungen zur LXX des Buches Isaias. ATA* XII,
(ii)   3 (1934).

Rev. Driver in *JTS* 36 (1935), 81-3.

Bertram in *TLZ* 1936, 176-80.

Humbert in *AfO* 10 (1935), 373-5.

37a ——: Textkritische Notizen zu den jüngeren Übersetzungen des Buches Isaias. *NGWGött* 1939, 75-102.

24, ——: Die Vorlage der Isaias-LXX und die erste Isaias-Rolle von
25 Qumran (IQIsᵃ). *JBL* 78 (1959), 34-59.

24 ZILLESSEN, A.: Bemerkungen zur alexandrinischen Übersetzung des Jesaja (c. 40-66). *ZAW* 22 (1902), 238-63.

24 ——: Die crux temporum in den griechischen Übersetzungen des Jesaja (c. 40-66) und ihren Zeugen. *ZAW* 23 (1903), 49-86.

24 ——: Jes. lii: 13-liii: 12 hebräisch nach LXX. *ZAW* 25 (1905), 261-84.

m. (i) *Jeremiah*

BEER, G.: Miscellen. *ZAW* 31 (1911), 152-4.

BURKITT, F. C.: Justin Martyr and Jer. xi: 19. *JTS* 33 (1932), 371.

DUVAL, E.: Le texte grec de Jérémie d'après une étude récente [Thackeray]. *RB* 12 (1903), 394-404.

FEIGIN, S.: The Babylonian Officials in Jeremiah 39: 3, 13. *JBL* 45 (1926), 149-55.

24 HANEMANN, G.: (LXX version of יתעל). (Jer. 50, 3) [In Hebrew]. *Leshonenu* 27/8 (1963), 179-80.

HASTOUPIS, A. P.: *The LXX text of the Book of Jeremiah ch. 1-25* (Diss. Northwestern University, 1951).

JANZEN, J. G.: Studies in the text of Jeremiah. *HTR* 59 (1966), 447 [Summary of thesis].

24 ——: Double readings in the text of Jeremiah. *HTR* 60 (1967), 433-47.

KÖHLER, L.: Kleine Beiträge zur LXX Forschung. *STZ* 26, 135-7. [Jer. v: 31].

24 ——: Beobachtungen am hebräischen und griechischen Text von Jeremia. c. I-IX. *ZAW* 29 (1909), 1-39.

MARTIN, R. A.: *The syntax of the Greek of Jeremiah* (Diss. Princeton, 1957).

RUDOLPH, W.: Zum Text des Jeremia. I, Zum griechischen Text. *ZAW* nF 7 (1930), 272-81.

24 SCHOLZ, A.: *Der masorethische Text und die LXX-Übersetzung des Buches Jeremias* (Regensburg, 1875).

24   SMITH, H. P.: Prof. Workman on the variations between the Hebrew
       and Greek text of Jeremiah. *JBL* 10 (1890), 107-17.

       SPOHN, M. G. L.: *Ieremias vates e versione Iudaeorum Alexandrino-
       rum ac reliquorum interpretum graecorum emendatus notisque
       criticis illustratus* (Leipzig, 1824; 2 vols.).

24   STREANE, A. W.: *The double text of Jeremiah (Massoretic and Alex-
       andrian) compared together with an appendix on the Old Latin
       evidence* (Cambridge, 1896).

       THACKERAY, H. ST. J.: The translators of Jeremiah. *JTS* 4 (1903),
       245-66.

       WICHELHAUS, I.: *De Jeremiae versione alexandrina* (Halle, 1847).

24   WORKMAN, G. C.: *The text of Jeremiah* (Edinburgh, 1889).

36f   YERKES, R. K.: The Lucianic version of the OT as illustrated from
       Jeremiah. *JBL* 37 (1918), 163-92.

38   ZIEGLER, J.: Die LXX Hieronymi im Buch des Propheten Jeremias
       In *Colligere fragmenta: Fs. A. Dold* (Beuron, 1952), 13-24.

31   ——: Jeremias-Zitate in Väter-Schriften. *Historisches Jahrbuch* 77
       (1958), 347-57.

15b   ——: *Beiträge zur Jeremias LXX. MSU* 6 (Göttingen, 1958).
(ii),
19,
24,
36a

(ii) *Lamentations*

BARDY, G.: Lam. Jer. iv: 20. *RechSR* 13 (1923), 166.

HASTOUPIS, A. P.: Χαρακτὴρ τῆς 'Αλεξανδρινῆς μεταφράσεως τοῦ
βιβλίου τῶν Θρήνων (Saloniki, 1962).

24   KELSO, J. A.: *Die Klagelieder. Der MT und die Versionen* (Diss.
       Leipzig, 1901).

(iii) *Baruch, Ep. Jeremiae*
(cp *BJHIL* 87-8)

ARTROM, E. S.: L'origine, la data e gli scopi dell'Epistola di Geremia. *Annuario Studi Ebraiche* 1 (1935), 49-74.

BEWER, J. A.: The river Sud in the Book of Baruch. *JBL* 42 (1923),
226-7.

DELLING, G.: *Jüdische Lehre und Frömmigkeit in den Paralipomena Jeremiae. BZAW* 100 (1967).

HARWELL, R. R.: *The principal versions of Baruch* (Diss. Yale, 1915).

HEINISCH, P.: Zur Entstehung des Buches Baruch. *Theologie und Glaube* 20 (1928), 704-10.

HERBST, A.: *Das apokryphische Buch Baruch aus dem Griechischen ins Hebräische übertragen* (Programm Hildesheim, 1886).

KALT, E.: *Das Buch Baruch übersetzt und erklärt* (Bonn, 1932).

KNEUKER, J. J.: *Das Buch Baruch* (Leipzig, 1879).

NAUMANN, W.: *Untersuchungen über den apokryphen Jeremiasbrief. BZAW* 25 (1913).

NESTLE, E.: Zum Buch Baruch; Zum Brief des Jeremias. In *LXX-Studien IV* (Stuttgart, 1903), 11-16, 16-19.

PESCH, W.: Die Abhängigkeit des 11. salomonischen Psalms vom letzten Kapitel des Buches Baruch. *ZAW* 67 (1955), 251-63.

ROCCO, B.: La μαννα di Baruch i: 10. *BibOr* 11 (1969), 273-7.

STODERL, W.: *Zur Echtheitsfrage von Baruch 1-3, 8* (Münster, 1922).

WAMBACQ, B. N.: Les prières de Baruch (i: 15-ii: 19) et de Daniel (ix: 5-19). *Biblica* 40 (1959), 463-75.

——: L'unité littéraire de Baruch i-iii: 8. *BEThL* 12 (1959), 455-60.

n. *Ezekiel*

BARNES, W. E.: see I-II Samuel.

BEWER, J. A.: On the Text of Ezechiel 7: 5-14. *JBL* 45 (1926), 223-231.

CORNILL, C. H.: *Das Buch des Propheten Ezechiel* (Leipzig, 1886). Rev. Lagarde in *GGA* 1886, 437-52.

DANIELSMEYER, W.: *Neue Untersuchungen zur Ezechiel-LXX* (Diss. Münster, 1936).

DAVIDSON, A. B.: The LXX and the MT (Ez. i: 13). *ET* 6 (1894), 283-4.

35b   FILSON, F. V.: The omission of Ezek. xii: 26-28 and xxxvi: 23b-38 in Codex 967. *JBL* 62 (1943), 27-32.

35b   GEHMAN, H. S.: The relations between the text of the John H. Scheide Papyri and that of the other Greek manuscripts of Ezekiel. *JBL* 57 (1938), 281-7.

24,   ——: The relation between the Hebrew text of Ezekiel and that of
35b   the John H. Scheide Papyri. *JAOS* 58 (1938), 92-102.

HERRMANN, J.: Die Gottesnamen im Ezechieltexte. *BWAT* 13 (1913), 70-87.

———: Die LXX zu Ezechiel das Werk dreier Übersetzer. *BWAT* nF 5 (1923), 1-19.

HIRSCHLER, G.: (The LXX translation of Ezekiel) [In Hebrew]. *Jubilee Volume in honour of B. Heller* (Budapest, 1941), 18-31.

JAHN, G.: *Das Buch Ezechiel auf Grund der LXX hergestellt, über- setzt und kritisch erklärt* (Leipzig, 1905).

36a   KATZ, P.: Zur Textgestaltung der Ezechiel-LXX. *Biblica* 35 (1954), 29-39.

11   LENNOX, R.: *The theological character of the book of Ezekiel in the LXX* (Diss. Princeton, 1947).

MARGOLIS, M. L.: Ezek. xxvii: 4. *ZAW* 31 (1911), 313-4.

31,   NEUSS, W.: *Das Buch Ezechiel in Theologie und Kunst bis zum Ende
41   des 12. Jahrh.* (Münster, 1912).

35b, PAYNE, J. B.: The relationship of the Chester Beatty Papyri of
c   Ezekiel to Codex Vaticanus. *JBL* 68 (1949), 251-65.

SCHÄFERS, J.: Ist das Buch Ezechiel in der LXX von einem oder mehreren Dolmetschern übersetzt? *Theologie und Glaube* 1 (1909), 289-91.

THACKERAY, H. ST. J.: The translators of Ezekiel. *JTS* 4 (1903), 398-411.

36f   TISSERANT, E.: Notes sur la recension lucianique d'Ézéchiel. *RB* ns 8 (1911), 384-90.

TURNER, N.: The Greek translator of Ezekiel. *JTS* ns 7 (1956), 12-24.

35c   ZIEGLER, J.: Die Bedeutung des Chester Beatty-Scheide Papyrus 967 für die Textüberlieferung der Ezechiel-LXX. *ZAW* nF 20 (1945/8), 76-94.

36a   ———: Zur Textgestaltung der Ezechiel-LXX. *Biblica* 34(1953), 435-55.

o. Daniel

ANDREWS, D. K.: The translations of the Aramaic *dî* in the Greek Bibles. *JBL* 66 (1947), 15-51.

BAUMGARTNER, W.: Susanna: die Geschichte einer Legende. *ARW* 24 (1926), 259-80 = *Zum AT und seiner Umwelt* (Leiden, 1959), 42-66.

———: Der weise Knabe und die des Ehebruchs beschuldigte Frau. *ARW* 27 (1929), 187-8 = *Zum AT und seiner Umwelt* (Leiden, 1959), 66-7.

BENJAMIN, C. D.: Collation of HP 23 (Venetus)-62-147 in Daniel from photographic copies. *JBL* 44 (1925), 303-26.

BÉVENOT, H.: Execratio vastationis. *RB* 45 (1936), 53-65.

BLUDAU, A.: *De alexandrinae interpretationis libri Danielis indole critica et hermeneutica* (Diss. Münster, 1891).

——: Die Apokalypse und Theodotions Danielübersetzung. *Theologische Quartalschrift* 79 (1897), 1-26.

24 ——: *Die alexandrinische Übersetzung des Buches Daniel und ihr Verhältnis zum MT.* (Freiburg, 1897).

DAUBNEY, W. H.: *The three additions to Daniel* (Cambridge, 1906).

26b DELCOR, M.: Un cas de traduction 'Targoumique' de la LXX à propos de la statue en or de Dan. iii. *Textus* 7 (1969), 30-5.

15c EISLER, R.: gśtj = κάστυ τοῦ γραμματέως = קסת הספר im Daniel-
(ii) kommentar des Hippolytos von Rom. *OLZ* 33 (1930), 585-7.

FORDERER, M.: Der Schild des Achilleus und der Lobgesang im Feuerofen. *Studium Generale* 8 (1955), 294-301.

36g GEHMAN, H. S.: The Hesychian influence in the versions of Daniel. *JBL* 48 (1929), 329-32.

GRELOT, P.: Les versions grecques de Daniel. *Biblica* 47 (1966), 381-402.

HELLER, B.: Die Susannaerzählung: ein Märchen. *ZAW* 54 (1936), 281-7.

39d HOWORTH, H. H.: Daniel and Chronicles. *PSBA* 29 (1907), 31-8,
(i) 61-9.

HUET, G.: Daniel et Susanne. *RHR* 65 (1912), 277-84; 76 (1917), 129f.

24 JAHN, G.: *Das Buch Daniel nach den LXX hergestellt, übersetzt und kritisch erklärt* (Leipzig, 1904).

9 JULIUS, C.: *Die griechischen Danielzusätze und ihre kanonische Geltung. Biblische Studien* VI, 3-4 (1901).

15c KATZ, P.: Πρεσβυτήριον in I Tim. iv: 14 and Susanna 50. *ZNW* 51
(ii), (1960), 27-30.
27

KUHL, C.: *Die drei Männer im Feuer. BZAW* 55 (1930).

LEVI, I.: L'histoire de Susanne et les vieillards. *REJ* 96 (1933), 157-71.

24 LÖHR, M.: Textkritische Vorarbeiten zu einer Erklärung des Buches Daniel. *ZAW* 15 (1895), 75-103, 193-225; 16 (1896), 17-39.

MACKENZIE, R. A. F.: The meaning of the Susanna Story. *Canadian Journal of Theology* 3 (1957), 211-8.

MONTGOMERY, J. A.: The 'two youths' in the LXX text to Daniel 6. *JAOS* 41 (1921), 316-7.

36e ——: Hexaplaric strata in the Greek texts of Daniel. *JBL* 44
        (1925), 289-302.
     ——: *The Book of Daniel*. I.C.C. (Edinburgh & New York, 1927),
        24-57.
34   NESTLE, E.: The song of the three holy children in Greek Bibles.
        ET 12 (1900/1), 527-8.
     ——: Zu Dan. xi: 18. *ZAW* 26 (1906), 169.
24   RIESSLER, P.: Zur Textgeschichte des Buches Daniel. *Theologische
        Quartalschrift* 79 (1897), 584-603.
16   RIFE, J. M.: *Some translation phenomena in the Greek versions of
        Daniel* (Diss. Chicago, 1931).
     SCHARFENBERG, J. G.: *Specimen animadversionum quibus loci non-
        nulli Danielis et interpretum eius veterum praesertim graecorum
        illustrantur emendantur* (Leipzig, 1774).
     SCHMIDT, N.: Daniel and Androcles. *JAOS* 46 (1926), 1-7.
     SCHMITT, A.: *Stammt der sogenannte 'Θ'-Text bei Daniel wirklich von
        Theodotion? MSU IX* (Göttingen, 1966).
     WIKGREN, A. P.: *A comparative study of the Theodotionic and LXX
        translations of Daniel* (Diss. Chicago, 1932).
40d WURMBRAND, M.: A Falasha variant of the story of Susanna.
        Biblica 44 (1963), 29-45.
31   ZIEGLER, J.: Der Bibeltext im Daniel-Kommentar des Hippolyt von
        Rom. *NGWGött* 1952, 163-99.
     ZIMMERMANN, F.: The story of Susanna and its original language.
        JQR 48 (1957/8), 236-41.
     ——: Bel and the Dragon. *VT* 8 (1958), 438-40.

40. VERSIONS

(See also 5, 10, 18, 31, 33, 35-9)

a. ARABIC

General

BAUMSTARK, A.: art. in *LTK* 2, 317-9.
DRIVER, G. R.: Supposed Arabisms in the OT. *JBL* 55 (1936), 101-
    20.
EURINGER, S.: Zum Stammbaum der arabischen Bibelhandschriften
    Vat. ar. 468 und 467. *ZfS* 7 (1929), 259-73.
GEHMAN, H. S.: The Arabic Bible in Spain. *Speculum* 1 (1926), 219-
    21.

——: The 'Polyglot' Arabic Text of Daniel and its affinities. *JBL* 44 (1925), 327-52.

GRAF, G.: Bibelübersetzungen. In: *Geschichte der christlichen arabischen Literatur* I = *SeT* 118 (1944), 85-137, 186-7.

34   HALL, I. H.: The Arabic Bible of Drs. Eli Smith and Cornelius V. A. van Dyck. [<Hebr.] *JAOS* 11 (1885), 1-11.

HENNINGER, J.: Arabische Bibelübersetzungen vom Frühmittelalter bis zum 19 Jahrhundert. *Neue Zeitschrift für Missionswissenschaft* 17 (1961), 201-33.

HYVERNAT, H.: art. 'Versions, arabes' in *DB* 1, 845-56.

KAHLE, P.: *Die arabischen Bibelübersetzungen* (Leipzig, 1904).

34   KLEINHANS, A.: De collaboratoribus franciscanis in Bibliis arabicis anno 1671 editis. *Antonianum* 4 (1929), 369-86.

34   MERCATI, G.: De versione bibliorum arabica a. 1671 edita. [<Vg.] *RB* ns 1 (1904), 250-1.

NESTLE, E.: art. in *PRE*² 3, 90-5.

PETERS, C.: Grundsätzliche Bemerkungen zur Frage der arabischen Bibeltexte. *RSO* 20 (1942), 129-43.

34   SARROUF, Th.: Περὶ τῶν ἀραβικῶν μεταφράσεων καὶ ἐκδόσεων τῆς θείας γραφῆς. In Πεντηκονταετηρὶς τῆς θεολογικῆς Σχολῆς τοῦ Σταυροῦ (Jerusalem, 1913).

34   THOMPSON, J. A.: The major Arabic Bibles. *The Bible Translator* 6 (1955), 1-12, 51-5, 98-106, 146-50.

TRITTON, A. S.: The Bible Text of Theodore Abu Kurra. *JTS* 34 (1933), 52-4.

34   VACCARI, A.: Un codice carsciunico della Casanatense e la Bibbia araba del 1671. *Biblica* 4 (1923), 96-108.

——: Una Bibbia araba per il primo Gesuita venuto al Libano. *MUSJ* 10 (1925), 79-104.

——: La storia d'una Bibbia araba. *Biblica* 11 (1930), 350-5.

Text and Concordance

3a   ANON: (Arabic Bible) (Beirut⁴, 1913).

     Rev. Torrey in *American Journal of Theology* 23 (1919), 105-7.

2   POST, G. E.: *Fihris al-kitāb al-muqaddas* [concordance] (Beirut, 1872-5).

Pentateuch

ALGERMISSEN, E.: *Die Pentateuchzitate Ibn Ḥazms. Ein Beitrag zur*

Geschichte der arabischen Bibelübersetzungen (Diss. Munich, 1933).

CHEIKHO, L.: Deux anciens manuscrits arabes du Pentateuque. *Mashriq* 21 (1923), 141-7.

DAVIDSON, H. S.: *De Lagardes Ausgabe der arabischen Übersetzung der Genesis (Cod. Leid. arab. 230) nachgeprüft* (Leipziger semit. Studien 3, 5; Leipzig, 1908).

EDELMANN, R.: (Features in Arabic translations of the Pentateuch) [Hebrew]. *Melilah* 5 (1955), 45-50.

HUGHES, C. J.: *De Lagardes Ausgabe der arabischen Übersetzung des Pentateuchs. Cod. Leid. arab. 377 nachgeprüft* (Leipziger semit. Studien 7, 3; Leipzig, 1920).

KÖBERT, R.: Die älteste arabische Genesisübersetzung. In: Altheim-Stiehl, *Die Araber in der Alten Welt*, II (Berlin, 1965), 333-43.

LAGARDE, P. A. DE: *Materialien zur Kritik und Geschichte des Pentateuchs*, I (Leipzig, 1867).

RHODE, J. F.: *The Arabic version of the Pentateuch in the Church of Egypt* (Diss. Catholic University, 1921; St. Louis/London, 1924). Rev. Vaccari in *Biblica* 4 (1923), 232-4.

TAESCHNER, F.: Die alttestamentlichen Bibelzitate, vor allem aus dem Pentateuch, in aṭ Ṭabarīs Kitāb ad-Dīn wad-Daula und ihre Bedeutung für die Frage nach der Echtheit dieser Schrift. *OC* 3 ser., (1934), 23-39, 277-8.

Historical Books

RÖDIGER, A.: *De origine et indole arabicae librorum V.T. historicorum interpretationis libri duo* (Halle, 1829).

Poetical books : Psalms-Sirach

BAUDISSIN, W. Graf. DE: *Translationis antiquae arabicae libri Jobi quae supersunt nunc primum edita.* [<Syh] (Leipzig, 1870) [cp also Fleischer in *ZDMG* 18 (1864), 288-91].

BAUMSTARK, A.: Der älteste erhaltene griechisch-arabische Text von Psalm 110 (109). *OC* 31 (1934), 55-66.

——: Minbar = Thron, und älteste arabische Psaltertexte. *OLZ* 46 (1943), 337-41.

COOK, S. A.: An Arabic version of the Prologue to Ecclesiasticus. *PSBA* 28 (1902), 173-84.

DÖDERLEIN, J. C.: Von arabischen Psaltern. *RBML* 2 (1778), 151-79; 4 (1779), 57-96.

LAGARDE, P. A. DE: *Psalmi 1-49 arabice* (Göttingen, 1875).

——: *Psalterium, Iob, Proverbia arabice* (Göttingen, 1876).

MᶜHARDY, W. D.: The Arabic text of Ecclesiasticus in the Bodleian ms. Hunt. 260. *JTS* 46 (1945), 39-41.

MITTWOCH, E.: Aus einer arabischen Übersetzung und Erklärung der Psalmen. *ZAW* 23 (1903), 87-93 [<Hebrew].

PETERS, C.: Arabische Psalmenzitate bei Abū Nu'aim. *Biblica* 20 (1939), 1-9.

34   SAYDON, P.: The origin of the 'Polyglot' Arabic Psalms [<Bohairic]. *Biblica* 31 (1950), 226-36.

VIOLET, B.: Ein zweisprachiges Psalmenfragment aus Damascus. *OLZ* 4 (1901), 384-403, 425-41, 475-88 (and separately, Berlin, 1902).

Prophetic Books

34   GEHMAN, H. S.: The 'Polyglot' Arabic of Daniel and its affinities. *JBL* 44 (1925), 327-52.

LÖFGREN, O.: *Studien zu den arabischen Danielübersetzungen mit besonderer Berücksichtigung der christlicher Texte. Nebst einem Beitrag zur Kritik des Peschittatextes* (UUÅ 1936: 4; Uppsala, 1936).

34   RYSSEL, V.: Die arabische Übersetzung des Micha in der Pariser und Londoner Polyglotte. *ZAW* 5 (1885), 102-38.

VACCARI, A.: Le versioni arabe dei Profeti. *Biblica* 1 (1920), 266-8; 2 (1921), 401-23; 3 (1922), 401-23.

b. ARMENIAN

General

ABEGHIAN, A.: *Vorfragen zur Entstehungsgeschichte der altarmenischen Bibelübersetzungen* (Marburg, 1906).

AKINIAN, N.: Zur 1500 Jahrfeier der armenischen Bibelübersetzung [Armenian]. *HA* 49 (1935), 449-54.

——: Die Armen. Übersetzung der Hl. Schrift [Armenian]. *HA* 49 (1935), 550-63, 634-5 (German summary).

ANON: *Célébration du quinzième centenaire de la traduction armé-nienne de la bible* (Paris, 1938).

AUCHER, J.: Un aperçu sur la version arménienne de la sainte bible [Armenian]. *Pazmaveb* 1935, 253-84.

34   BERBÉRIAN, H.: Rom und Oskans armenische Bibel nach J. B. van Neercassel [Armenian]. *HA* 80 (1966), 337-52.

CONYBEARE, F. C.: art. in *HDB* 1, 151-3.

34   DER NERSESSIAN, S.: (Arsen Bagratuni as editor of the Armenian Bible) [Armenian]. *Pazmaveb* 124 (1966), 344-53.

ERMONI, V.: Étude critique sur la version arménienne de la bible. *Pazmaveb* 58 (1900), 296-302, 346-52, 406-10, 451-4.

LELOIR, L.: art. in *DBS* 6, 810-18.

LÜDTKE, W.: Der Katalog der armenischen Bibelhandschriften von S. Lazzaro. *ZNW* 17 (1916), 68-77.

LYONNET, S.: Aux origines de l'Église arménienne. La traduction de la bible et le témoignage des historiens arméniens. *RechSR* 25 (1935), 170-87.

MACLER, F.: Les traducteurs arméniens ont-ils utilisé l'hébreu? *HA* 41 (1927), 609-16 = *Monumenta armenologica* (1927), 1-4.

TER-MOVSESIAN, M.: *Istorija nerevoda Biblij na armjanskij jazyk* (St. Petersburg, 1902).

34   VEER, A. C. DE: Rome et la bible arménienne d'Uscan d'après la correspondance de J-B van Neercassel. *REByz* 16 (1958), 172-82.

Text and Concordance

ASTAUCATUREAN, T.: *Hamabarbaṙ hin ew nor ktakaranacʻ* [Concor-dance of OT and NT] (Jerusalem, 1895).

ZOHRAB, H. Y.: *Astuacašunčʻ matean hin ew nor ktakaranacʻ* [Arme-nian Bible] (Venice, 1805).

Pentateuch

MERCIER, B.: Genèse 27, 41 et Job 30, 31 dans la bible arménienne. *RechSR* 37 (1950) 292-4.

Historical Books

BÉVENOT, H.: The Armenian text of Maccabees. *JPOS* 14 (1934), 268-83.

DZOVAGAN: (Koriun and the Armenian translator of Maccabees) [Armenian]. *Sion* ns ((1935), 181-7.

——: (The old Armenian translation of Chronicles) [Armenian]. *Sion* ns 11 (1937), 109-14.

GEHMAN, H. S.: The Armenian version of I and II Kings and its affinities. *JAOS* 54 (1934), 53-9.

36e JOHNSON, B.: *Die armenische Bibelübersetzung als hexaplarischer Zeuge im 1. Samuelbuch* (Coniectanea Biblica, OT series, 2; Lund, 1968).

40i KHALATHIANTZ, G.: (An important discovery in the Library of Eǰmiacin: the Armenian translation, from the Syriac, of I-II Chron.) [Armenian]. *Ararat* 29 (1896), 311-7.

——: *Girk' Mnac'ordac'* [Chronicles] (Moscow, 1899). see *Pazmaveb* 58 (1900), 117-22, 458-60.

KOGIAN, S.: (The Armenian version of 2 Maccabees) (Vienna, 1923).

Poetical Books: Psalms-Sirach

BAUMSTARK, A.: Der armenische Psaltertext: sein Verhältnis zum syrischen der Pe. und seine Bedeutung für die LXX-Forschung. *OC* ns 12-4 (1922/4), 180-213; 3 ser., 1 (1927), 158-69, 319-33.

40g ——: Armenischer und afrikanisch-lateinischer Proverbientext. *Biblica* 35 (1954), 346-56.

DURIAN, E.: (Newly found chapters of the Old Armenian translation of Sirach). [42, 25- 46, 6; Armenian]. *Sion* ns 1 (1927), 246-50.

DZOVAGAN: (The old Armenian translation of Sirach) [Armenian]. *Sion* ns 10 (1936), 150-3.

——: (The old Armenian translation of Ecclesiastes) [Armenian]. *Sion* ns 10 (1936), 45-8.

EURINGER, S.: Ein unkanonischer Text des Hohenliedes (Cant. 8, 15-20) in der armenischen Bibel. *ZAW* 33 (1913), 272-94.

——: Das Nomen gentilicium der Braut im armenischen Hohenliede. *HA* 41 (1927), 617-24 = *Monumenta armenologica* (1927), 5-8.

40c, FELDMANN, F.: *Textkritische Materialien zum Buch der Weisheit,*
k *gesammelt aus den sahidischen, syrohexaplarischen und armenischen Übersetzungen* (Freiburg i.B., 1902).

GRIGORIAN, M.: (Das Psalterium von Gregor II, Katholikos von Aghtamar) [Armenian]. *HA* 74 (1959), 533-40.

KALANANIAN, A.: (Why did Mesrop translate Proverbs?) [Armenian]. *Banber Matenadarani* Erevan 7 (1964), 113-24.

KAMINKA, A.: Altarmenische Psalmenüberschriften. *ZAW* 22 (102), 121-8.

MERCIER, B: see Pentateuch.

OSKIAN, H.: (The first and second translations of the Song of Songs) [Armenian]. (Vienna, 1924) = *HA* 38 (1924), 215-33, 297-311, 400-18.

WILLIAMS, C. S. C.: Armenian variants in the Book of Wisdom. *JTS* ns 7 (1956), 243-6.

Prophetic books

GEHMAN, H. S.: The Armenian Version of the Book of Daniel and its Affinities. *ZAW* 48 (1930), 82-99.

c. COPTIC

General

AMÉLINEAU, E. C.: Les travaux rélatifs à l'édition de la version copte de la Bible. *Journal des Savants* ns 10 (1912), 259-71.

BÖHLIG, A.: Art. in *LTK²* 2 (1958), 392-4.

——: Untersuchungen über die koptischen Proverbientexte. (Stuttgart, 1936).

BOTTE, B.: art. in *DBS* 6, 818-25.

DRESCHER, J.: The earliest biblical concordances. *BSAC* 15 (1958-60), 62-7.

GASELEE, S.: Notes on the Coptic versions of the LXX. *JTS* 11 (1910), 246-57.

GROSSOUW, W.: De koptische bijbelvertalingen. *Studia Catholica* 9 (1933), 325-53.

GUIDI, I.: Il canone biblico della chiesa copta. *RB* 10 (1901), 161-74.

HALLOCK, F. H.: The Coptic Old Testament. *AJSL* 49 (1932/3), 325-35.

HEBBELYNCK, A.: Les versions coptes de la Bible. *Le Muséon* 16 (1897), 91-3.

HYVERNAT, H.: Étude sur les versions coptes de la Bible [lists texts published; cp Vaschalde, Till] *RB* 5 (1896), 427-33, 540-69, 6 (1897), 48-74.

JERNSTEDT, P.: Graeco-Coptica IV. Zwei Bibelzitate aus dem AT bei Schenute. *ZäS* 64 (1929), 127-8.

KAMMERER, W.: *A Coptic Bibliography* (Ann Arbor, 1950), 32-47.

KASSER, R.: Le Papyrus Bodmer III et les versions bibliques coptes. *Le Muséon* 74 (1961), 423-34.

——: Les dialectes coptes et les versions coptes bibliques. *Biblica* 46 (1965), 287-310.

——: *L'Évangile selon S. Jean et les versions coptes de la Bible.* (Neuchâtel, 1966).

LAGARDE, P. A. DE: Die koptischen HSS der göttinger Bibliothek. *AbhKGWG* 1878, 3-62.

PAYNE, J. B.: Characteristics of Coptic Bible Translation. *The Ashbury Seminarian* 5 (Wilmore, Kentucky; 1950), 64-6.

PERICOLI RIDOLFINI, F.: art. in *Enc. Catt.* 4 (1950), 511-4.

PETERSEN, T.: The biblical scholar's concern with Coptic studies. *CBQ* 23 (1961), 241-9.

ROBINSON, F.: art. in *HDB* 1, 668-73.

TILL, W. C.: Coptic and its value. *BJRL* 40 (1957), 229-58.

——: Coptic biblical texts published after Vaschalde's lists. *BJRL* 42 (1959), 220-40.

VASCHALDE, A.: Ce qui a été publié des versions coptes de la Bible. *RB* ns 16 (1919), 220-43, 513-31; 17 (1920), 91-106, 241-58; 18 (1921), 237-46; 19 (1922), 81-8, 234-58.

——: Ce qui a été publié des versions coptes de la Bible. Deuxième groupe: textes bohairiques. *Le Muséon* 43 (1930), 409-31; 45 (1932), 117-56.

——: Ce qui a été publié des versions coptes de la Bible. Troisième groupe: textes en moyen égyptien. Quatrième groupe: textes akhmimiques. *Le Muséon* 46 (1933), 299-313.

WEIGANDT, P.: Zur Geschichte der koptischen Bibelübersetzungen [on Kasser, *Biblica*, 1965]. *Biblica* 50 (1969), 80-95.

Selections

AMÉLINEAU, E. C.: Fragments de la version thébaine de l'écriture (Ancien Testament). *Recueil de Travaux* 7 (1886), 197-217; 8 (1886), 10-62; 9 (1887), 101-30; 10 (1888), 67-96, 169-81.

BOURIANT, U.: Les papyrus d'Akhmim. *Mission arch. fr. mém.* 1 (1884-9), 243-304. [Ex., Ecclus., II Macch.].

BUDGE, E. A. W.: *Coptic Biblical Texts in the dialects of Upper Egypt* (London, 1912). [Dt., Jonah; cp Hebbelynck, Schleiffer, Thompson].

CIASCA, A.: *Sacrorum Bibliorum fragmenta copto-sahidica Musei Borgiani* (Rome, 1885-1904; 3 vols), [vol. 3 = NT].

ERMAN, A.: Bruchstücke der oberägyptischen Übersetzung des AT. *NAGW* 1880, 401-40.

GILMORE, J. E. and RENOUF, P. le P.: Coptic Fragments. *PSBA* 17 (1895), 251-3. [Gen. Pss.].

HEBBELYNCK, A.: L'unité et l'âge du papyrus copte biblique Or. 7594 du B.M. *Le Muséon* 34 (1921), 71-80 [cp Budge].

HYVERNAT, H.: *Bybliothecae Pierpont Morgan codices coptici photographice expressi* (Rome, 1922) [Lev. Nu. Dt. I-II Kms. Isai.; Sahidic].

KAHLE, P.: *Bala'izah* (Oxford, 1954), I, 293-333. [Gen. Dt. Kms. Pss. Isai].

LACAU, P.: Textes de l'AT en copte sahidique. *Recueil de travaux* 23 (1901), 103-24 [Isai. Jer. Tob. Jud.].

——: Textes coptes en dialectes akhmimique et sahidique. *BIFAO* 8 (1911), 43-109 [Ex. Ecclus. Macch.].

LAGARDE, P. A. DE: Bruckstücke der koptischen Übersetzung des AT. *Abh. GGW* 24 (1879), 63-104 = Orientalia I (Göttingen, 1879/80), 63-104.

——: *Aegyptica*. (Göttingen, 1883) [Wis. Ecclus.].

LEMM, O. VON: Sahidische Bibelfragmente. *BullAcadImpérSciences* (St. Petersburg), 25 (1906).

MASPERO, G.: Fragments de la version thébaine de l'AT. *Mission arch. fr. mém.* 6 (1892-7), 1-296 [cp Gaselee].

PETERSEN, T. C.: *A collection of Papyri, Egyptian, Greek, Coptic, Arabic*. (New York, 1964) [Pss. Dan.].

SCHLEIFFER, J.: Sahidische Bibelfragmente aus dem British Museum zu London. *SbAWWien* 162: 6, 164: 6, 173: 5 (1909-14).

——: Bruchstücke der sahidischen Bibelübersetzung. *SbAWWien* 170: 1 (1912).

——: Bemerkungen zu Budge's *Coptic Biblical Texts* ... (1912) *WZKM* 28 (1914), 253-60.

STERN, L.: Zwei koptische Bibelfragmente. *ZäS* 22 (1884), 97-9. [Ex. Ps.].

THOMPSON, SIR H.: *The Coptic (Sahidic) version of certain books of the OT from a papyrus in the British Museum* (London, 1908) [Prov. Job Eccles. Cant. Wis. Ecclus.].
    Rev. Crum in *JTS* 11 (1910), 300-2.
        Schleiffer in *RSO* 9 (1921/3), 183-7.

——: *A Coptic palimpsest containing Joshua, Judges, Ruth, Judith and Esther in the Sahidic dialect* (London, 1911) [<BM Add. 17183].
  Rev. Crum in *ZDMG* 65 (1911), 853-8.
    Rösch in *OLZ* 14 (1911), 550-3.
——: *The new biblical papyri.* (Privately printed, 1913) [recollation of Budge].
TILL, W.: *Koptische Pergamente theologischen Inhalts* (Vienna, 1934).
—: Wiener Faijumica. *Le Muséon* 49 (1936), 169-217. [Jer. Pss. Dan.].
——: Sahidische Fragmente des AT. *Le Muséon* 50 (1937), 175-237.
——: Kleine koptische Bibelfragmente. *Biblica* 20 (1939), 241-63. [4 Kms. Pss. Prov.].
——: Papyrussammlung der Nationalbibliothek in Wien. Katalog der koptischen Bibelbruchstücke. Die Pergamente. *ZNW* 39 (1940), 1-57.
——: Coptic Biblical fragments in the John Rylands Library. *BJRL* 34 (1951/2), 332-58.
——: Die koptischen Ostraca der Papyrussammlung der Österr. Nationalbibliothek. *Denkschr. Öst. Ak. Wiss., phil.-hist. Kl.* 78: 1 (Vienna, 1960).
WINSTEDT, E. O.: Sahidic Biblical fragments in the Bodleian Library. *PSBA* 25 (1903), 317-25; 26 (1904), 231-21; 27 (1905), 57-64.
——: Some unpublished Sahidic fragments of the OT. *JTS* 10 (1909), 233-54.
WORRELL, W. H.: *The Coptic Manuscripts of the Freer Collection* (New York, 1923) [Pss. Job].
——: *Coptic texts in the University of Michigan Collection* (Ann Arbor, 1942) [Ruth Eccl. Cant. Gen. Jer. Bar.].
  Rev. Crum in *JTS* 44 (1943), 122-8.

Pentateuch

ANDERSSON, E.: *Ausgewählte Bemerkungen über den bohairischen Dialect im Pentateuch koptisch* (Uppsala, 1904).
ANON: *Kitāb al-muqaddas al-ʿahd al-qadīm* (Cairo, 1939) [Gen.-Ex. Coptic and Arabic.].
BROOKE, A. E.: The Bohairic version of the Pentateuch. *JTS* 3 (1902), 258-78.

——: Sahidic fragments of the OT. *JTS* 8 (1907), 67-74. [Gen. Lev. Dt.].

CRUM, W. E.: The Decalogue and Deuteronomy in Coptic. *PSBA* 25 (1903), 99-101.

FALLET, A.: *La version copte du Pentateuche.* (Paris, 1854). [Gen. 1-27].

GIAMBERARDINI, G.: Testo copto sa'idico del Gen. xxiii: 18-20; xxiv: 1-24. *Studia Or. Chr. Coll.* 7 (Cairo, 1962), 207-20.

HEDLEY, P. L.: Three Graeco-Coptic Biblical texts. *JTS* 35 (1934), 58-60. [Gen. Ex. Ps.].

KASSER, R.: *Papyrus Bodmer III: Évangile de Jean et Génèse, ch. 1-3 (boh.) CSCO* 177-8 (Louvain, 1958).

——: *Papyrus Bodmer XVI: Exode i: 1-xv: 21 en sahidique* (Cologny-Geneva, 1961).

——: *Papyrus Bodmer XVIII: Deut. i: 1-x: 7 en sahidique* (Cologny-Geneva, 1962).

LAGARDE, P. A. DE: *Der Pentateuch koptisch* [Boh.] (Leipzig, 1865).

LEFORT, L. T.: Fragments bibliques en dialecte akhmimique. *Le Muséon* 66 (1953), 1-30. [Ex.].

MUNIER, H.: Sur deux passages de la Génèse en copte sahidique. *Annales du Service* 13 (1914), 187-92.

RICCI, S. DE: The Zouche Sahidic Exodus fragment (Exodus xvi: 6-xix: 11) from the original manuscript. *PSBA* 28 (1906), 54-67.

WILKINS, D.: *Quinque libri Moysis prophetae in lingua Aegyptia. Ex manuscriptis Vaticano Parisiensi et Bodleiano descripsit ac latine vertit* (London, 1731).

Historical Books

BELLET, P.: Un fragmento de la versión sahidica de 3 Reyes iv: 11-13, 15-19. *Studia Papyrologica* 3 (1965), 70-8.

BRÜGSCH, H. K.: Memphitisch-koptische Fragmente. *ZäS* 14 (1876), 119-20. [2 Kms vi: 1-20].

——: *Der Bau des Tempels Salomos nach der koptischen Bibelversion* (Leipzig, 1877).

BURMESTER, O. H. E.: The Bohairic Pericope of III Kingdoms xviii: 36-9. *JTS* 36 (1935), 156-60.

DIEU, L.: Le texte copte sahidique des livres de Samuel. *Le Muséon* 59 (1946), 445-52.

GIRARD, L. ST. P.: Un fragment inédit du livre de Tobie (ch. i: 7b à 20a). *BIFAO* 22 (1923), 115-8.

KASSER, R.: *Papyrus Bodmer XXI: Josue, ch. 6-11 et 22-4 (copte)* (Cologny-Geneva, 1963).

LEIPOLDT, J. and VIOLET, B.: Ein saidisches Bruchstück des vierten Esrabuches. *ZäS* 41 (1904), 137-40.

PAYNE, J. B.: *A critical and comparative study of the Sahidic Coptic texts of I Samuel* (Diss. Princeton, 1949).

——: The Sahidic Coptic text of I Samuel. *JBL* 72 (1953), 51-62.

SHORE, A. F.: *Joshua i-vi and other passages in Sahidic, edited from a fourth century Sahidic codex in the Chester Beatty Library.* (Chester Beatty Monographs 9; Dublin, 1963) [same manuscript as P. Bodmer xxi].

Psalms

ADLER, C.: Notes on the Johns Hopkins and Abbott collections of Egyptian antiquities with the translation of two Coptic inscriptions by Mr. W. Max Müller. *JAOS* 15 (1895), xxxi-iv. [Ps. ii: 3-5].

BRIGHTMAN, F. E.: The Sahidic Text of the Psalter. *JTS* 2 (1901), 275-6. [on Budge].

BUDGE, E. A. W.: *The earliest known Coptic Psalter* (London, 1898).

BURMESTER, O. H. E. and DÉVAUD, E.: *Psalterii versio memphitica e recognitione Pauli de Lagarde. Réédition avec le texte copte en caractères coptes* (Louvain, 1925).

CRUM, W. E.: Un psaume en dialecte d'Akhmim. *Mém. Inst. français d'arch. or.* 67 (1934), 73-6.

IDELER, J. L.: *Psalterium coptice: ad codicum fidem recensuit, lectionis varietatem et Psalmos apocryphos sahidica dialecto conscriptos ac primum a Woidio editos adjecit* (Berlin, 1837).

KORTENBEUTEL, H. and BÖHLIG, A.: Ostrakon mit griechisch-koptischem Psalmentext. *Aegyptus* 15 (1935), 415-8.

LAGARDE, P. A. DE: *Psalterii versio memphitica. Accedunt psalterii thebani fragmenta parhamiana, proverbiorum memphiticorum fragmenta berolinensia* (Göttingen, 1875) [Latin characters; cp Burmester-Dévaud].

LIEBLEIN, J. D. C.: Thebanskkoptisk oversaettelse af Davids 89 of 90 Psalme. *Oslo ak. Forh.* 1895, no. 5.

MALLON, A.: Un manuscrit du psautier copte-bohairique. *RB* ns 4 (1907), 557-9.

MÜLLER, W.: Koptische Psalmentexte. *Forschungen und Berichte: Staatliche Museen zu Berlin* (Berlin, 1967), 88-94.

PRINCE, J. D.: Two versions of the Coptic Psalter. *JBL* 21 (1902), 92-9.

QUECKE, H.: Ein koptisch-arabische Horologion in der Bibliothek des Katharinenklosters auf dem Sinai (Cod. Sin. ar. 389). *Le Muséon* 78 (1965), 99-117.

RAHLFS, A.: *Die Berliner Handschrift des sahidischen Psalters. Abh. KGWG* IV, 4 (Göttingen, 1901).

TILL, W. and SANZ, P.: *Eine griech.-koptische Odenhandschrift. MBE* 5 (Rome, 1939).

VIAUD, G.: Le Psaume 151 dans la liturgie copte. *BIFAO* 67 (1969), 1-8.

VITTI, A.: Le varianti del Salterio boairico del Cod. Vat. Copt. 5. *Biblica* 9 (1928), 341-9.

WESSELY, K.: Sahidisch-griechische Psalmenfragmente. *SbAWWien* 155: 1 (Vienna, 1908).

——: Die griechischen Lehnwörter der sahidischen und bohairischen Psalmenversion. *Denkschr. Öst.Ak. Wiss.* 54: 3 (1910).

WORRELL, W. H.: *The Coptic Psalter in the Freer Collection* (University of Michigan Humanistic Series 10, 1; New York-London, 1916).

Proverbs

BÖHLIG, A.: *Untersuchungen über die koptischen Proverbientexte* (Stuttgart, 1936).

——: Zur Berliner achmimischen Proverbienhandschrift. *ZäS* 83 (1958), 1-3.

——: *Der achmimische Proverbientext nach ms. Berol. orient. oct. 987. Teil I: Text und Rekonstruktion der sahidischen Vorlage* (Studien zur Erforschung des christlichen Aegyptens 3; Munich, 1958).
    Rev. Lefort in *Le Muséon* 71 (1958), 198-200.

——: Zur Berliner achmimischen Proverbienhandschrift. In *Gottes ist der Orient: Fs. O. Eissfeldt* (Berlin, 1959), 40-1.

——: *Proverbien-Kodex: Die Sprüche Salomos* (Leipzig, 1963) [Facsimile; 2 vols].

BOURIANT, U.: Les Proverbes de Salomon. Version copte publiée d'après deux manuscrits faisant partie de la bibliothèque du Patriarche copte-jacobite du Caire. *Recueil de travaux* 3 (1882), 129-47.

BSCIAI, A.: *Kitāb shudhūr al-amthāl wa-hikmat Sulaiman wa-Yashu' ibn Sīrakh* (Rome, 1886). [Prov. i-xiv: 26, xxxi: 10-20 in Bohairic Arabic translation; Wis. and Ecclus. not published, *pace* title].

BURMESTER, O. H. E., and DÉVAUD, E.: *Les Proverbes de Salomon. Texte bohairique* (Vienna, 1930).

KASSER, R.: *Papyrus Bodmer VI. Livre des Proverbes. CSCO* 194-5 (Louvain, 1960).

——: Origine de quelques variantes dans la version sahidique des Proverbes. *ÉTRel* 36 (1961), 359-66.

——: The old Coptic horoscope and P. Bodmer VI. *JEA* 49 (1963), 157-60.

SOBHY, G. P.: *The Book of the Proverbs of Solomon in the Dialect of Upper Egypt* (Cairo, 1927) [republished by Worrell].

STERN, L.: Kritische Anmerkungen zu der bohairischen Übersetzung der Proverbia Salomonis. *ZäS* 20 (1882), 191-202.

WORRELL, W. H.: *The Proverbs of Solomon in Sahidic according to the Chicago manuscript* (Chicago, 1931) [first published by Sobhy].

Job

AMÉLINEAU, E. C.: La version thébaine du livre de Job. *PSBA* 9 (1886/7), 109-12.

——: The Sahidic translation of the Book of Job. *TransSBA* 9 (1893), 405-75.

CHEYNE, T. K.: The Sahidic version of the Book of Job. *PSBA* 9 (1886/7), 374.

DIEU, L.: Nouveaux fragments préhexaplaires du livre de Job en copte-sahidique. *Le Muséon* ns 13 (1912), 147-85.

PORCHER, E.: *Le livre de Job. Version copte bohairique. Patrologia Orientalis* XVIII, 2 (1924), 209-340.

TATTAM, H.: *The ancient Coptic version of Job the Just, translated into English and edited* (London, 1846).

TORTOLI, G.: Sulla versione copta del Giob in dialetto saidico col saggio di un edizione di essa. *Atti 4 Int. Congr. Orient.*, Florence 1878; I, 79-90.

——: Un nuovo codice copto del museo egiziano di Torino continente ... con versetti di vari capitoli del 'Libro di Giobbe'. *Atti, Acc. Lincei*, ser. 5, 1 (1893), 3-136.

Wisdom-Ecclesiasticus

BUCKLE, D. P.: The 17th chapter of the Book of Wisdom. A translation of the Coptic (Sahidic) version with textual and lexical notes. *Int. Journal of Apocrypha* 39 (1914), 70-2.

——: The book of the Wisdom of Solomon, with special reference to the Coptic version. *Journal Manchester Egyptian Society* (1914/5), 14-6.

——: The Bohairic lections of Wisdom from a Rylands manuscript. *JTS* 17 (1916), 78-98.

BURMESTER, O. H. E.: The Bohairic Pericopae of Wisdom and Sirach. *Biblica* 15 (1934), 451-65; 16 (1935), 25-57, 141-74.

FELDMANN: see under Armenian.

HUSSELMAN, E. M.: A palimpsest fragment from Egypt. *Studi . . . A. Calderini e R. Paribeni* (Milan, 1956), II, 453-9.

PETERS, N.: *Die sahidisch-koptische Übersetzung des Buches Ecclesiasticus auf ihren wahren Werth für die Textkritik untersucht. Biblische Studien* 3, 3 (Freiburg i.B., 1898).

TILL, W.: Die koptischen Versionen der Sapientia Salomonis. *Biblica* 36 (1955), 51-70.

Prophetic Books

'ABD AL MASIH, Y.: The Hymn of the Three Children in the Furnace *BSAC* 12 (1946/7), 1-15.

BELL, H. I. and THOMPSON, H.: A Greek-Coptic glossary to Hosea and Amos. *JEA* 11 (1925), 241-6.

BARDELLI, G.: *Daniel, copto-memphitice* (Pisa, 1849).

BOURIANT, U.: Fragments des Petits Prophètes en dialecte de Panopolis. *Recueil de Travaux* 19 (1897), 1-12.

BSCIAI, A.: *Liber Baruch prophetae* (Rome, 1870).

CHASSINAT, E.: Fragments de manuscrits coptes en dialecte fayoumic. *BIFAO* 2 (1902), 171-206 [incl. Isai.].

DEIBER, A.: Fragments coptes inédits de Jéremie. *RB* 5 (1908), 554-66 (cp 6 (1909), 158-60).

DONADONI, S.: Una pergamena saidica dei θρῆνοι di Geremia. *Archiv Orientálni* 20 (1952), 400-6.

GEHMAN, H. S.: The Sahidic and Bohairic versions of the Book of Daniel. *JBL* 46 (1927), 279-330.

GROSSOUW, W.: Un fragment sahidique d'Osée ii: 9-v: 1 (BMOr. 4717). *Le Muséon* 47 (1934), 185-204.

——: *The Coptic versions of the Minor Prophets. A contribution to the study of the LXX. MBE* 3 (Rome, 1938).

    Rev. Bertram in *OLZ* 43 (1940), 425-8.

    Ziegler in *ThRev* 39 (1940), 105f.

HEBBELYNCK, A.: Fragments inédits de la version copte d'Isaie. *Le Muséon* 32 (1913), 177-227.

KABIS, M.: Das Buch Baruch koptisch. Mitgetheilt durch H. Brügsch. *ZäS* 10 (1872), 134-6; 11 (1873), 18-21; 12 (1874), 46-9; 14 (1876), 148.

KASSER, R.: *Papyrus Bodmer XXII et Missisippi Coptic codex II : Jer. xl : 3-lii : 34; Lam., Ep. Jer., Bar. i : 1-v : 5 en sahidique* (Cologny-Geneva, 1964).

——: *Papyrus Bodmer XXIII : Esaie xlvii : 1-lvi : 24 en sahidique* (Cologny-Geneva, 1965).

KETTER, P.: Ein koptischer Text von Joel i: 5-15. *OC* ns 5 (1915), 1-9.

MALININE, M.: Fragments d'une version achmimique des Petits Prophètes. *Coptic Studies . . . W. E. Crum* (Boston, 1950) 365-415.

SCHULTE, A.: *Die koptische Übersetzung der vier Grossen Propheten untersucht* (Munich, 1892).

——: Die koptische Übersetzung der kleinen Propheten untersucht. *Theol. Quartalschrift* 76 (1894), 605-42; 77 (1895), 209-29.

TATTAM, H.: *Duodecim Prophetarum Minorum libros in lingua aegyptiaca vulgo coptica seu memphitica ex manuscripto Parisiensi descriptos et cum manuscripto J. Lee . . . collatos latine edidit* (Oxford, 1836) [facing Latin translation].

——: *Prophetae Majores in dialecto linguae aegyptiacae memphitica seu coptica* (Oxford, 1852; 2 vols.) [facing Latin translation].

——: A Coptic version of Jeremiah xx: 4. *JSacredLit.* 2 (1863), 466-7.

TILL, W.: *Die achmimische Version der zwölf kleinen Propheten (Codex Rainerianus, Wien)* (Hauniae, 1927).

    Rev. Crum in *JTS* 29 (1928), 207-11.

——: Ein sahidisches Baruchfragment. *Le Muséon* 46 (1933), 35-41.

WESSELY, K.: *Duodecim Prophetarum Minorum versionis achmimi-cae codex Rainerianus* (Leipzig, 1915).
  Rev. Spiegelberg in *OLZ* 21 (1918), 22-9.
ZIEGLER, J.: Beiträge zur koptischen Dodekapropheton-Überset-zung. *Biblica* 25 (1944), 105-42.

d. ETHIOPIC

General

ALTHEIM, F. and STIEHL, R.: Zur Chronologie der äthiopischen Bibelübersetzung; Die älteste äthiopische Bibelübersetzung. In *Die Araber in den alten Welt* V/2 (Berlin, 1969), 345-52, 353-60.
BOTTE, B.: art. in *DBS* 6, cols 825-9.
CHARLES, R. H.: art. in *HDB* 1, 791-3.
DILLMANN, A.: art. in *PRE²* 1 (1877), 203-6.
HEIDER, A.: *Die äthiopische Bibelübersetzung. Ihre Herkunft, Art, Geschichte, und ihr Wert für alt- und neutestamentliche Wissen-schaft* (Leipzig, 1902).
LANTSCHOOT, A. VAN: Abbā Salāmā, métropolite d'Éthiopie (1348-1388) et son rôle de traducteur. *Atti del Conv. Internaz. di Studi Etiopici*, 1960.
34 LÖFGREN, O.: Die äthiopische Bibelausgabe der katholischen Mis-sion [= da Bassano], mit einer Kollation des Danieltextes. *Le Monde Oriental* 23 (1929), 174-80.
  ——: The necessity of a critical edition of the Ethiopian Bible, *3rd Internat. Conference, Ethiopic Studies, Addis Ababa*, 1966.
34 NEMBRO, M. DA: Traduzioni ed edizioni della Bibbia in lingua geʿez curate dai missionari in Etiopia. *Divinitas* (Rome), 9 (1965), 141-9.
PRÄTORIUS, F.: art. in *PRE²* 3 (1897), 87-90.
RAHLFS, A.: *Über einige alttestamentliche Handschriften des Abesse-nierklosters S. Stefano zu Rom. MSU* III, 1 (Berlin, 1918).
  Rev. Tisserant in *RB* 35 (1925), 292-6.
  ——: Die äthiopische Bibelübersetzung. In *Septuaginta-Studien²* (Göttingen, 1965), 659-81.
ROSSINI, CONTI C.: Sulla versione e sulla revisione delle sacre scritture in etiopico. *ZfA* 10 (1895), 236-41.
ULLENDORFF, E.: Bible translations. In *Ethiopia and the Bible* (London, 1968), 31-72.

Texts

BASSANO, F. DA: (Old Testament in Ge'ez) (Asmara, 1922-6; 4 vols).
DILLMANN, A.: *Biblia Veteris Testamenti Aethiopica* (Leipzig, 1853-94). Vol. I, *Octateuchus* (1853); II, 1-2, *Libri Regum* (1861, 1871); V, *Libri Apocryphi* (1894).

Pentateuch/Octateuch

BOYD, O.: *The text of the Ethiopic version of the Octateuch, with special reference to the age and value of the Haversford manuscript* (Bibliotheca Abessenica 2; Leiden, 1905).
——: *The Octateuch in Ethiopic, according to the text of the Paris Codex, with the variants of five other manuscripts. I, Genesis; II, Exodus, Leviticus.* (Bibliotheca, Abessenica 3-4; Leiden/ Princeton, 1909, 1911).
CAQUOT, A.: Un texte éthiopien sur les enseignes du camp d'Israel. *Annales d'Éthiopie* 2 (1957), 246-7.
RECKENDORF, S.: Über den Werth der altäthiopischen Pentateuch-übersetzung für die Reconstruction der LXX. *ZAW* 7 (1887), 61-90.

Historical Books (Joshua-Esdras)

DAVIES, D. M.: *The Old Ethiopic Version of Second Kings* (Diss. Princeton, 1944).
GEHMAN, H. S.: The Old Ethiopic version of I Kings and its affinities. *JBL* 50 (1931), 81-114.
GRÉBAUT, S.: *Les Paralipomènes*, I-II. *Patrologia Orientalis* XXIII, 4 (1932), 521-772.
——: *La troisième livre d'Esdras (Esdras et Néhémie canoniques).* *Patrologia Orientalis* XIII, 5 (1919), 641-738.
ROUPP, N.: Die älteste äthiopische Handschrift der vier Bücher der Könige. *ZfA* 16 (1902), 296-343.

id. (Esther - Maccabees)

DUENSING, H.: Mitteilung [Esther]. *TLZ* 37 (1912), 189.
HOROVITZ, J.: Das äthiopische Maccabäerbuch [text & transl.] *ZfA* 19 (1906), 194-233.
PEREIRA, F. M. E.: Le livre d'Esther, version éthiopienne. *Patrologia Orientalis* IX, 1 (1912), 1-56.

RAHLFS, A.: Über das Fehlen der Makkabäerbücher in der äthiopischen Bibelübersetzung. *ZAW* 28 (1908), 63-4.

Poetical Books: Psalms - Sirach

AHLMARK, A. S.: Den ethiopiska översättningen av Ben Sira textkritiskt behandlad. *Le Monde Oriental* 26/7 (1932/3), 257-304.

DORN, B.: *De Psalterio aethiopico commentatio* (Leipzig, 1825).

DUENSING, H.: Mitteilung [Eth. Psalms mss]. *TLZ* 56 (1931), 143.

EURINGER, S.: *Die Auffassung des Hohenliedes bei den Abessiniern* (Leipzig, 1900).

——: 'Schöpferische Exegese' im äthiopischen Hohenliede. *Biblica* 17 (1936), 327-44, 479-500; 18 (1937), 107; 20 (1939), 27-37.

——: Ein äthiopischer Scholienkommentar zum Hohenlied. *Biblica* 18 (1937), 257-76, 369-82.

GLEAVE, H. C.: *The Ethiopic version of the Song of Songs* (London, 1951).

Rev. Schall in *OLZ* 1954, 48-51.

34   LEFÈVRE, R.: Il salterio etiopico del 1513, primato della stampa romana. *Palatino: Rivista romana di cultura* 10 (1966), 15-20.

LUDOLF, H.: *Psalterium Davidis aethiopice et latine cum duobus impressis et tribus manuscriptis codicibus diligenter collatum et emendatum* (Frankfurt, 1701).

MERCER, S. A. B.: *The Ethiopic Text of Ecclesiastes* (Boston, Mass., 1931).

Rev. Littmann in *OLZ* 1933, 373-7.

Löfgren in *Le Monde Oriental*, 1933, 334-45.

PEREIRA, F. M. E.: *Le livre de Job. Patrologia Orientalis* II, 5 (1907), 561-688.

WEISCHER, B. M.: Die äthiopischen Psalmen- und Qērlosfragmente in Erevan/Armenien. *OC* 53 (1969), 113-58.

Prophetic Books

BACHMANN, J.: *Dodekapropheton Aethiopum ... I: Der Prophet Obadia* (Halle, 1892).

——: *Der Prophet Jesaia nach der äthiopischen Bibelübersetzung. I, Der äthiopische Text; II, Der äthiopische Text in seinem Verhältnis zur LXX* (Berlin, 1893).

———: *Die Klagelieder in der äthiopischen Bibelübersetzung, auf Grund handschriftlicher Quellen, mit textkritischen Anmerkungen* (Halle, 1893).

DILLMANN, A.: Der äthiop. Text des Joel. (In Merx, *Die Prophetie des Joel* (Halle, 1879), 449-58.).

FUCHS, H. F.: *Die äthiopische Übersetzung des Propheten Micha. Edition und textkritischer Kommentar nach den Handschriften in Oxford, London, Paris, Cambridge, Wien und Frankfurt* (Bonner biblische Beiträge 28; Bonn, 1968).

KRAMER, F. O.: *Die äthiopische Übersetzung des Zacharias. Der Text zum ersten Male herausgegeben.* (Leipzig, 1898).

———: *Die äthiopische Übersetzung des Zacharias. Eine Vorstudie zur Geschichte und Kritik des LXX-Textes.* (Leipzig, 1908).

LÖFGREN, O.: *Die äthiopische Übersetzung des Propheten Daniel* (Paris, 1927).

———: *Jona, Nahum, Habakuk, Zephanja, Haggai, Sacharja und Maleachi äthiopisch, unter Zugrundlegung des Oxforder MS. Huntingdon 625 nach mehreren Handschriften herausgegeben* (Uppsala, 1930).
Rev. Littmann in *OLZ* 1933, 373-7.

PEREIRA, F. M. E.: *O livro do profeta Amós e a sua versão etiópica. Estudio literário* (Academia das sciências de Lisboa. Boletim da segunda classe, 11; Coimbra, 1917).

PRAETORIUS, F.: Das apokryphe Buch Baruch im Äthiopischen. *ZWT* 15 (1871) 230-47. [cp Sachse in *ZWT* 17 (1873), 268f].

SCHÄFERS, J.: *Die äthiopische Übersetzung des Propheten Jeremias* (Freiburg i.B., 1912).
Rev. Rahlfs in *GGA* 176 (1914), 126-8.

e. GEORGIAN

General

BLAKE, R. P.: O drevnegruzinskich versijach vetchago zavjeta. *Izvestija kavkazkago otdelenija moskovskago archeologičeskago obščestva* 6 (Tiflis, 1921), 1-40.

———: Georgian Theological Literature. *JTS* 26 (1924), 50-64.

———: Ancient Georgian versions of the Old Testament. *HTR* 19 (1926), 271-97.

———: The Athos codex of the Georgian Old Testament. *HTR* 22 (1929), 33-56.

———: Catalogue of the Georgian manuscripts in the Cambridge University Library. *HTR* 25 (1932), 207-24.

34   BROSSET, M.: Notice sur la Bible géorgienne imprimée à Moscou en 1742. *JAs* II, 2 (1828), 42-50.

DZANASHVILI, M.: (The Georgian Bible) [In Georgian; on III-IV Kms]. *Nashromebi* [Works] (Tbilisi, 1910), III, 37-70.

GOUSSEN, H.: Die georgische Bibelübersetzung, *OC* 6 (1906), 300-18.

KLUGE, T.: Die Schriften des Alten Testaments und ihre georgischen Übersetzungen. *ZAW* 31 (1911), 304-7.

———: Studien auf dem Gebiete des georgischen Bibeltextes. *OC* ns 4 (1914), 120-2.

LELOIR, L.: La version géorgienne de la Bible. *Pazmaveb* 116 (1958), 197-203.

———: art. *DBS* 6, 829-34.

MARR, N.: Ečmiadzinskie otryki drevne-gruzinskago vetchago zavjeta. *Christianskii Vostok* 2, 378-88.

———: Zamutki k sv. pisaniu drevne-arman. i dr.-gruzin. *Christianskii Vostok* 2, 163-74, 263-74; 3, 249-62; 4, 229-45.

MOLITOR, J.: Die georgische Bibelübersetzung. *OC* 37 (1953), 23-9. [mostly on NT].

———: Georgien und seine Bibel. *Trierer Theol. Zeitschrift* 62 (1953), 91-8.

———: Zur Frage der Vorlage des altgeorgischen Bibeltextes. *Bedi Karthlisa* 26/7 (1957), 23-7.

———: Zur Textgeschichte des georgischen Alten Testamentes. *Bedi Karthlisa* 32/3 (1959), 53-5 [summary of Assfalg].

PALMIERI, A.: Le versioni Giorgiane della Bibbia. *Bessarione* II, 5 (1903), 259-68, 322-7; II, 6 (1904), 72-7, 189-94.

PÄTSCH, G.: Linguistische Bermerkungen zur Textgeschichte der georgischen Bibel. *Bedi Karthlisa* 50/1 (1966), 103-10.

ŠANIDZE, Mz.: (The rendering of the Hebrew Alphabet in Georgian manuscripts of the OT) [Georgian, Russian summary]. *Enat' mecnierebis institutis šromebi ,aḡmosavluri enat'a* seria 2 (Tiflis, 1957), 157-74.

TARCHNIŠVILI, M.: *Geschichte der kirchlichen georgischen Literatur.* *SeT* 185 (Rome, 1955), 313-28.

ZORELL, F.: Ursprung und Eigenart der georgischen Bibelübersetzung. *HA* 41 (1927), 669-80 = *Monumenta armenologica* I (1927), 31-6.

———: *Grammatik zur altgeorgischen Bibelübersetzung mit Textproben und Wörterverzeichnis* (Rome, 1930).

Selections

DŽAVACHIŠVILI, J.: (Recently discovered old Georgian mss.) [Georgian]. *Bulletin (Moambe) of University of Tiflis* 2 (1922/3), 313-91 [OT texts 371-89].

KEKELIDZE, K. S.: (Hanmeti and haemeti texts) [Georgian]. *Mimomhilveli* 1 (1926), 261-7 = *Etiudebi* VIII, 357-62.

IMNIAŠVILI, I.: (Concordance) (Tiflis, 1948-   ).

MOLITOR, J.: *Monumenta Iberica Antiquiora. Textus Chanmeti et Haemeti ex inscriptionibus, S. Bibliis et Patribus. CSCO* Subs. 10 (Louvain, 1956). [pp. 5-11: Gen., Prov., Jer.].

ŠANIDZE, A.: (Cambridge Hanmeti fragments) [Georgian]. *Enimkis Moambe* 2 (Tiflis, 1937).

———: (The Hanmeti Lectionary) [Georgian; Photographic reproduction] (Tiflis, 1945).

ŠANIDZE, A.; ABULADZE, I.; IMNIAŠVILI, I.; SCHMERLING, R.: (Critical edition of Athos manuscript) [Georgian].

    I. (Gen.-Ex.) (Tiflis, 1947).

    II. (Lev., Judges, Ruth, Job, Isaiah) (Tiflis, 1948).

ŠANIDZE, Mz.: (From the lexicon of the Old Georgian language). *Bulletin (Moambe) of the Georgian Academy of Sciences* (Institute of Manuscripts) 2 (1960), 55-63 [Some words in 2 Kms.].

———: (Two Hebrew words in the text of the OT). Ibid. 4 (1962), 53-5. [In 4 Kms.].

TARCHNIŠVILI, M.: Zwei georgische Lektionarfragmente aus dem 5. und 8. Jahrhundert. *Kyrios* 6 (1942/3), 1-28; reedited in *Le Muséon* 73 (1960), 261-96.

———: *Le grand lectionnaire de l'église de Jérusalem* (5e-8e siècle). *CSCO* 188-9 (Louvain, 1959).

Pentateuch - Historical Books

ABULADZE, I.: (Some leaves of an old manuscript of the Georgian Bible). [Georgian]. T'bilisis sahelmcip'o universitetis šromebi 18 (1941), 149-59 [Numbers xxiv: 6-xxv: 14; xxvi: 45-xxvii: 18].

BLAKE, R. P.: The Georgian version of 4th Esdras from the Jerusalem manuscript [Edition and Latin translation]. *HTR* 19 (1926), 299-375.

——: The Georgian text of 4th Esdras from the Athos manuscript. *HTR* 22 (1929), 57-105.

Poetical Books

GARITTE, G.: Une édition critique du Psautier géorgien. *Bedi Karthlisa* 36/7 (1961), 12-20 [on Šanidze's edition and Sinai papyrus Psalter].

KEKELIDZE, K. S.: (Historical and cultural significance of the terminology and textual peculiarities of the oldest Georgian Psalter) [Georgian; on Sinai papyrus Psalter]. *Studies in the history of ancient Georgian Literature*: [Georgian title] 3 (Tiflis, 1955), 120-6.

——: *Commentarii in Ecclesiastem Metrophanis Metropolitae Smyrnensis* [Georgian; 180-226=text of Ecclesiastes from modern transcript of Athos manuscript]. *Monumenta Georgica. Scriptores Ecclesiastici* I (Tiflis, 1920).

ŠANIDZE, A.: *Codex paleographicus: versio Cantici Canticorum* (Tiflis, 1924).

ŠANIDZE, Mz.: *Drevnegruzinskie redakcii Psaltyri po rukopisjam X-XIII vekov* (Tiflis, 1960).

Prophetic Books

ASSFALG, G.: *Altgeorgische Übersetzungen der Propheten Amos, Micheas, Sophonias und Zacharias: Texte aus den georgischen Handschriften Jerusalem nr 7 und 11 (11. Jh.), Athos nr 1 (AD 978), Sinai nr 37 (10. Jh.)* (Diss. Munich, 1958(?)) [Summary in Molitor].

BLAKE, R. P.: Khanmeti palimpsest fragments of the Old Georgian version of Jeremiah. *HTR* 25 (1932), 225-76.

—— and BRIÈRE, M.: *The Old Georgian version of the Prophets.* Minor Prophets: *Patrologia Orientalis* XXIX 2 (1961), 263-382.
Isaiah: *Patrologia Orientalis* XXIX 3 (1962), 383-510.
Jeremiah: *Patrologia Orientalis* XXIX 4 (1962), 511-694.
Ezekiel and Daniel: *Patrologia Orientalis* XXIX 5 (1962), 695-870.
Apparatus criticus: *Patrologia Orientalis* XXX 3 (1962), 345-601.

DANÉLIA, K.: Versions géorgiennes de Prophéties de Jérémie. *Bedi Karthlisa* 48/9 (1965), 215-6.

HEDLEY, P. L.: The Georgian fragments of Jeremiah. *JTS* 34 (1933), 392-5.

IMNIAŠVILI, I.: (Jonah; text taken from 10th century lectionary) [Georgian]. *Kart'uli enis istoriuli k'restomat'ia* I (Tiflis, 1953), 134-7.

MOLITOR, J.: Spuren altsyrischer Bibelübersetzung in den Chanmeti-Palimpsesten aus Jeremias. *Bedi Karthlisa* 43/4 (1963), 99-102.

f. GOTHIC

BEBB, LL. J. M.: art. in *HDB* 4, 861-3.

18a HOPPE, O.: Några iakttagelser om hebräiska namms behandling i gotiskan. *Nordisk Tidskrift for Filologi* 6 (1884), 245-7.

36f JÜLICHER, A.: Die griechische Vorlage der gotischen Bibel. *Zf deutsches Altertum und deutsche Literatur* 52 (1910), 365-87.

KAUFFMANN, F.: Beiträge zur Quellenkritik der gotischen Bibel-übersetzung. Vorbemerkungen. I, Die alttestamentlichen Bruchstücke. *Zf deutsche Philologie* 29 (1897), 306-37.

——: Zur Textgeschichte der gotischen Bibel. *Zf deutsche Philologie* 43 (1911), 118-32.

KISCH, A.: Der Septuagintacodex des Ulfilas. *MGWJ* 22 (1873), 42-6, 85-9, 215-9.

LANGNER, E.: *Die gotischen Nehemia-Fragmente* (Spottau, 1903).

MOSSÉ, F.: Bibliographia Gotica. A bibliography of writings on the Gothic language to the end of 1949. *Medieval Studies* 12 (1950), 237-324 [esp. 257f: texts and studies; 308f: translation technique].

OHRLOFF: Die alttestamentlichen Bruchstücke der gotischen Bibel-übersetzung. *Zf deutsche Philologie* 7 (1876), 251-95.

STREITBERG, W.: *Die gotische Bibel* (Heidelberg[5], 1965). [OT: xxxi-v; OT texts: 448-55 (Neh., with Greek retroversion)].

18a TEGNER, E.: Hebreiska namms behandling i gotiskan. *Nordisk Tidskrift for Filologi* 6 (1884), 304-14.

THOMPSON, E. A.: *The Visigoths in the time of Ulfila* (Oxford, 1966). Chaps. V and VI.

g. OLD LATIN
General

ADAMS, A. W.: The Old Latin version. *The Bible Translator* 5 (1954), 101-6.

ALLGEIER, A.: Haec vetus et vulgata editio. Neue wort- und begriffsgeschichtliche Beiträge zur Bibel auf dem Tridentinum. *Biblica* 29 (1948), 353-90.

ANON: The Old Latin version of the Old Testament. *ChQR* 52 (1901), 130-56.

AYUSO MARAZUELA, T.: El problema de la primitiva Biblia de España. *Arbor* 16 (1950), 426-32.

——: Una importante colección de notas marginales de la 'Vetus Latina Hispana'. *EstBibl* 9 (1950), 329-76.

——: La Liturgia Mozárabe y su importancia para el texto bíblico de la Vetus Latina Hispana. *EstBibl* 10 (1951), 269-312.

——: Origen español del Códice Lugdunense de la Vetus Latina. *EstBibl* 12 (1953), 377-95.

——: *La Vetus Latina Hispana*. I, *Prolegomenos* (Madrid, 1953).

BLONDHEIM, D. S.: *Les parlers judéo-romains et la vetus latina. Études sur les rapports entre les traductions bibliques de langue romane des juifs au moyen âge et les anciennes versions* (Paris, 1925).
Rev. Blau in *JQR* ns 19 (1928/9), 157-82.

BOSCHERINI, S.: Sulla lingua delle primitive versioni latine dell'AT. *Atti e Memorie AccadToscanScLett* 26 (1961/2), 205-29.

BOTTE, B.: art. 'Itala' in *DBS* 4 (1948), 777-82.

——: art. 'Latines' in *DBS* (1952), 334-9.

BRUYNE, D. DE: Encore l'Itala de S. Augustin. *RHE* 28 (1927), 779-85.

——: S. Augustin reviseur de la Bible. In *Miscellanea Agostiniana* (Rome, 1931), II, 521-606.

39f ——: Argarizim (II Mach. v: 23, vi: 2). *RBibl* 30 (1921), 405-7.

——: Les citations bibliques dans le 'De Civitate Dei'. *RB* 41 (1932), 550-60.

39b ——: Gofera (Jud. vi: 11, 24; viii: 27, 32; ix: 5). *RBibl* 30 (1921) 569-71.

39a ——: Subiunctorium (Ex. xxii). *RBibl* 30 (1921), 571-2.

BURKITT, F. C.: *The Rules of Tyconius. Texts and Studies* III, 1 (Cambridge, 1894).

——: *The Old Latin and the Itala. Texts and Studies* IV, 3 (Cambridge, 1896).

——: St. Augustine's Bible and the Itala. *JTS* 11 (1910), 258-68.

——: Itala problems. In *Miscellanea ... Amelli* (Montecassino, 1920), 25-41.

CANTERA, J.: En torno a la 'Vetus Latina Hispana'. *Sefarad* 15 (1955), 171-9.

——: Origin, familias y fuentes de la Vetus Latina. *Sefarad* 22 (1962), 296-311.

36d ——: La Vetus Latina y el texto masorético. Hipótesis de una revisión de la VL a base del texto hebreo. *Sefarad* 23 (1963), 252-64.

36f ——: Puntos de contacto de la Vetus Latina con la recensión de Luciano y con otras recensiones griegas. *Sefarad* 25 (1965), 69-72.

26 ——: Puntos de contacto de la Vetus Latina con el Targum Arameo y con la Pesitta. Hipótesis de un origen targúmico de la Vetus Latina. *Sefarad* 25 (1965), 223-40.

CARMODY, F. J.: Quotations in the Latin Physiologus from Latin Bibles earlier than the Vulgata. *Classical Philology* 1 (1944), 1-8.

36c CERIANI, A. M.: Le recensioni dei LXX e la versione latina detta Itala. *RRIL* II, 19.4 (Milan, 1886).

CONYBEARE, F. C.: On some fragments of a pre-Hieronymian Latin version of the Bible. *Expos* IV, 4 (1891), 63-80, 129-41.

CORSSEN, P.: Bericht über die lateinischen Bibelübersetzungen. *Jahrbuch für Altertumswissenschaft* 101 (1899), 1-83.

34 DENK, J.: Die Italazitate in der grossen Cambridger LXX. *BZ* 4 (1906), 19.

——: Wie ich mir einen neuen Sabatier vorstelle. *BZ* 6 (1908), 337-44.

——: Einiges über die Itala-Vogelnamen asida, calab(d)rio, cauua. *BZ* 6 (1908), 344-5.

——: *Sabatier redivivus: Die altlateinische Bibel in ihrem Gesamtbestand vom 1-9. Jahrh* (Leipzig, 1914) [Specimen Ruth]. Rev. Jülicher in *TLZ* 1917, 37.

——: *Der neue Sabatier und sein wissenschaftliches Programm* (Leipzig, 1914).

ECKER, J.: *Porta Sion. Lexicon zum lateinischen Psalter (Psalterium Gallicanum) unter genauer Vergleichung der LXX und des hebräischen Textes* (Trier, 1903).

FISCHER, B.: *Vetus Latina: Die Reste der altlateinischen Bibel nach*

Petrus Sabatier neu gesammelt und herausgegeben von der Erzabtei Beuron. I/1, *Verzeichnis der Sigel für Kirchenschriftsteller* (Freiburg, 1949; ²1963). [+Ergänzungslieferungen, 1963-]. II: *Genesis* (1964) [All published of OT books to date].

FISCHER, B.: Der Bibeltext in den Ps-Augustinischen 'Solutiones quaestionum ab haereticis objectarum'. *Biblica* 23 (1942), 139-64.

——: Die Lesungen der römischen Ostervigil unter Gregor d. Grossen. In *Colligere Fragmenta: Fs. A. Dold* (Beuron, 1952), 144-59.

——: Zur Liturgie der lateinischen Handschriften von Sinai. *RBén* 74 (1964), 284-97.

FREEMAN, A.: Further studies in the Libri Carolini (II, Patristic exegesis, Mozarabic antiphons and the Vetus Latina). *Speculum* 40 (1965), 203-89.

GALBIATI, E.: Volgata e antica latina nei testi biblici del rito Ambrosiano. *Ambrosius* 31 (1955), 157-71.

GRAY, L. H.: Biblical citations in Latin Lives of Welsh and Breton Saints differing from the Vulgata. *Traditio* 8 (1952), 389-97.

KENNEDY, H. A. A.: art. 'Latin versions, The Old' in *HDB* 3, 47-62.

KÖNIG, F.: Die Bedeutung der Vetus Latina. *Saeculum* 4 (1953), 267-73).

KUSCH, H.: Die Beuroner Vetus Latina und ihre Bedeutung für die Altertumswissenschaft. *FuF* 29 (1955), 46-57.

LAGARDE, P. A. DE: *Probe einer neuen Ausgabe der lateinischen Übersetzungen des AT* (Göttingen, 1885).

LAUCHERT, F.: Zu dem biblischen Vogelnamen asida. *BZ* 8 (1910), 184.

LINKE, H.: *Studien zur Itala* (Breslau, 1889).

LOWE, E. A.: The Codex Cavensis: new light on its later history. In *Quantulacunque: Fs. K. Lake* (London, 1937), 325-32.

MATZKOW, W.: *De vocabulis quibusdam Italae et Vulgatae christianis quaestiones lexicographicae* (Berlin, 1933).

MÉCHINEAU, L.: art. 'Latines, versions de la Bible' in *DB* 4, 97-123.

MOHRMANN, C.: *Études sur le latin des chrétiens*, I-III (Rome, 1958, 1961, 1965).
   Rev. Ehrhardt in *JTS* 1959, 401-7.

MONCEAUX, P.: La Bible latine en Afrique. *REJ* 42 (1901), 129-72; 43 (1901), 15-49.

34

MÜLLER, M. M.: *Der Übergang von der griechischen zur lateinischen Sprache in der abendländischen Kirche* (Rome, 1943).

MUÑOZ IGLESIAS, S.: La 'Vetus Latina Hispana'. *EstBibl* 14 (1955), 67-71.

NESTLE, E.: In *Urtext und Übersetzungen der Bibel* (Leipzig, 1897), 86-95.

PETERS, C.: Targum und Praevulgata des Pentateuchs. *OC* 31 (1934), 49-54.

POGGEL, H.: *Die vorhieronymianischen Bibelübersetzungen* (Paderborn, 1901).

QUENTIN, H.: La prétendue Itala de St. Augustin. *RB* 36 (1927), 216-25.

RÖNSCH, H.: Sprachliche Parallelen aus dem Bereiche der Itala. *ZWT* 11 (1868), 76-108.

——: *Itala und Vulgata* (Marburg, 1869;[2] 1875).

——: Die alttestamentliche Itala in den Schriften des Cyprian. *ZfHistTheol* 1875, 86-161.

——: Studien zur Itala. *ZWT* 18 (1875), 425-36; 19 (1876), 397-414; 20 (1877), 409-16; 21 (1878), 536-8; 24 (1881), 198-204; 25 (1882), 104-9.

——: Die Italaform Istrahel. *ZWT* 26 (1883), 497-9.

——: *Collectanea philologa* (Bremen, 1891).

——: *Die ältesten lateinischen Bibelübersetzungen nach ihrem Wert für die lateinische Sprachwissenschaft* (Bremen, 1891).

SABATIER, P.: *Bibliorum Sacrorum Latinae Versiones antiquae seu Vetus Italica.* 3 vols. (Rheims, 1743-9; Paris, 1751) [Under revision. See Fischer, above].

SALMON, P.: Le texte biblique des lectionnaires mérovingiens. In *La Bibbia nell'alto Medievo* (Spoleto, 1963), 491-517.

SCHAEFER, K. T.: *Die altlateinische Bibel* (Bonn, 1957) [32 pp].

SCHILDENBERGER, J.: Arbeit an der lateinischen Bibel. *Benediktinische Monatsschrift* 17 (1935), 401-8.

——: Die Itala des hl. Augustinus. In *Colligere Fragmenta: Fs. A. Dold* (Beuron, 1952), 84-102.

SCHULZ, F.: Die biblischen Texte in der 'Collatio legum mosaicarum et romanarum'. *Studia et Documenta Historiae et Iuris* (Rome) 2 (1936), 20-43.

SIMMS, G. O.: The doublet readings in the Book of Kells. *Hermathena* 94 (1960), 103-6.

STENZEL, M.: Zur Frühgeschichte der lateinischen Bibel. *ThRev* 49 (1953), 97-103.

STRECKER, A.: Die Cena Cypriani und ihr Bibeltext. *ZWT* 54 (1912), 61-78.

STUMMER, F.: Die lateinische Bibel vor Hieronymus und das Judentum. *Theologie und Glaube* 19 (1927) 184-99.

——: *Einführung in die lateinische Bibel* (Paderborn, 1928).

——: Beiträge zur Lexikographie der lateinischen Bibel. *Biblica* 18 (1937), 23-50.

——: Vom Satzrythmus in der Bibel und in der Liturgie der lateinischen Christenheit. *Archiv für Liturgiewissenschaft* III, 2 (1954), 233-81.

SÜSS, W.: *Studien zur lateinischen Bibel*. I, *Augustins Locutiones und das Problem der lateinischen Bibelsprache. Acta et Commentari Universitatis Tartuensis* B, 29, 4 (1932).

THIELE, W.: art. 'Lateinische altkirchliche Bibelübersetzungen'. *RGG*[3], i, 1196-7.

THIELMANN, P.: *Bericht über das gesammelte handschriftliche Material zu einer kritischen Ausgabe der lateinischen Übersetzungen biblischer Bücher des Alten Testaments. SbBayAkWissMünchen* II (1899).

ULLRICH, J. B.: *De Salviani scripturae sacrae versionibus*. Programm der kgl. Studienanstalt zu Neustadt, 1893.

VACCARI, A.: *Studi critici sopra le antiche versioni latine del Vecchio Testamento* (Rome, 1914).

——: Tranelli di citazioni bibliche. In *Scritti di Erudizione e di Filologia* (Rome, 1958), II, 3-16.

——: Le citazioni del Vecchio Testamento presso Mario Vittorino. *Biblica* 42 (1961), 459-64.

——: Les traces de la Vetus Latina dans le Speculum de S. Augustin. *Studia Patristica* 4 (1961) = *TU* 79, 228-33.

WALLACH, L.: The unknown author of the Libri Carolini. Patristic exegesis, Mozarabic antiphons, and the Vetus Latina. In *Didascaliae: Studies in honor of A. M. Albareda*, ed. S. Prete (New York, 1961), 469-515.

WEIHRICH, F.: Die Bibelexcerpte *de divinis scripturis* und die Itala des Augustinus. *SbAkWissWien* ph.-hist. Kl. 129 (1893).

WUNDERER, K.: *Bruchstücke einer africanischen Bibelübersetzung in der ps. cyprianischen Schrift Exhortatio de paenitentia* (Erlangen, 1889).

ZIEGLER, L.: *Die lateinischen Bibelübersetzungen vor Hieronymus und die Itala des Augustinus* (Munich, 1879).

Selections

BELSHEIM, J.: *Palimpsestus Vindobonensis antiquissimae veteris testamenti translationis latinae fragmenta* (Christiania, 1885).

BERGER, S.: Notice sur quelques textes latins inédits de l'AT. *Notes et Extraits* 34 (1895), 119-52.

BISCHOFF, B.: Neue Materialien zum Bestand und zur Geschichte der altlateinischen Bibelübersetzungen. In *Miscellanea G. Mercati. SeT* 121 (1946), 407-36 [Num., Esdr., Dan.].

BRUYNE, D. DE: Fragments d'anciennes versions latines tirés d'un glossaire. *Bulletin du Cange* 1927, 113-20.

CLARK, C. U.: Some Itala fragments in Verona. *Transactions, Connecticut Academy of Arts and Sciences* 15 (1909), 5-18.

DOBSCHÜTZ, E. VON: A collection of Old Latin Bible quotations (Somnium Neronis). *JTS* 16 (1915), 1-27.

DOLD, A.: *Das älteste Liturgiebuch der lateinischen Kirche. TuA* 26/8 (Beuron, 1936) [Some Old Latin texts].

——: Versuchte Neu- und Erstergänzungen zu den altlateinischen Texten im Cod. Clm. 6225 der Bayerischen Staatsbibliothek. *Biblica* 37 (1956), 39-58.

LOWE, E. A.: Two new Latin liturgical fragments on Mt. Sinai. *RBén* 74 (1964), 252-83.

MERCATI, G.: *Nuove note di letteratura biblica e cristiana* (Rome, 1941), 95-126 [Isaiah], 137-34. [2 Chron.].

MOLSDORF, W.: Fragment einer altlateinischen Bibelübersetzung in der Königlichen und Universitäts-Bibliothek zu Breslau. *ZAW* 24 (1904), 240-50.

RANKE, E.: *Par palimpsestorum Wirceburgensium. Antiquissimae Veteris Testamenti versionis latinae fragmenta* (Vienna, 1871).

VERCELLONE, C.: *Variae lectiones vulgatae latinae bibliorum editionis* (Rome, 1860, 1864; 2 vols.).

VOGEL, A.: *Beiträge zur Herstellung der alten lateinischen Bibelübersetzung* (Vienna, 1868).

Octateuch

ASHBURNHAM, LORD: *Librorum Levitici et Numerorum versio antiqua Itala* (London, 1868).

AYUSO MARAZUELA, T.: Origen de códice Ottoboniano del Eptateuco. *Misc. Biblica B. Ubach* (Montserrat, 1953), 115-29.

——: *Vetus Latina Hispana. II, El Octateuco.* Introducción general y edición critica. (Madrid, 1967).

BONNARDIÈRE, A. M. LA: *Biblica Augustiniana. AT, le Deutéronome* (Paris, 1967).

BILLEN, A. V.: *The Old Latin texts of the Heptateuch* (Cambridge, 1927).

——: The Old Latin version of Judges. *JTS* 43 (1942), 140-9.

BURKITT, F. C.: The Old Latin Heptateuch [on Billen]. *JTS* 29 (1928), 140-6.

——: The text of Exodus xl: 17-19 in the Munich Palimpsest. *JTS* 29 (1928), 146-7.

CANTERA ORTIZ DE URBINA, J.: *Vetus Latina. Rut: estudio critico de la versión latina prejeronimiana del libro de Rut, según el manuscrito 31 de la Universidad de Madrid. = Textos y Estudios del Seminaro Filológico Card. Cisneros,* 4 (Madrid, 1965). Rev. Baars in *VT* 18 (1968), 125-7.

DEGERING, H. and BOECKLER, A.: *Die Quedlinburger Italafragmente.* Cassiodor-Gesellschaft, Veröffentlichungen, I. (Berlin, 1932).

DOLD, A.: Versuchte Neu- und Erstergänzungen zu den altlateinischen Texten im Cod. Clm. 6225 der Bayerischen Staatsbibliothek. *Biblica* 37 (1956), 39-58 [Exodus xxxvi: 22-xl: 32, cp Ziegler].

41 DÜNING, A.: *Ein neues Fragment der Quedlinburger Italacodex* (Quedlinburg, 1888).

FRITZSCHE, O. F.: *Fragmenta libri Judicum post Petrum Sabatier paullo auctiora* (Zürich, 1867).

GERSTINGER, H.: Zwei Fragmente einer altlateinische Übersetzung des Buches der Richter. *Mitteilungen d. VereinsKlassPhilol Wien* 6 (1929), 94-107.

MARGOLIS, M. L.: Additions to Field from the Lyons Codex of the Old Latin. *JAOS* 33 (1913), 254-8 [For Joshua i-ix].

26b MAYOR, J. E. B.: *The Latin Heptateuch* (London, 1889).

PETERS, C.: Targum und Praevulgata des Pentateuchs. *OC* III, 9 (1934), 49-54.

ROBERT, U.: *Pentateuchi versio latina antiquissima e codice Lugdunensi* (Paris, 1881).

——: *Heptateuchi partis posterioris [Dt.-Judges] versio latina antiquissima e codice Lugdunensi* (Lyon, 1900).

41 SCHUM, W: Das Quedlinburger Fragment einer illustrierten Itala. *TSK* 1876, 121-34.

VACCARI, A.: Frammenti biblici latini dall'Egitto. *Biblica* 22 (1941), 1-12. [cp PapiriSocItal 12 (1951), 98f.].

——: Note lessicali. 3, vocabulo insussistente. *Archivum Latinum Medii Aevi* 1 (1924), 185-6. [Judges v: 8].

——: Occhio al commento! A proposito di 'ipse' o 'ipsa' in Gen. iii: 15. *Colligere Fragmenta: Fs. A. Dold.* (Beuron, 1952), 34-9.

ZIEGLER, L.: *Bruchstücke einer vorhieronymianischen Übersetzung des Pentateuch aus einem Palimpseste der K. Hof- und Staatsbibliothek zu München* (Munich, 1883).

Historical Books (Samuel, Kings, Chronicles, Ezra, Nehemiah).

BAARS, W.: Einige Bemerkungen zu einem altlateinischen Text von Nehemia. *VT* 8 (1958), 425 [cp Bischoff].

BENSLY, R. L.: *The Fourth Book of Ezra. The Latin version edited from the manuscripts. Texts and Studies* III, 2 (Cambridge, 1895).

BERGER, S.: *Notice sur quelques textes latins inédits de l'AT. Notices et extraits des manuscrits de la Bibliothèque Nationale*, XXXIV, 2 (Paris, 1893).

BOER, P. A. H.: Confirmatum est cor meum. Remarks on the Old Latin text of the Song of Hannah. *OTS* 13 (1963), 173-92.

——: De griekse en oud-latijnse tekst van I Sam. ii: 10a-3. *Theologie en Praktijk* (Lochem) 23 (1963), 49-57.

——: Once again the Old Latin text of Hannah's Song. *OTS* 14 (1965), 206-13.

BONNARDIÈRE, A. M. LA: Les livres de Samuel et des Rois, les livres de Chroniques et d'Esdras dans l'œuvre de Saint Augustin. *RevÉtAugustiniennes* 2 (1956), 335-63.

——: *Biblia Augustiniana*. II, *Livres historiques* (Paris, 1960).

36f DIEU, L.: Retouches lucianiques sur quelques textes de la vieille latine (I et II Samuel). *RB* ns 16 (1919), 372-403.

DOLD, A.: Honorificatus est rex Israel. Eine bedeutungsvolle Übersetzung von 2 Sam. vi: 20 aus der altlateinischen Bibel. *Benediktinische Monatschrift* (Beuron) 22 (1946), 292-5.

——: Ein altlateinisches Zitat aus dem Canticum Annae in einer der Vita des hl. Evurtius entnommenen Oration. *Libri* 2 (1952), 50-4.

FISCHER, B.: Lukian-Lesarten in der Vetus Latina der vier Königs-
bücher. *Studia Anselmiana* 27/8 (1951), 169-77.
HAUPT, P.: *Veteris versionis antehieronymianae libri II Reg. sive
Samuelis fragmenta Vindobonensia* (Vienna, 1877).

36f HAUPERT, R. S.: *The relation of codex Vaticanus and the Lucianic
text in the Books of Kings from the viewpoint of the Old Latin and
the Ethiopic versions* (Diss. Philadelphia, 1930).
MERCATI, G.: Quattro frammenti del II dei Paralipomeni. *SeT* 95
(1941), 127-34.
VOOGD, H.: *A critical and comparative study of the Old Latin texts
of I Samuel* (Diss. Princeton, 1947).
WEBER, R.: *Les anciennes versions latines du deuxième livre des
Paralipomènes. CBL* 8 (Rome, 1945).
——: Les interpolations de Samuel dans les manuscrits de la
Vulgata. *Misc. G. Mercati* (Rome, 1946), I, 19-39.
YORK, H. C.: The Latin version of First Esdras. *AJSL* 26 (1910),
253-302.

Historical Books (Esther - Maccabees)

BELSHEIM, J.: *Libros Tobiae, Judith, Ester ... e codice Monacense*
(Trondheim, 1893).
BOGAERT, M.: Un témoin liturgique de la vieille version latine du
livre de Judith. *RBén* 77 (1967), 1-26.
34 ——: La version latine du livre de Judith dans la première Bible
d'Alcala. *RBén* 78 (1968), 7-32, 181-212.
BRUYNE, D. DE: Notes de philologie biblique. *RB* 30 (1931), 400-8
[II Macc. v: 23, vi: 2, ix: 9].
——: *Les anciennes traductions latines des Macchabées. Anecdota
Maredsolana* IV (1932).
DÖRRIE, H.: *Passio SS. Machabaeorum: die antike lateinische
Übersetzung des IV. Maccabäerbuches* (Göttingen, 1938).
EIZENHÖFER, L.: Stellen aus der Passio SS. Macchabaeorum in der
westgotisch-mozarabischen Inlatio ihres Festes. *Archiv für
Liturgiewissenschaft* 7 (1961), 416-22.
LOWE, E. A.: A sixth century Italian uncial fragment of Maccabees
and its eighth century Northumbrian copy. *Scriptorium* 16
(1962), 84-5.
MARIOTTI, S.: Vetus Latina 2 Macc. i: 33f. *GiornaleItalFilol* 20
(1967), 159f.

MERCATI, G.: Frammenti urbinati d'un'antica versione latina del libro II de' Maccabei. *RB* 11 (1902), 184-211 = *SeT* 77 (1937), 320-39.

MOLSDORF, W.: Fragment einer altlateinischen Bibelübersetzung in der Königlichen und Universitäts-Bibliothek zu Breslau. *ZAW* 24 (1904), 240-50. [II Macc.].

MOREAU, J.: Un nouveau témoin du texte latin du livre d'Esther. *La Nouvelle Clio* 3 (1951), 398.

——: Un fragment de la versio antiquissima de la traduction latine de la LXX. *CdE* 27 (1952), 319-20.

MOTZO, B.: *La versione latina di Ester secondo i LXX. Annali della Facoltà di Lettere della R. Università de Cagliari* I-II (1928). Rev. Möhle in *Gnomon* 5 (1929), 565-8.

THIELMANN, P.: *Beiträge zur Textkritik der Vulgata, insbesondere des Buches Iudith* (Speyer, 1883).

TURNER, C. H.: I Macc. vi: 59-vii: 2. *JTS* 10 (1909), 541.

VOIGT, E. E.: *The Latin versions of Judith* (Leipzig, 1925).

Psalms

ALLGEIER, A.: Ist das Psalterium iuxta Hebraeos die letzte Psalmenübersetzung des hl. Hieronymus? *Theologie und Glaube* 18 (1925), 671-87.

——: Psalmenzitate und die Frage nach der Herkunft der Libri Carolini. *Historisches Jahrbuch* 46 (1926), 333-53.

——: Das Psalterium Casinense und die abendländische Psalmenüberlieferung. *Römische Quartalschrift* 34 (1926), 28-45.

——: Der lateinische Text in der bilinguen Psalmenhandschrift no. 10 der Spitalbibliothek in Cues. *Pastor Bonus* 1927, 261-71.

36e,
37a ——: Die Hexapla in den Psalmenübersetzungen des hl. Hieronymus. *Biblica* 8 (1927), 450-63.

36e,
37a ——: Schlussbemerkungen zum Gebrauch der Hexapla bei Hieronymus. *Biblica* 8 (1927), 468-9.

——: Vergleichende Untersuchungen zum Sprachgebrauch der lateinischen Übersetzungen der Psalmen und der Evangelien. *ZAW* 46 (1928), 34-49.

——: Die Psalmenzitate in der Vulgata des NT: *Römische Quartalschrift* 36 (1928), 21-42.

——: *Die altlateinischen Psalterien. Prolegomena zu einer Text-*

geschichte der Hieronymianischen Psalmenübersetzungen (Freiburg, 1928).

Rev. Capelle in *RTAM* 1 (1929), 112-4.

    Vaccari in *Biblica* 10 (1929), 108-12.

——: *Bruchstücke eines altlateinischen Psalters aus St. Gallen.* *SbHeidAkWiss* 1928/9, 2.

——: Lehrreiche Fehler in den altlateinischen Psalterien. *BZ* 18 (1929), 271-93.

——: Der Brief an Sunnia und Fretela und seine Bedeutung für die Textherstellung der Vulgata. *Biblica* 11 (1930), 86-107.

——: Die mittelalterliche Überlieferung des Psalterium iuxta Hebraeos von Hieronymus und semitische Kentnisse im Abendland. *OC* III, 3/4 (1930), 200-31.

——: Das afrikanische Element im altspanischen Psalter. *Spanische Forschungen der Görresgesellschaft* 2 (1930), 196-228.

——: *Die Überlieferung der alten lateinischen Psalmenübersetzungen und ihre kulturgeschichtliche Bedeutung* (Freiburg, 1931).

——: Die erste Psalmenübersetzung des hl. Hieronymus und das Psalterium Romanum. *Biblica* 12 (1931), 447-82.

——: Die Psalmen in der mozarabischen Liturgie und das Psalterium von Saint Germain des Près. *Spanische Forschungen der Görresgesellschaft* 3 (1931), 179-326.

——: Zwei griechisch-lateinische Bibelhandschriften aus Cues und ihre Bedeutung für die Frage der abendländischen Septuaginta-Überlieferung. *OC* III, 10 (1935), 139-60.

ALTANER, B.: Wann schrieb Hieronymus seine Ep. 106 ad Sunniam et Fretelam de Psalterio? *VC* 4 (1950), 246-8.

AMELLI, A. M.: *Liber Psalmorum iuxta antiquissimam latinam versionem. CBL* I (Rome, 1912).

ANON: *Biblia sacra iuxta latinam vulgatam versionem.* X, *Liber Psalmorum* [Hex. Psalter] (Rome, 1953).

Rev. Vaccari in *Biblica* 36 (1955), 101-3.

AYUSO MARAZUELA, T.: El salterio latino en la actualidad. *Sefarad* 15 (1955), 395-409.

——: *Biblia Polyglotta Matritensia* VII, 21. *Vetus Latina; Psalterium Visigothicum-Mozarabicum* (Madrid, 1957).

——: El salterio de Gregorio de Elvira y la Vetus Latina Hispana. *Biblica* 40 (1959), 135-59 (= SBO 1, 1-25).

——: Un autorizado testigo en el salterio de la Vetus Latina Hispana: el pseudo-Speculum. *Estudios Ecclesiasticos* 34 (1960),

689-704.

——: *Vetus Latina Hispana. V, El Salterio. Introducción general y edición crítica* (Madrid, 1962; 3 vols).

BAKKER, A.: Note sur le Psautier de S. Augustin. *RBén* 45 (1933), 20-8.

BARON, L.: Le manuscrit latin du Sinaï. *Revue du Moyen Age Latin* 1956, 267-80.

BIELER, L.: *Psalterium Graeco-Latinum. Codex Basiliensis A VII. 3* (Amsterdam, 1960).

BONACORSI, I.: *Psalterium latinum cum graeco et hebraico comparatum* (Florence, 1914/5).

BROU, L.: Le Psautier liturgique visigothique et les éditions critiques des psautiers latins. *Hispania Sacra* 8 (1955), 337-60.

BRUYNE, D. DE: La lettre de Jérôme à Sunnia et Frétela sur le Psautier. *ZNW* 28 (1929), 1-13.

36e,   ——: La reconstitution du psautier héxaplaire latin. *RBén* 41
37a   (1929), 297-324.

——: Le problème du psautier romain. *RBén* 42 (1930), 101-26.

——: Notes sur le Psautier de S. Augustin. *RBén* 45 (1933), 20-28.

BURKITT, F. C.: Jerome's work on the Psalter. *JTS* 30 (1929), 395-7.

CAPELLE, P.: *Le texte du Psautier latin en Afrique. CBL* 4 (Rome, 1913).

——: L'élément africain dans le Psalterium Casinense'. *RBén* 32 (1920), 113-31.

——: Deux psautiers gaulois dans Cod. Aug. CCLIII. *RBén* 37 (1925). 181-223.

DOLD, A.: *Lichtbildausgabe des Stuttgarter altlateinischen Unzialpsalters (aus dem 8. Jh.; Cod. Bibl. Fol. 12 der Württ. Landesbibliothek)* (Beuron, nd).

——: *Getilgte Paulus- und Psaltmentexte. TuA* 14 (Beuron, 1928).

——: *Der Palimpsestpsalter im Codex Sangallensis 912, eine altlateinische Übersetzung des frühen 6. Jhs. TuA* 21/4 (Beuron, 1933).

——: Ein Stuttgarter altlateinischer Unzialpsalter aus dem 8. Jh. *Römische Quartalschrift* 42 (1934), 251-77.

——: Stuttgarter Fragmente eines weiteren Folchart-Psalters neben dem bisher als einmalig angenommenen der Stiftsbibliothek von St. Gallen. *ZfLandesgeschichte* 1943, 145-60.

GRIBOMONT, J. and THIBAUT, A.: Méthode et esprit des traducteurs du Psautier grec. *CBL* 13 (Rome, 1959), 51-105.

HAMANN, C. L. F.: *Canticum Moysi ex psalterio quadruplici Salomonis III episcopi* . . . (Jena, 1874).

JEANNOTTE, H.: *Le Psautier de S. Hilaire de Poitiers* (Paris, 1917).

KNAUER, G. N.: *Psalmenzitate in Augustins Konfessionen* (Göttingen, 1955).

LAGRANGE, M. J.: De quelques opinions sur l'ancien psautier latin. *RB* 41 (1932), 161-86.

LOWE, E. A.: An unknown Latin Psalter on Mt. Sinai. *Scriptorium* 9 (1955), 177-99.

———: Two other unknown Latin liturgical fragments on Mt. Sinai. *Scriptorium* 19 (1965), 3-29 [Incl. Psalter].

34   MARTIMORT, A. G.: Travaux de l'Abbaye de S. Jérôme sur les Psaumes. *Maison Dieu* 59 (1959), 167-72.

MORIN, G.: La part de St. Isidore dans la constitution du texte du psautier mozarabe. In *Miscellanea Isidoriana* (Rome, 1936), 151-63.

NOHE, A.: *Der Mailänder Psalter. Seine Grundlage und Entwicklung* (Freiburg i.B., 1936).

ONGARO, G.: Saltero veronese e revisione agostiniana. *Biblica* 35 (1954), 443-76.

PUNIET, P. DE: *Le psauteur liturgique à la lumière de la tradition chrétienne* (Paris, 1935).

QUACQUARELLI, A.: Labores fructuum. Ps. cxxviii (cxxvii) 2. *Vetera Christianorum* 1 (1964), 15-26.

SAINTE-MARIE, H. DE: *S. Hieronymi Psalterium iuxta Hebraeos. CBL* 11 (Rome, 1954).

SALMON, P. (ed.): *Richesses et déficiences des anciens Psautiers latins. CBL* 13 (Rome, 1959).
    Rev. Capelle in *RHE* 55 (1960), 492-8.

———: Le problème des Psaumes. Le texte et l'interprétation des Psaumes au temps de S. Jérôme et S. Augustin. *Ami du Clergé* 64 (1954), 162-73.

SCHNEIDER, H.: Der altlateinische Palimpsest-Psalter in Cod. Vat. Lat. 5359. *Biblica* 19 (1938), 361-82.

———: *Die altlateinischen biblischen Cantica. TuA* 29/30 (Beuron, 1938).

———: Die Psalterteilung in Fünfziger- und Zehnergruppen. In *Universitas: Fs. A. Stohr*. (Mainz, 1960) I, 36-47.

SISAM, C. and K.: *The Salisbury Psalter, edited from Salisbury Cathedral ms. 150* (London, 1959).

36e, THIBAUT, A.: La revision héxaplaire de St. Jérôme. *CBL* 13 (1959),
37a   107-49.

THOUVENOT, R.: Une citation biblique dans l'épigraphie africaine. *Atti del III Congresso Internaz. di Epigrafia* (Rome, 1959), 381-5. [Ps. xxii: 1].

VACCARI, A.: *La Grecia nell'Italia meridionale.* 7, Il Saltero Cassinese. *Orientalia Christiana* III, 3 (Rome, 1925).

——: 'Psalterium Gallicanum' e 'Psalterium iuxta Hebraeos'. *Biblica* 8 (1927), 213-5.

——: I Psalteri di S. Girolamo e di S. Agostino. In *Scritti di erudizione e di filologia* (Rome, 1952) I, 207-55.

——: S. Augustin, S. Ambroise et Aquila. In *Augustinus Magister* (1955) III, 471-82 = *Scritti di erudizione e di filologia* (Rome, 1958) II, 229-43.

——: Psalterium S. Augustini in monte Sinai repertum. *Biblica* 36 (1956), 260 = *Scritti di erudizione e di filologia* (Rome, 1958) II, 242-3.

VOLK, P.: Das Psalterium des hl. Benediktus. *Studien und Mitteilungen zur Geschichte des Benediktinerordens* 18 (1930), 83-97.

WARD, A.: Jerome's work on the Psalter. *ET* 44 (1932/3), 87-92.

WEBER, R.: La traduction primitive de βάρις dans les anciens psautiers latins. *VC* 4 (1950), 20-32.

——: *Problèmes d'édition des anciens psautiers latins.* (Rome, 1951).

——: 'Vindica sanguinem' (Ps. lxxviii: 10). Une vieille faute des anciens psautiers latins. In *Colligere Fragmenta: Fs. A. Dold.* (Beuron, 1952), 45-8.

——: *Le psautier romain et les anciens psautiers latins. CBL* 10 (Rome, 1953).

ZEILLER, J.: La lettre de S. Jérôme aux Gothes Sunnia et Frétela. *CRAI* (1935), 238-50.

ZIEGLER, J.: *Antike und moderne lateinische Psalmenübersetzungen. SbBayerAkWiss* 1960, 3.

——: Altlateinische Psalterien. *BZ* 5 (1961), 94-117.

Proverbs - Song of Songs

40b BAUMSTARK, A.: Armenischer und Afrikanisch-lateinischer Proverbientext. *Biblica* 35 (1954), 346-56.

BONNARDIÈRE, A. M. LA: Le Cantique des Cantiques dans l'œuvre de S. Augustin. *RevEtAugustiniennes* 1 (1955), 225-37.

BRUYNE, D. DE: Les anciennes versions latines du Cantique des Cantiques. *RBén* 38 (1926), 97-122.

CASPARI, C. P.: *Das Buch Hiob i: 1 - xxxviii: 16 in Hieronymus' Übersetzung aus der alexandrinischen Version nach einer St. Galler Handschrift saec. VIII* (Christiania, 1893).

DOLD, A.: Die altlateinischen Proverbientexte im Codex 25.2.36 von St. Paul in Kärnten. *Biblica* 19 (1938), 241-59.

GAILEY, J. H.: *Jerome's Latin version of Job from the Greek, ch. 1-26; its text, character and provenience* (Princeton, 1945).

LAGARDE, P. A. DE: Das Hieronymus Übertragung der griechischen Übersetzung des Job. *Mitteilungen* II, 11 (Göttingen, 1887), 189-237.

SALMON, P.: Le texte de Job utilizé par S. Grégoire dans les Moralia. *Studia Anselmiana* 27/8 (1951), 187-94.

SCHILDENBERGER, J.: *Die altlateinischen Proverbien. Ein Beitrag zu ihrer Textgeschichte* (Beuron, 1934).

——: Die altlateinischen Proverbien-Randlesungen der Bibel von Valvanera. *Spanische Forschungen der Görresgesellschaft* 5 (1935), 97-107.

——: *Die altlateinischen Texte des Proverbienbuches untersucht und textgeschichtlich eingegliedert. I, Die alte afrikanische Textgestalt. TuA* 32/3 (Beuron, 1941).

36e, 37a VACCARI, A.: *La versione Geronimiana esaplare dei Proverbi* (Rome, 1913) [<*Civiltà Cattolica* 1913].

——: Navis pelagizans [Prov. xxx: 18]. *Biblica* 4 (1923), 179-80.

——: Latina Cantici Canticorum versio a s. Hieronymo ad graecam hexaplarem emendata. *Biblica* 36 (1955), 258-60.

——: Recupero d'un lavoro critico di s. Girolamo. In *Scritti di erudizione e di filologia* (Rome, 1958) II, 83-146.

——: *Cantici Canticorum vetus latina translatio a S. Hieronymo ad graecum textum hexaplarem emendata* (Rome, 1959).

——: Cantici Canticorum latine a s. Hieronymo recensiti emendatio [Cant. ii: 13]. *Biblica* 44 (1963), 74-5.

WILMART, A.: L'ancienne version latine du Cantique i-iii: 4. *RBén* 28 (1911), 11-36.

Wisdom - Ecclesiasticus

ANON: *Sapientia Salomonis, Liber Hiesu Filii Sirach.* = *Biblia Sacra iuxta Latinam Vulgatam Versionem* (Rome, 1964).

BAARS, W.: On a Latin fragment of Sirach. *VT* 15 (1965), 280-81.

BRUYNE, D. DE: Étude sur le texte latin d'Ecclésiastique. *RBén* 40 (1928), 5-48.

——: Le prologue, le titre et la finale de l'Ecclésiastique. *ZAW* 47 (1929), 257-63.

——: Étude sur le texte latin de la Sagesse. *RBén* 41 (1929), 101-33.

DOIGNON, J.: Sacrum-sacramentum-sacrificium dans le texte latin du livre de la Sagesse. *RevÉtLatines* 34 (1956), 240-53.

DOLD, A.: *Lateinische Fragmente der Sapientalbücher aus dem Münchener Palimpsest CLM 19105. TuA* 13 (Beuron, 1928).
Rev. Vaccari in *Biblica* 11 (1930), 242-7.

DOUAIS, C.: *Une ancienne version latine de l'Ecclésiastique* (Paris, 1895).

EBERHARTER, A.: The text of Ecclesiasticus in the quotations of Clement of Alexandria and St. Cyprian. *Biblica* 7 (1926), 79-83.

——: Die Ekklesiastikus-Zitate in den pseudo-cyprianischen Schriften. *Biblica* 7 (1926), 324-5.

HERKENNE, H.: *De veteris latinae Ecclesiastici capitibus i-xliii* (Leipzig, 1899).
Rev. Cowley in *JQR* 12 (1899/1900), 168-71.

LAGARDE, P. A. DE: Die Weisheiten der Handschrift von Amiata. *Mitteilungen* I (Göttingen, 1884), 283-378.

MOHRMANN, C.: À propos de Sap. xv: 18. *VC* 6 (1952), 28-30 = *Études sur le latin des chrétiens*, III, 273-5.

SKEHAN, P. W.: Notes on the Latin text of the Book of Wisdom. *CBQ* 4 (1942), 230-43.

STUMMER, F.: Via peccantium complanata lapidibus (Eccli. 21, 11). In *Colligere Fragmenta: Fs. A. Dold* (Beuron, 1952), 40-4.

THIELMANN, P.: Die lateinische Übersetzung des Buches der Weisheit. *ALL* 8 (1893), 235-77.

——: Die lateinische Übersetzung des Buches Sirach. *ALL* 8 (1893), 511-61.

——: Die europäischen Bestandteile des lateinischen Sirach. *ALL* 9 (1894), 247-84.

WILMART, A.: Nouveaux feuillets toulousains de l'Ecclésiastique. *RBén* 33 (1912), 110-23.

ZIEGLER, J.: Zur griechischen Vorlage der Vetus Latina in der Sapientia Salomonis. In *Lux tua veritas: Fs. H. Junker* (Trier, 1961), 275-91.

Prophetic Books

ALLGEIER, A.: Die Konstanzer altlateinische Propheten Handschrift. *Jahresbericht der Görresgesellschaft* (Köln) 1939, 79-95.

——: Der Text einiger kleiner Propheten bei Lucifer von Calaris. *Studia Anselmiana* 27/8 (1951), 286-300.

AMELLI, A.: *De libri Baruch vetustissima latina versione, usque adhuc inedita, in celeberrimo codice Cavense* (Monte Cassino, 1902).

BAARS, W.: Een weinig bekende oudlatijnse tekst van Jesaja 23. *NTT* 22 (1967), 241-8.

26b   BAUMSTARK, A.: Aramäischer Einfluss in altlateinischen Text von Hab. 3. *OC* III, 6 (1931), 163-81.

BONNARDIÈRE, A. M. LA: Les douze petits prophètes dans l'œuvre de S. Augustin. *RevÉtAugustiniennes* 3 (1957), 341-74.

——: *Biblia Augustiniana. AT: Les douze petits prophètes* (Paris, 1963).

BROU, L.: Les 'benedictiones' ou cantique des trois enfants dans l'ancienne messe espagnole. *Hispania Sacra* 1 (1948), 21-33.

BRUYNE, D. DE: Deux notes sur les prophètes en écriture onciale provenants de Constance. *RBén* 43 (1931), 159-60.

CORSSEN, P.: *Fragmente der Weingartner Prophetenhandschrift* (Berlin, 1899).

——: *Zwei neue Fragmente der Weingartner Prophetenhandschrift* (Berlin, 1899).

DOLD, A.: *Konstanzer altlateinische Propheten- und Evangelien-Bruchstücke mit Glossen. TuA* 7/9 (Beuron, 1923). Rev. Vaccari in *Biblica* 6 (1925), 237-41.

——: *Neue St. Galler vorhieronymianische Prophetenfragmente der St. Galler Sammelhandschrift 138b zugehörig. TuA* 31 (Beuron, 1940).

——: Was ein Vers der Vetus Latina uns nicht alles lehren kann. *Münchener Theologische Zeitschrift* 5 (1954), 273-5. [Isai. liii: 7].

HOBERG, G.: *Die älteste lateinische Übersetzung des Buches Baruch* (Freiburg, i.B.² 1902).

GUSTAFSSON, F.: *Fragmenta veteris testamenti in latinum conversi e palimpsesto vaticano eruta* (Helsingfors, 1881) = *AASF* 12 (1881), 243-67.

HUGLO, M.: Fragments de Jérémie selon la Vetus Latina. *VC* 8 (1954), 83-6.

KNAUER, G. N.: Sarabara (Dan. iii: 94 (27)) bei Aug. mag. 10, 33-11, 37. *Glotta* 23 (1954), 100-118.

LEHMANN, P.: *Die Konstanz-Weingartner Propheten-Fragmente in phototypischer Reproduktion* (Leiden, 1912).

MATTEI-CERASOLI, L.: *Liber Baruch secondo il testo del codice Cavense. Analecta Cavensia* I, (1935).

MERCATI, G.: Alcuni frammenti biblici di antica versione latina. I, Tre frammenti d'Isaia. *SeT* 95 (1941), 95-126.

MÜNTZER, F.: *Fragmenta versionis antiquae latinae antehieronymianae prophetarum Ieremiae, Ezechielis, Danielis et Hoseae ex codice rescripto Bibl. Univ. Wirceburgensis* (Hafniae, 1819).

OESTERLEY, W. O. E.: The Old Latin Texts of the Minor Prophets. *JTS* 5 (1904), 76-88, 242-53, 378-86, 570-9; 6 (1905), 67-70, 217-20.

PANYIK, A.: *A critical and comparative study of the Old Latin text of the Book Ezekiel and the Minor Prophets* (Diss. Princeton, 1938).

RANKE, E.: *Fragmenta versionis latinae antehieronymianae prophetarum Hoseae Amosi et Michae e codice Fuldense* (Marburg, 1856).

———: *Fragmenta versionis sacrarum scripturarum latinae antehieronymianae e codice manuscripto* (Marburg, 1860; Vienna², 1868).

———: *Antiquissimae veteris testamenti versionis latinae fragmenta Stuttgardiana* (Marburg, 1888).

SCHAUMBERGER, J. B.: Die Prophetentexte der Bronzetüre von St. Paul. *Römische Quartalschrift* 37 (1929), 41-56.

SCHEPENS, P.: Le prophète Malachiel. *RechSR* 12 (1921), 362-3; 13 (1922), 350-1.

SCHERER, C.: Neue Fuldaer Bruchstücke der Weingartener Prophetenhandschrift. *ZAW* 30 (1910), 161-200.

STENZEL, M.: *Das Dodekapropheton der lateinischen Septuaginta. Untersuchungen über die Herkunft und geschichtliche Entwicklung des nichthieronymianischen Dodekapropheton* (Diss. Würzburg, 1950).

———: Das Dodekapropheton in Übersetzungswerken lateinischer Schriftsteller des Altertums. *TZ* 9 (1953), 81-92.

———: Die Konstanzer und St. Galler Fragmente zum altlateinischen Dodekapropheton. *Sacris Erudiri* 5 (1953), 27-85.

———: Altlateinische Canticatexte im Dodekapropheton. *ZNW* 46 (1955), 31-60.

———: Das Zwölfprophetenbuch im Würzburger Palimpsest-Codex

(cod. membr. 64) und seine Textgestalt in Väterzitaten. *Sacris Erudiri* 7 (1955), 5-34.

VOGEL, A.: *Beiträge zur Herstellung der alten lateinischen Bibelübersetzung. Zwei handschriftliche Fragmente in dem Buche des Ezechiel und den Sprüchworten Salomos* (Vienna, 1868).

WILMART, A.: Trois nouveaux fragments de l'ancienne version des prophètes. *RBén* 26 (1909), 145-62, 384-6.

h. SLAVONIC

General

ALTBAUER, M.: (Traces of Hebrew commentaries in the Slavonic translations of the Bible) [In Hebrew]. *Tarbiz* 34 (1964), 379-81.

ANON: *Pravoslavnaja Bogoslovskaja Enciklopedija* (St. Petersburg, 1901) II, 374-597.

——: The Russian Bible. *ChQR* 41 (1895/6), 203-25.

BAUMSTARK, A.: Die altslawische Bibel. *LTK* 2 (1913), 322f.

BEBB, Ll. J. M.: The Slavonic Version. *HDB* 4, 863-4.

ČISTOVIČ, J.: Ispravlenie teksta Slavjanskoj Biblii. *Pravoslavnoje Obozrenje* 1 (1861), 479-510; 2, 41-72.

GLUBOKOWSKIJ, N. N.: *Die russische theologische Wissenschaft in ihrer historischen Entwicklung und ihrem gegenwärtigen Zustand* (Warsaw, 1928).

HADŽEGA, J.: Der Beitrag von Maximos Agioritis zur Verbesserung des Textes der altslavischen Bibel. *BZ* 23 (1935/6), 44-9.

JAKIMOV, I.: Kritičeskoje izsledovanie teksta slavjanskago perevoda vetchago zavjeta i jego zavisimosti ot teksta perevoda senidesjat tolkovnikov. *Christianskoje Čtenie* (1878).

JEVSEJEV, J.: Zamjetki po drevno slavjanskomu perevodu sv. pisania. *Bulletin of the Imperial Academy of Sciences* (St. Petersburg) 1898, 329-64; 1899, 355-73.

——: Rukopisnoje predanje slavjanskoj biblii. *Christianskoje Čtenie* 1911, 435-50, 644-60.

——: Očerki po istorii slavjanskago perevoda biblii. *Christianskoje Čtenie* 1912, 1261-85, 1372-74; 1913, 192-213, 350-73, 469-93.

LESKIEN, A.: Slawische Bibelübersetzungen. *PRE³* 3 (1913), 151-67.

MICHALJOV, A. V.: *Grečeskie i drevneslavjanskie parimejniki* (Warsaw, 1908).

MINNS, E. H.: Saint Cyril really knew Hebrew. In *Mélanges publiés en honneur de M. P. Boyer* (Paris, 1925), 94-7.

RAHLFS, A.: Zur Frage nach der Herkunft des glagolitischen Alphabets. *ZVS* 45 (1913), 285-7.

34 SCHWEIGL, J.: La Bibbia Slava del 1751 (1756). *Biblica* 18 (1937), 51-73.

——: art. Slavi, versione della Bibbia. *EC* 11 (1953), 798-9.

SEDLAČEK, J.: *Uvod do knih starého zákona*. (Prague, 1904), 89-139.

——: art. Slaves (versions). *DB* 5 (1912), 1800-8.

STEFANIĆ, V.: (Old Slavonic Bible) [In Serbian]. In *Enciklopedija Jugoslavije* (Zagreb, 1955), 494-504.

VAJS, J.: *Kritické studie staroslav. textu biblického* (Prague, 1927).

WEBER, K.: *Der Umfang der ältesten slavischen Bibelübersetzung. Nachrichten aus dem Benediktiner-Kolleg St. Peter in Salzburg* 5 (1928).

Prose Books

ARNIM, B. VON: Zur altbulgarischen Übersetzung der Genesis. *ZfSlavPhilologie* 13 (1936), 97.

ALTBAUER, M.: (Slavonic version of Ruth) [In Hebrew]. *Leshonenu* 25 (1961), 24-6.

——: (Criteria for reconstructing prototypes of Slavonic version, with special reference to Ruth) [In Czeck]. *Slavia* (Prague) 36 (1967), 510-66.

HAMM, J.: Judita u hrvatskim glagoljskim brevijarima. *Radovi Staroslavenskog Instituta* 3 (1958), 103-99, 200f. (resumé).

LEBEDEV, V.: *Slavjansky perevod knigi Jisusa Navina* (St. Petersburg, 1890).

VAJS, J.: *Liber Ruth* = Glagolitica 2, i (Veglae, 1905).

——: *Kniha Rut v překlade staroslovanském.* = *Kritické studie staroslovanského texta biblického* 2 (Prague, 1926).

Psalter

AMFILOCHY, ARCHIMANDRITE: *Drevne-slavjanskaja Psaltir XIII-XIV veku* (Moscow, 1879; 2 vols).

ARNIM, B. VON: *Studien zum altbulgarischen Psalterium Sinaiticum. Veröffentlichungen des slavischen Instituts und der Friedrich-Wilhelm-Universität Berlin* 3 (Leipzig, 1930).

DUJČEV, I.: *Bolonski Psaltir. Bulgarski knižovei pametnik ot XIII vek* (Sofia, 1968).

188 VERSIONS

GRÜNENTHAL, O.: *Das Eugenius-Psalterfragment mit Erläuterungen* (Heidelberg, 1930).

HAMM, J.: *Psalterium Vindobonense. Der glossierte glagolitische Psalter der Österr. Nationalbibliothek* (Graz/Köln, 1967).

HEINTSCH, K.: Staro-cerkiewno-slowiański Psałterz Eugeniusza. *Sprawozdania Wrocławskiego Tow. Naukowego* 5 (1950), 33-8.

JAGIĆ, V.: *Psalterium Bononiense* (Vienna, Berlin, St. Petersburg, 1907).

KURZ, J.: O nové nalezeném emauzském charvátskohlaholském zlomku žaltáře. *Slavia* (Prague) 22 (1953), 81-104.

LAURENČIK, J.: *Influxus textus psalterii latini in psalterium sinaiticum palaeoslavicum* (Diss. Prague, 1947) [Summary in *BALC* 3, 197-8].

——: Nelukianovská čteni v sinajském žaltáři. *Slovanské Studie* (Prague, 1948).

LÉPISSIER, J.: La traduction vieux-slave du Psautier. *RevÉt Slaves* 43 (1964), 59-72.

ONASCH, K.: Der Psalter in der byzantinisch-slavischen Orthodoxie. In *Gottes ist der Orient: Fs. O. Eissfeldt* (Berlin, 1959), 106-28.

POGORELOV, V.: *Čudovskaja Psaltyr XII veka* (St. Petersburg, 1910).

SEVERJANOV, S.: *Sinajskaja Psaltyr* (Petrograd, 1922).

VAJS, J.: *Psalterium palaeoslovenicum croatico-glagoliticum* (Prague, 1916).

——: *Solvenski psaltir: psalterii palaeoslovenici quinquagena prima* (Prague, 1920).

——: Zaltář Fraščićův. *Slavia* 1 (Prague, 1922), 269-84, 2 (1923), 304-9.

——: Které recense byla řecká předloha staroslovenského překladu žaltáře. *Byzantinoslavica* 8 (1939/46), 55-86 [With French resumé].

VERDIANI, C.: Il salterio Laurenziano-Voliniense. Codex paleoslavo del 1384. *Ricerche Slavistiche* 3 (1954), 1-29.

Other Poetical Books

HAMM, J.: Varijante u prijepisima hrvatskih glagoljasa. *Slovo* 2 (1953), 18-36 [Job i-ii].

——: Starohrvatski prijevod 'pjesme nad pjesmana'. *Slovo* 6/8 (1957), 195-229. [Cant.].

JEVSEJEV, J.: *Kniga Proroka Isaii v drevne-slavjanskom perevode* (St. Petersburg, 1897).

——: *Kniga Proroka Daniila v drevne-slavjanskom perevode* (Moscow, 1905).

KOPEČNY, F.: Stipate me malis (Cant. ii: 5) Ospete me jablky. *Slavia* 25 (1956), 322-7.

PECHUŠKA, F.: *Staroslovanský překlad knihy Job* (Prague, 1935).

VAJS, J.: *Liber Iob = Glagolitica* 2 (Veglae, 1903).

——: *Liber Ecclesiastis = Glagolitica* 2. ii (Veglae, 1905).

——: *Propheta Oseas = Analecta sacrae scripturae ex antiquioribus codicibus glagoliticis: Prophetae Minores* (Veglae, 1910).

——: *Zacharias-Malachias = Analecta sacrae scripturae ex antiquioribus codicibus glagoliticis: Prophetae Minores* 5 (Veglae, 1915).

i. PESHITTA

(Only for books translated direct from Greek, i.e., the so-called Apocrypha, less Ecclesiasticus.)

BAARS, W.: An additional fragment of the Syriac version of the Psalms of Solomon. *VT* 11 (1961), 222-3.

BARNES, W. E.: On the influence of the Septuagint on the Peshitta. *JTS* 2 (1901), 186-97.

BENSLEY, R. L.: *The Fourth Book of Maccabees and kindred documents in Syriac* (Cambridge, 1895).

BLOCH, J.: The influence of the Greek Bible on the Peshitta. *AJSL* 36 (1919/20), 161-6.

BURKITT, F. C.: A new manuscript of the Odes of Salomon. *JTS* 13 (1912), 372-85. [380-2 on Pss. Sol.].

CERIANI, A. M.: *Translatio Syra Pescitto Veteris Testamenti ex codice Ambrosiano sec. fere VI photolithographice edita* (Milan, 1876/83; 2 vols).

EMERTON, J. A.: *The Peshitta of the Wisdom of Solomon = Studia Post-Biblica* 2 (Leiden, 1959).

FELDMANN, F.: see above, 40b.

GOTTHEIL, R.: Peshitta Text of Gen. 32: 25. *JAOS* 33 (1913), 263-4.

HARRIS, J. R.: *The Odes and Psalms of Solomon* (Cambridge, 1909: ²1911).

HARWELL, R. R.: *The principal versions of Baruch* (Diss. Yale, 1915).

HOLTZMANN, J.: *Die Peschitta zum Buche der Weisheit* (Freiburg, i.B., 1903).

KUHN, K. G.: see 39.

LAGARDE, P. A. DE: *Libri veteris testamenti apocryphi syriace* (Leipzig, 1861).

LEBRAM, J. C. H.: Die Peschitta zu Tobit vii: 11-xiv: 15. *ZAW* 69 (1957), 185-211.

——: *Tobit*. In *The Old Testament in Syriac, Sample Edition* (Leiden, 1966).

MINGANA, A. and HARRIS, J. R.: *The Odes and Psalms of Solomon* (Manchester, 1916/20; 2 vols).

MINGANA, A.: Some uncanonical Psalms. In *Woodbrooke Studies* I (Cambridge, 1927), 145-7, 288-94.

NAU, F.: see 39.

NOTH, M.: Die fünf syrisch überlieferten apokryphen Psalmen. *ZAW* 48 (1930), 1-23.

PENNA, A.: Le spedizioni di Lisia nella versione Peshitta. *Studii Biblici Franciscani Liber Annuus* 13 (1962/3), 93-100.

——: I libri dei Maccabei nei manoscritti siriaci della Biblioteca Vaticana. In *Mélanges E. Tisserant* (Rome, 1964), I, 235-43.

——: I nomi propri dei primi due libri dei Maccabei nella Peshitta. *RSO* ns 4 (1965), 13-41.

Peshitta Institute: *List of OT Peshitta manuscripts* (Leiden, 1961) [Supplements in VT 12 (1962), 127-8, 237-8, 351; 13 (1963), 260-8; 18 (1968), 128-43].

RUNNING, L. G.: The problem of the mixed Syriac manuscripts of Susanna in the 17th century. *VT* 19 (1969), 377-83.

SCHMIDT, G.: Die beiden Syrischen Übersetzungen des I. Maccabäerbuches. *ZAW* 17 (1897), 1-47, 233-62.

TRENDELENBURG, J. G.: Primi libri Maccabaeorum Graeci textus cum versione Syriaca collatio instituta. *RBML* 15 (1784), 58-153.

WILKINS, G.: see 39 (Odes).

WILLEY, D.: The Odes and Psalms of Solomon. *JTS* 14 (1913), 293-8. [295-8 on Pss. Sol.].

WRIGHT, W.: Some apocryphal Psalms in Syriac. *PSBA* 9 (1887), 257-66.

j. Syro-Hexaplar

Altheim, F. and Stiehl, R.: Die Bibliotheken Alexandreias 2. Die Bibliothek des Serapeion in *Die Araber in der alten Welt* 2 (Berlin, 1965), 16-38.

Eichhorn, J.: Über den Verfasser der hexaplarisch-syrischen Übersetzung. *RBML* 7 (1780), 225-50.

Goshen-Gottstein, M. H.: Eine Cambridger Syrohexaplahandschrift. *Le Muséon* 67 (1954), 291-6.

——: Neue Syrohexaplafragmente. *Biblica* 37 (1956), 162-83.

——: The edition of Syro-hexaplar materials. *Textus* 4 (1964), 230-1.

Göttsberger, J.: Die syro-armenischen ... Bibelcitate ... des Barhebräus. *ZAW* 21 (1901), 101-27.

——: Die syro-koptischen Bibelcitate ... aus den Scholien des Barhebräus. *ZAW* 21 (1901), 128-41.

Gregory, C. R.: Die syrische Hexapla am Anfange des neunten Jahrhunderts. *Theol. Lit. Bl.* 23 (1902), 361-6.

Gwynn, J.: art. Paul of Tella. *DCB* 4 (1887), 266-71.

Lossen, M.: *Briefe von Andreas Masius und seinen Freunden 1538 bis 1573* (Leipzig, 1886).

Mercati, G.: Di varie antichissime sottoscrizioni a codici esaplari. *SeT* 95 (1941), 1-48.

——: Intorno all'onomastico della Siroesaplare. *SeT* 95 (1941), 85-91.

Nestle, E.: art. in *PRE*² 3 (1897), 175-6.

——: Zur syrischen Hexapla. *Th.Lit.Bl.* 23 (1902), 398-9.

Vocht, H. de: Andreas Masius (1514-73). *SeT* 125 (1946), 425-41.

Vosté, J. M.: Les textes bibliques dans le Pontifical de Michel le Grand. *Biblica* 27 (1946), 107-12.

——: Les deux versions syriaques de la Bible d'après Mar Išoʻdad de Merw. *Biblica* 33 (1952), 235-6.

Selections

Baars, W.: *New Syro-hexaplaric texts, edited, commented upon and compared with the LXX* (Leiden, 1968) [pp. 25-7: list of OT passages *not* available in Syh.].

Ceriani, A. M.: *Codex syro-hexaplaris Ambrosianus photographice editus. Monumenta Sacra et Profana* VII (Milan, 1874).

Gwynn, J.: *Fragments of the later Syriac versions of the Bible* (London, 1909) [Gen. Lev. Chron. Neh.].

LAGARDE, P. A. DE: *Veteris Testamenti ab Origene recensiti fragmenta apud Syros servata quinque* (Göttingen, 1880) [in Hebrew characters].

——: *Bibliothecae syriacae... quae ad philologiam sacram pertinent.* (Göttingen, 1892) [cp. Die Interpunction in meiner Bibliotheca Sacra. *Mitteilungen* III, 24 (1889), 281].

Pentateuch

BAUMSTARK, A.: Griechische und hebräische Bibelzitate in der Pentateucherklärung Išoʿdads von Merw. *OC* ns 1 (1911), 1-19.

CERIANI, A. M.: *Pentateuchus syrohexaplaris quae supersunt cum notis. Monumenta Sacra et Profana*, II, 1-4 (Milan), 1863.

KERBER, G.: Syrohexaplarische Fragmente zu Leviticus und Deuteronomium aus Bar-Hebraeus gesammelt. *ZAW* 16 (1896), 249-64.

Historical Books

BOER, P. A. H. DE: A Syro-hexaplar text of the Song of Hannah. I Samuel ii: 1-10. *Hebrew and Semitic Studies presented to G. R. Driver* (Oxford, 1963), 8-15.

KERBER, G.: Syrohexaplarische Fragmente zu den beiden Samuelis-büchern aus Bar-Hebraeus. *ZAW* 18 (1898), 177-96.

LEBRAM, J. C. H.: *Tobit*. In *The OT in Syriac: Sample Edition* (Leiden, 1966).

RØRDAM, S.: *Libri Judicum et Ruth secundum versionem syriaco-hexaplarem* (Copenhagen, 1859-61) [pp. 1-59: Dissertatio de regulis grammaticis quas secutus est Paulus Tellensis in Veteri Testamento ex graeco syriace vertendo].

TORREY, C. C.: Portions of First Esdras and Nehemiah in the Syro-hexaplar Version. *AJSL* 23 (1906/7), 65-74.

Poetical and Prophetic Books

CERIANI, A. M.: *Baruch, Threni et epistola Jeremiae versionis syriacae Pauli Tellensis cum notis et initio prolegomenon. Monumenta Sacra et Profana* I, 7 (Milan, 1861).

FRITSCH, C. T.: The treatment of the hexaplaric signs in the Syro-hexaplar of Proverbs. *JBL* 72 (1953), 169-81.

KRUSE-BLINKENBERG, L.: The Book of Malachi according to Codex Syro-Hexaplaris Ambrosianus. *Studia Theologica* 21 (1967), 62-82.

PIGULEVSKAYA, N.: Greko-siro-arabskaja rukopis IX veka. *Palestinskij Sbornik* 1 (63) (1954), 59-90.

SCHNEIDER, H.: Biblische Oden im syrohexaplarischen Psalter. *Biblica* 40 (1959), 199-209.

VOSTÉ, J. M.: Les citations syro-hexaplaires d'Išo'dad de Merw dans le commentaire sur les Psaumes. *Biblica* 26 (1945), 12-36.

——: La version syro-hexaplaire de la Sagesse. *Biblica* 30 (1949), 213-7.

k. SYRIAC: JACOB OF EDESSA

BAARS, W.: Ein neugefundenes Bruchstück aus der syrischen Bibelrevision des Jakob von Edessa. *VT* 18 (1968), 548-54.

CERIANI, A. M.: *Monumenta sacra et profana*, II, 1 (Milan, 1863) [Gen.].

——: *Monumenta sacra et profana*, V, 1 (Milan, 1868) [Isai.].

DELEKAT, L.: Die syrolukianische Übersetzung des Buches Jesaja und das Postulat einer alttestamentlichen Vetus Syra. *ZAW* 69 (1957), 21-55.

SACY, S. DE: Notice d'un manuscrit syriaque, contenant les livres de Moïse (Paris, syr. 26 in Syr.). *Notices et Extraits des Manuscrits de la Bibliothèque Nationale*, IV (Paris, 1798/9), 648-68.

UGOLINI, M.: Il ms Vat. syr. 5 e la recensione del VT di Giacomo d'Edessa. *OC* 2 (1902), 409-20.

l. PALESTINIAN SYRIAC *(Christian Palestinian Aramaic)*

BAARS, W.: A Palestinian Syriac Text of the Book of Lamentations. *VT* 10 (1960), 224-7.

——: Two Palestinian Syriac texts identified as parts of the Epistle of Jeremy. *VT* 11 (1961), 77-81.

BAUMSTARK, A.: Neue orientalische Probleme biblischer Textgeschichte. *ZDMG* nf 14 (1935), 89-118.

——: Das Problem des christlich-palästinischen Pentateuchtextes. *OC* 3 ser. 10 (1935), 201-24.

BLACK, M.: *A Christian Palestinian Horologian. T&S* ns 1 (Cambridge, 1953) [Pss.].

DELEKAT, L.: Die syropalästinische Jesaja-Übersetzung. *ZAW* 71 (1959), 165-201.

DUENSING, H.: *Christlich-palästinisch-aramäische Texte und Fragmente nebst einer Abhandlung über den Wert der palästinischen Septuaginta* (Göttingen, 1906).
  Rev. Schulthess in *ZDMG* 61 (1907), 210-22.

GWILLIAM, G. H.: *The Palestinian Version of the Holy Scriptures. Anecdota Oxoniensia, Semitic Series* I, 5 (Oxford, 1893) [Num. Dt. Pss. Prov. Job Isai.].

——, BURKITT, F. C., and STENNING, J. F.: *Biblical and Patristic relics of the Palestinian Literature. Anecdota Oxoniensia, Semitic Series* I, 9 (Oxford, 1896) [Ex. 3 Kms. Job Wis.].

LAND, J. P. N.: *Anecdota Syriaca* IV (Leiden, 1875) [Dt. Pss. Prov. Job Isai.].

LEWIS, A. S.: *A Palestinian Syriac Lectionary containing lessons from the Pentateuch, Job, Prophets, Acts and Epistles. Studia Sinaitica* 6 (London, 1897; Supplement, 1907).

—— and GIBSON, M. D.: *Palestinian Syriac Texts from Palimpsest Fragments in the Taylor-Schechter Collection* (Cambridge, 1900). [cp. A. S. Lewis, *Studia Sinaitica* 11 (1902), xlvii, 133-8].

——: *Codex Climaci Rescriptus. Horae Semiticae* 8 (Cambridge, 1909).

MARGOLIOUTH, G.: The Liturgy of the Nile. *JRAS* 28 (1896), 577-731. [OT texts also published in next item].

——: More fragments of the Palestinian Syriac version of the Holy Scriptures. *PSBA* 18 (1896), 223-36; 19 (1897), 39-60.

PIGOULEWSKI, N.: Fragments syro-palestiniens des Psaumes CXXIII-IV. *RB* 43 (1934), 519-23.

SCHULTHESS, F.: Christlich-palästinische Fragmente. *ZDMG* 56 (1902), 249-61.

——: *Lexicon Syropalaestinum* (Berlin, 1903) [pp. vii-xvi: list of biblical texts published].

——: *Christlich-palästinische Fragmente aus der Omayyaden-Moschee zu Damaskus. Abh. KGWGött.* VIII, 3 (Berlin, 1905).

41. ILLUSTRATION OF LXX

(See also 35c, 36b, 40g)

ALPATOFF, M.: A Byzantine illuminated manuscript of the Palaeo-
logue epoch in Moscow. *Art Bulletin* 12 (1930). [Psalter].

ANON: *Il Rotulo di Giosuè* (Codices e Vaticanis selecti, 5; Milan,
1905).

ANON: *Miniature della bibbia cod. Vat. Reg. gr. 1 e del salterio cod.
Vat. Palat. gr. 381* (Collezione palaeografica vaticana, 1; Milan,
1905).

ASTRUC, C.: Un psautier à frontispiece: le supp. gr. 610. *Cahiers
archéologiques* 3 (1948), 106-13.

BAUMSTARK, A.: Frühchristlich-syrische Psalterillustration in einer
byzantinischen Abkürzung. *OC* 5 (1905), 295-320.

——: Zur byzantinischen Odenillustration. *Römische Quartalschrift*
21, 4 (1907), 167-75.

——: Ein rudimentäres Exemplar der griechischen Psalterillustration durch Ganzseitenbilder. *OC* II, 2 (1912), 107-19.

——: Frühchristlich-syrische Prophetenillustration durch stehende
Autorenbilder. *OC* III, 9 (1934), 99-104.

BERNHEIMER, R.: The martyrdom of Isaiah. *Art Bulletin* 34 (1952),
19-34.

BIANCHI-BANDINELLI, O.: La composizione del diluvio nella Genesi
di Vienna. *Mitteil. Deutsch. Arch. Inst. (Röm. Abt.)* 62 (1955),
66-77.

BISCHOFF, B., MÜTHERLICH, F., FREDE, H. J., and FISCHER, B.: *Der
Stuttgarter Bilderpsalter*. I, *Facsimile*; II, *Untersuchungen*
(Stuttgart, 1968).

BLANC, LE: La connaissance des Livres Saints et les artistes chrétiens
des premiers siècles. *Mém. Académie des Inscriptions* 36, 2
(1899).

BLOCH, P.: Nachwirkungen des Alten Bundes in der christlichen
Kunst. *Monumenta Judaica, 2000 Jahre Geschichte und Kultur
der Juden am Rhein* (Köln, 1963), 737-81.

BUBERL, P.: *Die Miniaturhandschriften der Nationalbibliothek in
Athen. Denkschrift d. Kais. Wiener Ak. Wiss., phil.-hist. Kl.* 60,
2; 1917.

——: Das Problem der Wiener Genesis. *Jahrbuch der kunsthistori-
schen Sammlungen in Wien*, nF 10 (1936), 9-58.

——: *Der Wiener Dioscorides und die Wiener Genesis* (Leipzig-
Vienna, 1937).

———: *Die Wiener Genesis. Beschreibendes Verzeichnis der illuminierten Handschriften in Österreich*, 8, 4; 1937.

BUCHTAL, H.: *The miniatures of the Paris Psalter* [gr. 139] (London, 1938).

CAHN, A. S.: The missing model of the S. Julien de Tours frescoes and the Ashburnham Miniatures. *Cahiers archéologiques* 16 (1966), 203-7.

DEGERING, H., and BOECKLER, A.: *Die Quedlinburger Itala-Fragmente* (Cassiodor-Gesellschaft, Veröffentlichungen, 1; Berlin, 1932. [two vols].

DER NERSESSIAN, S.: A Psalter and New Testament Manuscript at Dumbarton Oaks. *Dumbarton Oaks Papers* 19 (1965), 153-83 [= Athos, Pantokrator-Psalter 49].

DUFRENNE, S.: Le psautier de Bristol et les autres psautiers byzantins. *Cahiers archéologiques* 14 (1964), 159-82. [BM Add. 40731].

———: Une illustration 'historique', inconnue, du Psautier du Mont-Athos, Pantocrator no. 61. *Cahiers archéologiques* 15 (1965), 83-95.

———: *L'illustration des psautiers grecs du moyen âge* [Pantokrator 61, Paris gr. 20, BM Add. 40731] (Paris, 1966).

ESCHWEILER, J.: Illustrationen zu altlateinischen Texten im Stuttgarter Bilderpsalter. *Colligere fragmenta: Fs. A. Dold* (Beuron, 1952), 49-51.

FABRICIUS, U.: *Die Legenden im Bild des ersten Jahrtausends der Kirche* (Kassel, 1958).

FINK, J.: *Noë der Gerechte in der frühchristlichen Kunst* (Beiheft, Archiv für Kulturgeschichte, 4; Münster-Köln, 1955).

FROLOW, A.: La fin de la querelle iconoclaste et la date des plus anciens psautiers grecs à illustrations marginales. *RHR* 163 (1963), 201-23.

GEBHARDT, O. VON: *The miniatures of the Ashburnham Pentateuch* (London, 1883).

GERSTINGER, H.: *Die Wiener Genesis* (Vienna, 1931) [colour facsimile and study].

GRABAR, A.: Images bibliques d'Apamée et fresques de la synagogue de Doura. *Cahiers archéologiques* 5 (1951), 9-14.

———: Fresques romanes copies sur les miniatures du Pentateuque de Tours. *Cahiers Archéologiques* 9 (1957), 329-41.

———: Les sujets bibliques au service de l'iconographie chrétienne. *La Bibbia nell'Alto Medievo* (Spoleto, 1963), 387-411.

——: Quelques notes sur les psautiers illustrés byzantins du IXe siècle. *Cahiers archéologiques* 15 (1965), 61-82.

GRAEVEN, H.: Il rotulo di Giosuè. *L'arte* 1 (1898), 221ff.

GRONDIJS, L.: La datation des psautiers byzantins et en particulier du psautier Chloudoff. *Byzantion* 25/7 (1955/7), 591-616.

GUTMANN, J.: Jewish elements in the Paris Psalter. *Marsyas* 6 (1950/3), 42-9.

——: The Jewish origin of the Ashburnham Pentateuch miniatures. *JQR* ns 44 (1953/4), 55-72.

HARTEL, W. VON, and WICKHOFF, F.: *Die Wiener Genesis* (Vienna, 1895).

HEMPEL, H. L.: *Die Bedeutung des AT für die Programme der frühchristlichen Malerei* (Diss. Mainz, 1956).

——: Zum Problem der Anfänge der AT-Illustration. *ZAW* 69 (1957), 103-31; 73 (1961), 299-302.

HESSELING, D. C.: *Miniatures de l'Octateuque grec de Smyrne* (Codices Graeci et Latini photographice depicti; suppl. 6; Leiden, 1909).

KONDAKOV, N. P.: *Miniatjury grečeskoj rukopisi psaltiri IX veka is sobranija A. I. Chludova v Moskve* (Moscow, 1878).

KOSTECKAYA, A. O.: (Iconography of resurrection in miniatures of Chludov Psalter) [Russian]. *Seminarium Kondakovinum* 2 (1928), 61-70.

KRETSCHMAR, G.: Ein Beitrag zur Frage nach dem Verhältnis zwischen jüdischer und christlicher Kunst in der Antike. *Abraham unser Vater: Fs. O. Michel* (Leiden-Köln, 1963), 295-319.

KURZ, O.: Ein insulares Musterbuchblatt und die byzantinische Psalter-Illustration. *Byz.-neugr. Jahrb.* 19 (1938), 84-93.

LASSUS, J.: Les miniatures byzantines du Livre des Rois d'après un manuscrit de la bibliothèque vaticane [Vat. gr. 333 = Rahlfs 244]. *Mélanges d'archéologie et d'histoire* 45 (1928), 38-74.

——: Quelques représentations du passage de la Mer rouge dans l'art chrétien de l'Orient et d'Occident. *Mélanges d'archéologie et d'histoire* 46 (1929), 159-82.

LEROY, J.: *Les manuscrits syriaques à peintures* (Paris, 1964; 2 vols).

LETHABY, W. R.: The painted book of Genesis in the British Museum. *Archeological Journal* 69 (1912), 88-111; 70 (1913), 162.

MALICKIJ, N. V.: (Palestinian iconography in the Chludov Psalter) [Russian]. *Seminarium Kondakovinum* I (1927), 49-64.

——: Le psautier à illustrations marginales du type Chludov est-il de provenance monastique? *Mélanges Th. Uspensky.* II, 2 (Paris, 1932), 235-43.

MARIÈS, L.: Le Psautier à illustration marginale. Signification théologique des images. *Actes VIe congrès internat. d'études byzantines*, 1948 (Paris, 1951), II, 261-72.

——: L'irruption des saints dans l'illustration du psautier byzantin. *Analecta Bollandiana* 58 (1950), 153-62.

MILLET, G. and DER NERSESSIAN, S.: Le psautier arménien illustré. *Revue des Études Arméniennes* 9 (1929), 137-81.

MILLET, G.: L'Octateuque byzantin après une publication de l'institut russe de Constantinople. *Revue archéologique* 16 (1910) [On Ouspensky].

——: Le psautier byzantin à illustrations marginales: survivance du style illusioniste. *IIIe congrès internat. d'études byzantines*, 1930 (Athens, 1932), 242.

MINER, D. E.: The monastic psalter of the Walters Art Gallery. *Late Classical and Medieval Studies in honor of A. M. Friend* (Princeton, 1955), 232-53.

MITIUS, O.: *Jonas auf den Denkmälern des christlichen Altertums* (Freiburg i.B., 1897).

MOREY, C. R.: Notes on east Christian miniatures. *Art Bulletin* II (1929).

——: The Byzantine Renaissance. *Speculum* 14 (1939), 139-59.

——: Castelseprio and the Byzantine Renaissance. *Art Bulletin* 34 (1952), 173ff.

MUÑOZ, A.: Alcune osservazioni intorno al Rotulo di Giosuè e agli Ottateuchi illustrati. *Byzantion* I (1924), 475-83.

——: *Tre codici miniati della biblioteca del Serraglio a Constantinopli.* Pubblicazioni dell'Instituto per l'Europa orientale, II, 5, Studi bizantini (Rome, 1925).

NARKISS, B.: Towards a further study of the Ashburnham Penta-teuch (Pentateuque de Tours). *Cahiers Archéologiques* 19 (1969), 45-60.

NIKOLASCH, F.: Zur Ikonographie des Widders von Gen. 22. *VC* 23 (1969), 197-223.

NORDSTRÖM, C. O.: The Octateuch of the Seraglio and the history of its picture recension. *Xe congrès internat. d'études byzantines*,

1955 (Istanbul, 1957), 183-6.

——: Some Jewish legends in Byzantine Art. *Byzantion* 25/7 (1955/7), 487ff.

——: The water miracles of Moses in Jewish legend and Byzantine art. *Orientalia Suecana* 7 (1958), 78-109.

——: Rabbinische Einflüsse auf einige Miniaturen des serbischen Psalters in München (Staatsbibl. cod. slav. 4). *Akten des XI. internat. byz. Kongresses,* 1958 (Munich, 1960), 416-21.

——: Rabbinica in frühchristlichen und byzantinischen Illustrationen zum 4. Buch Mose. *Figura* ns 1 (Uppsala, 1960), 24-44.

——: *The Duke of Alba's Castilian Bible. Acta Univ. Uppsal.,* 1967. Rev. Gutmann in *Art Bulletin* 51 (1969), 91-6.

OMONT, H.: Peintures de l'ancien testament dans un manuscrit syriaque du VII ou VIII siècle. *Monuments Piot* 17 (1909), 85-98.

OUSPENSKY, T.: *L'Octateuque de la Bibliothèque du Sérail à Constantinople* (Sofia, 1907).

PÄCHT, J. and O.: An unknown cycle of illustrations of the life of Joseph. *Cahiers archéologiques* 7 (1954), 35-49.

PÄCHT, O.: Ephraimillustration, Haggadah und Wiener Genesis. *Fs. K. M. Swaboda* (Vienna-Wiesbaden, 1959), 213-21.

PERRY, M. P.: An unnoticed Byzantine Psalter [BM Add. 40731]. *Burlington Magazine* 38 (1921), 119-28, 282-9.

SCHULTZE, V.: *Die Quedlinburger Itala-Miniaturen der Königlichen Bibliothek in Berlin* (Munich, 1898).

ŠEVČENKO, I.: The anti-iconoclast poem in the Pantocrator Psalter. *Cahiers archéologiques* 15 (1965), 39-60.

SLOANE, J.: The Torah shrine on the Ashburnham Pentateuch. *JQR* ns 25 (1934/5), 1-12.

SMITH, A. M.: The iconography of the sacrifice of Isaac in early Christian art. *AJA* II, 26 (1922), 159-173.

SPEYART VAN WOERDEN, I.: The iconography of the sacrifice of Abraham. *VC* 15 (1961), 214-55.

STERN, H.: Quelques problèmes d'iconographie paléochrétienne et juive. *Cahiers archéologiques* 12 (1962), 99-113.

STUHLFAUTH, G.: A Greek Psalter with Byzantine miniatures. *Art Bulletin* 15 (1933), 311ff.

STRZYGOWSKI, J.: *Der Bilderkreis des griechischen Physiologus, des Kosmas Indicopleustes und Octateuch nach Handschriften der Bibliothek zu Smyrna.* Byzantinisches Archiv 2 (Leipzig, 1899).

——: *Die Miniaturen des serbischen Psalters der königl. Hof- und Staatsbibliothek in München. Denkschr. Kais. Akad. Wiss., phil.-hist. Kl.* 52 (Vienna, 1906).

TIKKANEN, J. J.: *Die Psalterillustration im Mittelalter. I. Byzantinische Psalter-Illustration* (Helsingfors, 1895).
Rev. Strzygowski in *Byz. Z.* 6 (1897), 424-6.

——: *Die Genesismosaiken von San Marco in Venedig und ihr Verhältnis zu den Miniaturen der Cottonbibel. Acta Societatis Scientiarum Fennicae* 17 (Helsingfors, 1889).

——: *Die Psalterillustration im Mittelalter. Acta Societatis Scientiarum Fennicae* 31, 5 (Helsingfors, 1903).

TSELOS, D.: The Joshua Roll: original or copy? *Art Bulletin* 32 (1950), 275ff.

TSUJI, S.: La chaire de Maximien, la Genèse de Cotton et les mosaïques de St. Marc à Venise: à propos du cycle de Joseph. In A. Grabar et al., *Synthronon* (Paris, 1968), 43-52.

WALD, E. T. DE: A fragment of a 10th century Psalter. *Medieval Studies in Memory of A. Kingsley Porter* (Cambridge, Mass., 1939).

——: *The illustrations in the manuscripts of the LXX.* Vol. III, Part 1: Vat. gr. 1927 (Princeton, 1941).
Vol. III, Part 2: Vat. gr. 752 (Princeton, 1942).
[For planned volumes see Weitzmann, Die Ill. der LXX, p. 96, n. 1].

——: The Comnenian portraits in the Barberini Psalter. *Hesperia* 13 (1944), 78-86.

WEITZMANN, K.: Der Pariser Psalter ms. grec 139 und die mittelbyzantinische Renaissance. *Jahrb. für Kunstwissenschaft* 1929, 178ff.

——: The Psalter Vatopedi 761. *Journal of the Walters Art Gallery* 10 (1947), 38ff.

——: *Illustrations in Roll and Codex: a study of the origin and method of text illustration* (Princeton, 1947).

——: *The Joshua Roll: a work of the Macedonian Renaissance* (Princeton, 1948).

——: Die Illustration der Septuaginta. *Münchener Jahrbuch der Bildenden Kunst*, 3 Folge, 3/4 (1952/3), 96-120.

——: Observations on the Cotton Genesis Fragments. *Late Classical and Medieval Studies in honor of A. M. Friend* (Princeton, 1955), 112-31.

——: The Octateuch of the Seraglio and the history of its picture recension. *Actes du Xe congrès internat. d'études byzantines* 1955 (Istanbul, 1957).

——: *Ancient Book Illumination* (Cambridge, Mass., 1959).

——: The survival of mythological representations in early Christian and Byzantine art and their impact on Christian Iconography. *Dumbarton Oaks Papers* 14 (1960), 43-68.

——: Zur Frage des Einflusses jüdischer Bilderquellen auf die Illustration des Alten Testaments. *Mullus: Fs. für T. Klauser = Jahrbuch für Antike und Christentum, Ergänzungsband* I (1964), 401-15.

WELLESZ, E.: *The Vienna Genesis* (Faber Library of Illuminated Manuscripts; London, 1960).

WILLOUGHBY, H. R.: Representational biblical cycles: Antiochian and Constantinopolitan. *JBL* 69 (1950), 129-36.

INDEX OF AUTHORS

Abbott, T. K.   74
'Abd al Masih, Y.   158
Abeghian, A.   147
Abel, F.-M.   21, 23, 115, 132
Abelesz, A.   51
Abrahams, I.   45, 116
Abrahams, M.   93
Abuladze, I.   165
Ackroyd, P. R.   119, 132
Adams, A. W.   168
Adler, C.   155
Aerts, W. J.   25
Ahlmark, A. S.   162
Aiura, T.   59
Akinian, N.   147
Albertson, J.   68
Albright, W. F.   39, 50, 98
Aldema, J. A. de   60
Alès, A. d'   87
Alfrink, B.   37
Algermissen, E.   145
Allen, H. F.   25
Allen, L. C.   107, 109
Allen, W. C.   30, 54
Allgeier, A.   69, 74, 88, 98, 102, 110,
   119, 134, 168, 177, 178, 184
Allrik, H. L.   110
Alpatoff, M.   195
Altaner, B.   178
Altbauer, M.   186, 187
Altheim, F.   41, 91, 92, 160, 191
Amann, F.   66
Amélineau, E. C.   150, 151, 157
Amelli, A. M.   178, 184
Amersfoordt, J.   98
Amfilochy, Archimandrite   187
Amir, J.   57
Amstutz, J.   30
Amusin, I. D.   30
Andersson, E.   153
Andrews, D. K.   34, 142
Andrews, H. T.   44
Anger, R.   93
Anlauf, G.   25
Anon   48, 74, 87, 145, 148, 153, 168,
   178, 182, 186, 195
Anz, H.   30
Aptowitzer, V.   47, 105

Arbesmann, E.   60
Argyle, A. W.   18, 25
Armstrong, G. T.   60
Armstrong, J. F.   137
Arndt, W. F.   29
Arnim, B. von   187
Arnold, W. R.   100
Artrom, E. S.   140
Ashburnham, Lord   173
Assfalg, G.   166
Astaucaturean, T.   148
Astruc, C.   195
Atkinson, B. F. C.   53
Aucher, J.   148
Audet, J.-P.   14, 42, 56
Auerbach, M.   30
Auvray, P.   13, 129
Ayuso Marazuela, T.   168, 174,
   178, 179

Baab, O. J.   16, 34, 99
Baars, W.   69, 74, 105, 132, 175,
   183, 184, 189, 191, 193
Bacher, W.   48, 109
Bachmann, J.   162, 163
Bacon, B. W.   54
Baethgen, F.   119
Bahrdt, C. G.   88
Bakker, A.   179
Baldi, D.   82
Bank, J. S.   21
Barber, E. A.   29
Bardelli, G.   158
Bardy, G.   13, 64, 69, 74, 87, 110,
   140
Barnard, L. W.   59
Barnard, P. M.   60
Barnes, W. E.   11, 51, 66, 105,
   107, 141, 189
Barns, J. W. B.   70
Baron, L.   179
Barr, J.   21, 30, 34, 48
Barrois, A.   17, 43
Barry, P.   30
Bartelink, G. J. M.   31, 60
Barthélemy, D.   10, 14, 74, 86, 95
Bartina, S.   74
Barton, G. A.   123

Bartsch, H. W.   74
Bassano, F. da   161
Bataille, A.   70
Batten, L. W.   105
Baudissin, W. W. G. von   37, 146
Bauer, A.   9
Bauer, J.   25
Bauer, W.   29, 66, 88
Bauernfeind, O.   58
Baumgärtel, F.   34, 35, 37, 98, 137
Baumgartner, A. J.   122
Baumgartner, W.   142
Baumstark, A.   1, 14, 54, 82, 98,
    119, 134, 144, 146, 149, 181, 184,
    186, 192, 193, 195
Bayer, E.   45, 110
Beare, F. W.   70
Beauchamp, P.   125
Bebb, Ll. J. M.   1, 167, 186.
Beckwith, I. T.   25
Beegle, D. M.   39
Beer, G.   123, 132, 139
Bees, N. A.   74
Begrich, J.   132
Beling, W. A.   105
Belkin, S.   57
Bell, H. I.   70, 158
Belléli, L.   97
Bellet, P.   89, 154
Belsheim, J.   173, 176
Bender, A.   98
Benediktsson, J.   40
Benjamin, C. D.   74, 142
Bennett, W. H.   105
Benoit, P.   14, 56, 80
Bensly, R. L.   175, 189
Berbérian, H.   148
Berg, J. F.   51, 119
Berger, S.   173, 175
Bergmann, J.   40
Bergmeier, R.   99
Berlinger, J.   51
Bernheimer, R.   195
Bertholet, A.   45
Bertini, U.   81
Bertram, G.   8, 9, 11, 17, 18, 19, 20,
    31, 37, 43, 48, 53, 60, 66, 84, 122
Bethune-Baker, J. F.   68
Betz, O.   58
Bevan, A. A.   116
Bévenot, H.   114, 134, 143, 148
Bewer, J. A.   134, 137, 140, 141
Beyer, K.   25

Bianchi-Bandinelli, O.   195
Bickell, G.   123
Bickermann, E. J.   16, 45, 84, 86,
    98, 112, 116
Biel, J. C.   29
Bieler, L.   75, 179
Billen, A. V.   75, 89, 98, 104, 174
Bischoff, B.   173, 195
Björck, G.   25
Black, M.   194
Blake, R. P.   163, 165, 166
Blakeney, E. H.   123
Blank, S. H.   31, 34
Blass, F.   24
Blau, J.   34, 48
Blau, L.   16, 37, 42, 69, 91
Bloch, J.   51, 96, 189
Bloch, P.   195
Blomqvist, J.   25
Blondheim, D. S.   16, 92, 93, 168
Bludau, A.   54, 60, 143
Boeckler, A.   174, 196
Boehmer, J.   11, 19
Boer, P. A. H. de   1, 105, 175, 192
Bogaert, M.   176
Böhl, E.   53, 80
Böhlig, A.   150, 155, 156
Böklen, E.   105
Boling, R. G.   103, 104
Bonaccorsi, G.   24
Bonacorsi, I.   179
Bonicatti, M.   75
Bonnardière, A. M. la   174, 175,
    181, 184
Bonner, C.   80
Boon, R.   65
Boscherini, S.   168
Bosse, A.   50
Bosshard, E.   134
Boström, O. H.   105
Botte, B.   75, 150, 160, 168
Bouriant, U.   151, 157, 158
Bousset, W.   17, 59, 88
Boyd, O.   161
Bratsiotis, P. I.   1, 8, 11, 60, 82,
    119, 137
Bratsiotis, N. P.   31
Braun, F.-M.   125
Braun, H.   132
Brenton, L. C. L.   7
Brightman, F. E.   155
Brinktrine, J.   37, 119
Brock, S. P.   16, 87, 106

Brockington, L. H.   19, 52, 53, 137
Brønno, E.   39, 42, 91
Brooke, A. E.   4, 66, 153, 154
Brou, L.   179, 184
Brownlee, W. H.   112
Bruce, F. F.   1, 11
Brügsch, H.   75, 154
Brunello, A.   7
Brunner, G.   113
Bruns, P. J.   92
Bruppacher, H.   116
Bruston, C. H.   42
Bruyne, D. de   31, 60, 89, 116, 119,
    130, 168, 173, 176, 179, 182, 183,
    184
Buberl, P.   195, 196
Büchel, C.   54
Bucher, P.   80
Büchler, A.   106, 130, 134
Büchsel, F.   21
Buchtal, H.   196
Bückers, H.   125
Buckle, D. P.   158
Budde, K.   37
Budge, E. A. W.   151, 155
Buhl, F.   1
Buresch, K.   25
Burkitt, F. C.   1, 9, 59, 65, 70, 75,
    82, 84, 93, 96, 107, 134, 168, 169,
    174, 179, 189
Burmester, O. H. E.   82, 154, 157,
    158
Burn, J. H.   9
Burney, C. F.   116

Cabaniss, A.   125
Cadbury, H. J.   130
Cadiou, R.   61
Cahn, A. S.   196
Caird, G. B.   31
Calderini, A.   73
Calès, J.   66
Cambe, P.   54
Campenhausen, H. von   14
Camps, G. M.   125
Canet, L.   106
Cannon, W. W.   94
Cantera, J.   87, 169, 174
Capelle, P.   94, 179
Caquot, A.   161
Carmody, F. J.   169
Caspari, C. P.   182
Caspari, W.   98

Cassuto, U.   93
Castell, E.   29
Cavaignac, E.   116
Cavallo, G.   69
Cazelles, H.   113
Ceresa-Gastaldo, A.   31
Cerfaux, L.   37
Ceriani, A. M.   75, 89, 169, 189, 191,
    192, 193
Černý, J.   39
Cervall, L.   82
Ceuppens, F.   125
Chabot, J. B.   75
Chambers, C. D.   25
Chantraine, P.   25, 29
Charles, R. H.   160
Chassinat, E.   158
Cheikho, L.   146
Cheyne, T. K.   157
Christianssen, I.   57
Christou, P. K.   87
Churgin, P.   52
Ciasca, A.   152
Čistovič, J.   186
Clark, C. U.   173
Clark, P. O.   10
Clarke, W. K. L.   54
Cohen, J.   116
Cohen, N. G.   58
Cohen, S.   1
Coleman, N. D.   25
Collart, P.   70, 80
Collomp, P.   70, 84
Colombo, D.   125
Colorni, V.   82
Colson, F. H.   57
Colwell, E. C.   7, 21, 85
Constantelos, D. J.   83
Conybeare, F. D.   5, 57, 148, 169
Cook, H. J.   112
Cook, S. A.   146
Cooper, C. M.   94, 104
Cornill, C. H.   37, 141
Corssen, P.   169, 184
Coste, J.   16, 31, 137
Cozza, J.   75, 79
Crönert, W.   24
Cross, F. M.   50
Crum, W. E.   154, 155

Dahood, M.   54
Dahse, J.   66, 84, 87, 99, 109
Dain, A.   69

Danélia, K.   167
Daniel, S.   31, 34
Daniélou, J.   56, 61, 65
Danielsmeyer, W.   141
Danker, F. W.   11
Danon, M.   97
Darlow, T. H.   5
Dathe, J. A.   89, 93
Daube, D.   21, 31
Daubney, W. H.   14, 143
Davidson, A. B.   141
Davidson, H. S.   146
Davies, D. M.   161
Dean, J. E.   61
Debrunner, A.   8, 21, 24, 26, 34, 86
Debus, J.   107
Degani, E.   102
Degering, H.   174, 196
Deiber, A.   158
Deissmann, (G) A.   17, 21, 22, 26,
   31, 66, 70, 75, 80, 130
Delcor, M. L.   38, 113, 125, 130, 143
Delekat, L.   51, 52, 119, 137, 193,
   194
Delitzsch, F.   67
Delling, G.   39, 57, 140
Denk, J.   67, 169
Dennefeld, L.   14
Denter, T.   110
Derjugin, T.   11
Der Nersessian, S.   148, 196, 198
Descamps, A.   19
Desečar, E.   130
Dévaud, E.   155, 157
Devreesse, R.   48, 61, 69, 81
Dickson, W. P.   93
Dieterich, K.   22
Diettricht, G.   51
Dieu, L.   106, 123, 154, 157, 175
Dillmann, A.   1, 26, 122, 160, 161,
   163
Dingermann, F.   134
Dittmar, W.   53
Dobschütz, E. von   48, 173
Dodd, C. H.   22, 31
Doderlein, J. C.   89, 147
Doignon, J.   183
Dold, A.   75, 173, 174, 175, 179, 182,
   183, 184
Dölger, F. J.   132
Donadoni, S.   158
Donovan, B. E.   70
Dorn, B.   162

Dörrie, H.   48, 86, 176
Dörries, H.   61
Douais, C.   61, 183
Drachmann, A. B.   40
Dräseke, J.   45, 96
Drescher, J.   4, 83, 150
Dreyfus, F.   14
Driver, G. R.   22, 137, 144
Driver, S. R.   106
Druce, G. C.   123
Drusius, J.   89
Dubarle, A. M.   14, 113, 119, 125
Du Brau, R. T.   19
Duensing, H.   161, 162, 194
Dufrenne, S.   196
Dujčev, I.   187
Dulière, W. L.   125
Dumeste, M.-L.   70
Dumézil, G.   31
Dummer, J.   125
Dunand, F.   70
Dunbar, G. R.   26
Düning, A.   174
Dupont, J.   54, 137
Dupont-Sommer, A.   125
Durian, E.   149
Duval, E.   139
Dzanashvili, M.   164
Džavachišvili, J.   165
Dzovagan,   149

Eberharter, A.   14, 19, 130, 183
Ecker, J.   169
Edelmann, R.   146
Edersheim, A.   57
Edgar, S. L.   53
Edwards, C. E.   11
Eerdmans, B. D.   38
Egli, C.   34, 98, 103
Ehrlich, E. L.   112
Eichgrun, E.   70
Eichhorn, J.   191
Eising, H.   125, 126
Eisler, R.   143
Eissfeldt, O.   16, 38, 89
Eizenhöfer, L.   176
Elliott, C. J.   61
Emerton, J. A.   91, 189
Englert, D. M. C.   52
Erman, A.   152
Ermoni, V.   148
Erradonea, I.   24
Erwin, H. M.   119

Eschweiler, J. 196
Euler, K. F. 137
Euringer, S. 123, 144, 149, 162
Every, G. 10

Fabricius, U. 196
Fallet, A. 154
Fang Che-Yong 130
Farmer, G. 47
Farrar, F. W. 11
Fascher, E. 31, 61
Faulhaber, M. 81
Fedalto, G. 97
Feigin, S. 134, 139
Feinberg, L. 70
Feldman, L. H. 57, 58
Feldmann, F. 126, 149, 158, 189
Fell, W. 14
Fenton, J. C. 31
Février, J. G. 45
Fichtner, J. 126
Field, F. 89, 92
Filson, F. V. 53, 141
Finan, T. 126
Finet, A. 31, 107
Fink, J. 196
Finn, A. H. 100
Fischer, B. 61, 106, 107, 169, 170, 176, 195
Fischer, J. 1, 43, 99, 135, 137
Fitzmyer, J. A. 53
Flashar, M. 42, 120
Focke, F. 126
Fonseca, L. G. da 31
Forderer, M. 143
Forster, A. H. 11, 32, 43
Förster, J. 87
Frankel, Z. 11, 17, 100
Frankenberg, W. 132
Frankl, P. F. 52, 123
Frede, H. J. 195
Freed, E. D. 54
Freeman, A. 170
Freudenthal, J. 18, 126
Frey, J. B. 133
Friedmann, M. 93
Friedrich, G. 29
Friedrichsen, A. 32
Fritsch, C. T. 19, 20, 99, 137, 192
Fritzsche, O. F. 104, 174
Froidevaux, L. M. 61
Frolow, A. 196
Fruhstorfer, K. 11

Fuchs, H. 1
Fuchs, H. F. 163
Fürst, J. 3, 18, 85, 99

Gailey, J. H. 123, 182
Galbiati, E. 170
Galiano, M. F. 70
Gamber, K. 83
Gamberoni, J. 114
Gard, D. H. 123
Gardthausen, V. 69
Garitte, G. 166
Garofalo, S. 75
Gärtner, E. 126
Gaselee, S. 150
Gaster, M. 47, 103
Gebhardt, O. von 5, 98, 133, 196
Gehman, H. S. 1, 22, 32, 48, 71, 75, 85, 88, 100, 106, 123, 141, 143, 144, 145, 147, 149, 150, 159, 161
Geiger, A. 11, 94
Geiger, E. E. 133
Geissen, A. 70
Gelin, A. 116
Gemoll, W. 126
Georgacas, D. J. 32
Gerhardsson, B. 83
Gerhardt, M. I. 61, 123
Gerhäusser, W. 76
Gerleman, G. 1, 109, 122, 123
Gerstinger, H. 76, 174, 196
Ghedini, G. 22, 26
Giamberardini, G. 154
Giannakopoulos, I. 5, 7
Giguet, P. 7
Gil, L. 1, 94, 95, 116
Gill, D. 126
Gilmore, G. W. 26
Gilmore, J. E. 152
Gingrich, F. W. 29
Ginsburg, M. S. 116
Ginsburger, M. 42, 91
Ginzberg, L. 18, 93
Girard, L. St. P. 155
Girdlestone, R. B. 110
Gitschel, J. 97
Giversen, S. 61
Glasson, T. F. 19, 114
Glaue, P. 96
Gleave, H. C. 162
Glenn, M. G. 100
Glubokowskij, N. N. 186
Golega, J. 97

Gonda, J. 26
Good, E. M. 135
Goodenough, E. R. 57
Gooding, D. W. 45, 48, 86, 99, 101, 102, 107, 108, 120
Goodspeed, E. J. 76
Gordis, R. 10
Gordon, C. H. 100
Goshen-Gottstein, M. H. 48, 84, 191
Gotch, F. W. 76
Gottheil, R. 1, 10, 189
Göttsberger, J. 4, 43, 101, 108, 122, 191
Goulder, M. D. 54
Goussen, H. 164
Grabar, A. 196, 197
Gradenwitz, O. 29
Graetz, H. 47, 85, 99, 124
Graeven, H. 197
Graf, G. 145
Grafe, E. 126
Grant, F. C. 17
Grant, R. M. 61, 126
Grassi, G. 26
Gray, G. B. 1, 34, 124, 133, 137
Gray, L. H. 170
Grébaut, S. 161
Greenberg, M. 50
Gregory, C. R. 191
Grelot, P. 14, 126, 143
Grenfell, B. P. 71
Gribomont, J. 120, 179
Grieve, A. J. 1
Griffiths, J. G. 40
Grigorian, M. 149
Grimm, W. 116
Grindel, J. M. 86
Grinfield, E. W. 12
Grintz, Y. M. 113
Grobel, K. 32
Grondijs, L. 197
Grosart, J. B. 32
Grosse-Brauckmann, E. 8, 120
Grossouw, W. 150, 159
Grünenthal, O. 188
Gry, L. 133
Gryglewicz, F. 19, 116
Guey, J. 124
Guidi, I. 14, 150
Guirau, J. M. 61
Gundry, R. H. 54
Günther, E. 116

Gustafsson, F. 184
Gutmann, J. 45, 197
Gwilliam, G. H. 194
Gwynn, J. 94, 95, 191
Gwynn, R. M. 34, 110, 122

Haag, E. 114
Haag, H. 12
Hadas, M. 5, 44, 116
Hadidian, D. Y. 11
Hadžega, J. 186
Haelst, J. van 71
Haenchen, E. 54
Haendler, G. 62
Halévy, J. 91
Halkin, F. 14, 114
Hall, I. H. 145
Hallock, F. H. 150
Hamann, C. L. F. 180
Hamm, J. 187, 188
Hamm, W. 71
Hamp, V. 3
Hänel, J. 52, 108
Hanemann, G. 139
Hanhart, R. 1, 5, 11, 47, 67, 116
Hanson, A. T. 54, 57
Hanson, R. P. C. 65
Harder, G. 55
Harford, J. B. 38
Harl, M. 62
Harman, H. M. 26
Harris, J. R. 22, 40, 55, 56, 59, 76, 114, 116, 117, 126, 189, 190
Harrison, E. F. 11
Hart, J. H. A. 6, 76, 130
Hartel, W. von 197
Hartmann, L. F. 1, 130
Hartmann, W. 10
Hartung, K. 22
Harwell, R. R. 141, 190
Hasenzahl, W. 120
Hastoupis, A. P. 139, 140
Hatch, E. 3, 22
Haupert, R. S. 43, 108, 176
Haupt, P. 114, 135, 176
Hauschild, G. R. 26
Hautsch, E. 1, 99.
Hebbelynck, A. 150, 152, 159
Hedley, P. L. 67, 154, 167
Hegermann, H. 137
Heidenheim, M. 95
Heider, A. 160
Heiming, O. 83

Heinemann, I.   21, 126
Heinisch, P.   18, 57, 126, 127, 141
Heinrici, G. F. G.   71
Heintsch, K.   188
Hejcl, J.   42
Helbing, R.   22, 24
Helfritz, H.   59
Heller, B.   143
Heller, Ch.   4, 43
Heller, J.   35
Hemmerdinger, B.   89
Hempel, H. L.   197
Hempel, J.   12, 102.
Herkenne, H.   117, 183
Herrmann, J.   35, 38, 134, 141,
   152
Herrmann, L.   45
Herwerden, H. van   29
Hesseling, D. C.   26, 97, 197
Higgins, M. J.   26
Highfield, H.   12, 32
Hilgenfeld, A.   133
Hill, D.   32
Hindley, J. C.   35
Hirsch, E. G.   94
Hirschler, G.   142
Hlubovskyj, N. N.   24
Hoberg, G.   184
Hody, H.   1, 44
Hody, H.   1, 44
Hoeg, C.   83
Hofbauer, J.   102
Holladay, W. L.   32
Hollenberg, J.   103
Holm-Nielsen, S.   133
Holmes, R.   6
Holmes, S.   103
Hölscher, G.   58
Holtz, T.   55
Holtzmann, J.   190
Holzmann, M.   85
Hommel, E.   130
Hommel, H.   38
Hommes, N. J.   56
Hooykaas, I.   12
Hoonacker, A. van   135
Hoppe, O.   167
Hoppmann, O.   81
Horovitz, J.   161
Hoskyns, E. C.   55
Howard, G.   1
Howard, H. E. J.   8
Howard, W. F.   26

Howorth, H. H.   15, 67, 90, 110,
   111, 121, 124, 143
Huber, K.   26, 101
Huckle, J. J.   120
Huet, G.   114, 143
Hughes, C. J.   146
Huglo, M.   184
Huhn, E.   53
Hulley, K. K.   65
Humbert, P.   43
Hunger, H.   76, 137
Hunkin, J. W.   117
Hunt, A. S.   71
Hyldahl, N.   55
Hyvernat, H.   145, 150, 152

Ideler, J. L.   155
Imniašvili, I.   165, 167
Irigoin, J.   69
Irmscher, J.   22
Irwin, W. A.   2
Jacques, X.   32
Jadrijevic, A.   117
Jager, J. N.   6, 8
Jäger, J. G.   122
Jagić, V.   188
Jahn, G.   11, 111, 112
Jakimov, I.   186
Jalabert, L.   80
James, M. R.   7, 133
Jannaris, A. N.   24
Janssens, G.   91
Jansen, H. L.   114
Jansma, T.   135
Janzen, J. G.   139
Jeannotte, H.   62, 180
Jeffery, A.   1
Jeffrey, J.   124, 134
Jellicoe, S.   1, 8, 45, 88, 93
Jenni, E.   8
Jentsch, W.   19
Jepsen, A.   15
Jeremias, J.   71
Jernstedt, P.   150
Jerphanion, G. de   80
Jervell, J.   55
Jevsejev, J.   189
Johannessohn, M.   26, 27, 65, 67,
   92
Johnson, A. C.   71
Johnson, B.   106, 149
Johnson, S. E.   35, 53, 55, 135
Johnston, J. B.   47

Jones, D. 55
Jones, H. S. 29
Jonge, M. de 133
Joosen, J. C. 21
Jouassard, G. 62, 65, 83
Joüon, P. 32, 114, 117
Jülicher, A. 167
Julius, C. 143
Jung, L. 85

Kabis, M. 159
Kahana, A. 44
Kahle, P. 152
Kahle, P. E. 12, 47, 49, 53, 65, 99,
    135, 145
Kahler, E. 62
Kalananian, A. 150
Kalt, E. 141
Kamentzky, A. S. 52
Kaminka, A. 117, 122, 135, 150
Kamerer, W. 151
Kappler, W. 5, 67, 117
Karnetzki, M. 53
Karo, G. 81
Karpp, H. 14, 62
Kase, E. H. 71
Kasser, R. 71, 151, 154, 155, 157,
    159
Kasterer, J. P. van 15
Katz, P. 9, 15, 32, 35, 38, 47, 55,
    57, 59, 69, 71, 85, 86, 93, 100, 103,
    117, 124, 138, 142, 143
Kauffmann, F. 167
Kaufmann, D. 85
Kaupel, H. 18, 27, 35
Kayser, C. 120
Kearns, C. 130
Kelly, B. H. 35, 106
Kelso, J. A. 35, 140
Kennedy, H. A. A. 32, 170
Kennedy, J. 49
Kenyon, F. G. 2, 38, 69, 71, 76,
    84, 88
Kerber, G. 192
Kerrigan, A. 62
Ketter, P. 159
Khalathiantz, G. 149
Kiessling, E. 29
Kilpatrick, G. D. 70, 72, 120, 130
Kipper, B. 97
Kircher, C. 3

Kirkpatrick, A. F. 11
Kisch, A. 167
Kisser, G. 29
Kistemaker, S. 55
Kittel, G. 29
Kittel, R. 38, 133
Klein, S. 58
Klein, R. W. 108, 110, 111
Kleinhans, A. 145
Klijn, A. F. J. 46, 89
Klima, O. 112
Klostermann, E. 40, 65, 76, 89,
    122, 123
Kluge, T. 164
Knauer, G. N. 180, 184
Kneuker, J. J. 141
Knox, W. L. 57
Köbert, R. 146
Koenig, J. 84
Kogian, S. 149
Köhler, L. 12, 35, 40, 100, 124,
    138, 139
Kohn, S. 96
Kondakov, N. P. 197
König, E. 43
König, F. 170
Könnecke, C. 40
Koole, J. L. 15, 130
Kopečny, F. 189
Korn, J. H. 32
Korsunskij, J. 2
Kortenbeutel, H. 155
Kosteckaya, A. O. 197
Kraetzschmar, R. 117
Kraft, H. 87
Kraft, R. A. 59, 72, 100
Kramer, F. O. 163
Krauss, S. 93, 97, 100
Kremer, J. 62
Kretschmer, G. 197
Kretschmer, P. 29
Kruse-Blinkenberg, L. 193
Kuhl, C. 143
Kuhn, G. 127, 131
Kuhn, K. G. 3, 133, 190
Kühner, R. 24
Kuhring, W. 27
Kunze, G. 83
Kurz, J. 188
Kurz, O. 197
Kusch, H. 170

Lacau, P. 152

Lagarde, P. A. de   6, 12, 41, 62, 67, 76, 120, 122, 124, 138, 146, 147, 151, 152, 154, 155, 170, 182, 183, 190, 192
Lagrange, M. J.   19, 76, 127, 180
Lake, K.   76
Lambertz, M.   22
Lampe, G. W. H.   29, 62
Land, J. P. N.   194
Landschreiber, K. W.   67
Lange, S.   127
Langen, J.   112
Langner, E.   167
Lantschoot, A. van   160
Lanz-Liebenfels, J.   6
Larcher, C.   127
Lassus, J.   197
Lauch, E.   76
Lauchert, F.   170
Lauer, S.   117
Laurenčik, J.   188
Laurentin, R.   62
Lauterbach, J. Z.   38
Lawlor, H. J.   135
Lazarus, A.   8
Lebedev, V.   187
Lebram, J. C. H.   114, 190, 192
Leclerq, H.   80
Ledogar, R. J.   35
Lee, J. A. L.   32
Leeuwen, W. S. van   32
Lefebvre, M.   115
Lefèvre, R.   162
Lefort, L.-Th.   15, 27, 154
Lehmann, P.   185
Leipoldt, J.   16, 21, 131, 155
Lella, A. Di   131
Leloir, L.   148, 164
Lemke, W. E.   110
Lemm, O. von   152
Lemoine, E.   22
Lennox, R.   142
Lépissier, J.   188
Lerch, D.   62
Leroy, J.   197
Leskien, A.   186
Lethaby, W. R.   197
Levi, I.   35, 117, 133, 143
Lewis, A. S.   194
Lewis, J. J.   46
Lewy, J.   112
Liddell, H. G.   29
Lieberman, S.   32, 131

Lieblein, J. D. G.   155
Liebreich, L. J.   93, 95
Lietzmann, H.   6, 72, 76
Lifshitz, B.   76, 96
Lindblom, J.   40
Lindhagen, C.   32
Lindl, E.   81
Linke, H.   170
Lipsius, K. H. A.   27
Lisowsky, G.   4, 40
Ljungvik, H.   27
Locker, E.   29
Loewe, R.   20, 117
Löfgren, O.   147, 160, 163
Löhr, M.   114, 143
Loi, V.   62
Lommatzsch, E.   111
Lossen, M.   191
Lowe, A. D.   32
Lowe, E. A.   170, 173, 176, 180
Ludlum, J. H.   104
Ludolf, H.   162
Ludtke, W.   148
Ludwich, A.   97
Lütkemann, L.   89, 135, 138
Lyon, R. W.   76
Lyonnet, S.   33, 127, 148
Lys, D.   19
MacDonald, D. B.   127
MacKenzie, R. A. F.   143
Macler, F.   148
Maldfeld, G.   72
Malha, L.   12
Malickij, N. V.   198
Malinine, M.   159
Mallon, A.   156
Mandelkern, S.   4
Mangenot, E.   10
Manson, T. W.   33, 133
Marbury, C. H.   53
Marcus, R.   7, 18, 38, 57, 112, 117
Margoliouth, D. S.   127
Margoliouth, G.   194
Margolis, M. L.   2, 6, 35, 36, 42, 43, 49, 67, 77, 84, 85, 89, 91, 100, 103, 120, 131, 135, 142, 174
Mariès, L.   127, 198
Mariotti, S.   176
Marr, N.   164
Marshall, F. H.   97
Martimort, A. G.   180
Martin, R. A.   27, 100, 139
Martini, C. M.   9

Marx, A. 127
Maspero, G. 152
Mattei-Cerasoli, L. 185
Matzkow, W. 170
Mauersberger, A. 29
Mayor, J. E. B. 174
Mayser, E. 24
McHardy, W. D. 147
McLean, N. 66
Mearns, J. 121
Méchineau, L. 86, 89, 170
Meecham, H. G. 44
Meek, T. J. 36, 99
Meershoek, G. Q. A. 65
Meinhold, J. 6
Meister, R. 27, 42
Meisterhans, K. 24
Melamed, E. Z. 117, 118, 135
Menzel, P. 127
Mercati, G. 12, 15, 38, 41, 53, 62,
    67, 72, 77, 87, 89, 90, 91, 92, 94,
    95, 96, 98, 102, 120, 135, 145, 173,
    176, 177, 185, 191
Mercer, S. A. B. 162
Mercier, B. 148, 150
Méritain, J. 106
Merk, A. 15
Merx, A. 41, 135
Metzger, B. M. 2, 87, 111
Meyer, C. 114
Meyer, R. 90, 121
Meysing, J. 50
Mez, A. 58
Michaelis, W. 2, 33
Michaljov, A. V. 186
Michel, O. 46, 55, 58
Milik, J. T. 115
Miller, A. 114
Miller, P. S. 97
Millet, G. 198
Milligan, G. 29
Milne, H. J. M. 77, 83
Miner, D. E. 198
Mingana, A. 190
Minns, E. H. 186
Mitius, O. 198
Mittwoch, E. 147
Möhle, A. 92
Mohrmann, C. 22, 33, 127, 170, 183
Moir, I. 77
Molitor, J. 164, 165, 167
Molsdorf, W. 173, 177
Momigliano, A. 46

Monceaux, P. 170
Montevecchi, O. 22, 23, 38
Montgomery, J. A. 36, 38, 56, 108,
    143, 144
Moore, C. A. 112
Moore, G. F. 33, 88, 104
Moreau, J. 117, 177
Moreau, J. L. 17
Morenz, S. 18, 131
Morey, C. R. 198
Morgenthaler, R. 33
Moriarty, F. L. 12
Morin, G. 90, 180
Morrish, G. 3
Morus, S. F. N. 93
Mossbacher, H. 27
Mossé, F. 167
Motzo, B. 46, 112, 113, 127, 177
Moule, H. F. 5
Moulton, J. H. 23, 24, 29
Moulton, W. J. 111
Mozley, F. W. 27, 120
Mugler, C. 117
Muhl, J. 62
Müller, J. 115
Müller, M. M. 171
Müller, W. 156
Muneles, O. 40
Munier, H. 154
Muñoz, A. 198
Muñoz Iglesias, S. 171
Müntzer, F. 185
Muraoka, T. 27
Murphy, J. L. 19, 33
Murphy, R. E. 127
Murray, O. 46
Muses, C. A. 8
Mütherlich, F. 195
Mutschmann, H. 100
Mutzenbecher, E. H. 29

Nachmanson, E. 24, 27
Naldini, M. 72
Narkiss, B. 198
Nau, F. 121, 190
Naumann, W. 141
Negoitsa, A. 83, 120
Nembro, M. da 160
Nestle, E. 2, 3, 6, 9, 10, 11, 12, 15,
    21, 36, 38, 40, 41, 42, 55, 58, 62,
    67, 77, 80, 83, 84, 90, 94, 95, 96,
    99, 100, 104, 106, 108, 115, 117,
    121, 131, 141, 144, 145, 171, 191

Neuss, W. 142
Neves, J. C. M. das 138
Newman, H. L. 127
Newton, W. L. 65
Nida, E. A. 17
Niederwimmer, K. 72
Niese, B. 58, 117
Nikolasch, F. 198
Nohe, A. 120, 180
Nöldeke, T. 33, 115
Norden, E. 100
Nordstrom, C. O. 198, 199
Noth, M. 190
Nyberg, H. S. 49, 135

O'Callaghan, J. 72
O'Connell, K. G. 94, 101
O'Dell, J. 133
Oesterley, W. O. E. 77, 136, 185
Ohrloff 167
Oikonomos, C. 2
Oikonomou, E. B. 60
Olmstead, A. T. 100, 108
Olsson, B. 28
Omont, H. 77, 199
Onasch, K. 188
Ongaro, G. 180
Oort, H. 68
Opitz, H. G. 102
Oppenheim, B. 52
Orbe, A. 63
Orlinsky, H. M. 2, 9, 10, 17, 20, 47,
  49, 51, 72, 90, 100, 103, 106, 108,
  124, 138
Oskian, H. 150
Ottley, R. R. 2, 6, 138
Ouspensky, T. 199

Paap, A. H. R. 38, 39
Pächt, J. 199
Pächt, O. 199
Paeslack, M. 33
Pallia, J. J. 12
Palm, J. 28
Palmer, L. R. 24
Palmieri, A. 164
Panyik, A. 185
Parsons, E. A. 46
Parsons, J. 6
Pascal, P. 8
Paton, L. B. 113
Pätsch, G. 164
Patterson, G. H. 136

Pautrel, R. 115, 131
Pax, E. 33, 118
Payne, J. B. 142, 151, 155
Pechuška, F. 189
Pelletier, A. 44, 46, 58, 99, 101
Pelletier, A. 44, 46, 58, 99, 101
Pells, S. F. 8
Penna, A. 118, 190
Pépin, J. 21
Pericoli Ridolfini, F. 151
Pereira, F. M. E. 161, 162, 163
Perler, O. 118
Perles, F. 95, 131, 133
Perles, J. 96
Pernot, H. 23
Perry, M. P. 199
Pesch, W. 133, 141
Peters, C. 145, 147, 171, 174
Peters, N. 127, 158
Petersen, T. C. 151, 152
Peterson, E. 80
Pfeiffer, R. H. 2, 50
Pflaum, H. G. 127
Philippides, L. I. 43, 46
Phillips, G. A. 72, 77, 102
Phillips, W. J. 49
Philonenko, M. 106, 127
Piattelli, D. 63
Piccoli, G. 33
Pick, B. 15
Pigulevskaya (Pigoulewski), N.
  193, 194
Pilarczyk, D. E. 63
Pinkuss, H. 52
Pirot, L. 111
Pitra, J. B. 90
Places, E. des 127
Planas, F. 128
Plath, M. 115
Plessner, M. 9
Ploeg, J. van der 55
Podlaka 2
Poggel, H. 171
Pogorelov, V. 188
Poque, S. 63
Porcher, E. 157
Porter, F. C. 128
Posnanski, A. 63
Posner, A. 120
Post, G. E. 145
Prado, J. 115
Prätorius, F. 160, 163
Préaux, C. 80, 118

Preisigke, F.   29
Prestige, G. L.   33
Pretzl, O.   90, 91, 103, 104
Preuschen, E.   65
Preuss, E.   50
Price, I. M.   2
Priero, G.   115
Prigent, P.   57, 60
Prijs, L.   12, 18
Prince, J. D.   156
Procksch, O.   68, 91, 134, 136
Psaltes, S. B.   24
Psichari, J.   23
Puniet, P. de   180
Purinton, C.   128

Quacquarelli, A.   63, 113, 180
Quecke, H.   156
Quentin, H.   171
Quispel, G.   63

Rabin, C.   16, 36, 51
Rabinowitz, J. J.   101
Radermacher, L.   23, 25
Rahlfs, A.   6, 7, 10, 12, 15, 63, 68,
   69, 77, 81, 83, 89, 93, 94, 96, 105,
   108, 118, 120, 138, 156, 160, 162,
   187
Rahmer, M.   41
Ranke, E.   173, 185
Raurell, F.   33
Ravenna, A.   118
Reckendorf, S.   161
Redpath, H. A.   2, 3, 4, 9, 18, 36,
   39, 78, 92
Reese, J. M.   128
Rehm, M.   66, 106, 108, 110
Rehrl, S.   19
Reider, J.   5, 9, 49, 72, 94
Reinke, L.   136
Renaud, B.   118
Rengstorf, K. H.   30, 58
Renouf, P. le P.   152
Repo, E.   33
Rese, M.   55
Revilla, R. M.   68
Rhode, J. F.   146
Ricardo, B. I.   28
Ricci, S. de   154
Richard, M.   63, 81, 82
Richnow, W.   118
Ricken, F.   128
Riddle, D. W.   36

Riesenfeld, B.   30
Riesenfeld, H.   30, 33
Riessler, P.   44, 144
Rife, J. M.   36, 144
Rinaldi, G.   2, 106
Ringgren, H.   113
Risberg, B.   118, 128
Rist, M.   115
Robert, U.   174
Roberts, B. J.   2, 15, 49
Roberts, C. H.   69, 72, 73
Robertson, A. T.   25, 28
Robinson, F.   151
Robinson, H. W.   2
Roca Puig, R.   73
Rocco, B.   60, 78, 141
Rödiger, A.   146
Rogers, V.   110
Rokeah, D.   41
Romaniuk, C.   128
Romeo, A.   33
Rönsch, H.   171
Rørdam, S.   192
Ros, J.   10, 23
Rose, A.   55, 63, 120
Rossberg, C.   28
Rossi, S.   63
Rossini, Conti C.   160
Rouffiac, J.   28
Roupp, N.   161
Rousseau, O.   121
Routh, M. J.   88
Rowley, H. H.   47, 106
Rozemond, K.   68
Rudberg, G.   73
Rudolph, W.   111, 139
Ruelle, C.-E.   78
Rüger, H. P.   94
Rundgren, F.   111
Running, L. G.   190
Ruwet, J.   15
Růžička, R.   42
Ryan, J. K.   111
Rydbeck, L.   23
Ryden, L.   131
Ryle, H. E.   7, 15, 58, 133
Ryssel, V.   147

Sabatier, P.   171
Sacchi, P.   84
Sacy, S. de   193
Sahlin, H.   111
Sainte-Marie, H. de   180

Salkind, J. M.   52
Salmon, G.   94
Salmon, P.   171, 180, 182
Salonius, A. H.   28
Salzberger, M.   122
Sandy, W.   2, 14, 15
Sanders, H. A.   73, 78
Sanderson, M. L.   54
Šanidze, A.   165, 166
Šanidze, Mz.   164, 165, 166
Sant, C.   63
Sanz, P.   156
Sarrouf, Th.   145
Sauermann, O.   131
Saydon, P.   115, 147
Scazzocchio, L.   138
Schade, L.   118
Schaeder, H. H.   102
Schäfer, K. T.   3, 171
Schäfers, J.   36, 142, 163
Schalit, A.   58
Schaller, B.   59
Scharfenberg, J. G.   144
Schaumberger, J. B.   185
Schecker, H.   59
Schedl, C.   120
Scheftelowitz, J.   113
Schepens, P.   185
Scherer, C.   185
Schermann, Th.   78, 84
Schiby, J.   96
Schildenberger, J.   171, 182
Schlatter, A.   59, 131
Schleiffer, J.   152
Schleusner, J. F.   13, 30
Schlütz, K.   138
Schlutz, S. J.   49
Schmerling, R.   165
Schmid, J.   106
Schmid, U.   18
Schmidt, C.   73, 78
Schmidt, G.   190
Schmidt, K. L.   33
Schmidt, N.   144
Schmidtke, F.   43
Schmitt, A.   94, 144
Schmitt, C.   115
Schneider, B.   113
Schneider, H.   68, 121, 180, 193
Schneider, J.   19
Schnierla, W.   15
Schoemaker, W. R.   39
Schoeps, H. J.   95, 101, 133

Scholz, A.   138, 139
Schreiner, J   13, 49, 104
Schroeder, A.   58
Schroyer, M. J.   21
Schubart, W.   69
Schulte, A.   104, 115, 118
Schultess, F.   194
Schultz, S. J.   102
Schultze, V.   199
Schulz, F.   171
Schulz, T. N.   20
Schum, W.   175
Schürer, E.   2, 13, 128
Schütz, R.   128
Schuurmans Stekhoven, J. Z.   136
Schwabe, M.   118
Schwartz, E.   33, 52, 90
Schwartz, J.   80, 101
Schwarz, W.   17
Schweigl, J.   187
Schweitzer, A.   118
Schwyzer, E.   25, 33
Scott, R.   29
Sebök, M.   52
Sedlaček, J.   187
Seebass, H.   109
Seeligmann, I. L.   9, 49, 85, 138
Segal, M. H.   51
Segalla, G.   36
Segert, S.   136
Seider, R.   69
Sellin, E.   13
Selwyn, W.   101, 102
Semple, W. H.   66
Sereni, E.   115
Servin, A.   101
Ševčenko, I.   199
Severjanov, S.   188
Seyberlich, R. M.   113
Sheehan, J. F. X.   53
Shenkel, J. D.   109, 110
Sheppard, H. W.   105, 138
Shore, A. F.   155
Shotwell, W. A.   60
Shutt, R. J. H.   59
Siebeneck, R. T.   128, 131
Siegfried, C.   58, 59
Sigwalt, C.   118
Silberstein, S.   109
Silverstone, A. E.   94
Simke, H.   63, 123
Simms, G. O.   171
Simonetti, M.   63

Simotas, P. N.   36, 73, 106
Simpson, D. C.   115
Sisam, C.   180
Sisam, K.   180
Skeat, T. C.   69, 77, 78
Skehan, P. W.   2, 46, 51, 86, 114, 128, 183
Skinner, J.   39
Slater, T.   97
Sloane, J.   199
Smend, R.   131
Smit Sibinga, J.   55, 60
Smith, A. M.   199
Smith, H. P.   13, 78, 140
Smith, J. A.   39
Smith, M.   86
Smith, W. R.   2
Smits, C.   53
Smolar, L.   107
Smoroński, K.   63
Smothers, E. R.   73
Smythe, H. R.   63
Sobhy, G. P.   157
Soffer, A.   20, 99, 120
Soisalon-Soininen, I.   13, 28, 78, 87, 104
Solyom, J.   121
Sophocles, E. A.   30
Souter, A.   13
Spanneut, M.   88
Speiser, E. A.   91, 128
Sperber, A.   9, 13, 42, 47, 49, 53, 68, 78, 86, 92, 105, 109
Speyart van Woerden, I.   199
Spicq, C.   20, 33, 55, 131
Spinka, M.   78
Spitaler, A.   10
Spoer, H. H.   121
Spohn, M. G. L.   140
Spródowsky, H.   59
Stade, B.   39
Staerk, W.   53, 120, 138
Stählin, G.   20, 46, 59
Stählin, O.   63
Staples, W. E.   42
Starratt, A. B.   63
Stefanič, V.   187
Stegmüller, G.   64, 138
Stegmüller, O.   73, 84
Stein, E.   18, 21, 46, 58, 113, 128
Steininger, P. P.   4
Stenzel, M.   172, 185
Stern, H.   199

Stern, L.   157
Steuernagel, C.   114
Steinmüller, J. E.   33
Stendahl, K.   55
Stengel, P.   13
Stenzel, M.   15, 107
Stephanus, H.   30
Sterenberg, J.   28
Stern, L.   152
Steve, M. A.   80
Stiehl, R.   41, 92, 113, 160, 191
Stock, St. G.   5
Stockmayer, T.   88
Stoderl, W.   141
Stoebe, H. J.   107
Stoerig, H. J.   17
Stöger, A.   131
Stokes, G. T.   88
Streane, A. W.   140
Strecker, A.   172
Streitberg, W.   167
Stricker, B. H.   46
Strömberg, R.   28
Strugnell, J.   121
Strzygowski, J.   199, 200
Stuhlfauth, G.   199
Stummer, F.   66, 114, 172, 183
Suggs, M. J.   128
Sundberg, A. C.   15, 57
Surkau, H. Q.   118
Süss, W.   172
Sutcliffe, E. F.   66
Svennung, J.   28
Swanson, D. C.   33
Sweet, J. P. M.   129
Swete, H. B.   2, 7, 13, 47
Swetnam, J.   34

Tabachovitz, D.   23, 53
Taeschner, F.   146
Talmon, S.   49, 138
Tarchnišvili, M.   164, 165
Tarelli, C. G.   34
Tarn, W. W.   46
Tasker, R. V. G.   68
Tattam, H.   157, 159
Taylor, C.   78, 90
Tcherikover, V.   46
Techen, L.   10
Tedesche, S.   5, 111
Tegner, E.   167
Tennant, F. R.   131
Ter-Movsesian, M.   148

Testuz, M.   71, 73
Thackeray, H. St. J.   3, 13, 25, 30, 36, 45, 59, 107, 109, 121, 122, 134, 136, 140, 142
Thibaut, A.   120, 179, 181
Thiele, E. R.   50
Thiele, W.   172
Thielmann, P.   172, 177, 183
Thierry, G. J.   39
Thiersch, H. G. S.   99
Thomas, D. W.   49, 85, 131
Thomas, K. J.   56
Thompson, E. A.   167
Thompson, E. M.   69, 79
Thompson, H.   152, 153, 158
Thompson, J. A.   145
Thomsen, P.   90
Thomsen, C.   8
Thornhill, R.   99, 105, 107
Thouvenot, R.   80, 181
Thrall, M. E.   28
Thumb, A.   23
Thunberg, L.   64
Tièche, E.   65
Tikkanen, J. J.   200
Till, W. C.   151, 153, 156, 158, 159
Tindall, C.   79
Tischendorf, A. F. C. von   7, 79
Tisserant, E.   41, 79, 88, 142
Torm, F.   28
Torrey, C. C.   16, 110, 111, 113, 115, 118, 192
Tortoli, G.   157, 158
Toy, C. H.   54
Tracy, S.   119
Tramontano, R.   45
Traube, L.   39
Traversa, A.   73
Treitel, L.   10, 136
Trencsényi-Waldapfel, I.   20, 107
Trendelenburg, J. G.   190
Treu, K.   41, 73, 79
Treves, M.   129, 131
Tripolitis, A.   72
Tritton, A. S.   13, 145
Tromm, A.   3
Trudinger, L. P.   56
Tselos, D.   200
Tsuji, S.   200
Turner, C. H.   16, 177
Turner, N.   23, 36, 94, 142
Tychsen, O. G.   43

Ugolini, M.   193
Ullendorff, E.   160
Ullrich, J. B.   172
Unnik, W. C. van   56

Vaccari, A.   3, 9, 46, 64, 66, 79, 88, 90, 94, 102, 114, 119, 121, 131, 138, 145, 147, 172, 175, 181, 182
Vajda, G.   48
Vajs, J.   187, 188, 189
Vandervorst, J.   3
Vanhoye, A.   129
Vannutelli, P.   7, 54
Vaschalde, A.   151
Vattioni, F.   7
Veer, A. C. de   148
Veilleux, A.   64
Vellas, B.   13, 36, 102, 129, 136
Vellas, V.   48, 84
Venard, L.   54
Venetianer, L.   84
Vercellone, C.   79, 173
Verdiani, C.   188
Vergote, J.   23
Viaud, G.   156
Vigouroux, F. G.   8
Vincent, H.   46
Violet, B.   79, 147, 155
Visser, E.   13
Viteau, J.   28, 133
Vitti, A.   156
Vocht, H. de   191
Voeltzel, R.   64
Vogel, A.   173, 186
Vogels, H. J.   1, 54
Vogt, E.   3, 51, 73, 80
Vogué, A. de   121
Voigt, E. E.   177
Volk, P.   181
Vollers, K.   136
Vollmer, H.   56
Volterra, E.   64
Volz, H.   121
Vööbus, A.   3, 96
Voogd, H.   176
Vosté, J.-M.   64, 191, 193
Votaw, C. W.   28

Wacholder, B. Z.   50
Wackernagel, J.   23
Waddell, W. G.   39
Wahl, C. A.   30
Wahl, O.   134

Wainwright, G. A.   18, 40
Wald, E. T. de   200
Walde, B.   4, 112
Waldis, J.   28
Waldis, J. K.   93
Walker, N.   39
Wallach, L.   172
Walter, N.   21
Wambacq, B. N.   141
Ward, A.   66, 181
Waszink, J. H.   21
Watson, N. M.   34
Weber, K.   187
Weber, R.   176, 181
Weber, W.   129
Weierholt, M.   119
Weigandt, P.   151
Weihrich, F.   172
Weingreen, J.   107
Weinheimer, H.   4
Weinstein, N. J.   18
Weischer, B. M.   162
Weisengoff, J. P.   129
Weitzmann, K.   81, 200, 201
Welch, A. C.   101
Welles, C. B.   74
Wellesz, E.   201
Wellhausen, J.   3, 134
Wendland, P.   45, 46, 48, 58
Wessely, C.   95
Wessely, K.   156, 160
Westermann, W. L.   47
Wevers, J. W.   3, 9, 36, 48, 68, 85,
    107, 109
Whittaker, J.   101
Wichelhaus, I.   140
Wickenhauser, A.   34
Wickhoff, F.   197
Wiener, H. M.   49, 100, 101
Wiessert, D.   138
Wifstrand, A.   28, 56
Wikgren, A. P.   7, 81, 121, 144
Wilbrand, W.   41
Wilcken, U.   74
Wilhelm, A.   119
Wilkins, D.   154
Wilkins, G.   122, 190
Willey, D.   190
Williams, C. S. C.   150
Williger, E.   18
Willis, W. H.   74

Willoughby, H. R.   80, 201
Willrich, H.   47
Wilmart, A.   182, 183, 186
Wilson, J. B.   37
Wilson, R. McL.   64
Winardy, J.   56
Winder, J. C. M. van   64
Winstedt, E. O.   153
Winter, P.   132, 138
Witkowski, S.   23
Wittek, M.   69
Wolfson, H. A.   34
Wölker, W.   64
Woods, F. H.   107
Workman, G. C.   140
Worrell, W. H.   153, 156, 157
Wright, A. G.   129
Wright, W.   190
Wunderer, K.   172
Wurmbrand, M.   144
Würthwein, E.   3
Wutz, F. X.   41, 42, 43, 44

Yadin, Y   132
Yerkes, R. K.   140
Yoder, Y. O.   34
York, H. C.   176
Youtie, H.   74

Zahn, G.   95
Zandstra, S.   52, 136
Zeiller, J.   181
Zeitlin, S.   5, 16
Zenner, J. K.   129
Ziegler, J.   3, 6, 10, 13, 20, 41, 64,
    68, 80, 93, 102, 124, 129, 132, 136,
    138, 139, 140, 142, 144, 160, 181,
    183
Ziegler, K.   100
Ziegler, L.   173, 175
Ziener, G.   129
Zillessen, A.   139
Zimmermann, F.   5, 112, 114, 129,
    144
Zimmermann, L.   124
Zink, J. K.   16
Zohrab, H. Y.   148
Zorell, F.   39, 40, 164, 165
Zuntz, G.   47, 74, 83, 84, 92, 122
Zwaan, J. de   74